Relapse and Addictive Behaviour

Relapse and Addictive Behaviour

Edited by

Michael Gossop

Tavistock/Routledge
London and New York

First published in 1989
by Routledge
11 New Fetter Lane, London EC4P 4EE
29 West 35th Street, New York, NY 10001

Typeset by Mayhew Typesetting, Bristol

Printed in Great Britain by
Billing & Sons Ltd, Worcester

British Library Cataloguing in Publication Data

Relapse and addictive behaviour
1. Addiction. Psychological aspects
I. Gossop, Michael
157'.6

Library of Congress Cataloging in Publication Data

Relapse and addictive behaviour / edited by Michael Gossop.
p. cm.
Includes bibliographies and index.
1. Compulsive behaviour. 2. Substance abuse–Psychological aspects. I. Gossop, Michael, 1948–
[DNLM: 1. Compulsive Behavior–psychology.
2. Substance
Dependence–psychology. WM 270 R3818]
RC533.R45 1989
616.85'227–dc19
DNLM/DLC
for Library of Congress 88–29691
CIP

ISBN 0–415–02354–8

Contents

Part II

Contributors

Steven Allsop, Co-ordinator
Drug Education Centre, Western Australia Alcohol and Drug Authority, Perth, Western Australia.

Virginia Berridge
Institute of Historical Research, University of London, London, England.

Brendan P. Bradley
Department of Experimental Psychology, University of Cambridge, Downing Street, Cambridge CB2 3EB, England.

R. Iain F. Brown
Department of Psychology, University of Glasgow, Glasgow, Scotland.

J. Richard Eiser
Department of Psychology, Washington Singer Laboratories, University of Exeter, Exeter, England.

Judith R. Gordon
Department of Psychology, University of Washington, Seattle, Washington 98195, USA.

Michael Gossop
The Bethlem Royal Hospital and the Maudsley Hospital, Beckenham BR3 3BX, England.

Nick Heather
National Drug and Alcohol Research Centre, University of New South Wales, Australia.

G. Alan Marlatt
Department of Psychology, University of Washington, Seattle, Washington 98195, USA.

Janice K. Marques, Project Director, Sex Offender Treatment and Evaluation Project
California State Department of Mental Health, 1600, 9th Street, Rm. 120, Sacramento, California 95814, USA.

Craig Nelson, Treatment Director, Sex Offender Treatment and Evaluation Project
Atascadero State Hospital, P.O. Box 7001, Atascadero, California, 93423–7001, USA.

Howard Rankin
Hilton Head Health Institute, Hilton Head Island, South Carolina, USA.

Bill Saunders, Principal Lecturer
Addiction Studies Unit, Curtin University of Technology, Perth, Western Australia.

Saul Shiffman
Clinical Psychology Center, University of Pittsburgh, 604 Engineering Hall, 4015 O'Hara Street, Pittsburgh PA 15260, USA.

Anna Stallard
Department of Clinical Psychology, Stobhill Hospital, Glasgow, Scotland.

Stephen Sutton
Imperial Cancer Research Fund Health Behaviour Unit, Institute of Psychiatry, 101 Denmark Hill, London SE5 8AF, England.

Chapter One

Introduction

Michael Gossop

Mark Twain once remarked that giving up smoking was easy – so easy that he had done it a hundred times. In this observation, he neatly summed up the problem of relapse as the central problem of addiction. With an addiction to heroin, alcohol, cigarettes, or any other addictive behaviour, the problem is not so much getting off as staying off.

This book is concerned with the different ways in which people can become addicted. It may be seen as part of a trend towards reconstructing the notion of 'addictive behaviour' which looks more closely at the common ground shared by the different types of addictions. In particular, the book examines a problem that stands at the very heart of the many different types of addictive behaviours – the great difficulty that people experience in trying to escape from their addiction. This has usually been referred to as the problem of relapse. However, this concept carries a number of implicit assumptions that make it far from satisfactory to many of the contributors to this book. Indeed, the problems inherent in the concept of relapse are widely recognized but the concept lingers on in the absence of any satisfactory or generally agreed alternative. To those who are impatient to escape the fog of conceptual confusion surrounding the book's title, I would offer an apology but also ask for their forbearance. The book is part of 'work in progress' and its contents illustrate the research and thought on this complex and important issue that are part of current attempts to find a way through the fog.

It also has to be admitted that the definition of what is to count as 'addictive behaviour' is far from a straightforward matter. None the less, some of the following are important or essential elements of what we mean by an addiction.

1. A strong desire or sense of compulsion to engage in the particular behaviour (especially when the opportunity to engage in such behaviour is not available).

2. Impaired capacity to control the behaviour (notably in terms of controlling its onset, staying off, or controlling the level at which the behaviour occurs).
3. Discomfort and distress when the behaviour is prevented or stops.
4. Persisting with the behaviour despite clear evidence that it is leading to problems.

Not all of these features need be present in every instance of addictive behaviour, but most of them are usually evident, and the first element, the sense of compulsion, would seem to be an essential ingredient. It contradicts our understanding of what we mean by an 'addiction' that someone could be said to be addicted to something but not experience a strong need for it. Together these four features provide a good picture of addictive behaviour with its sense of compulsion, the difficulty of maintaining control over the behaviour, the distress associated with withdrawal, and the persistence that such behaviours show once they have become established.

For many years the notion of 'addiction' has been virtually synonymous with drug addiction. And of the various forms of drug addiction, one in particular has had a quite disproportionate influence upon thinking about the problem, namely addiction to heroin and to other opiates. Certainly the behaviour of the heroin addict meets all the defining characteristics stated above. There is a strong compulsion to take the drug (craving). There is impaired control, most conspicuously shown by the repeated failures to give up the drug based on will-power alone. There is the distress caused by withdrawal symptoms; and there is the continued use of the drug despite many and various problems caused by the habit (the financial costs, the criminal risks, the dangers of infection and ill-health).

The fact that heroin has always been linked to such clear cases of addictive behaviour has undoubtedly helped to mislead many people into the belief that addictiveness could be understood as being a property that was *intrinsic* to certain drugs. This produced futile arguments along the lines of whether this or that drug was 'really addictive'. Also, because of the stigma that surrounds heroin addiction, there has been a popular tendency to link addiction to illegal and prohibited substances. However, addictive behaviour is not just a problem related to the use of certain illegal drugs. Indeed, in many respects it needs to be emphasized that some of the most prevalent and most damaging forms of addiction are not linked to the illicit drugs at all.

There are many other drugs which can produce those psychological and physiological changes that some people are so eager to experience. It has always been clear that alcohol leads many people into an addictive pattern of use. Both the *Bible* and the Hindu *Ayurveda* (dating from about 1000 B.C.) refer to the perils of intoxication and habitual drinking. The prophet Isaiah complained that 'Priests and profits are addicted to strong drink and bemused with wine; clamouring in their cups, confirmed topers, hiccuping in drunken stupor; every table is covered with vomit.' None the less, because alcohol is such a familiar intoxicant (and possibly because there are so many economic vested interests in its production and distribution), there is a tendency to underplay the enormous damage that it can do to individuals and to societies.

A 1978 survey of drinking in England and Wales suggested that 5 per cent of men and 2 per cent of women reported alcohol-related problems and, at a conservative estimate, there may be as many as half a million people in Britain with problems of such severity that they could be regarded as addicted to alcohol. One measure of the scale of the problem can be taken from recent research in general hospitals that showed that approximately 25 per cent of acute male admissions to medical wards were directly or indirectly due to alcohol: an even higher proportion of surgical emergencies were related to alcohol (Report of the Royal College of Psychiatrists 1986).

Until quite recently there was a similar tendency to underrate the addictive potential of smoking and to underplay the damage done by this habit. However, the habit of cigarette smoking has also demonstrated its own powerful addictive capacity to trap and to harm smokers. It is somewhat surprising that this was so slow to be fully acknowledged. When the first Spanish settlers in the New World were reproached for their indulgence in 'such a disgusting habit' as smoking they replied that they found it impossible to give up (Corti 1932). During the four-and-a-half centuries since then, smoking has continued to cause dependence, though it is only in recent years that it has been possible to take it seriously in this respect. Earlier this century is was possible for such an authoritative member of the medical 'establishment' as Sir Humphrey Rolleston to assert that tobacco could only be regarded as a drug of addiction 'in a humorous sense' (Rolleston 1926), a view which has shown remarkable persistence. As the evidence for the health hazards of smoking has strengthened and people have continued to find it so difficult to give up, the humour of its addictiveness has lessened somewhat. It is interesting that some heroin addicts have suggested that it would be easier for them to give up heroin than to give up smoking, and in a survey of British opiate addicts it was found that addicts described their 'need' for cigarettes as being at least as great as their 'need' for heroin (Blumberg *et al.* 1974).

But even a definition of drugs which is extended to include such legally available substances as alcoholic drinks or cigarettes is not sufficient to encompass the various forms of addictive behaviour. There are addictive behaviours which do not involve the taking of drugs at all. Compulsive gambling is one such activity. There are many people for whom gambling has passed beyond the occasional placing of bets into a realm of behaviour which can lay strong claims to being an 'addictive behaviour' with its associated implications of compulsion, preoccupation, difficulties of control, and persisting with it despite the obvious financial and social harm that it causes. One rough estimate of the number of people with compulsive gambling problems suggests that it may be a little under 1 per cent of the population or, in the United States, about one million people (Dickerson 1984). Like drinking and drug taking, gambling is an ancient activity, and is a recorded part of ancient Egyptian, Chinese, Greek, and Roman civilizations. One of the main influences upon Chinese thought has been Confucian philosophy, according to which alcohol, opium, womanizing, and gambling are identified as the four major vices (Singer 1974). The Roman historian Tacitus also wrote that compulsive gambling was so great a problem among the German tribal chiefs that 'Under the influence of uncontrollable ecstasy the players gambled their wives, their children and ultimately themselves into captivity'.

Of the addictive behaviours mentioned above, none is in any way essential to human survival. One way of coping with such problems as compulsive gambling, alcoholism, or drug addiction could involve total abstinence. This is not possible for eating, an activity which for many people can cause similar problems to the other addictive behaviours. Orford in his book *Excessive Appetites* (1985) cites several such cases. Instances are given of people craving food, being unable to control their eating, stealing food or money to buy food, hiding and hoarding food, and lying about their eating. Such addictive behaviour is capable of leading to its own adverse consequences (often associated with obesity) and can be just as resistant to change as any other addiction.

A similar example of a normal human need and activity which can become excessive and compulsive is sex. Krafft-Ebbing's *Psychopathia Sexualis*, first published in 1886, dealt at some length with those sexual problems which are characterized by compulsive need, and described these as capable of developing

> to such an extent that it permeates all . . . thoughts and feelings, allowing of no other aims in life, tumultuously, and in rut-like

> fashion demanding gratification without granting the possibility of moral and righteous counter-presentations, and resolving itself into an impulsive, insatiable succession of sexual enjoyments.
> (Krafft-Ebbing 1965).

During the same period of nineteenth-century enthusiasm for identifying different addictive behaviours in the form of 'manias', a sexual counterpart to 'morphinomania', 'dipsomania', and 'narcomania' was 'nymphomania' (or its male equivalent, satyriasis), and, whereas such pseudo-medical terms have long since perished through disuse, there still remains the problem of the compulsive behaviours to which they referred.

The first part of *Relapse and Addictive Behaviour* looks at some of the most important forms of addictive behaviour. Not all forms of addiction are covered here. There are many other drugs of abuse that could have been included (the benzodiazepine tranquillizers or cocaine, for example), and there are other addictive behaviours which do not involve the administration of drugs. Humankind has always sought doors in the wall of reality, and, quite apart from the vast range of chemicals which can help to produce altered states of consciousness, there are many activities that can do this. Loud music, rhythmic dancing, meditation, exercise, and many different varieties of thrill seeking can all serve as escape routes from the ordinariness of reality (Gossop 1987). And some of these activities can become sufficiently compulsive to qualify as addictive behaviours. Exercise, for example, can act as a stimulant which produces physiological changes in the brain, and for a few people their addiction to exercise is such that being deprived of it can cause such withdrawal symptoms as depressed mood, irritability, impaired concentration, and sleep disturbance (de Coverley Veale 1987). However, it was felt that it would be unnecessarily repetitive for *Relapse and Addictive Behaviour* to attempt to be fully inclusive in covering all forms of addictive behaviour. The presence of relapse as a common theme that unites the different addictive behaviours will be apparent in the following chapters.

In chapter 2, Steve Allsop and Bill Saunders look at one of the most common addictions, that to alcohol. In their discussion of relapse and alcohol problems they point to the importance of seeing relapse as a process and not merely as an event. (The importance of this is taken up by other authors in the book.) Allsop and Saunders also indicate how the individual's beliefs and decisions operate as significant components in initiating and maintaining commitment to change. Stephen Sutton, in chapter 3, deals with one of the other major addictions of our time, that to cigarette smoking. Sutton provides a detailed and up-to-date review of the four major approaches to understanding smoking relapse, and goes on to compare their various strengths and weaknesses. He points to the merits of the self-efficacy model and also stresses the value of studying relapse from a decision-making standpoint. Sutton cautions us that the relapse field is 'long on theory but short on data'. In chapter 4, Brendan Bradley presents a more empirically based discussion of the problem of relapse among a group of opiate addicts who had been successfully withdrawn from drugs. This study points to the extremely rapid lapse to opiate use that occurs among many such drug takers and identifies some of the factors found to be associated with the return to opiates. More encouragingly, the study also shows how this initial lapse does not necessarily presage a return to addictive use.

Howard Rankin's discussion of eating disorders (chapter 5) offers a challenge to views of these problems that too readily assume the relevance of an addictive-behaviours perspective, and suggests that the notion of relapse may be misleading in this context. In chapter 6, Janice Marques and Craig Nelson look at the problem of relapse among sexual offenders, a form of behaviour which can manifest itself as child molesting or rape and which can have devastating consequences for the victims. Iain Brown's discussion of gambling (chapter 7) looks at psychological explanations of this behaviour and points to the experience of arousal as a powerful but largely neglected determinant.

One of the most serious threats to public health in recent years has been the appearance and spread of HIV infection and AIDS. This problem is linked in at least two separate ways to the concerns of this book since HIV can be spread both by sexual contact and by the sharing of injecting equipment. In the last chapter of the first part of *Relapse and Addictive Behaviour*, Anna Stallard and Nick Heather look at the problem of HIV infection and AIDS among intravenous drug takers. Until effective medical treatments and vaccines are available, AIDS and HIV may be seen as behavioural problems in which behaviour change and relapse are centrally important issues in the effort to check the spread of infection.

Part II looks at the issue of relapse from perspectives other than those of the specific types of addictive behaviour. This second part of the book begins with Saul Shiffman's valuable and scholarly review of the conceptual issues involved in the study of relapse (chapter 9). Shiffman's chapter looks not at the particular causes of relapse but at the conceptual framework within which we attempt to describe and explain this problem, at the ways in which the study of different relapse factors is related to particular models of relapse, and at commonalities and differences in relapse across the addictive behaviours. In chapter 10, Nick Heather and Anna Stallard take a more specific point of focus. They look at one particular model of relapse which has had considerable impact upon thinking about the problem of relapse (that of Alan Marlatt and his colleagues) and draw attention to what they see as its neglect of craving as a determinant of relapse. The chapter goes on to suggest how social learning and conditioning models of relapse might be reconciled and what implications this might have for treatment. Two theoretical traditions in psychology that have tended to develop somewhat independently of each other are the investigation of attitudes and of learning. In chapter 11, Richard Eiser examines some of the assumptions inherent in different models and theories, and looks at how such models may illuminate our understanding of the problem of relapse in the addictions. Our views of such problems are influenced not only by recent research but also by more distant historical events. Virginia Berridge provides a different perspective upon relapse and addictive behaviour by looking back to some of the ways in which notions of relapse emerged as part of new medical and psychological approaches to addiction and its treatment (chapter 12). In chapter 13, Bill Saunders and Steve Allsop have undertaken the difficult task of preparing a critique of relapse. Their analysis shows up many of the problems that are inherent in the concept (or at least in the ways in which it is commonly used), but Saunders and Allsop also do much to clarify and extend our understanding of this important but curiously elusive concept. Finally, in chapter 14, Alan Marlatt and Judith Gordon look forward to some future directions. They discuss the problems of the focus and timing of relapse prevention interventions and the question of how best to match relapse prevention treatments to different stages of the process of change. Their discussion is illustrated by an example of one such application aimed at changing the sexual habits of individuals at risk of acquiring or transmitting HIV infection.

References

Blumberg, H., Cohen, S., Dronfield, B., Mordecai, E., Roberts, J., and Hawks, D. (1974) 'British opiate users: I. people approaching London treatment centres', *International Journal of the Addictions* 9: 1–23.

Corti, C. (1932) *A History of Smoking*, New York: Harcourt.

Coverley Veale, D. de (1987) 'Exercise dependence', *British Journal of Addiction* 82: 735–40.

Dickerson, M. (1984) *Compulsive Gamblers*, London: Longman.

Gossop, M. (1987) *Living with Drugs*, Aldershot: Wildwood House/Gower.
Krafft-Ebbing, R. (1965) *Psychopathia Sexualis*, translated by F. Klaf, New York: Stein & Day.
Orford, J. (1985) *Excessive Appetites: A Psychological View of Addictions*, Chichester: Wiley.
Rolleston, H. (1926) 'Medical aspects of tobacco', *Lancet* 1: 961–5.
Royal College of Psychiatrists (1986) *Alcohol: Our Favourite Drug*, London: Tavistock.
Singer, K. (1974) 'The choice of intoxicant among the Chinese', *British Journal of Addiction* 69: 257–68.

Part One

Chapter Two

Relapse and alcohol problems

Steven Allsop and Bill Saunders

Introduction

It is pertinent to commence this chapter by asking the question 'why is relapse so important?' The simple answer is that relapse occurs with alarming regularity, leading many to identify 'alcoholism' as a 'relapsing condition' (Litman 1980). For many clinicians, clients, and the public at large, this fact reinforces the view that problem drinkers are often 'unmotivated' and are at worst 'hopeless cases', exhibiting an exotic condition quite isolated from ordinary human behaviour. Further testament to the importance of relapse is contained in the truism – treatment that prevents and manages relapse is more effective treatment.

The definition that is applied to relapse will obviously influence the understanding or explanation of the phenomenon. We would agree with Grabowski (1986) that 'application of the word to the behavioural phenomenon falling under the rubric of "relapse" is unfortunate' and at the very least is 'ungainly'. In addition, as argued in chapter 13, a strong case can be made for perceiving 'relapse' as a breakdown in a resolution to change any behaviour. However, the term 'relapse' is brief and widely employed and so we will use it throughout this chapter. Employing traditional definitions, if a single drink after a period of abstinence denotes relapse, then 90 per cent of problem-drinking clients are likely to relapse within a twelve-month period (Orford and Edwards 1977). If it is defined as a return to pre-treatment levels of morbidity, 45 per cent to 50 per cent of clients will relapse within twelve months (Armor *et al.* 1978). Without entering into debate about the appropriateness of any definition, it is clear that a substantial proportion, if not a majority, of clients are likely to return to some drinking and experience some negative consequences of this drinking after treatment. Theoretical and clinical endeavour must be brought to bear on this issue.

Unfortunately, until the late 1970s, relapse received very little attention from clinicians or researchers. The background for this neglect can be found in the disease models of alcohol problems, specifically the concepts of craving and loss of control. Craving, as described by Isbell (1955) and Mardones (1955), was defined as an overwhelming desire to drink experienced by abstaining 'alcoholics'. Loss of control, a physical demand for alcohol, following the ingestion of the initial drink, was a drive which overrode the ability of the 'alcoholic' to control how much or how often she/he drank (Jellinek 1952, 1960). It was postulated that factors (either as a result of years of heavy alcohol use or even pre-existing the onset of drinking) internal to the 'alcoholic' meant that the condition was irreversible.

Although there were modifications to these concepts, specifically relating to the inevitability and immediacy of loss of control (see e.g., Keller 1972), the essential message was that relapse was fully understood, being due to factors beyond the influence of either the clinician or the drinker. The only preventive was the prescription of lifelong abstinence. Many clinicians failed even to raise the issue of relapse on the pretext that to discuss it could precipitate a return to drinking.

The utility of the concepts of 'craving' and 'loss of control' has been put to the test in a large number of studies. Generally, the conclusion is that the traditional conceptualizations are not useful in helping us understand problem drinking or relapse, nor in designing clinical responses (see e.g., Heather and Robertson 1981; Marlatt 1978). The major influence on the experience of craving appears to be the individual's expectations (Maisto *et al.* 1977; Marlatt *et al.* 1973; Merry 1966). However, one group of researchers has suggested that the subjective experience of craving in severely dependent drinkers may be influenced by factors in addition to expectations: even when drinkers were unaware of whether or not a priming dose of alcohol had been given, craving (operationally defined by the researchers as speed of drinking) increased after a priming dose of alcohol had been given (Stockwell *et al.* 1982).

Other studies have similarly questioned the value of the concept of loss of control (e.g., Bigelow and Liebson 1972; Mendelson and Mello 1966), indicating that, although problem drinkers may drink large quantities of alcohol when given the opportunity, their drinking is still responsive to subjectively perceived costs and benefits: environmental conditions can be manipulated to influence how much, and how often, problem drinkers drink. Thus, the same factors that influence everyday behaviour and so-called normal or social drinking are at play and 'the constructs of craving and loss of control as key concepts in the disease model of alcoholism have received little or no empirical support' (Marlatt 1978).

Such criticisms prompted a renewed interest in the investigation of relapse. Foremost in this work have been the extensive contributions made separately by Gloria Litman (e.g., Litman 1980; Litman *et al.* 1977, 1979, 1983a, 1983b, 1984) and Alan Marlatt (e.g., Marlatt 1978; Marlatt and Gordon 1980; Marlatt and George 1984; Marlatt and Gordon; 1985; Curry *et al.* 1987). Their work has stimulated theoretical and clinical developments that have done much to oppose the air of pessimism surrounding the treatment of problem drinkers. The core of the relapse literature is based on mainstream developments in psychology, especially social learning theory. The following is an attempt to utilize this work as a framework for understanding and for responding to the common occurrence of problem drinkers not keeping their resolves to cut down or stop drinking. It is important to note that relapse is not a distinct entity and can only be understood if its position in the process of behaviour change is acknowledged constantly.

The initial resolution and commitment

In order for a problem drinker to be labelled a 'relapser' he or she must have embarked on the process of changing his or her problematic use of alcohol. Any analysis of relapse must, therefore, commence at the beginning of the process of remission – the initiation of change. Support for this contention can be found in a paper drawing on knowledge from across the addiction behaviours (Brownell *et al.* 1986). These authors noted that relapse 'must be considered in the light of the stages that precede it'. Brownell and colleagues stressed the importance of decision-making and commitment, and lamented the paucity of research on these factors, especially in relation to relapse. In studies of people who give up their addiction, either with or without treatment, a two-staged process of remission has been identified (see e.g., Saunders and Kershaw 1979; Stimson and Oppenheimer 1982; Tuchfeld 1981; Vaillant 1983; Wille 1980). In two separate reviews of the literature it was concluded that remission involves the recognition that the costs of drug use outweigh the benefits and the decision to change the behaviour (Saunders and Allsop 1985; Stall and Biernacki 1986). The accumulation of costs and their subjective appraisal may occur over a long period of time with frequent shifting of the balance of costs and benefits. This makes a longitudinal perspective essential, along with the recognition that remission is a process not an event (Orford 1985). The final stage of the process involves the development and availability of a range of maintenance factors including the development of coping skills and the opportunity to take up a new lifestyle.

In this process some emphasis is placed on the decision making of the person. As described by Janis and Mann (1977), decision making can be of varying types which may influence the degree of adherence to a particular decision. Decisions made under stress, aptly named 'hot cognitions' by Abelson (1963), are particularly vulnerable to reversal. As Janis and Mann have outlined, decisions that have serious implications for the individual, or may involve loss, indeed may literally be life or death decisions, are seldom made coolly and calmly. When in conflict individuals are likely to adopt one of five decision-making styles. These are:

Unconflicted adherence – whereby an individual continues doing what she/he was doing, because with minimal evaluation it appears to be the best option.

Unconflicted change – whereby an individual adopts a new course of action because with minimal evaluation the old way appears flawed and the new course is perceived as being better, or comes highly recommended by a superior or trusted colleague.

Defensive avoidance – whereby an individual undertakes a behaviour knowing it to be undesirable but perceiving it as the only solution or the best of a very poor range of alternatives. Information that confirms the fatuity of the behaviour is ignored or avoided and rationalizations to bolster the choosing of the course of action may be made.

Hypervigilance – whereby an individual, realizing that some urgent action is required, hastily scans possible courses of action and, driven by much anxiety, selects one and literally hopes for the best. As the consequences of the behaviour are seldom evaluated, the outcome can be disastrous.

Vigilance – whereby an individual, aroused by a moderate degree of stress, is sufficiently encouraged to scrutinize the available options carefully, work through possible outcomes, assimilate any new information that could be of value, and then select a course of action that maximizes the chances of success and minimizes potential adverse consequences.

Obviously, the last type of decision-making style is more likely to result in a robust resolution and high-quality commitment. Unfortunately, the very nature of addiction behaviour wherein the individual is in conflict over drug use would suggest that defensive avoidance and hypervigilance will be styles of decision making that are frequently employed.

As Orford (1985) has argued, ambivalence is an important characteristic of addictive or 'appetitive' behaviour, in that the individual simultaneously experiences attachment and incentives to continue drug use along with increased costs and disincentives. This push and pull generates conflict. Orford has noted, 'What characterises an "ism" or "mania", or a strong and troublesome appetite, as distinct from a relatively trouble-free, restrained, moderate or normal appetitive behaviour, is the upgrading of a state of balance into one of conflict' (Orford 1985: 233).

In Orford's arguments it is the simultaneous experience of being attracted to use but being held back by awareness of possible adverse consequences that generates conflict. Janis and Mann have argued that it is under these conditions that poor types of decision-making will be employed and any resulting decision will be vulnerable to challenge. Basically, the capacity to stand back and view the information is impaired. The individual cannot 'think straight' and is thus more likely to act impulsively or make a decision on inadequate information.

This tendency for reduced information processing is likely to be increased in problem drinkers by the existence of cognitive impairment. It is firmly accepted that regular heavy alcohol use impairs cognitive capacity, especially in terms of visual-spatial ability, problem solving and information processing (e.g., Chelune and Parker 1981; Gregson and Taylor 1977). Thus, many problem drinkers have high conflict over their use of alcohol coupled with reduced cognitive ability. The frequent fluctuations in decisions and behaviour – frequent breakdowns or reversals in resolution – are therefore not to be unexpected. It is likely that, given such circumstances, a person will not develop a strong commitment to change. Indeed, it would be argued that this pattern of intermittent resolutions to stop drinking followed by changes of mind is a hallmark feature of problem drinking.

At this point it is pertinent to refer to our other chapter in this volume. We have argued there that in the relapse literature the terms 'commitment' and 'resolution' have been frequently misused. In our view, it is useful to separate the terms and make clear the distinctions between them. Resolution is defined as the making of a decision to act in a specific way, and commitment is the carrying out of this intention. Thus, the intention to stop alcohol use is a resolution and the keeping of that intent, through various means, is the commitment.

With this caveat in mind, support for the importance of resolution can be found in a report from Hall and Havassy (1986). Using data from a study of problem drinkers, tobacco and opiate users, the authors tested the hypothesis that greater commitment to abstinence (or in our terms high resolution) was associated with a longer time to relapse. They employed a 'Commitment to Abstinence' questionnaire in which subjects were asked to select from six treatment goals (e.g., 'no clear goal', 'controlled use', to 'total lifelong abstinence') the one which best fitted their current status. On twelve weeks' follow-up, the authors concluded that:

> Independent of drug group, if subjects endorsed a statement indicating that they intended to be abstinent and never use the problem drug again, they were slower to return to daily use. They also were more likely to be abstinent at the end of 3 months.
>
> (Hall and Havassy 1986: 131)

The quality and type of the initial resolution therefore has a bearing on eventual outcome. Obviously, further investigation needs to be conducted with such constructs. One major avenue of enquiry will relate to the dynamics of constructs such as resolution and commitment. Both are likely to be unstable, but will be influenced by the ongoing perceptions of costs and benefits of the particular course of action on which the individual has embarked.

Resolve is likely to be enhanced and commitment maintained if a person keeps salient the reasons that prompted the initial decision to change. The work by Litman and her colleagues supports this contention. In a study of problem drinkers, these researchers reported that a major difference between 'relapsers' and 'survivors' was that the latter were more likely to remember their reasons for changing their drinking behaviour (e.g., 'Remembering how I've let my friends down in the past') (Litman *et al.* 1983a).

The probability of relapse will therefore be decreased to the extent that the person can develop a high-quality resolution to change and maintain a high degree of commitment. In such circumstances the person's ability to tolerate challenges to the decision will be high. However, there is a substantial body of evidence which suggests that the nature and frequency of such challenges have an impact on the process of relapse; even the strongest of resolves can be eroded in the face of certain kinds of challenges or consistent challenges. A coherent understanding of the relapse process requires a recognition of the interaction of resolution, commitment, and high-risk situations.

Warning signs and high-risk situations

As argued in the above section, the process of relapse commences well before the first 'lapse'. Poor-quality resolutions, low commitment to the decision to change can result in minimal or low-level challenges prompting the initial breaking of the resolve to stop or cut down alcohol use. From reports of problem drinkers and their 'significant others', it is apparent that there are clear warning signs about an oncoming change in resolution. Gorski and Miller (1979) identified factors such as 'apprehension about well being' and 'lack of confidence to stay sober'. Similarly, Marlatt and Gordon (1985) have suggested a process whereby problem drinkers engage in covert planning of a lapse – a process they labelled 'Apparently Irrelevant Decisions'. Marlatt has suggested that this process involves a series of mini-decisions, each one moving the person closer to situations of extreme temptation: situations in which it would take an almost superhuman effort to avoid drinking. Thus, rather than the individual being an unwitting victim of circumstance, it is suggested he or she is an aware and active participant in the outcome.

In the initial outlines of his model, Marlatt placed much emphasis on high-risk situations (Marlatt 1978; Marlatt and Gordon 1980). This emphasis arose from investigations into the effectiveness of aversive conditioning techniques with problem drinkers (Marlatt *et al.* 1973). Drawing on the reports of subjects who experienced a drinking episode during follow-up, Marlatt identified the factors presented at the time of the first drink. He noted that feelings of frustration and anger, social pressure to drink, negative mood states (e.g., depression) and temptations to drink ('one drink will be OK') accounted for over 80 per cent of reported drinking episodes. Later work across the addiction behaviours (Cummings *et al.* 1980) identified eight main categories of relapse precipitant that could be further reduced to two broad classes: intrapersonal determinants (negative emotional states, negative physical states, positive emotional states, testing personal control, and urges/temptations) and interpersonal determinants (interpersonal conflict, social pressures to drink, and positive emotional states). For problem drinkers, intrapersonal determinants, specifically negative emotional states, were identified as the most commonly reported precipitant.

Similarly, Litman and her colleagues (1983b) have developed an instrument which assesses the number of situations a problem drinker perceives as 'high risk'. The Relapse Precipitants Inventory (RPI) was developed from the reports of problem drinkers about the kinds of situations they anticipated would put them at risk of drinking heavily. The researchers noted that there was 'a direct relationship between the total number of situations seen as being dangerous . . . and subsequent outcome from 6 to 15 months later' (Litman *et al.* 1983b: 388).

Reports of high-risk situations should, however, be interpreted with a degree of caution. Relevant information is usually from clinical samples after a 'relapse' (i.e., drinking that resulted in people going back into a clinical situation) which is an outcome that is likely to have important bearings on attribution. Attribution theory (e.g., Weiner *et al.* 1971) would indicate that such 'failure' experiences are usually attributed to external factors, while experiences of success are attributed internally. Thus, the readmitted client is unlikely to report 'it was great fun. I really enjoyed it. I decided to ignore your advice and go drinking', but much more likely to say, 'I couldn't help it – I was overwhelmed by the circumstances I suddenly found myself in'. This is especially so if the client has a sense of letting down his/her clinician, or perhaps being barred from further counselling.

An analysis of 'relapse' episodes outside clinical jurisdiction can serve to emphasize this point. For example, in our own work (Allsop *et al.* 1989) and that of a colleague (Fulton 1983) it became apparent that an emphasis on high-risk situations and lack of coping skills as precipitators of 'bad relapses' was often inappropriate. Subjects reported relapses occurring in situations in which they had previously coped quite adequately, and it was clear that they had chosen not to deploy skills which were in their repertoire. Furthermore, some 'relapses' were planned in advance and many reported their 'relapses' in quite a different light to that often related in a clinical context. Two examples of such 'relapses' illustrate these points:

> It was Wednesday. I was down the town doing the shopping and I met a friend on the corner. He had a big win on the horses. He asked me to go for one and I thought that one drink would be alright, but it wasn't. I was as happy as hell that day.
>
> I met an old friend in the high street and made arrangements to meet him the next day. I knew I would take a drink when I was to meet him. Next day I met him in the pub. I was feeling guilty about drinking but pleased to have met him. I was reasonably happy. I was thinking I shouldn't be doing this. I had nothing better to do, but there's no harm done.
>
> (Fulton 1983)

Care needs to be taken not to overemphasize high-risk situations and the capacity of the person to respond to these. In both the above reports the subjects chose not to employ coping skills, skills which they did possess. There is a very real difference between being skill deficient and having skills but deciding not to use them. Some of the emphasis in Marlatt's model is akin to suggesting that problem drinkers are hapless victims in a sea of high-risk circumstance. We would argue that the role of decision making (ineffective as this may sometimes be) has been underplayed. Keeping a decision is a matter of balance between good-quality resolution and having the abilities to carry out the resolution. Without coping skills, adherence to any decision will be short-lived (Janis and Mann 1977). Even given vigilant decision making and strong resolution, lack of skills may result in a highly resolved incompetent. Any analysis of relapse should, therefore, include a recognition of the importance of interaction of decision making, commitment, and coping skills. Good-quality coping skills will not be used if the resolution is of poor quality and commitment weak; similarly, high-quality resolve will be undone by poor coping abilities.

Coping skills

High-risk situations are often responded to with ineffective and/or inappropriate responses. Problem drinkers do require a repertoire of coping skills if they are to adhere to any initial decision to change drinking behaviour. Evidence relating to coping skills can be found in three broad areas: analyses of remission, assessment of skill deficits exhibited by problem drinkers, and treatment programmes with a skills component.

Billings and Moos (1983) analysed factors associated with remission in a group of problem drinkers who had participated in a treatment programme. They noted the importance of the gradual development of problem-solving skills after a period of abstention. Essentially, after a period of 'survival', the subjects learnt ways of responding to high-risk situations. Similarly, Litman and colleagues (1984) noted that there appears to be a gradual acquisition of coping skills at different points in the remission process. Subjects who were identified as 'survivors' had apparently commenced by avoiding risky situations, and then gradually developed more complex coping strategies.

It has also been reported that problem drinkers who are deficient in skills are likely to have poor outcomes. For example, Chaney *et al.* (1978) reported that the speed at which a subject could provide a description of a coping response to a given high-risk situation was a significant predictor of outcome. The quicker the response the less likely it was that the subject would relapse or, if he or she did relapse, it would be less severe in terms of duration and intensity.

Coping skill development may, however, be mediated by cognitive ability and impairment (see e.g., Acker 1980; Sanchez-Craig and Walker 1982; Wilkinson and Sanchez-Craig 1981). For example, in one study it was noted that verbal and visual memory impairment was associated with low treatment compliance (Guthrie and Elliot 1980). In another study, it was noted that, when compared to a whole range of variables (e.g., locus of control, drinking history, demographic details), indices of cognitive dysfunction were the best predictors of poor outcomes (Abbott and Gregson 1981).

Inherent in these reports are major implications for any analysis of relapse and the design of intervention strategies. Some researchers have suggested that it may be appropriate to withhold treatment until reversible deficits have had time to improve (e.g., Goldman and Rosenbaum 1977). Alternatively, it may be appropriate that intervention should include techniques to compensate for cognitive deficits (Donovan and Chaney 1985) and that accompanying written material (e.g., outlining content, methods and instructions) should be an adjunct to treatment (Heather and Robertson 1981). Gorski and Miller (1979) reported employing methods similar to the problem-solving techniques described by D'Zurilla and Goldfried (1971) in a direct attempt to compensate for the neuropsychological impairment experienced by problem drinkers.

A review of treatment studies in which skills training was employed as a major component supports the use of skills training in general, but especially problem-solving techniques. Intagliata reported that problem-solving skills training helped subjects develop problem-solving abilities, especially in terms of difficult social situations and in the development of plans for dealing with potential difficulties upon discharge from treatment. In addition, a majority of subjects who were contacted at follow-up reported using such techniques (Intagliata 1978, 1979). Although methodological problems, including poor contact rates at follow-up, limited the implications of this study, other studies support the value of problem-solving techniques.

Chaney (Chaney 1976; Chaney *et al.* 1978) employed problem solving with problem drinkers, training them to generate solutions to a range of 'high-risk' situations, which were then modelled and role-played. Subjects who received this training had better outcomes, compared to a discussion group and no-additional-treatment control group. This improved functioning was evident in terms of a skills assessment immediately after treatment and drinking behaviour at one-year follow-up. The experimental group reported fewer 'days drunk', 'days continuous drinking', and amount of alcohol consumed.

Chaney's study has been replicated by Jones and colleagues (Jones *et al.* 1982), although with subjects of generally higher socio-economic standing and better employment and marital status. Two treatment packages (skills or discussion) were conducted as an adjunct to an AA-orientated programme. The skills training and discussion group were functioning better (fewer days 'drunk' and lower alcohol consumption) at follow-up than the no-additional-treatment control group, although there were no differences in outcome between the 'skills' and 'discussion group'. Unfortunately, interpretation of these results is difficult as only 45 per cent of the sample were contacted at follow-up.

Jackson and Oei (1978) compared a traditional treatment package with social and assertive skills training and cognitive restructuring (i.e., restructuring of beliefs). The experimental packages were associated with better outcome at follow-up. The authors suggested that different approaches may be appropriate for different subjects, with some requiring an emphasis on social skills, some on cognitive restructuring, and others requiring a combination of both. Social skills training, especially assertiveness training and relaxation training, has been variously supported as being appropriate for problem drinkers, especially as part of broader intervention packages (e.g., Freedberg and Johnston 1978; Miller and Taylor 1980).

However, as noted by several authors (e.g., Brownell *et al.* 1986; Donovan and Chaney 1985), which clients require what type of training and when remains to be resolved. For example, cognitively impaired drinkers may, for a short period or even permanently, be unable to benefit from certain or all kinds of skills training. Skills training may be inappropriate for clients who have not yet decided to alter their drinking behaviours. Thus, 'problem drinkers no doubt differ not only in their need for skills training, but also in their ability to benefit from specific treatment components' (Donovan and Chaney 1985: 385).

As mentioned above, having the requisite skills is no guarantee of them being employed. An individual may decide not to use them or may not believe that she/he can respond effectively or may fail to persist in their application in the face of difficulty or discouragement. As Litman and her colleagues have suggested, this may be because the person has not experienced the coping behaviours being effective: 'the use of coping behaviours *per se* is not related significantly to outcome, whereas the reported effectiveness of these coping behaviours is related significantly to outcome' (Litman *et al.* 1984: 290).

It is an important distinction that good outcome is due not so much to the existence of coping skills themselves as to the individual's belief that their coping skills work. This raises the whole issue of self-efficacy and outcome expectancy: that people achieve what they think they can achieve, and what they think is worthwhile achieving.

Outcome expectancy

Within the framework of social learning theory, Bandura has argued that behaviour is a function of two expectancies: outcome expectancy and self-efficacy (Bandura 1977a, 1977b).

Outcome expectancy is the expectancy of what will happen if a particular behaviour or behaviour pattern is deployed. It is the anticipated effects of a behaviour which are important in determining whether a behaviour is used. Expectancy is influenced by both anticipation of outcome and the history of actual outcomes. Several authors have reported on the varied positive outcome expectancies people have in relation to alcohol and its effect on behaviour (e.g., Brown 1985; Brown *et al.* 1980; McAndrew and Edgerton 1969). These expectancies include the benefits of intoxication, the social effects of drinking, expectation about sexual performance, and anticipation of tension reduction. It has been acknowledged that these expectancies are powerful predictors of behaviour, often being more powerful than the pharmacological impact of alcohol.

Outcome expectancies may be both positive and negative. For example, Rollnick and Heather (1982) suggested that a strong positive outcome expectancy of abstinence would be associated with longer periods of abstinence, while a strong negative outcome expectancy that one drink would result in continued drinking is likely to be associated with 'relapse' following initial alcohol use.

In support of this prediction, Heather and his colleagues (1982) reported that problem-drinking subjects who held negative outcome expectancy of taking a drink (e.g., 'If I had one drink, I would continue drinking until I was drunk') were more likely to be drinking problematically at six-month follow-up. Further study showed the power of this prediction (Heather *et al.* 1983), with this subjective outcome expectancy being more predictive of outcome than an objective measure of alcohol dependence.

Similarly, Eastman and Norris (1982) have reported that problem drinkers who maintained positive outcome expectancies about drinking and intoxication were more likely to relapse. This is consistent with Marlatt's model of relapse (Marlatt 1978; Marlatt and Gordon 1985), wherein it is posited that positive outcome expectancies of a return to drinking or continued drinking will increase the probability of relapse. Marlatt has also argued that the relative strength of positive outcome expectancies may increase as the salience of negative outcome expectancies decrease. That is, as the person forgets the bad times and reminisces about the good, resolution wavers and decisional conflicts may increase the probability of relapse. Obviously this event will be balanced out by the occurrence and recognition of any positive outcomes resulting from cutting down or stopping drinking, and the negative outcome expectancies of a return to or increase in drinking.

In this respect, it is pertinent to draw on another addiction behaviour – smoking. Mausner and Platt (1971) have shown that an increase in the outcome expectancy that there will be benefits from stopping smoking is predictive of a reduction in smoking. This was a better discriminator of outcome than an increase in the negative expectancies of continued smoking alone.

It can be postulated that a further influence on outcome expectancy is the availability of coping skills and the person's expectancy that he/she can effectively engage in them. Marlatt and Donovan have suggested that if a person is low in self-efficacy and/or has no appropriate coping responses to high-risk situations, then it is likely that positive outcome expectancies of drinking will be increased. In a difficult situation over which the person has no sense of mastery, drinking will be the line of least resistance and will appear attractive, especially if the situation is one in which the person drank in the past (Donovan and Marlatt 1980; Marlatt and Donovan 1981).

Some support for this suggestion can be found in a study reported by Cooney and his colleagues (Cooney *et al.* 1987). Problem and non-problem drinkers were engaged in cue exposure and response prevention, whereby they held and smelt, but did not drink, their favourite alcoholic beverage. Both groups reported an increased desire to drink and increased positive outcome expectancies about drinking. The problem drinkers also reported an increase in physical symptoms (i.e., shakes and sweating) and a decrease in confidence about coping with future tempting situations. Thus, a high-risk situation was followed by a decrease in self-efficacy and an increase in the positive outcome expectancy of drinking.

This implies that a commitment to change will be enhanced and maintained if the person develops an outcome expectancy that stopping/changing drinking behaviour will be beneficial and if the negative outcome expectancies of returning to heavy drinking are kept salient. Some attempt to gauge the individual's expectations could therefore be important, not only in preventing the advent of relapse but also in determining the probability of 'some drink' becoming a relapse. This is more likely to occur if the individual concerned expects one drink to equal one drunk.

Self-efficacy

Self-efficacy was defined by Bandura (1977a) as the subjective expectation that one can execute a behaviour within a given situation. It has been argued that self-efficacy is an important factor in the analysis of relapse, predicting the initiation and persistence of the deployment of coping skills (Annis 1986; Rollnick and Heather 1982; Marlatt 1978; Marlatt and Gordon 1985; Wilson 1978). Low self-efficacy would militate against the effective application of coping skills in a high-risk situation. This in itself would increase the expectancy of future failure, increasing the probability of continued drinking after any 'lapse'. In relation to learned helplessness (Abramson *et al.* 1978, 1980), the expectation of future 'failure' would be increased if the individual attributes any lapse or 'failure' to internal, global, and stable factors (e.g., 'I have a disease', 'I'm an alcoholic') rather than to external, specific, and controllable factors (e.g., 'I'm at my brother's wedding', 'My friends are putting pressure on me to drink').

The predictive utility of self-efficacy has been indirectly and directly tested. In a study of smokers, Sjoberg and Johnson (1978) suggested that there was a 'domino effect' – once a lapse or breakdown in resolution had occurred, the second and third lapses tended to occur more easily. More directly, methods of rating self-efficacy are currently being developed (e.g, Annis, 1986) and their predictive utility tested. For example, Rist and Watzl (1983) reported that low self-efficacy ratings by problem drinkers were associated with an increased probability of relapse at six-month follow-up. The current authors have also noted a strong relationship between post-treatment self-efficacy ratings and drinking behaviour over a six-month follow-up: high self-efficacy scores were associated with better outcome (Allsop *et al.* 1989). These findings are supported by reports in other addiction behaviours, such as smoking (e.g., Condiotte and Lichtenstein 1981).

It would therefore be appropriate for any intervention strategy to be gauged in terms of the degree to which it enhances a client's self-efficacy to cope with subjective high-risk situations. However, this should be in conjunction with the development and enhancement of coping skills, otherwise the client may develop an inappropriate sense of confidence that is not matched by competence.

Bandura has argued that the least effective way to increase self-efficacy is through verbal persuasion (Bandura 1977a). More effective is the opportunity to observe role models carry out the behaviour, although the most effective method is via personal experience of mastery. This may be obtained through cognitive and behavioural rehearsal of coping skills, through role plays in the treatment setting and/or success experiences in the real world (Annis 1986; Heather and Robertson 1981; Wilson 1978).

Accordingly, Marlatt has suggested employing a 'dry run' in the clinical setting wherein a client observes role models coping in a high-risk situation and/or cognitively rehearses the successful engagement of coping responses (Marlatt 1979). This is similar to procedures adopted by Sanchez-Craig (1975) as part of a larger package aimed at encouraging clients to recognize high-risk situations and develop a subjective belief in the capacity to cope with them.

In summary, if a person maintains a high positive outcome expectancy of drinking, the probability of relapse is increased. This may occur in the clinical setting because the clinician has failed to address the client's outcome expectancies, by not assessing them or by failing to match treatment goals to client expectations or in not attempting to influence them.

Intervention packages will be effective to the extent that they increase self-efficacy with an appropriate and complementary repertoire of coping skills. This should include a sense of mastery over situations after an initial lapse has occurred. If a lapse does occur, continued heavy drinking will be minimized if the drinker does not have the outcome expectancy 'one lapse = relapse'. It is also important that a lapse is attributed to specific factors that can be influenced, as opposed to global, internal, and irreversible factors.

From re-use to problem use

Obviously, some of the factors that are involved in the initial breakdown of resolution are also involved in a 'relapse'. However, many analyses and discussions of relapse suggest that there are specific mediators in a lapse becoming a relapse.

In this model of relapse, Marlatt has proposed the Abstinence Violation Effect (AVE) as such a mediator (Marlatt and Gordon 1985). This concept is a dynamic one in which the more intense the AVE the greater the probability of relapse. As proposed in the most recent description (Marlatt and Gordon 1985), the AVE involves two processes: the attributions made by the individual regarding the initial lapse and the subsequent emotional response. If a person attributes a slip to irreversible, global, and internal factors then self-efficacy may be decreased and the individual may experience a sense of helplessness; in which case the intensity of the AVE will be increased and the probability of relapse greater. If a 'lapse' is attributed to specific controllable factors then the intensity of the AVE will be diminished as will the probability of relapse.

The next process relates to the emotional reaction of the person. Marlatt has suggested that if the lapse is attributed to global, irreversible, and internal factors, the individual may experience a negative emotional response to the discrepancy between his/her self-image (e.g., 'I'm an abstainer') and his/her actual behaviour (e.g., 'I'm drinking'). This reaction may be experienced in the form of guilt, depression, or lowered self-esteem. The process is similar to that of Festinger's concept of cognitive dissonance (Festinger 1964). The person will seek to alleviate the discomfort by making behaviour and cognition consonant. To the extent that the lapse has decreased self-efficacy and the attributions are made to global, irreversible factors, and if there is a degree of positive outcome expectancy about continued drinking (e.g., 'It will make me feel better/more in control') the intensity of the AVE will be increased along with the probability of continued drinking and relapse.

While the AVE is an interesting concept, with direct clinical implications, empirical support is limited. However, two separate research endeavours do offer some support. In the previously mentioned study by Cooney and his colleagues (1987) some of the data are consistent with Marlatt's speculations. When problem drinkers were allowed to hold and smell their favourite drink, an immediate response was an increase in positive outcome expectancies about drinking, accompanied by a decrease in self-confidence about coping with future temptations to drink. A sense of guilt was also engendered.

More specifically, although related to smokers, Curry and her colleagues (1987) reported results that were consistent with the AVE as described by Marlatt. Subjects who were in a treatment programme to quit smoking were asked for causal attributions for smoking and abstinence in a hypothetical high-risk situation before the subjects actually stopped smoking. Any subjects who 'lapsed' over the follow-up also provided retrospective attributions for the initial lapse. Although the initial prospective attributions in the hypothetical situation were not related to attributions for smoking there was a significant relation between the attributions for the lapse and subsequent smoking behaviour: those subjects whose lapse was followed by a relapse were more likely to have made global, internal, and stable causal attributions about the initial lapse (i.e., a more intense AVE) than those subjects who returned to abstinence. The predictive strength of the AVE as defined in this study was demonstrated by the fact that a discriminant analysis indicated that the AVE was the single strongest predictor of subsequent smoking following a lapse.

Nevertheless, some concerns have been raised about the AVE (Saunders and Allsop 1987). These, in part, relate to our lack of knowledge of the proportion of relapses in which the AVE occurs. Unfortunately, as previously discussed, our current conceptualizations of relapse are largely influenced by retrospective reports from clinical samples who have usually experienced a return to problematic use. In this respect, it is important to note that only retrospective rather than prospective attributions were predictive of outcome in the report by Curry and her colleagues. Attributional processes are likely to underestimate the role of decision making and personal responsibility and increase the perceived role of 'out-of-my-control' factors. We have certainly been impressed by a significant proportion of clients who, out of the context and confines of the treatment setting, have, under close examination, explained to us that when they said 'I decided to go for a drink' they actually decided to 'go drinking'. This raises the question: what other processes might influence a lapse resulting in a relapse? Indeed, it is pertinent to question whether relapse is a two-staged process, as suggested by Marlatt. This question is debated in chapter 13.

Drinking behaviour, from its inception, is influenced by the actual and expected consequences, and addiction behaviour in general can be said to be characterized by the selection of short-term benefits over longer-term adverse consequences. These very influences are likely to impact upon an individual recommencing an old drinking pattern. Positive outcome expectancies of continued drinking and the fading of the salience of previous reasons for cutting down or stopping drinking may tip the motivational balance in favour of continued drinking. In view of the emotional reaction to a lapse, as described by Marlatt, or in a state of conflict brought about by the probable experience of strong incentives and disincentives to continue the drinking pattern (Orford 1985), the conditions are optimal for poor decision making, especially 'defensive avoidance': the individual is likely to maximize the benefits of drinking and either ignore or minimize the costs. This would increase the probability of relapse.

Other influences are worthy of note. Problem drinking develops over many years and is a highly overlearned behaviour. Like other addiction behaviours, it is characterized by predictability (Peele 1985). A feature of such overlearned behaviours is the process of 'spontaneous recovery'. Pavlov was the first to report on the rapid reinstatement of a conditional response after a period of absence (Pavlov 1927). With problem drinkers this process is likely to be facilitated in that a lapse is likely to occur in a situation replete with drinking cues. One drink is usually found in close proximity to a readily available supply of alcohol (e.g., in a bar), with heavy-drinking friends, and will have provided internal cues associated with a raised blood alcohol level. It has already been noted that the knowledge of having consumed alcohol (Marlatt *et al.* 1973) and the experience of drinking, especially for those individuals defined as 'severely dependent', are powerful incentives for continued use (Stockwell *et al.* 1982). This would mean that an initial 'lapse' will be a high-risk situation in and of itself for which the person needs appropriate coping skills and self-efficacy to employ these skills.

Summary

A range of factors has been identified as relevant to relapse. As with the process of remission, there is a need to address initiators of change as well as maintenance factors. In this review, a number of factors that may discriminate between those who maintain a resolution to change and those who do not have been identified.

The process of relapse is influenced by the quality of the initial resolution to alter drinking behaviour. The probability of relapse will be minimized to the extent that a person engages in vigilant decision making and makes a robust resolution to change. The quality of this initial resolution will have a large influence on the quality of ensuing action, the commitment to change. Commitment to change will also be enhanced if the person continues to be vigilant, especially in keeping the reasons for change salient. In addition, it is imperative that the person experiences the anticipated benefits from her/his behaviour change. All individuals embarking on change will encounter challenges to their resolves. In the early and vulnerable stages of change, it may be appropriate to avoid these situations. However, eventually, avoidance strategies should be replaced by appropriate coping skills, and in this regard the use of problem-solving skills training appears warranted.

It is appropriate, in any strategy for problem drinkers, to consider the implications of cognitive impairment. In some cases this may require the development of responses to specific key situations rather than more generalizable responses. In all cases it will mean providing written material or other recall aids. Finally, for those clients with cognitive impairments, performance-based, rather than verbally mediated, interventions will be more appropriate.

Performance-based interventions are also more likely to increase self-efficacy, especially if a person experiences success in situations perceived as challenging. An increase in self-efficacy will increase the probability that coping skills will be employed and persisted with and decrease the probability of relapse.

In any intervention package, assessment of a client's outcome expectancy is merited. Are the goals of treatment consistent with the client's? In addition, a client who holds the negative outcome expectancy 'one drink = one drunk' or 'lapse = relapse' is more likely to relapse following a lapse.

Several processes have been identified as mediators of a lapse developing into a relapse. In the concept of the AVE, the person's causal attributions about the initial lapse and his/her emotional reaction to this are important mediators. In addition, it is important that the person has a readily available repertoire of alternatives to continued and/or heavy drinking and a sense of mastery over any situation in which a lapse occurs, including the lapse itself.

Clinical practice

A good deal of clinical practice can be criticized because it is not based on the theoretical or empirical literature. While a good deal of research is required to assess the value of many of the clinical strategies discussed in this chapter, it is nevertheless unfortunate that much clinical practice is in direct contradiction of what limited evidence is available (Miller and Hester 1986).

The acceptance of traditional concepts of alcohol problems, especially that of 'loss of control', imposes limitations on any clinical programme. The role of the client as a decision maker, albeit a frequently inefficient one, is minimized or ignored: consequently there is little or no attempt at influencing the quality of decision making. In traditional programmes only one goal of treatment is advocated – abstinence, irrespective of the client's preferences. Orford has commented that the demand made by many such programmes, that the client acknowledges that she/he is an 'alcoholic' and accepts abstinence as the only means of recovery 'may be thought of as the very antithesis of brainstorming' (Orford 1985: 283). Thus, vigilant decision making is not encouraged, but rather adherence to a goal selected by the clinician. In addition, the development of coping skills, especially problem solving, is limited.

Emphasis is frequently given to the development of an internalized 'will-power' rather than the attainment of desirable goals and the employment of coping skills. If there is any development of coping skills, the focus is usually on avoiding the first drink with a parallel encouragement of the outcome expectancy 'one drink = one drunk'. The development of such a belief system is likely to minimize a client's efficacy expectations about being able to cope with a lapse. In addition, this emphasis will encourage causal attributions for a lapse to be made to internal, global, and irreversible factors such as 'I have a disease'. Thus, traditional programmes may increase the probability of a lapse becoming a relapse.

Many programmes are predominantly verbally delivered, despite the limited effectiveness of this approach in increasing a client's skills repertoire or self-efficacy. Little emphasis is given to performance-based strategies or even the writing down of the basic content of any programme – despite the argument that such strategies are important given the specific cognitive impairments experienced by a substantial proportion of problem drinkers.

Finally, many programmes are conducted in a clinical setting with little or no direct reference to or application within the client's broader environment. Even when programmes include components such as skills training, they are restricted to verbalization and rehearsal in the clinical setting – rarely extending to rehearsal and application in the 'real world'. It is not surprising that if clinical endeavour is restricted to the clinical setting then so too will treatment effects be similarly limited.

The above discussion has implications for the development of a relapse prevention and management programme. Such a programme might commence by developing a high-quality resolution to change, at the same time assessing a client's outcome expectancies of such a change and matching these to treatment goals. The maintenance of this resolution would be enhanced by the individual keeping salient the initial reasons for change.

The development of coping skills might then be the next stage of the programme. These would be developed in relation to subjectively perceived high-risk situations. The development of a sense of self-efficacy would be enhanced, if the programme is performance-based, by cognitively rehearsing the coping skills or employing them in role plays or in real life. The probability of relapse will be reduced to the extent that an individual views a lapse in terms of specific and reversible, as opposed to global and irreversible, factors. Thus, an individual might be encouraged to develop strategies on how to avoid a lapse precipitating continued and heavy drinking. This could include teaching her/him an alternative pattern of drinking, even if he/she is engaged in an abstinence programme. If an individual on an abstinence programme does have a lapse, and the evidence suggests most will, it is not surprising that in the absence of any other patterns of alcohol use, then return to the previous, long-standing, problematic pattern of drinking is quickly achieved. The possibility of teaching moderate use even to abstainers has much to support it. It would go some way towards dispelling the outcome expectancy 'one drink = one drunk' and would encourage a sense of mastery in the event of a lapse, the availability of the alternative drinking behaviour minimizing the probability that a lapse would become a relapse.

Research engaged in by Rankin and his colleagues may be of

relevance in this regard (e.g., Rankin *et al.* 1983). Arguing that a priming dose of alcohol may result in a 'compulsion to continue to drink' they focused their strategy on the client's sense of inability to stop once started. Problem-drinking subjects were given sufficient alcohol to raise their blood alcohol levels to between 65 and 100 mg per cent. Next, in the presence of more alcohol the subjects were encouraged to resist the temptation to drink. Scales measuring 'desire for drink' and 'difficulty in resisting' showed a shift over six consecutive experimental sessions: subjects demonstrated an increase in their ratings of their ability to refuse further alcohol as compared to the control group. Further work is required on the clinical applicability of these techniques, but this and other studies highlight the value of attending to the management of a lapse not just its prevention. The evidence that most clients will experience a lapse should make such undertakings of paramount importance.

From theory to practical application – putting relapse prevention to the test

The arguments presented above formed the basis of an experimental relapse prevention and management package for problem drinkers (Allsop *et al.* 1989). This cognitive–behavioural package was compared to a relapse discussion group and no-additional-treatment control group with male subjects recruited in an alcohol treatment unit located in Scotland.

The cognitive–behavioural package consisted of a detailed assessment of subjective high-risk situations, the employment of motivational interviewing (Miller 1983) to develop a high-quality resolution to change, and problem-solving techniques. The package was performance based, over eight one-hour sessions, with one nurse acting as therapist. Subjects worked in pairs.

The discussion group was conducted over the same time period with the same nurse-to-subject ratio. The programme was, however, discussion- as opposed to performance-based, encouraging subjects to examine past relapse experiences, consider potential high-risk factors in the future, and discuss strategies that might minimize the risk of relapse.

Two weeks after entering the treatment unit, and therefore after at least two weeks without any alcohol, subjects were recruited into the programme. Subjects were randomly allocated to one of the three treatment groups. A total of sixty subjects were thus recruited, twenty in each group. Assessment was conducted, including drinking history, subjective high-risk situations, and self-efficacy ratings for coping with future high-risk situations.

The first treatment session for the cognitive–behavioural group was conducted with one subject and the nurse-therapist, employing motivational interviewing: encouraging the subject to verbalize his perceptions of the costs of his alcohol use and eliciting concerns about these. In the next session in pairs, subjects were taught the application of problem solving, through verbal instruction, modelling, and rehearsal. Over the ensuing four sessions, the problem-solving techniques were applied to the high-risk situations identified in assessment, which had been hierarchically structured from least to most threatening, thus increasing the probability of success experiences. Solutions were either cognitively or behaviourally rehearsed in the treatment setting. In addition, homework assignments involved the application of problem-solving techniques outside the treatment setting.

Sessions five and six emphasized the development of responses to minimize the risk of a lapse developing into a relapse. Subjects identified specific factors that may facilitate a lapse developing into a relapse: responses to these factors were brainstormed, and this 'list' was then employed by each subject to develop a personally relevant list of potential responses. Subjects were encouraged to be specific, and to initiate action. For example, if a subject responded 'I would call a friend', the nurse would ask which friend and what her/his telephone number was. Next the subject was encouraged to think through how the friend might help him. The nurse might then role-play the friend, asking the subject to rehearse how he might seek help after a lapse had occurred. Finally, thc nursc would contract with the patient that he would see his friend to discuss any support in the event of a lapse. This process was repeated for a range of potential responses.

The seventh session involved each subject engaging in a subjectively challenging but not too risky real-life high-risk situation. Selection was based on initial assessment and negotiation between the nurse and each subject. For example, for some subjects, the situation involved walking past an alcohol retailers, while others might socialize in a setting where alcohol was available and being consumed (e.g., in a pub). The nurse and each subject commenced by identifying risk factors and employed problem solving to develop appropriate responses. All subjects successfully avoided drinking in these situations. Upon return, debriefing involved encouraging subjects to attribute their success experience to themselves.

In the final session, after a review of all the previous sessions, subjects were introduced to a decision matrix, similar to that outlined by Marlatt (Marlatt and Gordon 1985): subjects reviewed the benefits and costs, short-term and long-term, of starting drinking and avoiding drinking. This was intended to keep salient their reasons for altering their drinking behaviour.

In order to facilitate recall and practice of the techniques, each subject kept a self-generated manual: this included a record of 'the problems I have as a result of my drinking', 'the reasons I have for changing my drinking', an outline of problem-solving techniques (based on Robertson and Heather 1983), 'what to do in a lapse', and decision matrices, for completion in the eight sessions and to be reviewed 'from time to time thereafter'.

This experimental package was superior to the discussion and control groups in terms of impact upon self-efficacy ratings and drinking behaviours and related problems at six-month follow-up. For example, on pre-post-treatment measures of self-efficacy, seventeen subjects in the experimental group increased their self-efficacy ratings compared to nine in the discussion group and eleven in the control group. The actual changes in ratings were significantly greater in the experimental group compared to the other two groups.

At six-month follow-up 95 per cent of the subjects were contacted for interview. Subjects in the discussion and control groups reported twice as many weeks 'heavy drinking' and were more likely to have 'relapsed' (defined as consuming 240 grams of absolute alcohol or more in three days or less) and more rapidly than the experimental group. For example, in the first three months eleven subjects in the discussion group and fifteen in the control group had 'relapsed' compared to four in the experimental group.

Unfortunately, at twelve-month follow-up, although 80 per cent of subjects were contacted for interview, there was a disparity in the number contacted in each group. This makes interpretation of any analyses difficult. However, it did appear that differences between the experimental and other groups were reduced.

Finally, a discriminant function analysis indicated that post-treatment self-efficacy rating was the best predictor of outcome at six months compared to a range of factors such as initial dependence rating, alcohol consumption, prior to admission to the treatment unit, and measures assessing memory functioning.

These results are consistent with those reported by Chaney and his colleagues (1978), and support the argument that performance-based treatment packages are superior to verbally mediated ones. The contention that high self-efficacy will be associated with improved outcome was also supported. While attesting to the value of such programmes, a major limitation of the study was the failure to address broader changes in the subject's environment and lifestyle, which have been identified by several researchers as of paramount importance in maintaining changes in drinking behaviour (e.g., Grabowski 1986, Saunders and Allsop 1985). Perhaps a more comprehensive and more enduring programme would include components aimed at helping the client restructure her/his environment similar to those employed by Azrin and his colleagues (Azrin 1976; Azrin *et al.* 1982; Hunt and Azrin 1973). This issue is examined in more detail in chapter 13.

Conclusions

In the current chapter, it has been argued that relapse should be perceived in terms of a process rather than an event. Our understanding of this process will be enhanced by the recognition of decision making as an integral part of initiating and maintaining commitment to change. In presenting this argument we hope we have emphasized the need to remove relapse, or more appropriately 'resolution breakdown', from the clinical context in which it has been approached and place it fairly and squarely in the context of ordinary human behaviour. In addition, we have identified relapse as part of the 'giving up' process.

There are, of course, some special concerns regarding problem drinkers. The role of cognitive functioning appears to be a major factor in the relapse process, one requiring recognition in clinical practice as well as in our theoretical debates. As more fully discussed in chapter 13, we would also lament the fact that much of the existing knowledge about relapse in problem drinkers is predominantly based on studies conducted with male subjects. There is good reason to expect that gender differences do exist and that these differences have ramifications for the development of theory and clinical practice.

There is no doubt that the last decade has witnessed a move from the perception that relapse in problem drinkers is mysterious and uncontrollable to the view that it is predictable, with constructive responses available to both clinician and client.

A major catalyst in this development has been a move away from purely alcohol-focused explanations towards employing general principles of human behaviour, especially learning, decision making, and the making and breaking of resolutions. Perhaps this is well expressed by a participant on one of our workshops: 'I'm always making New Year's resolutions. I always find it hard to keep them. Why should problem drinkers be any different?'

Acknowledgements: The research into relapse prevention undertaken by the authors and cited in this chapter was supported by a grant from the Alcohol Education and Research Council, London. We would also like to acknowledge the endeavours of Vanda Brown, Pamela Marshall, Brian McCann, Sue McKenna, and Frank Rush.

The secretarial expertise and good humour of Maureen Bright in the preparation of this paper is much appreciated.

References

Abelson, R. (1963) 'Computer simulation of "hot" cognition', in S. Tomkins and S. Messick (eds) *Computer Simulation of Personality*, New York: Wiley.

Abbott, M. and Gregson, R. (1981) 'Cognitive dysfunction in the prediction of relapse in alcoholics', *Journal of Studies on Alcohol* 42(3): 230–43.

Abramson, L.Y., Garber, J., and Seligman, M.E.P. (1980) *Human Helplessness: Theory and Application*, New York: Academic Press.

Abramson, L.Y., Seligman, M.E.P., and Teasdale, J. (1978) 'Learned helplessness in humans: critique and reformulation', *Journal of Abnormal Psychology* 87: 49–74.

Acker, W. (1980) 'A microcomputer based neuropsychological assessment system for use with chronic alcoholics', *Drug and Alcohol Dependence* 6: 84.

Allsop, S., Saunders, W., and Carr, A. (1989) 'Relapse, prevention and management: a controlled trial with problem drinkers', in preparation.

Annis, H.K. (1986) 'A relapse prevention model for treatment of alcoholics', in D. Curson, H. Rankin, and E. Shepherd (eds) *Relapse in Alcoholism*, Northampton: Alcohol Counselling and Information Service.

Armor, D.J., Polich, J.M., and Stambul, H.B. (1978) *Alcoholism and Treatment*, New York: Wiley.

Azrin, N. (1976) 'Improvements in the community – reinforcement approach to alcoholism', *Behaviour Research and Therapy* 14: 339–48.

Azrin, N., Sissons, R., Meyers, R., and Godfrey, M. (1982) 'Alcoholism treatment by disulfiram and community reinforcement therapy', *Journal of Behaviour Therapy and Experimental Psychiatry* 13: 105–12.

Bandura, A. (1977a) 'Self-efficacy: toward a unifying theory of behavioral change', *Psychological Review* 84: 191–215.

Bandura, A. (1977b) *Social Learning Theory*, Englewood Cliffs, NJ: Prentice-Hall.

Bigelow, G. and Liebson, I. (1972) 'Cost factors controlling alcoholics' drinking', *Psychological Record* 22: 305–10.

Billings, A. and Moos, R. (1983) 'Psychosocial processes of recovery among alcoholics and their families: implications for clinicians and programme evaluators', *Addictive Behaviors* 8: 205–18.

Brown, S.A. (1985) 'Reinforcement expectancies and alcoholism treatment after a one year follow-up', *Journal of Studies on Alcohol* 46: 304–8.

Brown, S.A., Goldman, M.S., Inn, A., and Anderson, L.R. (1980) 'Expectations of reinforcement from alcohol: their domain and relation to drinking patterns', *Journal of Consulting and Clinical Psychology* 48: 419–26.

Brownell, K., Marlatt, G., Lichtenstein, E., and Wilson, G. (1986)

'Understanding and preventing relapse', *American Psychologist* July: 765–82.

Chaney, E.F. (1976) *Skill Training with Alcoholics*, doctoral dissertation, University of Washington: University Microfilms No. 77–557.

Chaney, E.F., O'Leary, M.R., and Marlatt, G.A. (1978) 'Skill training with alcoholics', *Journal of Consulting and Clinical Psychology* 46: 1092–104.

Chelune, G.J. and Parker, J.B. (1981) 'Neurosychological deficits associated with chronic alcohol abuse', *Clinical Psychology Review* 1: 181–95.

Condiotte, M.M. and Lichtenstein, E. (1981) 'Self-efficacy and relapse in smoking cessation programs', *Journal of Consulting and Clinical Psychology* 49: 648–58.

Cooney, N.L., Gillespie, R.A., Baker, L.H., and Kaplan, R.F. (1987) 'Cognitive changes after alcohol cue exposure', *Journal of Consulting and Clinical Psychology* 55: 150–5.

Cummings, C., Gordon, J., and Marlatt, G.A. (1980) 'Relapse: prevention and prediction', in W.R. Miller (ed.) *The Addictive Behaviors*, New York: Pergamon.

Curry, S., Marlatt, G.A., and Gordon, J.R. (1987) 'Abstinence Violation Effect: validation of an attributional construct with smoking cessation', *Journal of Consulting and Clinical Psychology* 55: 145–9.

Donovan, D.M. and Chaney, E.F. (1985) 'Alcoholic relapse prevention and intervention: models and methods', in G.A. Marlatt and J.R. Gordon (eds) *Relapse Prevention: Maintenance Strategies in the Treatment of Addictive Behavior*, New York: Guilford Press.

Donovan, D.M. and Marlatt, G.A. (1980) 'Assessment of expectancies and behaviours associated with alcohol consumption: a cognitive behavioural approach', *Journal of Studies on Alcohol* 41: 1153–85.

D'Zurilla, T. and Goldfried, M. (1971) 'Problem solving and behaviour modification', *Journal of Abnormal Psychology* 78: 107–26.

Eastman, C. and Norris, H. (1982) 'Alcohol dependence, relapse and self-identity', *Journal of Studies on Alcohol* 43: 1214–31.

Festinger, L. (1964) *Conflict, Decision and Dissonance*, Stanford, California: Stanford University Press.

Freedberg, E.J. and Johnston, W.E. (1978) *The Effects of Relaxation Training within the Context of a Multi-Modal Alcoholism Treatment Program for Employed Alcoholics*, Substudy No. 988, Toronto, Ontario: Alcoholism and Addiction Research Foundation.

Fulton, A. (1983) *Relapse Fantasies*, Postgraduate Diploma in Alcohol Studies, dissertation, Alcohol Studies Centre, Paisley College of Technology.

Goldman, M.S. and Rosenbaum, G. (1977) 'Psychological recoverability following chronic alcholol abuse', in F.A. Seixas (ed.) *Currents in Alcoholism, Vol. II*, New York: Grune & Stratton, pp. 187–96.

Gorski, T.T. and Miller, M. (1979) *Counselling for Relapse Prevention*, Hazel Crest, Illinois: Alcoholism Systems Associates.

Grabowski, J. (1986) 'Acquisition, maintenance, cessation and reacquisition: an overview and behavioural perspetive of relapse to tobacco use', in F.M. Tims and C.G. Leukefeld (eds) *Relapse and Recovery in Drug Abuse*, National Institute on Drug Abuse Research Monograph 72, Rockville, Maryland: Department of Health and Human Services.

Gregson, R.A.M. and Taylor, G.M. (1977) 'Prediction of relapse in men alcoholics', *Journal of Studies on Alcohol* 38: 1749–60.

Guthrie, A. and Elliot, W.A. (1980) 'The nature and reversibility of cerebral impairment in alcoholism: treatment implications', *Journal of Studies on Alcohol* 41: 156–8.

Hall, S.M. and Havassy, B.E. (1986) 'Commitment to abstinence and relapse to tobacco, alcohol and opiates', in F.M.Tims and C.G. Leukefeld (eds) *Relapse and Recovery in Drug Abuse*, National Institute on Drug Abuse Research Monograph 72, Rockville, Maryland: Department of Health and Human Services.

Heather, N. and Robertson, I. (1981) *Controlled Drinking*, London: Methuen.

Heather, N., Rollnick, S., and Winton, M. (1983) 'A comparison of objective and subjective measures of alcohol dependence as predictors of relapse following treatment', *British Journal of Clinical Psychology* 22: 11–17.

Heather, N., Winton, M., and Rollnick, S. (1982) 'An empirical test of "a cultural delusion of alcoholics"', *Psychological Reports* 50: 379–82.

Hunt, G.M. and Azrin, N.H. (1973) 'A community reinforcement approach to alcoholism', *Behaviour Research Therapy* 11: 91–104.

Intagliata, J.C. (1978) 'Increasing the interpersonal problem-solving skills of an alcoholic population', *Journal of Consulting and Clinical Psychology* 46: 489–98.

Intagliata, J.C. (1979) 'Increasing the responsiveness of alcoholics to group therapy: an interpersonal problem-solving approach', *Group* 3: 106–20.

Isbell, H. (1955) 'Craving for alcohol', *Quarterly Journal of Studies on Alcohol* 16: 38–42.

Jackson, P. and Oei, T.P.S. (1978) 'Social skills training and cognitive restructuring with alcoholics', *Drug and Alcohol Dependence* 3: 369–74.

Janis, I. and Mann, L. (1977) *Decision Making: A Psychological Analysis of Conflict, Choice and Commitment*, New York: Free Press.

Jellinek, E.M. (1952) 'Phases of alcohol addiction', *Quarterly Journal of Studies on Alcohol* 13: 673–84.

Jellinek, E.M. (1960) *The Disease Concept of Alcoholism*, New Haven, Connecticut: Hillhouse Press.

Jones, S.L., Kanfer, R., and Lanyon, R.I. (1982) 'Skill training with alcoholics: a clinical extension', *Addictive Behaviors* 7: 285–90.

Keller, M. (1972) 'On the loss-of-control phenomenon in alcoholism', *British Journal of Addiction* 67: 153–66.

Litman, G.K. (1980) 'Relapse in alcoholism: traditional and current approaches', in G. Edwards and M. Grant (eds) *Alcoholism: Treatment in Transition*, London: Croom Helm.

Litman, G.K., Eiser, J.R., Rawson, N.S.B., and Oppenheim, A.N. (1977)

'Towards a typology of relapse: a preliminary report', *Drug and Alcohol Dependence* 2: 157–62.

Litman, G.K., Eiser, J.R., Rawson, N.S.B., and Oppenheim, A.N. (1979) 'Differences in relapse precipitants and coping behaviours between alcohol relapsers and survivors', *Behaviour Research and Therapy* 17: 89–94.

Litman, G.K., Stapleton, J., Oppenheim, A.N., and Peleg, M. (1983a) 'An instrument for measuring coping behaviours in hospitalised alcoholics: implications for relapse prevention treatment', *British Journal of Addiction* 78: 269–76.

Litman, G.K., Stapleton, J., Oppenheim, A.N., Peleg, M., and Jackson, P. (1983b) 'Situations related to alcoholism relapse', *British Journal of Addiction* 78: 381–9.

Litman, G.K., Stapleton, J., Oppenheim, A.N., Peleg, M., and Jackson, P. (1984) 'The relationship between coping behaviours, their effectiveness and alcoholism relapse and survival', *British Journal of Addiction*, 79: 283–91.

McAndrew, C. and Edgerton, R.B. (1969) *Drunken Comportment: A Social Explanation*, Chicago: Aldine.

Maisto, S.A., Laverman, R., and Adesso, V.J. (1977) 'A comparison of two experimental studies investigating the role of cognitive factors in excessive drinking', *Journal of Studies on Alcohol* 30: 145–9.

Mardones, J. (1955) '"Craving" for alcohol', *Quarterly Journal of Studies on Alcohol* 16: 51–3.

Marlatt, G.A. (1978) 'Craving for alcohol, loss of control and relapse: a cognitive-behavioural analysis', in P. Nathan, G. Marlatt and T. Loberg (eds) *Alcoholism: New Directions in Behavioral Research and Treatment*, New York: Plenum.

Marlatt, G.A. (1979) 'Alcohol use and problem drinking: a cognitive behavioural analysis', in P. Kendall and S. Hollow (eds) *Cognitive Behavioral Interventions: Theory and Research Procedures*, New York: Academic Press.

Marlatt, G.A., Demming, B., and Reid, J.B. (1973) 'Loss of control drinking in alcoholics: an experimental analogue', *Journal of Abnormal Psychology* 81: 233–41.

Marlatt, G. A. and Donovan, D.M. (1981) 'Alcoholism and drug dependence: cognitive social-learning factors in addictive behaviours', in W.E. Craighead, A.E. Kazdin, and M.J. Mahoney (eds) *Behaviour Modification: Principles, Issues and Applications*, Boston: Houghton Mifflin.

Marlatt, G.A. and George, W. (1984) 'Relapse prevention: introduction and overview of the model', *British Journal of Addiction* 79: 261–73.

Marlatt, G.A. and Gordon, J.R. (1980) 'Determinants of relapse: implications for the maintenance of behaviour change', in P.O. Davidson and S.M. Davidson (eds) *Behavioral Medicine: Changing Health Lifestyles*, New York: Brunner/Mazel.

Marlatt, G.A. and Gordon, J.R. (1985) *Relapse Prevention: Maintenance Strategies in the Treatment of Addictive Behavior*, New York: Guilford Press.

Mausner, B. and Platt, E. (1971) *Smoking: A Behavioral Analysis*, New York: Pergamon.

Mendelson, J.J. and Mello, N.K. (1966) 'Experimental analysis of drinking behaviour of chronic alcoholics', *Annals of the New York Academy of Sciences* 133: 828–45.

Merry, J. (1966) 'The "loss of control" myth', *Lancet* 4: 1257–8.

Miller, W.R. (1983) 'Motivational interviewing with problem drinkers', *Behavioural Psychotherapy* 11: 147–82.

Miller, W.R. and Hester, R.K. (1986) 'The effectiveness of alcoholism treatment: what research reveals', in W.R. Miller and N. Heather (eds) *Treating Addictive Behaviors: Processes of Change*, New York: Plenum.

Miller, W.R. and Taylor, C. (1980) 'Relative effectiveness of bibliotherapy, individual and group self-control in the treatment of problem drinkers', *Addictive Behaviors* 5: 13–24.

Orford, J. (1985) *Excessive Appetites: A Psychological View of Addiction*, Chichester: Wiley.

Orford, J. and Edwards, G. (1977) *Alcoholism*, Oxford: Oxford University Press.

Pavlov, I.P. (1927) *Conditional Reflexes*, translated by G.V. Anrep, Oxford: Oxford University Press.

Peele, S. (1985) *The Meaning of Addiction: Compulsive Experience and its Interpretation*, Massachusetts: Lexington Books.

Rankin, H., Hodgson, R., and Stockwell, T. (1983) 'Cue exposure and response prevention with alcoholics: a controlled trial', *Behaviour Research and Therapy* 21: 435–46.

Rist, F. and Watzl, H. (1983) 'Self-assessment of relapse risk and assertiveness in relation to treatment outcome of female alcoholics', *Addictive Behaviors* 8: 121–7.

Robertson, I. and Heather, N. (1983) *So You Want to Cut Down Your Drinking? A Self-Help Manual for Controlled Drinking*, Edinburgh: Scottish Health Education Group.

Rollnick, S. and Heather, N. (1982) 'The application of Bandura's self-efficacy theory to abstinence oriented alcoholism treatment', *Addictive Behaviors*: 243–50.

Sanchez-Craig, M. (1975) 'A self-controlled strategy for drinking tendencies', *Ontario Psychologist* 7: 25–9.

Sanchez-Craig, M. and Walker, K. (1982) 'Teaching coping skills to chronic alcoholics in a co-educational halfway house: I. assessment of programme effects', *British Journal of Addiction* 77: 35–50.

Saunders, W. and Allsop, S.J. (1985) 'Giving up addiction', in F. Watts (ed.) *New Developments in Clinical Psychology* (British Psychological Society), Chichester: Wiley.

Saunders, B. and Allsop, S. (1987) 'Relapse: a psychological perspective', *British Journal of Addiction* 82: 417–29.

Saunders, W. and Kershaw, P. (1979) 'Spontaneous remission from alcoholism – a community study', *British Journal of Addiction* 74: 251–6.

Sjoberg, L. and Johnson, T. (1978) 'Trying to give up smoking: a study of

volitional breakdowns', *Addictive Behaviors* 4: 339–59.
Stall, R. and Biernacki, P. (1986) 'Spontaneous remission from the problematic use of substances: an inductive model derived from a comparative analysis of the alcohol, opiate, tobacco and food/obesity literature', *International Journal of the Addictions* 21: 1–23.
Stimson, G. and Oppenheimer, E. (1982) *Heroin Addiction: Treatment and Control in Britain*, London: Tavistock.
Stockwell, T.R., Hodgson, R., Rankin, H., and Taylor, C. (1982) 'Alcohol dependence, beliefs and the priming effect', *Behaviour Research and Therapy* 20: 513–22.
Tuchfeld, B. (1981) 'Spontaneous remission in alcoholics – empirical observations and theoretical implications', *Journal of Studies on Alcohol* 42: 626–41.
Vaillant, G. (1983) *The Natural History of Alcoholism: Courses, Patterns and Paths to Recovery*, Cambridge, Massachusetts: Harvard University Press.
Weiner, B., Frieze, J., Kukla, A., Reed, L., Rest, S., and Rosenbaum, R. (1971) *Perceiving the Courses of Success and Failure*, Morristown, NJ: General Learning Press.
Wilkinson, D.A. and Sanchez-Craig, M. (1981) 'Relevance of brain dysfunction to treatment objectives: should alcohol related cognitive deficits influence the way we think about treatment?', *Addictive Behaviors* 6: 253–60.
Wille, R. (1980) 'Processes of recovery among heroin users', in G. Edwards and A. Arif (eds) *Drug Problems in the Sociocultural Context*, Public Health Paper No. 73, Geneva: World Health Organization.
Wilson, G.T. (1978) 'Booze, beliefs and behaviour: cognitive processes in alcohol use and abuse', in P.E. Nathan, G.A. Marlatt, and T. Loberg (eds) *Alcoholism: New Directions in Behavioral Research and Treatment*, New York: Plenum.

Chapter Three

Relapse following smoking cessation: a critical review of current theory and research

Stephen Sutton

Introduction

It is convenient to divide the smoking career into the four major stages of initiation, maintenance, cessation, and relapse. For whatever reasons, historical or otherwise, the last of these has received the least attention from smoking researchers. However, the situation appears to be changing rapidly. In recent years there has been increased interest in the study of relapse as a topic in its own right rather than as a sideline of studies whose primary focus was the smoking withdrawal syndrome or the prediction of outcome. In 1986 a special issue of the journal *Health Psychology* was devoted to smoking relapse (Shumaker and Grunberg 1986) and a National Institute on Drug Abuse research monograph was published on relapse and recovery in drug abuse that included several contributions on smoking (Tims and Leukefeld 1986). This increased interest may have stemmed in part from the realization that many treatments are effective in helping the majority of smokers to quit in the short term but that the most common long-term outcome of treatment is relapse.

This chapter reviews current theories and data relating to relapse in smoking. After considering the thorny question of definition and reviewing existing data on rates and patterns of relapse, I discuss, in turn, conditioning approaches, Marlatt's cognitive-behavioural theory, Shiffman's situational approach, and self-efficacy theory. All these approaches are applicable to addictive behaviours in general rather than to smoking in particular. Indeed, the commonalities among the addictive behaviours with regard to relapse have been repeatedly stressed by researchers in the field, beginning with the publication of 'Hunt's curves' (Hunt *et al.* 1971) and most recently with an article in *American Psychologist* jointly authored by four specialists in smoking, alcohol, drugs, and eating disorders (Brownell *et al.* 1986). However, since the subject of the present chapter is relapse in smoking rather than relapse in general, the various theories are described as they apply to smoking, and citations of relevant evidence are largely restricted to work on smoking.

Definitional issues

In a sense, everyone knows what 'relapse' means. It means going back to smoking after a period of (usually voluntary) abstinence. However, a strict application of this behavioural definition requires that we specify, first, what minimum period of abstinence is necessary before a smoker is eligible for relapse, and second, what counts as 'going back to smoking'. With respect to the first point, clearly the minimum period of abstinence should be substantially longer than the usual interval between cigarettes. Thus, one hour would not be sufficient but twenty-four hours or forty-eight hours might be appropriate. Beyond that, the choice will reflect the researcher's theoretical and empirical interests. For example, those who are interested specifically in the factors influencing late relapse might choose three months or six months as the criterion. However, the advantage of using a relatively short period such as twenty-four hours is that it enables one to incorporate time off cigarettes as an independent or moderating variable in the analysis so that it is possible to examine, for example, the question of whether the factors influencing early relapse differ from those influencing late relapse.

With regard to the second half of the definition, given the predominant abstinence orientation of smoking treatment and intervention and given theories such as Marlatt's (Marlatt and Gordon 1985) that stress the psychological significance of a single violation of the abstinence rule, then it may be appropriate to regard the smoking of even one cigarette after a suitable period of abstinence as a relapse. In fact, a number of researchers have distinguished between 'lapses' or 'slips', on the one hand, and full-blown relapses on the other, and this seems to be a useful distinction even though these terms are not defined precisely.

In the smoking field there have been numerous studies that have examined prospective predictors of outcome. It might be thought that such studies would provide much information that is relevant to understanding relapse. However, this is not necessarily the case. Whether or not such studies are relevant to relapse will depend on the following two characteristics: (a) the sample that is analysed; and (b) the definition of outcome. To be directly relevant to relapse, the sample for analysis should consist only of smokers who have stopped smoking for some minimum period of time. For example, in a treatment study in which outcome at six months is predicted from various measures assessed at the end of treatment, the relevant sample might be all those abstinent at the termination of treatment. This has the additional advantage of controlling for the confounding effects of end-of-treatment smoking status. Unfortunately, most studies do not report analyses based on abstinent subjects only.

Turning to the question of definition of outcome, it is common practice to employ a point abstinence criterion which enables a comparison of those subjects who are not smoking at a given follow-up point with those who are. If we restrict the sample to those who were abstinent initially (as recommended earlier), then, in addition to subjects who have been continuously abstinent, the first group may include some 'lapsers' (those who have smoked one or more cigarettes but have since regained abstinence) and possibly some 'relapsers' (those who have experienced a full relapse but have made a renewed attempt to stop). The second group will consist of relapsers and possibly some subjects who have lapsed immediately prior to follow-up but who have not (yet) relapsed completely. Alternatively, some studies have employed a criterion of sustained abstinence which allows one to compare those who haven't smoked at all throughout the follow-up period with those who have smoked at least one cigarette but who may or may not be currently smoking. Thus, this outcome criterion effectively gives us continuous abstainers, on the one hand, versus lapsers and relapsers, on the other. Clearly, the sustained-abstinence criterion is more relevant to relapse. However, verification of self-report is more of a problem with this outcome criterion. In particular, it is generally not possible to validate, biochemically or otherwise, a subject's claim to have been continuously abstinent over a period of time. Other studies have employed continuous or nearly continuous measures such as 'per cent rate cigarette consumption' (daily consumption at follow-up expressed as a percentage of baseline consumption) or number of days to first lapse or to resumption of regular smoking.

Where they are available, this chapter focuses on prospective studies in which initially abstinent subjects were followed over time. Such studies enable stronger inferences to be drawn than retrospective studies in which ex-smokers and current smokers are asked about their past attempts to quit. However, some aspects of relapse are difficult, if not impossible, to study prospectively. For example, studies investigating the immediate antecedents and consequences of smoking lapses require a retrospective design; we have to wait for a lapse to occur before questioning the subject about the attendant circumstances.

Relapse rates

There are few systematic data on patterns and rates of relapse following smoking cessation. In the early 1970s, Hunt and his colleagues published relapse curves obtained by averaging the results of a large number of treatment studies. Figure 3.1 is from Hunt and Bespalec (1974) and shows the cumulative survival curves for two sets of studies; the 1971 curve is based on eighty-seven studies,

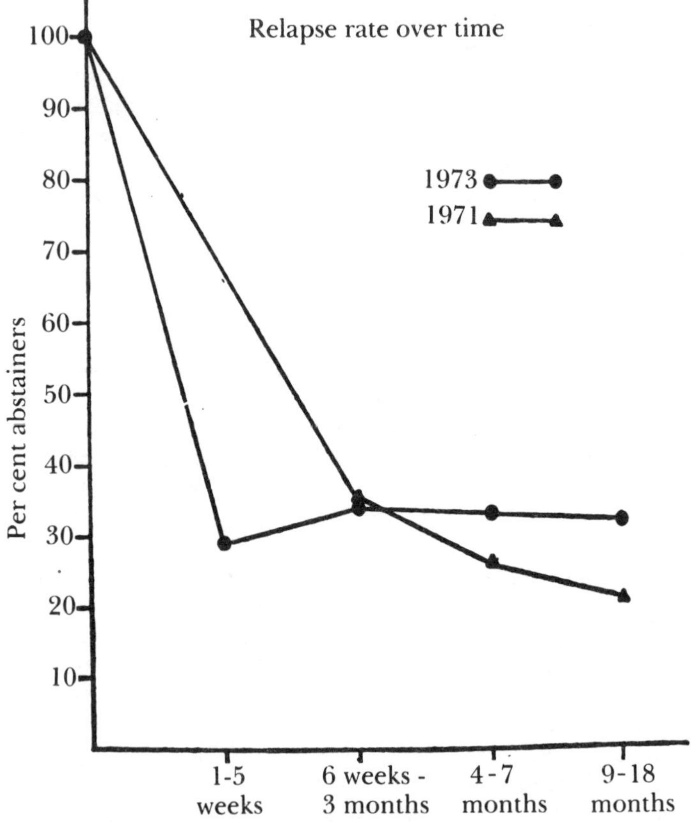

Source: Reproduced from Hunt and Bespalec (1974)

Figure 3.1 Cumulative survival curves for two sets of treatment studies

the 1973 curve on eighty-nine studies. Of those subjects abstinent at the end of treatment, the proportions still abstinent at the 9–18-month point are in the range 20–35 per cent. Note that the 1973 curve shows an increase in per cent abstainers between the first and second follow-up points instead of the expected monotonic decrease. This anomaly is presumably a result of combining disparate studies using varying follow-up periods, treatments, and subject samples. It is unclear whether the cumulative percentages are really based on sustained abstinence rates. If they are based on point abstinence rates, then the published curves probably give a flattering picture of the true state of affairs, since the sustained abstinence rate at a given time will always be less than or equal to the corresponding point abstinence rate. Some cautionary comments on the interpretation of relapse curves can be found in Litman *et al.* (1979) and Sutton (1979).

The best data on long-term relapse rates in a treatment or intervention setting come from the Multiple Risk Factor Intervention Trial (MRFIT), a six-year clinical trial of heart disease prevention through risk factor modification conducted in the United States. Men aged 35–57 at high risk for heart disease were randomly assigned to Special Intervention (SI) and Usual Care (UC) groups. Cigarette smokers in the SI group (n = 4,103) attended ten weekly group sessions incorporating both health education and behaviour modification components and then entered either a maintenance or an extended intervention programme which involved regular attendance (at least every four months) at the MRFIT centres. Figure 3.2 shows the survival curve for the SI group based on data from Hughes *et al.* (1981). There were 3,596 men who were cigarette smokers at first screen and who attended the forty-eight-month follow-up visit. Of these, 1,676 (46.6 per cent) had stopped by the four-month follow-up (which marked the end of the intensive intervention stage). This group is represented by the first point on the curve. At forty-eight months 56.2 per cent were still abstinent. It should be noted that these data are based on subjects' self-reports and that those who switched to a pipe or cigars were counted as successes. Although most relapses occurred in the first half of the period, significant relapse nevertheless took place after the sixteen-month follow-up (i.e., approximately one year from the end of intensive intervention); 33.2 per cent of those who relapsed between four months and forty-eight months did so after the sixteen-month point. The data of Hughes *et al.* (1981) also indicate that lighter smokers (1–19 cigarettes per day) not only had a higher cessation rate than heavier smokers but also a better maintenance rate; the percentages still abstinent at forty-eight months were 72.6 per cent in the 1–19 per

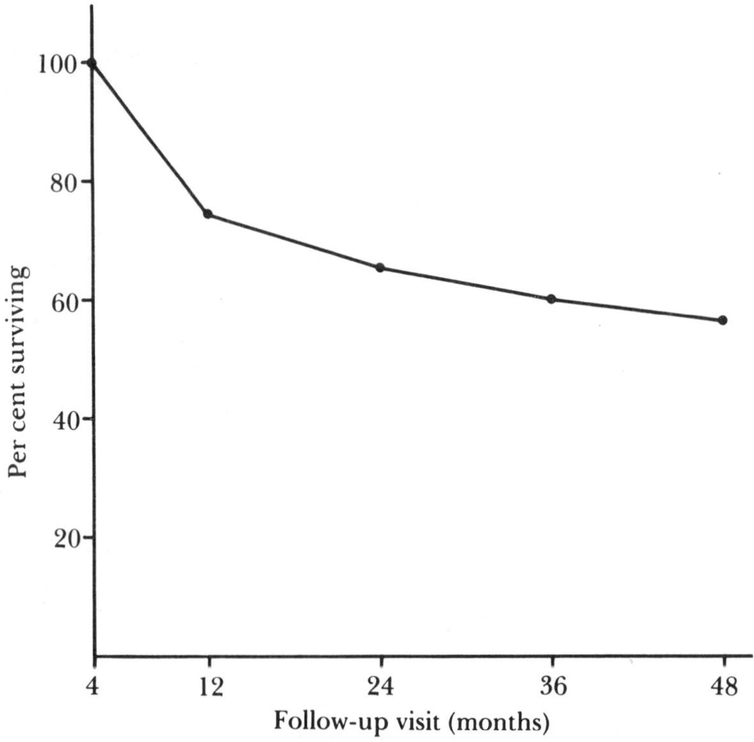

Source: Based on data from table 7, p.492, in Hughes, Hymowitz, Ockene, Simon, and Wogt (1981).

Figure 3.2 Cumulative survival curve for the Special Intervention (SI) group in the Multiple Risk Factor Intervention Trial (MRFIT)

day group compared with 53.1 per cent and 52.5 per cent in the 20–39 per day and 40+ per day groups.

Finer-grained analyses of relapse patterns have been conducted by Brandon *et al.* (1986) and Scott *et al.* (1986). These papers report data on such questions as the interval between first and second lapse and the rate of escalation to regular smoking, albeit in rather small samples.

I am not aware of any comparable data on natural recidivism in large population samples of smokers. There are obvious difficulties in obtaining detailed and accurate information on the timing and duration of periods of abstinence in such samples. Nevertheless, prospective studies are able to give an indication of the relapse rate in the population over a given period of time. For instance, Hammond and Garfinkel's (1964) data showed that of 96,890 ex-smokers at initial assessment 7.9 per cent had resumed cigarette smoking by the two-year follow up stage.

Conditioning, craving, and withdrawal

It is now recognized that cessation of smoking is associated with a syndrome of withdrawal symptoms which may last days or weeks. Commonly reported symptoms include craving, irritability, anxiety, inability to concentrate, and hunger (e.g., Cummings *et al.* 1985a; Hughes and Hatsukami 1986; Shiffman and Jarvik 1976; West *et al.* 1987). A simple model of (early) relapse would hold that smokers resume smoking in order to relieve such symptoms. A few studies have attempted to relate the experience of withdrawal to the probability of early relapse to smoking, with mixed success (Gunn 1986; Hughes and Hatsukami 1986; Manley and Boland 1983; Stitzer and Gross 1988; Subcommittee of the Research Committee of the British Thoracic Society (SRCBTS) 1984; West *et al.* 1987). There is a clear need for systematic prospective studies of smoking withdrawal and relapse.

In the literature on opiate and alcohol dependence, the idea that withdrawal symptoms may be classically conditioned to environmental cues and that relapse may be due to conditioned withdrawal has received considerable attention (e.g., Wikler 1980). A number of different versions of this conditioning theory have been proposed. The key ideas are as follows. Abrupt cessation of smoking (unconditional stimulus, UCS) is reliably followed by withdrawal symptoms, including craving (unconditional response, UCR). Environmental stimuli (conditional stimulus, CS) that are repeatedly associated with withdrawal may come to elicit conditioned withdrawal symptoms and conditioned craving (conditional response, CR). For example, a smoker who is unable to smoke in regular meetings and who experiences withdrawal symptoms may experience conditioned withdrawal in that situation when he or she subsequently stops smoking.

One advantage claimed for this model is that it is potentially able to account for relapse which occurs after months or even years of cessation when the 'real' withdrawal symptoms would be expected to have subsided. In keeping with the learning theory emphasis, smoking to relieve real or conditioned withdrawal could be explained in terms of operant conditioning, the withdrawal symptom being a negative reinforcer which is terminated by the resumption of smoking (although Grabowski and O'Brien (1981) argue that smoking in the presence of withdrawal symptoms is more accurately described in terms of *positive* reinforcement).

The cues that elicit conditioned withdrawal symptoms may include those associated with the act of smoking itself. Siegel and his colleagues point out that responses conditioned to the administration of some drugs are often opposite in direction to the drug effect (MacRae *et al.* 1987). They suggest that such compensatory CRs may be interpreted as withdrawal symptoms. As an example, they cite the glycemic effect of nicotine:

> Nicotine elevates blood glucose concentration. When the experienced smoker tries to stop smoking, we might expect that cigarette-associated environmental cues would elicit a cigarette-compensatory conditional decrease in blood sugar concentration, in anticipation of the hyperglycemic effect of nicotine usually occurring in the presence of these cues. The hypoglycemic CR is, on this occasion, not modulated by the hyperglycemic effect of nicotine (since the individual is abstaining from cigarettes). Thus, the nicotine addict, in the presence of nicotine-associated cues, might be expected to be hungry. Indeed, excessive eating (and resulting weight gain) is a commonly reported nicotine 'withdrawal symptom'.
>
> (MacRae *et al.* 1987: 378)

They argue that because of their anticipatory nature such 'withdrawal symptoms' might better be characterized as 'preparation symptoms'.

The above accounts may help to explain why an initial slip or lapse occurs. However, the conditioning approach has also been used to explain the consequences of an initial lapse. In discussing alcohol, Ludwig *et al.* (1974) argue that in dependent alcoholics the acute effects of consuming a small amount of alcohol may acquire the properties of a conditional stimulus that evokes conditioned withdrawal responses, including craving. Thus, in detoxified alcoholics the interoceptive actions of alcohol would stimulate craving for alcohol and further drinking ('loss of control').

Marlatt has suggested that the conditioned craving response is not aversive, as Ludwig *et al.* (1974) would argue, but appetitive and positive. Exposure to smoking-related cues (e.g., seeing a pack of cigarettes) will elicit positive expectancies and an increased desire for cigarettes (Marlatt 1985).

There have been no systematic attempts to investigate these ideas using cigarette smoking. One approach would be to obtain a detailed reinforcement history for a group of current smokers concerning the past occasions on which they have gone without cigarettes and the withdrawal symptoms they experienced and then to relate these experiences to subsequent relapse. A second approach would be to try to condition withdrawal symptoms in laboratory studies, perhaps using a paradigm similar to the one used by O'Brien and colleagues (1977) in studying opiate dependence. In their studies, withdrawal (UCR) was precipitated in former opiate addicts maintained on methadone by an injection of the opiate antagonist naloxone (UCS) in the presence of a distinctive conditional stimulus (peppermint odour plus tone). After a number of conditioning trials, a test trial was conducted in which the CS was presented on its own. This was found to elicit withdrawal symptoms. In principle, a similar paradigm could be employed to study the conditioning of withdrawal symptoms in smokers, if a suitable nicotine antagonist were available.

A number of studies in the literature on alcoholism have investigated the effect of a priming dose of alcohol on craving and/or subsequent consumption of alcohol in abstinent alcoholics. Several of these studies have controlled for the effects of expectancy (the belief that one is consuming alcohol) by means of the *balanced placebo design* (e.g. Engle and Williams 1972; Stockwell *et al.* 1982). In its simplest form, this consists of four conditions (2 × 2) under which the priming dose is administered: (i) given alcohol, told alcohol; (ii) given alcohol, told soft drink; (iii) given soft drink, told alcohol; (iv) given soft drink, told soft drink (Marlatt and Rohsenow 1980). With this design it is possible to examine the separate and interactive effects of alcohol and expectancy on craving and subsequent drinking. In principle, a similar approach could be applied to smoking to examine the following questions: What are the effects of smoking a single cigarette (or taking nicotine in some other form) on smokers who have recently stopped smoking? Do any of the effects resemble withdrawal symptoms, for example, heightened craving? Are the effects primarily due to the intake of nicotine or to the belief that one is taking in nicotine?

Marlatt's cognitive–behavioural approach

One of the most important theoretical contributions to relapse has been Marlatt's cognitive–behavioural approach (Cummings *et al.* 1980; Marlatt 1982; Marlatt and George 1984; Marlatt and Gordon 1980; Marlatt and Gordon 1985), although empirical tests of his ideas have lagged far behind the theoretical statements. Marlatt's theory is a rich blend of elements from social learning theory, social psychology, and psychodynamic theory, and it is difficult to do justice to his ideas in the space available. Perhaps as a corollary of this wealth of ideas, it is not always possible to derive tightly specified hypotheses from Marlatt's writings. This section attempts to give a brief outline of his theory and to review the relevant data in the smoking field.

As soon as the individual embarks on an attempt to stop smoking, he or she will encounter what Marlatt calls 'high-risk' situations, that is situations, occasions, or mood states that are frequently associated with relapse. Examples of such high-risk situations are feeling bored, having an argument with one's spouse, being at a party with other smokers, and finding a packet of cigarettes in the glove compartment. The individual's sense of perceived control or self-efficacy will increase to the extent that he/she deals with each high-risk situation as it arises using an effective coping response or strategy. The probability of a lapse decreases accordingly. Coping strategies may be cognitive or behavioural. If, for whatever reason, the person fails to apply an effective coping strategy, he/she will experience a decrease in self-efficacy. If the individual also holds positive outcome expectancies about smoking (e.g., that smoking will help them to relax in a stressful situation), then the probability of an initial lapse is increased.

Perhaps the most interesting part of the theory concerns the person's cognitive and affective reactions to the initial lapse and the implications these have for the probability of escalation to a full-blown relapse as opposed to a return to the abstinent state. This reaction is termed the Abstinence Violation Effect (AVE). The intensity of the AVE is postulated to be a function of a number of factors (e.g., the duration of the abstinence period, the presence of significant others) and to involve two components: (a) a cognitive dissonance effect; and (b) an attribution effect. To the extent that the violation (i.e., smoking a cigarette) is perceived to be inconsistent with one's self-image as a (would-be) ex-smoker, then dissonance will be aroused and is likely to be resolved in ways that increase the probability that the lapse will escalate to a full relapse. If smoking has been used in the past to cope with conflict and tension, then it may be used in a similar way in the high-risk situation. Alternatively, one way of reducing dissonance is to alter one's self-image so as to bring it into line with the new behaviour (e.g., 'This just goes to show that I am a smoker after all.').

With regard to the second, attributional, component of the AVE, if the person sees the lapse as due to stable personal or internal factors such as lack of will-power rather than as due to the particular situation (external, unstable), then again the probability of a subsequent relapse will increase.

As yet, there is little empirical evidence bearing directly on

Marlatt's theory. Cummings *et al.* (1980) categorized the initial relapse episodes of sixty-four smokers who had attended a treatment programme and identified three main high-risk situations. These were negative emotional states (accounting for 37 per cent of relapses), interpersonal conflict (15 per cent), and social pressure (32 per cent). 'Negative emotional states' refers to frustration, anxiety, depression, boredom, and so on, associated with intrapersonal factors and/or reactions to non-personal environmental events. 'Interpersonal conflict' refers to ongoing or relatively recent conflict involving family, friends, or workmates. 'Social pressure' was subdivided into direct social pressure, involving verbal persuasion from others to smoke, and indirect social pressure, which refers simply to being in the presence of people who are smoking. For smokers, the latter subcategory accounted for the majority of social pressure relapses. Only 2 per cent of relapses were associated with negative physical states (physical states specifically associated with prior smoking, such as 'withdrawal discomfort', and other physical states such as pain, illness, injury, and fatigue) and only 5 per cent were associated with urges and temptations, whether these occurred in the presence of smoking cues or 'out of the blue'. However, temporal factors were not taken into account in the analysis and it may be that the latter situations would occur more frequently among early relapsers, that is, smokers who relapse very soon after embarking on an attempt to quit. Other retrospective studies of the situational factors surrounding relapse are discussed in the following section.

Although situations such as negative emotional states may be regarded as 'high-risk' in the sense that a substantial proportion of relapses occur in such situations, they may nevertheless be low risk in so far as many smokers who are trying to quit may experience numerous episodes of boredom or depression without relapsing. From this standpoint, the riskiness of a particular situation is defined as the conditional probability of relapsing given exposure to that situation. In the same way, situations that are associated with relatively few relapses (e.g., testing personal control) may in fact be high risk in the sense that the chances of relapse are high if that situation is encountered. This raises the question of the frequency of exposure to different kinds of situations among smokers who are trying to stop smoking. For instance, do those smokers who relapse within a given time period tend to be those who have been exposed to a greater number of high-risk situations or to different kinds of situations than those who survive that period? What determines differential exposure to high-risk situations? Do some smokers covertly seek out high-risk situations so that they can give a convincing excuse for having smoked? By focusing on the situation in which relapse occurs rather than looking at prior exposure to different kinds of situations, one misses an important part of the complete picture. Another question that is not fully dealt with by Marlatt and his co-workers is what is it about high-risk situations that makes them high risk? To a large extent they may be situations in which the person has in the past usually or frequently smoked. This suggests that it would be helpful to try to link the following three sets of situations: usual smoking situations (i.e., prior to any attempt to stop), situations encountered when the person tries to quit, and the particular situation in which relapse occurs.

Two recent studies have investigated the factors influencing escalation to full-blown relapse to smoking once an initial lapse has occurred and hence have a direct bearing on the second part of Marlatt's theory. In the study reported by Curry *et al.* (1987), heavy smokers participating in a treatment programme were given smoking episode description forms and postage-paid envelopes and were asked to complete them and send them in if they smoked at least one cigarette after forty-eight hours or more of abstinence. The form asked subjects to specify one major cause for having smoked and to rate on seven-point scales (a) the degree to which this cause was due to them or to other people or circumstances (locus of causality), (b) whether the cause would be present in similar situations in the future (stability), and (c) whether the cause influenced other areas of their lives besides smoking (specificity). They were also asked whether they subsequently returned to regular smoking ('relapsers') or regained abstinence ('slippers'). Thirty-six subjects provided complete attribution and outcome data. Bearing in mind that it is not known what proportion of those who smoked this represents and that there may have been a self-selection bias associated with returning the forms, the results indicated that relapsers gave significantly more internal, stable, and global attributions for having smoked a single cigarette than slippers, which confirmed the authors' hypothesis. Relapsers also reported significantly more guilt after smoking their first cigarette but described the situation as less stressful. They also tended to report no change in perceived control from immediately before to immediately after smoking whereas slippers reported an increase in control.

Unfortunately the authors give no information on the causes reported by the subjects and there was no attempt to link the findings with Marlatt's classification of high-risk situations. It is possible that relapsers and slippers may differ in this regard and that differences in attributions may simply reflect differences in the type of situation associated with the initial smoking episode. For example, if I cite 'boredom' as the main cause of my initial smoking episode, I may be more likely to make an internal attribution than if I say that someone offered me a cigarette, which seems to imply an external attribution.

Prior to treatment Curry *et al.* (1987) also presented their subjects with a set of six hypothetical high-risk situations (e.g., feeling depressed, being at a party with other smokers) and asked them to suggest one major cause for having smoked (or not smoked) and to make the same three attribution ratings in each case. Interestingly, they found that two of these ratings (internal–external and stable–unstable) predicted relapse outcome. Compared with slippers, relapsers made significantly more internal and stable attributions for smoking in these hypothetical situations. However, there was no correlation between the attributions given for the hypothetical smoking situations and those given for the initial smoking episodes on these attribution dimensions. Thus, attributions for hypothetical situations appeared to be an independent predictor of relapse outcome.

In a similar study using a much larger sample, O'Connell and Martin (1987) interviewed subjects three months after they had taken part in a community-based smoking cessation clinic. Subjects who had smoked since the end of the programme were asked about the first cigarette smoked. Situations were classified using Marlatt's scheme. In addition, subjects were asked to rate the extent to which the smoking episode was due to will-power (internal) and to environmental (external) factors. The frequencies of situations were broadly similar to those reported by Marlatt (1985). The most frequently occurring items were 'negative emotional states – other' (26 per cent), 'social pressure – indirect' (25 per cent), and 'interpersonal conflict' (19 per cent). Loglinear modelling was used to compare 'relapsers' (those who stopped for twenty-four hours or more but then went back to smoking; n = 451) and 'lapsers' (those who stopped for twenty-four hours or more, lapsed temporarily, but then returned to abstinence; n = 60). The results showed that, compared with lapsers, relapsers tended to cite situations involving negative affect and made more internal and less external attributions. The attributional findings are consistent with those of Curry *et al.* (1987).

One problem with this study is that information was obtained from the two groups in different ways. Relapsers were interviewed by telephone whereas lapsers were interviewed in person so that a saliva sample could be obtained for biochemical validation of abstinence. A third group of subjects (abstainers) were also interviewed and asked about the situation in which they had been most tempted to smoke. Although they report that abstainers cited similar types of situations to lapsers (and that both these groups tended to differ from relapsers), it is not clear whether this is a valid comparison.

Other studies that have examined the immediate impact of relapse crises are also relevant to Marlatt's theory. Brandon *et al.* (1986) report that the predominant cognitive and affective responses of their subjects to the first lapse were self-blame/self-deprecation and depression/hopelessness. However, there was no evidence that reacting in this way was associated with more rapid escalation to regular smoking. The findings of Condiotte and Lichtenstein (1981) appear inconsistent with these results. Compared with those who lapsed but regained abstinence, those who relapsed completely were more likely to report that they felt guilty following the first relapse episode, that their confidence in their ability to resist further cigarettes had been reduced, and that they had made no attempt to control their smoking after the first cigarette. Finally, Shiffman (1984a) found that subjects who smoked in a relapse crisis were more likely to report feelings of guilt and less likely to report feeling worried than those who resisted temptation. The two groups did not differ in the frequency with which they reported positive feelings or feelings of failure. Surprisingly, lapsers had significantly higher pre-crisis self-efficacy ratings and both groups showed a similar reduction in self-efficacy from before to after. Shiffman's work is discussed in detail in the following section.

Shiffman's situational approach

Like Marlatt, Shiffman emphasizes the immediate situational antecedents of relapse (Shiffman 1982, 1984a, 1984b, 1986; Shiffman and Jarvik 1987; Shiffman *et al.* 1985a, 1985b). Although similar in many ways, his approach is less theoretical and more empirically based than Marlatt's. Unlike Marlatt, he has focused on smoking rather than on other addictive behaviours. Shiffman's approach employs a novel methodological device, a telephone hotline service for ex-smokers seeking help to stay off cigarettes. Callers to the Stay–Quit Line were interviewed, usually for 20 to 30 minutes, to obtain information on the antecedents and impact of the 'relapse crisis' (similar to Marlatt's high-risk situation). Shiffman (1982) reports that the hotline was successful in obtaining reports of relapse crises soon after they occurred; over 80 per cent of interviews took place within two days of the crisis. Over half the sample had abstained for less than ten days. Thus, the paradigm was useful in obtaining information on early relapse episodes. The data reported by Shiffman in a series of papers are based on overlapping samples obtained at various periods in the history of the hotline. In all the analyses, the sample was limited to those ex-smokers who used to smoke at least ten cigarettes a day and who reported having been abstinent from smoking for at least two days. No systematic data have been published on long-term outcome.

Shiffman (1982) describes the characteristics of relapse crises based on a sample of 183 ex-smokers, reporting, for instance, that 56 per cent took place in subjects' homes, that 29 per cent occurred when the ex-smokers had been eating or drinking, that 71 per cent occurred in the presence of negative affect, and that 54 per cent of subjects experienced withdrawal symptoms of one kind or another during the crisis. These findings are suggestive but they are subject to the same problem of interpretation as Marlatt's data on high-risk situations, namely that they are based only on positive instances (a relapse crisis occurred) whereas there is no information on negative instances (no crisis occurred). It would be useful to know, for example, how many times subjects had experienced negative affect without this precipitating a relapse crisis.

Of more relevance are the correlates of whether or not the person actually smoked in the situation, that is, whether the relapse crisis became a relapse episode. Shiffman (1982) reports that 39 per cent of callers said they had smoked a cigarette (usually one) in the situation. A number of variables were identified as correlates of smoking. Compared with those who did not smoke, lapsers were significantly more likely to report that other smokers were present, that they experienced *no* withdrawal symptoms in the situation, that they had consumed alcohol, and that the crisis took place at sites other than home or work. However, the most important predictor of outcome was performance of a coping response. Ex-smokers who reported using either behavioural coping (e.g., refusing the offer of a cigarette, leaving the situation) or cognitive coping (e.g., mentally reviewing the benefits of quitting) were much less likely to smoke than those who performed no coping response (28 per cent vs. 58 per cent for behavioural coping; 30 per cent vs. 55 per cent for cognitive coping; $p < 0.001$). (The relationship between coping and survival was in fact more complicated than this. Behavioural coping was associated with success only when subjects had not consumed alcohol and only when they were not feeling depressed.)

Other correlates of whether subjects smoked in the relapse crisis are mentioned by Shiffman (1984a). In response to a question on what effects they expected from smoking in that situation, those who smoked cited 'reduction of tension' more frequently and 'reduction of craving' less frequently than those who resisted the temptation to smoke.

Shiffman (1984b) replicated the main findings on an additional sample of eighty-one new cases. He also performed more detailed analyses of coping responses on the combined sample of 264 ex-smokers. The number of coping responses was unrelated to survival. Subjects who performed two or more cognitive or two or more behavioural responses were no more likely to survive the relapse crisis than those who performed only one. Coping responses were categorized into a number of different types. For example, behavioural coping was divided into the following categories: eating or drinking; distracting activity; escape; delay; physical activity; relaxation; and other behaviour. Cognitive coping responses were also categorized into seven types. With two exceptions, all coping responses seemed to be about equally effective.

Shiffman and Jarvik (1987) further analysed the hotline data with respect to the correlates of coping in relapse crises. They found evidence for decay of coping over time; the longer the subject had been abstinent, the less likely they were to perform a coping response. Characteristics of the situation also varied with length of abstinence. Later crises were less likely to be associated with withdrawal symptoms, alcohol, stress, and unusual locations.

Shiffman (1986) derived a taxonomy of relapse crises by subjecting the data on situational characteristics to cluster analysis. Four clusters emerged, which he labelled Social, Relaxation, Work, and Upset. These types of situations differed in the frequency of both coping and smoking. Social situations were significantly more likely to result in smoking than each of the other three types, and the frequency of smoking was higher in Upset situations than in Relaxation situations. The frequency of behavioural coping accounted for the higher lapse rates in Upset but not in Social situations. Shiffman *et al.* (1985a) reported broadly similar findings from a cluster analysis based on a small subsample of fifty-three cases.

Shiffman interprets these findings as support for a coping skill model of relapse. Given exposure to a relapse crisis, whether or not a lapse occurs will depend in part on whether the individual does something in an attempt to cope with the temptation to smoke; precisely what the person does seems to be less important. Shiffman does, however, mention the alternative possibility that subjects who survived may have been motivated to construct coping responses to which they could attribute their success.

The major problem with Shiffman's approach is that his findings and conclusions are based on a sample of ex-smokers who chose to call the hotline to seek help. Nothing is known about those who did not call. Self-selection bias could account for many of his findings. Suppose, for example, that ex-smokers who survived a relapse crisis without employing any coping response were less likely to telephone the hotline. These people would then be underrepresented in the sample, and, conversely, survivors who performed a coping response would be overrepresented. The overall effect would be to produce a positive association between coping and survival among the sample of callers. Although Shiffman (1982) employs this argument to explain the unexpected inverse relationship between withdrawal symptoms and smoking, he does not apply it to his main findings. The problem is that he is unable to rule out this alternative explanation, except on the grounds of plausibility.

Several studies have attempted to replicate aspects of Shiffman's findings using different sampling procedures. Cummings *et al.* (1985b), Brandon *et al.* (1986), and Baer and Lichtenstein (1988) used coding schemes similar to Shiffman (1982) to characterize the relapse episodes of subjects who had stopped smoking during a smoking cessation programme and then relapsed during a one- or two-year follow-up period (ns = 69, 54, and 176, respectively). In these studies, all those who relapsed were interviewed, thus eliminating the possibility of self-selection bias arising from the use of the hotline methodology. The frequencies of endorsement of various characteristics of the relapse situations were quite similar across all four samples. In addition, both Cummings *et al.* (1985b) and Brandon *et al.* (1986) reported tentative evidence that the circumstances leading to relapse varied with length of abstinence. In the Baer and Lichtenstein study, the data were analysed using the same clustering procedure as in Shiffman (1986) but yielded a simpler solution. Two clusters emerged, labelled Nonsocial/Negative (68 per cent of cases) and Social/Positive (32 per cent of cases), representing rather loose groupings of situational characteristics. Categorization of relapse episodes in terms of the two clusters was not related to length of abstinence, the time between relapse and interview, or to various prospective measures including the characteristics of a relapse occurring prior to intervention, prior smoking behaviour, perceived stress, nicotine dependence, and self-efficacy. However, there was tentative evidence that the situational characteristics of isolated incidents of smoking (slips) prior to relapse were related to cluster membership of the relapse episode, suggesting some individual consistency during the maintenance phase of quitting. Baer and Lichtenstein conclude that situational characteristics of relapse episodes are not as patterned or as predictable as previous descriptive studies have suggested.

Finally, support for some of Shiffman's findings with regard to coping responses comes from a study of unaided quitters reported by Curry and Marlatt (1985). Subjects were interviewed by telephone approximately one and four months after the cessation date. As

Shiffman found, the probability of surviving a high-risk situation was related to whether or not a coping response was performed. Among the eighty-eight subjects who described high-risk situations at one month, the survival rate was 63 per cent among those who reported both behavioural and cognitive coping compared with only 3 per cent among those who reported no coping. Again, as in Shiffman's results, the different types of coping strategies seemed to be about equally effective. Curry and Marlatt suggest that treatment participants should be encouraged to 'think *and* do something' when they encounter a high-risk situation. Although they go on to examine predictors of coping, they unfortunately did not test whether the same variables predicted smoking in the situation.

Self-efficacy theory

Self-efficacy theory (Bandura 1977, 1982) holds that the main factor mediating behavioural change is the individual's self-efficacy expectations, that is, the belief that they can successfully perform a given task in a given situation. A number of studies have applied self-efficacy theory to smoking relapse. This section focuses on prospective studies in which the self-efficacy expectations of recent quitters (e.g., subjects abstinent at the end of treatment) are used to predict subsequent relapse or maintenance of abstinence (Baer *et al.* 1986; Coelho 1984; Colletti *et al.* 1985; Condiotte and Lichtenstein 1981; DiClemente 1981; DiClemente *et al.* 1985; Killen *et al.* 1984; McIntyre *et al.* 1983). In these studies self-efficacy expectancies were measured by means of questionnaires listing a number of situations in which smoking may occur (e.g., when you want to relax, when you feel angry with yourself, when you have finished a meal or snack). Subjects were asked to rate their confidence that they would be able to resist the urge to smoke in each situation. The total or mean score was used as an index of the strength of efficacy expectations. Although there is no a priori reason to expect the items to reflect a single common factor, the evidence suggests that such questionnaires are primarily or approximately undimensional (Baer *et al.* 1986; DiClemente 1981).

DiClemente (1981; see also DiClemente and Prochaska 1982) interviewed sixty-three smokers who had recently stopped smoking, defined as 99 per cent free of their former habit (number of cigarettes per day) for at least two weeks. All subjects were interviewed within seven weeks of their quitting and completed a twelve-item Self-Efficacy questionnaire. They were re-interviewed by telephone five months after quitting and divided on the basis of self-report into successful maintainers (those who remained 99 per cent free of their habit over the five-month follow-up period) and recidivists. There were no significant differences between the two groups on any of the demographic or smoking history variables. The only significant predictor of smoking status was self-efficacy, with successful maintainers having higher scores than recidivists ($r = 0.35$, calculated from the F-value cited).

DiClemente *et al.* (1985) assigned 957 volunteers who were not involved in any formal treatment programme to one of five groups based on their smoking status and followed them up three to five months later. Of most relevance for present purposes is their 'recent quitters' group (143 subjects who were currently not smoking and had maintained abstinence for at least one day but not more than six months prior to the initial assessment). At follow-up, they were divided into three groups: long-term quitters, who had maintained non-smoking status for six months or more; relapsers; and those who had maintained recent quitter status. (Note that the last of these is a mixed group that would include both people who had been abstinent throughout the follow-up period and those who had relapsed but had then made a renewed attempt to stop.) A one-way ANOVA comparing these three groups indicated a significant difference in self-efficacy scores at initial assessment based on a thirty-one item questionnaire, with long-term quitters having higher scores than the other two groups. Temptation scores based on the same thirty-one situations correlated −0.18 with self-efficacy scores among recent quitters and did not significantly differentiate between the three follow-up groups. In a discriminant analysis of the same sample, self-efficacy emerged as one of only three significant predictors of smoking status from a set of fourteen predictors (Prochaska *et al.* 1985). Smoking status at follow-up was not significantly predicted from a variety of baseline variables including demographics and smoking history (Wilcox *et al.* 1985).

Coelho (1984), who used the same questionnaire as DiClemente *et al.* (1985), found that among forty-two subjects who were abstinent at termination of smoking treatment, end-of-treatment efficacy expectations correlated 0.43 ($p < 0.01$) with smoking status at three-month follow-up (sustained abstinence vs. relapse). Similar results were obtained by Condiotte and Lichtenstein (1981) in a sample of seventy-eight subjects participating in three different treatment programmes. End-of-treatment efficacy scores (based on forty-eight items) were significantly correlated ($r = 0.59$, $p < 0.0001$) with subsequent relapse (defined as whether or not the subject had resumed smoking at the rate of more than one cigarette a week) assessed at three months post-treatment. However, their base included ten subjects who were smoking at the end of treatment.

Consequently, the effects of end-of-treatment smoking status were not adequately controlled for. An interesting aspect of this study is that they obtained a high degree of correspondence between the situation in which subjects subsequently relapsed and end-of-treatment efficacy scores based on a cluster analysis which grouped situations into seven different types. Thus, those who expressed low confidence that they would be able to resist smoking in a social situation (e.g., when someone offers you a cigarette) tended to relapse in that type of situation. However, Baer *et al.* (1986) report that they have been unable to replicate this finding.

In a similar study using a virtually identical questionnaire, McIntyre *et al.* (1983) obtained a correlation of 0.37 ($p < 0.01$) between end-of-treatment efficacy and three-month follow-up smoking status (defined as not smoking during the week prior to follow-up vs. smoked during that week) among forty-one subjects who were abstinent at the end of treatment. However, the correlations for six months and one year were not significant ($r = 0.18$ and 0.00 respectively).

In a third study using a similar design, subjects, and measures, Baer *et al.* (1986) reported a failure to replicate their previous findings. Among subjects abstinent at end of treatment ($n = 64$), end-of-treatment efficacy ratings and smoking status at the one-, two-, three-, and six-month follow-ups were at best only marginally related (maximum $r = 0.21$, $p < 0.10$). In this study, the one-, two-, and three-month follow-ups were conducted by telephone, and subjects who were abstinent or nearly abstinent (smoking no more than one cigarette a day) rated their confidence on four items from the full forty-six item questionnaire. In sharp contrast to the results for end-of-treatment efficacy, at each follow-up efficacy based on this four-item scale was strongly correlated with smoking status at subsequent follow-ups. For example, two-month efficacy correlated 0.55 ($p < 0.001$) with three-month smoking status and 0.56 with six-month smoking status. These findings are intriguing and suggest the need for a more detailed analysis. Length of abstinence may play a role here. At each follow-up those defined as abstinent or nearly abstinent would comprise three subgroups: (a) those who had remained abstinent since the end of treatment; (b) those who had smoked since end of treatment but had not smoked during the week prior to follow-up; and (c) those who had smoked during this week but not more than one cigarette a day on average. These three subgroups would be expected to differ with regard to self-efficacy scores. Controlling for the effect of length of abstinence may well attenuate the observed relationship between efficacy and subsequent status and indicate that length of abstinence is a stronger predictor than efficacy. Alternatively, to the extent that the self-efficacy measure can be interpreted as a kind of self-prediction of one's future behaviour, it may be the case that people's predictions improve in accuracy over time as they encounter tempting situations of the kind included in the Confidence questionnaire.

Colletti *et al.* (1985) developed a seventeen-item Smoking Self-Efficacy Questionnaire (SSEQ) similar to those used in the studies discussed above. A clinic sample of smokers ($n = 56$) who were abstinent at post-maintenance (i.e., at the end of therapeutic contact) were divided into three groups: those who relapsed within the first month after post-maintenance; those who relapsed between one and three months after post-maintenance; and those who relapsed between three months and one year afterwards. Relapse was defined as having smoked more than one cigarette in any three-day period during follow-up. A one-way ANOVA revealed a significant difference in post-maintenance SSEQ scores, with those who relapsed before the one-month follow-up having lower efficacy scores than those who relapsed after three-month follow-up. By contrast, a simple global expectancy measure which asked subjects whether they would smoke again in the future did not significantly predict relapse. However, subjects who remained abstinent throughout the follow-up period were apparently excluded from these analyses.

Finally, Killen *et al.* (1984), using the Condiotte and Lichtenstein (1981) questionnaire, reported that, among initially successful quitters, post-treatment (six-week) self-efficacy scores significantly predicted outcome at fifteen-week follow-up ($r = 0.34$, $p < 0.02$) but not at long-term (ten-and-a-half-month) follow-up.

Overall, this review of self-efficacy theory as applied to smoking relapse shows fairly consistently that abstinent subjects' self-efficacy expectations predict subsequent relapse, at least in the short term. Although concurrent smoking status was controlled for in the analyses reported, it is also necessary to demonstrate that the observed correlation is not due to other antecedent variables that may influence both self-efficacy and the probability of relapse. In practice, this means controlling for the effects of any variable (in a multiple regression analysis, for instance) that correlates with self-efficacy even if its correlation with the criterion (relapse vs. abstinence) is zero. A number of correlates of efficacy expectations have been reported. For example, Baer *et al.* (1986) obtained significant correlations between end-of-treatment efficacy and baseline smoking rate, perceived stress, and perceived social support, among other things. However, to my knowledge, no studies have examined the correlates of efficacy expectations among the most relevant group of subjects, that is, those who have recently stopped smoking.

As it has been applied to smoking, self-efficacy theory is a one-variable theory. However, the belief that one can do something is clearly insufficient as a predictor or a determinant of behaviour. A key factor that is ignored (and this is true generally of cognitive–behavioural approaches) is motivation. As well as believing one can do something, it is also necessary to want to do it. This writer believes (possibly erroneously) that he has the ability to learn Italian (high self-efficacy expectations) but he lacks the required motivation and is therefore unlikely to do so. Although Bandura emphasizes efficacy expectations, he also defines a second kind of expectancy, namely outcome expectancy, which is the belief that a given behaviour will or will not lead to a given outcome. This is one way of conceptualizing motivation. An individual will be motivated to perform a behaviour to the extent that he or she believes that it will lead on balance to highly desired outcomes. Studies that have applied self-efficacy theory to smoking relapse have not investigated this second component of the model, though Godding and Glasgow (1985) have used outcome expectations together with efficacy expectations to predict controlled smoking status.

A concept which seems to be closely related to self-efficacy is behavioural expectation or self-prediction (Warshaw and Davis 1985). This is simply the individual's expectancy or subjective probability that he or she will perform the behaviour in question. In principle, behavioural expectations should integrate information about self-efficacy, motivation, and prior behaviour to provide a better predictor of behaviour than any of these variables would on their own. A number of prospective studies have used simple measures of success expectancy to predict relapse among abstinent subjects (Colletti *et al.* 1985; Eisinger 1971; Hall and Havassy 1986; Horwitz *et al.* 1985; Ockene *et al.* 1982; O'Connell 1984; Pederson *et al.* 1982; SRCBTS 1984). In Eisinger's (1971) study, a US national sample of 570 former cigarette smokers (those who had smoked as many as 100 cigarettes in their entire life but did not currently smoke cigarettes) were re-interviewed two years later. Eighty-seven per cent were again classified as former smokers. A higher proportion of abstainers than recidivists believed at the initial interview that they would not be smoking in five years (97.2 per cent vs. 81.9 per cent, $p < 0.001$). Pederson *et al.* (1982), in their multivariate analysis of factors predicting recidivism among respiratory patients, found that subjects' self-prediction ('What do you think the chances are that you will quit smoking in the next six months?') was the best predictor of outcome. In the SRCBTS (1984) study, a large-scale trial of nicotine chewing-gum in patients with smoking-related diseases, successes and failures at one year were compared with regard to their responses at three months. Among subjects who were abstinent at three months (n = 226), 85 per cent of eventual successes were certain they would remain abstinent compared with 59 per cent of eventual failures ($p < 0.005$). O'Connell (1984) found that those who relapsed had a higher expectancy of smoking in the three months after the cessation programme than did abstainers, although the two groups apparently did not differ with regard to their expectancy of success ('certainty of remaining a non-smoker'). The other studies did not find a relationship between success expectancy and relapse.

The accuracy of prediction is likely to be improved by reducing the time interval between the measurement of expectation and behaviour. The shorter the interval, the lower the chances are that events will occur that produce changes in expectations. Thus, it is not surprising that pre-treatment efficacy ratings do not usually predict subsequent behaviour, particularly as these ratings appear to be influenced by treatment (Coelho 1984; Colletti *et al.* 1985; Condiotte and Lichtenstein 1981; Killen *et al.* 1984; McIntyre *et al.* 1983; Nicki *et al.* 1984).

A second factor that may influence the accuracy of prediction has received a great deal of attention in the literature on attitude–behaviour relations (e.g., Ajzen and Fishbein 1980) but has been largely overlooked in applications of self-efficacy theory. This concerns the degree of 'correspondence' between the measures of behavioural expectation or self-efficacy and the criterion measure of behaviour. In order to predict behaviour accurately, the two concepts must be measured at the same level of specificity or generality. For example, Eisinger's (1971) measures of expectation and smoking status do not correspond in so far as the first refers to 'five years' time' whereas the second interview actually took place two rather than five years later. Taking this argument to the extreme, in order to maximize prediction, subjects should be made familiar with the definition of the criterion behaviour: 'This is the question we will be asking you in three months' time to assess your smoking status. Please indicate what you think your answer will be at that time.'

It should be noted that none of this makes any assumptions about the causal influence, as opposed to the predictive validity, of behavioural self-predictions. Behavioural expectations may themselves have a direct causal effect on subsequent behaviour (the 'self-fulfilling prophecy'). Alternatively, they may correlate with subsequent behaviour because both variables have correlated or common causes. For example, behaviour at time 2 may be correlated with behaviour at time 1 because they have causes in common; behavioural expectations measured at time 1 may reflect behaviour at time 1: that is, people's predictions about their future behaviour may be based on their current or prior behaviour; as a consequence, expectations at time 1 and behaviour at time 2 will be correlated.

Discussion and conclusion

The four theoretical approaches to smoking relapse that have been considered differ in a number of ways. First, they differ in the extent to which they have been applied to smoking. Although learning theory ideas are pervasive in the smoking field, there have been no systematic applications of what we have characterized as the 'conditioning, craving, withdrawal' approach to understanding relapse in smoking. This would seem to be a fruitful area for research. Similarly, Marlatt's ideas have in the main been applied in the field of alcoholism and little work has yet been conducted on smoking. By contrast, Shiffman's work has been confined to smoking, although Neidigh *et al.* (1988) have recently extended his approach to alcohol use. Self-efficacy theory has been widely applied to addictive and other health-related behaviours (see the reviews by DiClemente 1986 and O'Leary 1985).

The approaches also differ in the extent to which they focus on lapses, relapses, or both. The conditioning approach has not made this distinction, although the work on priming effects can be seen as a way of investigating the consequences of an initial lapse. Marlatt's approach is grounded on the lapse-relapse distinction and attempts to account for both stages. Shiffman's work focuses almost exclusively on lapses, or, more accurately, on crises which may or may not result in a lapse. To date, he has published no long-term data from his hotline studies. The work on self-efficacy largely ignores the lapse-relapse distinction. However, this could be usefully incorporated in future work. For example, two kinds of self-efficacy expectations could be assessed, those related to avoiding a lapse in a particular situation and those related to avoiding a full-blown relapse given that an initial lapse occurs.

The conditioning approach and those of Marlatt and Shiffman tend to emphasize situational rather than individual factors in relapse, although in the latter two cases, individual factors enter in the form of the coping skills and strategies that people bring with them to the situation. The self-efficacy approach, on the other hand, is situational only in respect of the way in which efficacy expectations are usually assessed. Even here, the usual practice is to employ an overall score rather than to study situation-specific expectations. Self-efficacy is seen as a relatively enduring, individual factor which is nevertheless susceptible to change, that is, it is more akin to an 'attitude' than to a personality trait. The situational emphasis evident in much work on relapse is perhaps not surprising given that relapse, or at least the first cigarette smoked after a period of abstinence, is a discrete event occurring in a particular situation.

The four approaches have different implications for treatment and intervention. To the extent that withdrawal symptoms are considered to be the main problem, some form of nicotine replacement to alleviate withdrawal would seem to be indicated. To date, there have been no controlled studies of nicotine replacement as a relapse prevention technique. However, a large-scale evaluation (n = 1,938) of nicotine chewing-gum as an adjunct to general practitioners' advice to stop smoking (Russell *et al.* 1983) found that the offer and prescription of the gum significantly reduced the relapse rate between the four-month and one-year follow-ups as compared with advice only (41 per cent vs. 55 per cent, $p < 0.05$). It should be noted that, from a strict learning theory perspective, nicotine replacement on its own would not be regarded as sufficient since it does not involve any systematic extinction of smoking behaviour. The nicotine antagonist mecamylamine is one potential agent of extinction (Nemeth-Coslett *et al.* 1986).

The approaches of Marlatt and Shiffman both imply that treatment should incorporate relapse prevention procedures designed to prepare the client for the inevitable encounter with high-risk situations or relapse crises and to teach appropriate coping skills and strategies. Thus, the problem is seen as one of lack of preparedness and deficient coping skills. There have been several controlled studies of skills training but these have yielded generally negative results (Brandon *et al.* 1987; Brown *et al.* 1984; Davis and Glaros 1986; Hall *et al.* 1984; Supnick and Colletti 1984). However, all these studies suffer from serious methodological deficiencies such as low statistical power and failure to compare conditions in terms of relapse or survival rates rather than simply the percentage of abstainers at various follow-up points.

There have been no experimental studies of the self-efficacy approach in the field of smoking relapse. Self-efficacy theory implies that treatments should incorporate efficacy-enhancing or confidence-boosting procedures. Bandura (1977) suggests a number of ways in which efficacy can be enhanced but argues that performance-based methods are likely to prove the most powerful. In the treatment of smoking, this might involve inducing clients to perform relatively minor tasks successfully (e.g., cutting down on the number smoked, not smoking in particular situations) and thus building their confidence for the major task of quitting smoking altogether.

Current approaches to relapse tend to make the implicit assumption that relapse is an event, something that happens to smokers who are trying to quit. An alternative view is that relapse is a decision. Saunders and Allsop have laid the groundwork for this approach in a stimulating paper in which they consider the question 'do relapses happen to people – or do people decide to make a relapse happen?' (Saunders and Allsop 1987: 421). Marlatt and Gordon (1985) have suggested that in some cases the initial lapse may be covertly planned or set up by the individual, though this notion is not emphasized in their theoretical statements. Elsewhere (Sutton 1987), I have presented a decision-making approach to understanding smokers' decisions to try to stop smoking based on their confidence that they could stop smoking if they tried (a kind of global self-efficacy) and their motivation to quit (conceptualized in terms of their subjective expected utility (SEU) with respect to the available courses of action). I have also suggested that these ideas can be extended to smoking cessation and relapse. The decision to stop smoking is, of course, always revocable. Once the smoker has embarked on an attempt to quit, he or she is repeatedly faced with another decision, namely whether to persevere with the attempt or to abandon it. According to the model, the same factors that influenced the original decision to try to stop will also influence the decision to persist with the attempt, namely confidence and SEU. For many smokers, trying to stop smoking will provide much new information, for example, withdrawal symptoms and reactions of friends and relatives. This new information will produce changes in the smoker's confidence of succeeding and his/her subjective probabilities and utilities with respect to the consequences of persevering or abandoning the attempt. The model predicts that if at any stage during the attempt the matrix of perceived benefits and costs changes such that resuming smoking is seen as the more attractive alternative, then the person will be highly vulnerable to relapse.

An additional hypothesis suggested by this analysis is that, to the extent that the smoker has accurately anticipated the unpleasant consequences associated with trying to stop smoking, he or she will be likely to adhere to the original decision. This will be the case even if the smoker expects to suffer very severe withdrawal symptoms. It is only unforeseen negative consequences that will lead to a decision to resume smoking. Unanticipated positive consequences will reinforce the original decision. To my knowledge, the process of relapse in smoking has not been studied from a thoroughgoing decision-making perspective.

This review has necessarily been selective. I have not referred to every published paper on relapse in smoking, although for each of the four main approaches considered I have attempted to be as comprehensive as possible in the limited space available. The relapse field was once described as being 'long on theory but short on data'. To an extent this is still true. There is certainly an ample supply – some would say a surfeit – of theoretical ideas in circulation. But if progress is to be made towards understanding the process and causes of relapse, these ideas need to be sharpened into refutable hypotheses and these hypotheses subjected to rigorous empirical investigation. It is hoped that this chapter has brought some order to existing theory and data and will help to guide future research in this difficult but important area.

Acknowledgements: I would like to thank my colleagues in the Smoking Section of the Addiction Research Unit for their helpful comments on an earlier draft of this chapter. The Medical Research Council and the Imperial Cancer Research Fund provided financial support.

References

Ajzen, I. and Fishbein,M. (1980) *Understanding Attitudes and Predicting Social Behavior*, Englewood Cliffs, NJ: Prentice-Hall.

Baer, J.S., Holt, C.S., and Lichtenstein, E. (1986) 'Self-efficacy and smoking re-examined: construct validity and clinical utility', *Journal of Consulting and Clinical Psychology* 54: 846–52.

Baer, J.S. and Lichtenstein, E. (1988) 'Classification and prediction of smoking relapse episodes: an exploration of individual differences', *Journal of Consulting and Clinical Psychology* 56: 104–10.

Bandura, A. (1977) 'Self-efficacy: toward a unifying theory of behavioral change', *Psychological Review* 84: 191–215.

Bandura, A. (1982) 'Self-efficacy mechanism in human agency', *American Psychologist* 37: 122–47.

Brandon, T.H., Tiffany, S.T., and Baker, T.B. (1986) 'The process of smoking relapse', in F.M. Tims and C.G. Leukefeld (eds) *Relapse and Recovery in Drug Abuse*, National Institute on Drug Abuse Research Monograph 72, Rockville, Maryland: Department of Health and Human Services, pp. 104–17.

Brandon, T.H., Zelman, D.C., and Baker, T.B. (1987) 'Effects of maintenance sessions on smoking relapse: delaying the inevitable?', *Journal of Consulting and Clinical Psychology* 55: 780–2.

Brown, R.A., Lichtenstein, E., McIntyre, K.O., and Harrington-Hotspur, J. (1984) 'Effects of nicotine fading and relapse prevention on smoking cessation', *Journal of Consulting and Clinical Psychology* 52: 307–8.

Brownell, K.D., Marlatt, G.A., Lichtenstein, E., and Wilson, G.T. (1986) 'Understanding and preventing relapse', *American Psychologist* 41: 765–82.

Coelho, R.J. (1984) 'Self-efficacy and cessation of smoking', *Psychological Reports* 54: 309–10.

Colletti, G., Supnick, J.A., and Payne, T.J. (1985) 'The Smoking Self-Efficacy Questionnaire (SSEQ): preliminary scale development and validation', *Behavioral Assessment* 7: 249–60.

Condiotte, M.M. and Lichtenstein, E. (1981) 'Self-efficacy and relapse in smoking cessation programs', *Journal of Consulting and Clinical Psychology* 49: 648–58.

Cummings, C., Gordon, J.R., and Marlatt, G.A. (1980) 'Relapse: prevention and prediction', in W.R. Miller (ed.) *The Addictive Behaviors*, New York: Pergamon, pp. 291–321.

Cummings, K.M., Giovino, G., Jaén, C.R., and Emrich, L.J. (1985a) 'Reports of smoking withdrawal symptoms over a 21 day period of abstinence', *Addictive Behaviors* 10: 373–81.

Cummings, K.M., Jaén, C.R., and Giovino, G. (1985b) 'Circumstances surrounding relapse in a group of recent ex-smokers', *Preventive Medicine* 14: 195–202.

Curry, S. and Marlatt, G.A. (1985) 'Unaided quitters' strategies for coping with temptations to smoke', in S. Shiffman and T.A. Wills (eds) *Coping and Substance Use*, New York: Academic Press, pp. 243–65.

Curry, S., Marlatt, G.A., and Gordon, J.R. (1987) 'Abstinence Violation Effect: validation of an attributional construct with smoking cessation', *Journal of Consulting and Clinical Psychology* 55: 145–9.

Davis, J.R. and Glaros, A.G. (1986) 'Relapse prevention and smoking cessation', *Addictive Behaviors* 11: 105–14.

DiClemente, C.C. (1981) 'Self-efficacy and smoking cessation maintenance: a preliminary report', *Cognitive Therapy and Research* 5: 175–87.

DiClemente, C.C. (1986) 'Self-efficacy and the addictive behaviors', *Journal of Social and Clinical Psychology* 4: 302–15.

DiClemente, C.C. and Prochaska, J.O. (1982) 'Self-change and therapy change of smoking behavior: a comparison of processes of change in cessation and maintenance', *Addictive Behaviors* 7: 133–42.

DiClemente, C.C., Prochaska, J.O., and Gibertini, M. (1985) 'Self-efficacy and the stages of self-change of smoking', *Cognitive Therapy and Research* 9: 181–200.

Eisinger, R.A. (1971) 'Psychosocial predictors of smoking recidivism', *Journal of Health and Social Behavior* 12: 355–62.

Engle, K.B. and Williams, T.K. (1972) 'Effect of an ounce of vodka on alcoholics' desire for alcohol', *Quarterly Journal of Studies on Alcohol* 33: 1099–105.

Godding, P.R. and Glasgow, R.E. (1985) 'Self-efficacy and outcome expectations as predictors of controlled smoking status', *Cognitive Therapy and Research* 9: 583–90.

Grabowski, J. and O'Brien, C.P. (1981) 'Conditioning factors in opiate use', *Advances in Substance Abuse* 2: 69–121.

Gunn, R.C. (1986) 'Reactions to withdrawal symptoms and success in smoking cessation clinics', *Addictive Behaviors* 11: 49–53.

Hall, S.M. and Havassy, B.E. (1986) 'Commitment to abstinence and relapse to tobacco, alcohol, and opiates', in F.M. Tims and C.G. Leukefeld (eds) *Relapse and Recovery in Drug Abuse*, National Institute on Drug Abuse Research Monograph 72, Rockville, Maryland: Department of Health and Human Services, pp. 118–35.

Hall, S.M., Rugg, D., Tunstall, C., and Jones, R.T. (1984) 'Preventing relapse to cigarette smoking by behavioral skill training', *Journal of Consulting and Clinical Psychology* 52: 372–82.

Hammond, E.C. and Garfinkel, L. (1964) 'Changes in cigarette smoking', *Journal of the National Cancer Institute* 33: 49–64.

Horwitz, M.B., Hindi-Alexander, M., and Wagner, T.J. (1985) 'Psychosocial mediators of abstinence, relapse, and continued smoking: a one-year follow-up of a minimal intervention', *Addictive Behaviors* 10: 29–39.

Hughes, G.H., Hymowitz, N., Ockene, J.K., Simon, N., and Vogt, T.M. (1981) 'The Multiple Risk Factor Intervention Trial (MRFIT). V. intervention on smoking', *Preventive Medicine* 10: 476–500.

Hughes, J.R. and Hatsukami, D. (1986) 'Signs and symptoms of tobacco withdrawal', *Archives of General Psychiatry* 43: 289–94.

Hunt, W.A., Barnett, L.W., and Branch, L.G. (1971) 'Relapse rates in addiction programs', *Journal of Clinical Psychology* 27: 455–6.

Hunt, W.A., and Bespalec, D.A. (1974) 'An evaluation of current methods of modifying smoking behavior', *Journal of Clinical Psychology* 30: 431–8.

Killen, J.D., Maccoby, N., and Taylor, C.B. (1984) 'Nicotine gum and self-regulation training in smoking relapse prevention', *Behavior Therapy* 15: 234–48.

Litman, G.K., Eiser, J.R., and Taylor, C. (1979) 'Dependence, relapse and extinction: a theoretical critique and a behavioral examination', *Journal of Clinical Psychology* 35: 192–9.

Ludwig, A.M., Wikler, A., and Stark, L.H. (1974) 'The first drink: psychobiological aspects of craving', *Archives of General Psychiatry* 30: 539–47.

McIntyre, K.O., Lichtenstein, E., and Mermelstein, R.J. (1983) 'Self-efficacy and relapse in smoking cessation: a replication and extension', *Journal of Consulting and Clinical Psychology* 51: 632–3.

MacRae, J.R., Scoles, M.T., and Siegel, S. (1987) 'The contribution of Pavlovian conditioning to drug tolerance and dependence', *British Journal of Addiction* 82: 371–80.

Manley, R.S. and Boland, F.J. (1983) 'Side-effects and weight gain following a smoking cessation program' *Addictive Behaviors* 8: 375–80.

Marlatt, G.A. (1982) 'Relapse prevention: a self-control program for the treatment of addictive behaviors', in R.B. Stuart (ed.) *Adherence, Compliance, and Generalization in Behavioral Medicine*, New York: Brunner/Mazel, pp. 329–78.

Marlatt, G.A. (1985) 'Cognitive factors in the relapse process', in G.A. Marlatt and J.R. Gordon (eds) *Relapse Prevention: Maintenance Strategies in the Treatment of Addictive Behaviors*, New York: Guilford Press, pp. 128–200.

Marlatt, G.A. and George, W.H. (1984) 'Relapse prevention: introduction and overview of the model', *British Journal of Addiction* 79: 261–73.

Marlatt, G.A. and Gordon, J.R. (1980) 'Determinants of relapse: implications for the maintenance of behavior change', in P.O. Davidson and S.M. Davidson (eds) *Behavioral Medicine: Changing Health Lifestyles*, New York: Brunner/Mazel, pp. 410–52.

Marlatt, G.A. and Gordon, J.R. (1985) *Relapse Prevention: Maintenance Strategies in the Treatment of Addictive Behaviors*, New York: Guilford Press.

Marlatt, G.A. and Rohsenow, D.J. (1980) 'Cognitive processes in alcohol use: expectancy and the balanced placebo design', *Advances in Substance Abuse* 1: 159–99.

Neidigh, L.W., Gesten, E.L., and Shiffman, S. (1988) 'Coping with the temptation to drink' *Addictive Behaviors* 13: 1–9.

Nemeth-Coslett, R., Henningfield, J.E., O'Keefe, M.K., and Griffiths, R.R. (1986) 'Effects of mecamylamine on human cigarette smoking and subjective ratings', *Psychopharmacology* 88: 420–5.

Nicki, R.M., Remington, R.E., and MacDonald, G.A. (1984) 'Self-efficacy, nicotine-fading/self-monitoring and cigarette-smoking behaviour', *Behaviour Research and Therapy* 22: 477–85.

O'Brien, C.P., Testa, T., O'Brien, T.J., Brady, J.P., and Wells, B. (1977) 'Conditioned narcotic withdrawal in humans', *Science* 195: 1000–2.

Ockene, J.K., Benfari, R.C., Nuttall, R.L., Hurwitz, I., and Ockene, I.S. (1982) 'Relationship of psychosocial factors to smoking behavior change in an intervention program', *Preventive Medicine* 11: 13–28.

O'Connell, K.A. (1984) 'Identification of variables associated with maintenance of nonsmoking in ex-smokers', Report Number HR-0-2917-F, Bethesda, Maryland: National Heart, Lung and Blood Institute.

O'Connell, K.A. and Martin, E.J. (1987) 'Highly tempting situations associated with abstinence, temporary lapse, and relapse among participants in smoking cessation programs', *Journal of Consulting and Clinical Psychology* 55: 367–71.

O'Leary, A. (1985) 'Self-efficacy and health', *Behaviour Research and Therapy* 23: 437–51.

Pederson, L.L., Baskerville, J.C., and Wanklin, J.M. (1982) 'Multivariate statistical models for predicting change in smoking behavior following physician advice to quit smoking', *Preventive Medicine* 11: 536–49.

Prochaska, J.O., DiClemente, C.C., Velicer, W.F., Ginpil, S., and Norcross, J.C. (1985) 'Predicting change in smoking status for self-changers', *Addictive Behaviors* 10: 395–406.

Russell, M.A.H., Merriman, R., Stapleton, J., and Taylor, W. (1983) 'Effect of nicotine chewing gum as an adjunct to general practitioners' advice against smoking', *British Medical Journal* 287: 1782–5.

Saunders, B. and Allsop, S. (1987) 'Relapse: a psychological perspective', *British Journal of Addiction* 82: 417–29.

Scott, R.R., Prue, D.M., Denier, C.A., and King, A.C. (1986) 'Worksite

smoking intervention with nursing professionals: long-term outcome and relapse assessment', *Journal of Consulting and Clinical Psychology* 54: 809–13.
Shiffman, S. (1982) 'Relapse following smoking cessation: a situational analysis', *Journal of Consulting and Clinical Psychology* 50: 71–86.
Shiffman, S. (1984a) 'Cognitive antecedents and sequelae of smoking relapse crises', *Journal of Applied Social Psychology* 14: 296–309.
Shiffman, S. (1984b) 'Coping with temptations to smoke', *Journal of Consulting and Clinical Psychology* 52: 261–7.
Shiffman, S. (1986) 'A cluster-analytic classification of smoking relapse episodes', *Addictive Behaviors* 11: 295–307.
Shiffman, S.M. and Jarvik, M.E. (1976) 'Smoking withdrawal symptoms in two weeks of abstinence', *Psychopharmacology* 50: 35–9.
Shiffman, S.M. and Jarvik, M.E. (1987) 'Situational determinants of coping in smoking relapse crises', *Journal of Applied Social Psychology* 17: 3–15.
Shiffman, S., Read, L., and Jarvik, M.E. (1985a) 'Smoking relapse situations: a preliminary typology', *International Journal of the Addictions* 20: 311–18.
Shiffman, S., Read, L., Maltese, J., Rapkin, D., and Jarvik, M.E. (1985b) 'Preventing relapse in ex-smokers: a self-management approach' in G.A. Marlatt and J.R. Gordon (eds) *Relapse Prevention: Maintenance Strategies in the Treatment of Addictive Behaviors*, New York: Guilford Press, pp. 472–520.
Shumaker, S.A. and Grunberg, N.E. (eds) (1986) *Proceedings of the National Working Conference on Smoking Relapse: Health Psychology* 5 (supplement).
Stitzer, M.L. and Gross, J (1988) 'Smoking relapse: the role of pharmacological and behavioral factors' in O.F. Pomerleau and C.S. Pomerleau (eds) *Nicotine Replacement: A Critical Evaluation*, New York: Alan.R.Liss, Inc., pp. 163–84.
Stockwell, T.R., Hodgson, R.J., Rankin, H.J., and Taylor, C. (1982) 'Alcohol dependence, beliefs and the priming effect', *Behaviour Research and Therapy* 20: 513–22.
Subcommittee of the Research Committee of the British Thoracic Society (SRCBTS) (1984) 'Smoking withdrawal in hospital patients: factors associated with outcome', *Thorax* 39: 651–6.
Supnick, J.A. and Colletti, G. (1984) 'Relapse coping and problem solving training following treatment for smoking', *Addictive Behaviors* 9: 401–4.
Sutton, S.R. (1979) 'Interpreting relapse curves', *Journal of Consulting and Clinical Psychology* 47: 96–8.
Sutton, S.R. (1987) 'Social-psychological approaches to understanding addictive behaviours', *British Journal of Addiction* 82: 355–70.
Tims, F.M. and Leukefeld, C.G. (eds) (1986) *Relapse and Recovery in Drug Abuse*, National Institute on Drug Abuse Research Monograph 72, Rockville, Maryland: Department of Health and Human Services.
Warshaw, P.R. and Davis, F.D. (1985) 'Disentangling behavioral intention

and behavioral expectation', *Journal of Experimental Social Psychology* 21: 213–28.

West, R.J., Hajek, P., and Belcher, M. (1987) 'Time course of cigarette withdrawal symptoms during four weeks of treatment with nicotine gum', *Addictive Behaviors* 12: 199–203.

Wikler, A. (1980) *Opioid Dependence: Mechanisms and Treatment*, New York: Plenum.

Wilcox, N.S., Prochaska, J.O., Velicer, W.F., and DiClemente, C.C. (1985) 'Subject characteristics as predictors of self-change in smoking', *Addictive Behaviors* 10: 407–12.

Chapter Four

Heroin and the opiates

Brendan P. Bradley

The term relapse is used in a number of ways in the drug dependence literature. It has been taken to refer to any drug use following a period of abstinence and it has also been used to mean a return to pre-treatment levels of morbidity. The first usage is overinclusive and, as argued later in this chapter, gives an unduly pessimistic impression of the outcome following treatment. According to this usage, an individual who uses once following a period of abstinence would be regarded as having relapsed, as would an individual who returned to daily use. The second usage is also unsatisfactory. There are multiple dimensions on which a drug abuser may improve or deteriorate, such as drug dose, number of type of drugs, frequency of drug taking, route of ingestion, social adjustment, work performance, and criminal involvement. It therefore seems appropriate, when considering outcome in a comprehensive way, to examine a number of dimensions, bearing in mind that there are degrees of improvement or deterioration in each.

Hunt *et al.* (1971) presented data which suggested that relapse rates in different addictions were similarly high, the majority, approximately 80 per cent, returning to drug use within a few months after treatment. However, their study overstates the relapse rate since relapse appears to have been taken as any drug use following treatment. In a study carried out by the author and colleagues, and summarized below, the outcome for opiate addicts six months after treatment was more favourable than Hunt and colleagues' study would suggest.

One approach which sheds light on the process of relapse is to investigate predictive factors. A recent example of this type of study is that of McAuliffe and co-workers (1986) who found the following factors to predict relapse in opiate addicts six months after discharge: time since detoxification, craving, physical dependence, number of extinction trials (when drugs were available but not used), the tendency to seek euphoria, and dysphoria. These authors concluded that, excepting physical dependence, most other predictors appeared to affect relapse through their ability to produce craving. Such an approach is indeed useful; it can allow the identification of high-risk groups, and suggests factors which may be addressed during treatment.

Another way of investigating relapse is to study the immediate precipitants of renewed drug use following a period of abstinence. Litman and colleagues have conducted systematic studies of this type with alcohol abusers. They found three factors to be particularly significant, namely, unpleasant moods, external events and euphoria, and lessened cognitive vigilance (Litman *et al.* 1983). There have been few studies of circumstances surrounding relapse in opiate addicts. Cummings *et al.* (1980) investigated such circumstances in two groups of opiate addicts, one of which was being treated by methadone maintenance while the other was undergoing an out-patient drug-free programme. Relapse in the sense used here is only applicable to those who used drugs following a state of abstinence so only the first group is directly relevant. They reported that the following factors prompted relapse, in decreasing order of importance: social pressure, negative emotional states, interpersonal conflict, positive emotional states (intrapersonal), negative physical states, urges and temptations, positive emotional states (interpersonal), and testing personal control. These results have considerable implications for treatment aimed at reducing the risk of relapse. Marlatt and colleagues have written extensively about such a treatment programme, Relapse Prevention (Marlatt and Gordon 1985).

The follow-up study

In this chapter the focus is on renewed opiate use following a period of abstinence. The initial use of opiates following abstinence is termed 'lapse' rather than 'relapse' to avoid pre-judging the issue of whether a more general deterioration had taken place. A summary is given of the major findings of the only British study which has systematically investigated the event of relapse following treatment for opiate abuse (Gossop *et al.* 1987; Bradley *et al.* 1988; Gossop *et al.* 1988). Eighty opiate addicts, sixty men and twenty women, who were admitted to a Drug Dependence Unit and who achieved a drug-free state, were followed up for six months following discharge. There was considerable heterogeneity within the sample. Age range from 15 to 38 years (mean 27). Drug use began between the ages of 11 and 30 years (mean 16), and regular opiate use started between 12 and 35 years (mean 21). Most used heroin (n = 47) as the main opiate, usually by intravenous injection. Seven used

Table 4.1 Outcome at six-month follow-up (n=77*)

	m	%
Opiate-free at six months		
for entire period	15	19.5
used at least once during the period	24	31
Total opiate-free at six months	39	51
Using opiates at six months		
Occasional use	11	14
Regular use	25	32.5

Source: Gossop *et al.* 1988.
* 2 subjects died from drug overdose

methadone, five used another opiate, and twenty-one used more than one opiate on a regular basis. Most abused other drugs in addition to opiates, most commonly amphetamines, barbiturates, and tranquillizers.

The first stage of treatment was a twenty-one-day methadone detoxification schedule. Subsequently, patients attended group therapy sessions and had individual counselling from nursing, medical, and psychological staff. Patients were generally seen weekly by a psychiatric nurse and less often by a psychiatrist in training. In these sessions social, occupational, and psychological difficulties were identified and the patient was encouraged to take an active part in their solution. This sometimes involved referral to a psychologist or social workers. Patients regularly attended an occupational therapy programme which included group sessions aimed at training them how to return to life outside the unit without using drugs. At the time of this study there were no resources for systematic follow-up support after discharge, although all patients were offered the option of attending as out-patients.

Two trained interviewers conducted semi-structured interviews on admission and two weeks after discharge. Those who had not used opiates in the two weeks after discharge were followed up again four weeks later. A six-month follow-up was conducted on all subjects. Outcome data are available for seventy-seven of the eighty subjects. At six months 51 per cent of those whose status was known (thirty-nine subjects) were opiate-free (Table 4.1). This was confirmed by urine tests. Twenty per cent (fifteen subjects) had remained totally abstinent from opiates during the six-month follow-up period, while 31 per cent (twenty-four subjects) had used opiates at some point since leaving the unit but were no longer using at the six months interview. Fourteen per cent (eleven subjects) were using opiates on a less than daily basis, while 33 per cent (twenty-five subjects) were daily users. Two subjects died during the follow-up period, as a result of drug overdose.

The figure of 51 per cent drug free at six-month follow-up is encouraging. However, six were in prison and four were receiving some form of in-patient or residential treatment for drug dependence. This leaves 45 per cent of those living in the community who were abstinent. This figure is still encouraging and suggests that the outcome for severely dependent opiate addicts is not as pessimistic as is widely believed. Our team was surprised at the proportion of individuals who had given up opiates at six months. Our impression had been that most of those who left the unit relapsed quickly. When we examined the data we found that 71 per cent of the sample had lapsed within six weeks of leaving the unit (figure 4.1). Therefore, a substantial proportion of those who lapsed had subsequently given up opiate use again. We had unwittingly made the assumption that renewed drug use following treatment would probably lead on to addictive use again. This assumption is one which is widely held among staff of drug treatment centres and it probably contributes to the disillusionment felt by many treatment staff. Such an impression is understandable because, if renewed drug use occurs, it is likely to do so within the first few weeks of leaving an in-patient unit. This is the time when information about outcome is most likely to be relayed back to staff by other patients or visitors.

Since the drug-taking behaviour changed over the follow-up period, the six-month period was divided into three equal segments and subjects were asked to describe their predominant pattern of drug taking during these times (figure 4.2). In the first two months 31 per cent were mainly drug free, 25 per cent were occasional users, while 44 per cent were daily users. In the final two-month period the number of non-users had risen to 44 per cent, the proportion of occasional users had fallen to 13 per cent, while the proportion of daily users was similar (43 per cent).

Thus, the first lapse to opiate use does not necessarily lead to complete relapse. Instead, some subjects show a recovery after lapse, an effect which can be obscured by traditional ways of presenting relapse data such as that used by Hunt *et al.* (1971) and as shown in figure 4.1. Moreover, despite the high initial lapse rate, 65 per cent were not re-addicted at the six months point. Excluding those in prison and those in residential treatment lowers the figure to 60 per cent. Even this figure represents a good outcome in comparison with previous estimated relapse rates.

It may be argued that the high abstinence rate stems from addicts

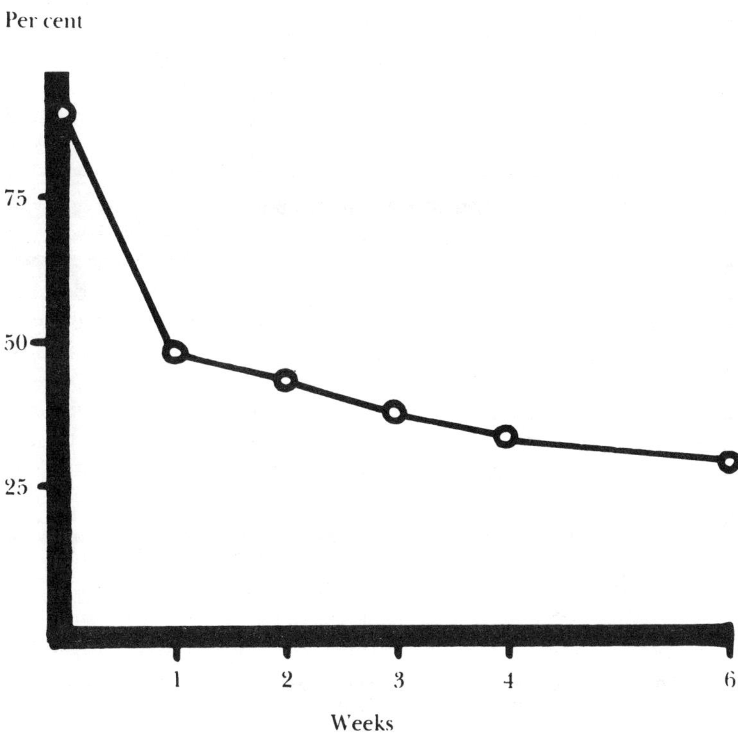

Figure 4.1 Cumulative survival curve for the first six weeks after leaving treatment

substituting other drugs. Although many of the abstinent subjects took other drugs, dependent use was not common. Only two of the thirty-nine abstinent individuals were using alcohol heavily (Litman's criteria) at six months, while another two had used it heavily at some stage between discharge and six months. About a quarter of the opiate-abstinent subjects had used cannabis since discharge but none used it daily. Two reported occasional use of amphetamines and

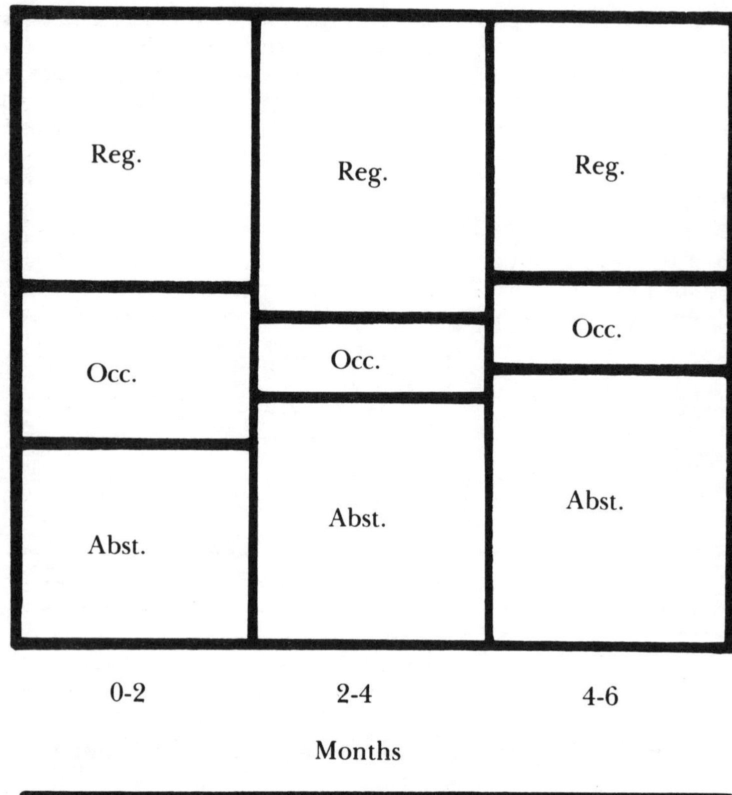

Source :Gossop *et al.* 1988

Figure 4.2 Patterns of opiate use during the six-month follow-up period

three were using tranquillizers. None of the abstinent subjects was using cocaine.

While it is therefore apparent that lapse to renewed drug use does not invariably lead to continued or dependent drug taking, nevertheless such an event is a critical step in every relapse. Therefore, it is important to examine the circumstances and precipitants of lapses.

Circumstances and precipitants of lapse

Subjects were asked to describe the first occasion of opiate use following discharge. Eleven different types of lapse precipitant were identified and are described below.

Cognitive Factors: an intention or plan to use again. *Mood States*: mainly unpleasant states such as boredom, anger, sadness, loneliness. *External Influences*: situations or events which were not drug-related. *Withdrawal Symptoms*: in practice, insomnia was the most common symptom. *Interpersonal Influences*: where another person contributed to the lapse. If drugs were offered this counted as 'Social Pressure'. If the other person was 'stoned' this was coded as a 'Drug-related Cue'. *Social Pressure*: a direct or indirect offer of drugs. *Leaving a Protected Environment*: usually a clinic, hostel or prison. *Drug Availability*: where subjects indicated that ready access to drugs was a pertinent factor. *Drug-related Cues*: drug-related items (e.g., syringes) or seeing people stoned. *Craving*: a strong desire or preoccupation with opiates. *Priming*: where subjects used another drug immediately prior to opiate use.

Cognitions, moods, and external events were the most commonly mentioned factors associated with the initial lapse (see Table 4.2). Almost two-thirds of those who lapsed regarded cognitive factors as influential, while half regarded both mood states and external events as contributors. These same three factors were also most commonly mentioned as leading to continued opiate use following the initial lapse. Cognitive and mood factors were judged to be the most important of all the factors in leading to renewed opiate use. These same two factors, together with leaving a protected environment were reported to be the most common initial factors in the chain of events leading up to the first lapse.

Cognitive factors usually involved an explicit decision or plan to use opiates, often stemming from boredom or from curiosity to experience the effects again. Some individuals convinced themselves that they could control opiate use, while others regarded their initial use as a test of whether they really were dependent. Of course, thoughts and plans concerning drug taking do not arise in a vacuum. There is evidence that the presence of drug-related cues can change individuals' expectations about drug effects (Cooney *et al.* 1987) so that drug use becomes more likely. Therefore, cognitions which result in renewed drug use are likely to arise from the individual's experience. Furthermore, some opiate users come into treatment at a time when their drug-taking has produced highly aversive outcomes, for example, arrest, disease, or the break-up of an important relationship. It is not surprising that initially, being aware of the

Table 4.2 Information about the circumstances of initial use of opiates following detoxification (n=58)

	1	2	3	4
	Total mentions[a]	*No. subjects mentioning factor*[b]	*Most important factor*[c]	*First factor*[d]
Cognitive	59	37	12	7
Mood	54	30	10	11
External	52	29	2	4
Withdrawal	23	16	5	2
Interpersonal	20	16	2	2
Leaving clinic, hostel, or prison	18	17	3	7
Drug availability	15	14	3	4
Drug-related cues	14	13	3	4
Craving	14	12	3	3
Priming	10	10	2	3
Social pressure	5	5	1	1

Source: Bradley *et al.* 1988.
[1] Total number of times each factor was mentioned
[2] Number of drug users who mentioned each factor
[3] Number of drug users who judged each factor to be the most important one
[4] Number of drug users who indicated each factor to have been the first in a sequence leading to lapse

aversive consequences, they are resolved to quit. After a few weeks or months, these aversive outcomes may no longer be so salient, and coping with life without drugs often requires considerable adjustment, so that the balance shifts towards drug use again.

More than half of the subjects indicated that negative mood states, such as sadness, loneliness, boredom, tension, or anxiety, were directly associated with lapse. A convincing reason for this is that in these circumstances drug use acts as a negative reinforcer by removing unpleasant effect. After years of drug use many individuals lack alternative strategies for dealing with unpleasant mood states and therefore are more likely to use drugs in these circumstances.

The majority of lapses occurred within a few weeks of leaving treatment, suggesting that environmental influences can have a major impact on relapse. Most individuals returned to their normal environment where drugs were readily available and where drug-related cues were common.

Our results are generally compatible with those of Marlatt, although we differ on the importance ascribed to social pressure. Marlatt found this to be the most important factor associated with relapse while we found it to be the least important. This apparent discrepancy may arise from our strict definition of social pressure in contrast to Marlatt's broad definition: what we classified as 'interpersonal', 'drug availability', or 'drug-related cues' may have been regarded by Marlatt as constituting social pressure. A further discrepancy is that there was little evidence that positive emotional states were associated with lapse in our sample, a factor identified by Marlatt as increasing the risk of relapse. We have also drawn attention to the importance of cognitive factors, such as plans and decisions to use opiates again, as lapse influences. Marlatt's (1985) model does indeed take account of cognitions despite the fact that he does not explicitly mention their role in his classification of high-risk situations. Our findings are generally compatible with those of Litman and colleagues (1983) who found that alcoholics perceived the same three influences, unpleasant mood states, external events, and cognitive factors, to be most important in relapse.

More than a quarter of those who lapsed indicated that withdrawal symptoms contributed to the lapse, supporting the behavioural view that drug taking is negatively reinforced. However, we did not find direct evidence in support of Wikler's (1980) theory that conditioned withdrawal symptoms, elicited by environmental stimuli, play an important role in relapse. Drug-related cues were present in approximately one-fifth of lapse episodes but in only one-quarter of this small group did the users consider them to be the most influential factors in their lapse. Moreover, these cues, being so intimately connected with the act of drug taking, should stand the best chance of eliciting conditioned withdrawal reactions, but again our users did not spontaneously report withdrawal-like reactions. We do not dispute the observations that such conditioned withdrawal can occur, but our users' reports suggest that conditioned withdrawal, in so far as this can be identified by the subject, is rarely a relapse precipitant. Nevertheless, these results should not be taken as disconfirming a conditioning model. There remains the possibility that environment, mood, or other cues elicit reactions, based on the ex-addict's previous learning history, which increase the likelihood of relapse.

About one-fifth reported craving in association with lapse but less than one-quarter of these judged it to be the most influential factor in returning to opiates. In a similar number of subjects, priming, that is, the prior use of another drug or alcohol, influenced lapse, but it was rarely mentioned as the most important factor.

The finding that craving was rarely reported to be influential in leading to renewed opiate use appears to be discrepant with McAuliffe and co-workers' (1986) finding that craving acted as a mediating variable in relapse. This apparent discrepancy may result from a tendency for individuals to report craving spontaneously only if it reached an extreme level or if it persisted over a long period.

Our findings suggest that cognitions, mood, and external factors are extremely important in leading to renewed drug taking. While we have classified these factors separately, it should be borne in mind that they do not, in general, act in isolation. For example, many individuals returned to their previous environment after discharge. In such an environment there was often a combination of drug availability, social pressure to use, and the presence of drug-related cues. Other ex-users left the treatment unit without arranging suitable accommodation or work. In this situation it is especially tempting to re-establish contact with drug-using friends in order to find a place to live or for social reasons. Those who resist re-establishing contact may feel lonely or bored, feelings which are again commonly associated with lapse.

Predictors of opiate use at six months follow-up

We investigated the factors identified at the initial in-patient interview which predicted opiate use at the six-month follow-up in the hope that this information would help us to understand better the process of renewed drug use and in order to identify factors which could be addressed during in-patient treatment so as to minimize the risk of return to drug use.

Four variables predicted opiate use at six months: the number of Protective Factors, Length of Admission, Length of the Previous Period of Abstinence, and Confidence in Remaining Abstinent. Taken together these four variables accounted for 41 per cent of the variance in the outcome variable. Protective factors were any factors which subjects thought made it easier to remain drug free. These included friends, work, accommodation, and hobbies or pastimes. Therefore, addicts' views at the beginning of their admission of whether these factors are helpful are valuable indicators of the likelihood of being drug free at six months. Accordingly, this information should be obtained early on in treatment so that attempts can be made to change any factors which are perceived to be detrimental to remaining drug free.

Those who remained in treatment longest were also more likely to be opiate free or to be using less heavily than those who spent less time in treatment. This finding may be interpreted in two ways: since treatment is designed to help addicts to give up drugs and to remain drug free, it is plausible that the longer the individual remains in treatment (and the more treatment is received) then the more beneficial change is likely to take place so that relapse is less likely. However, an alternative explanation is that those who remained longest in treatment were already highly motivated and that it was this which produced a better outcome. As noted, those who previously showed longer periods of abstinence were less likely to be using opiates at six-month follow-up. This may simply reflect the fact that those who remained off opiates for longer are more highly motivated to give up or are less heavily addicted. Alternatively, it is possible that there is a causal connection; the longer one remains off opiates and experiences a wide range of high-risk situations without using, the longer one will remain off drugs in a further period of abstinence.

Addicts who were more confident, at presentation for treatment, that they would stay off drugs were more likely to do well. Again, this result is difficult to interpret unambiguously, although in general it supports Marlatt's (1985) view that self-efficacy is an important variable in successful abstinence. Some addicts may be confident because they have a very strong resolve to give up drugs, while others may simply know that they are less addicted. Whatever the explanation, the finding underlines the importance of obtaining the addict's judgement of the likelihood of remaining abstinent. Those who express less confidence should be encouraged to anticipate difficulties which can then be addressed by cognitive–behavioural methods such as those included in Marlatt's account of relapse prevention treatment.

Implications for treatment

Most lapses occur within the first month after leaving treatment. This constitutes a critical period in recovery. Those who remain drug free beyond this point have a much reduced risk of returning to opiate use. It would appear that after-care services should be focused on this stage for maximal effect.

Some drug abusers lapse without showing a complete relapse while others become re-addicted. It may be possible to teach individuals how to prevent lapses becoming relapses, instead of ignoring this issue as many treatment programmes do. Marlatt describes techniques which may prove helpful. Even among those patients who returned to opiate use there are grounds for optimism. In general they used less opiates than at admission and fewer injected opiates. This indicates that drug abusers can modify their hazardous behaviour and this can help reduce the risk of AIDS and other infectious diseases. Such findings suggest that 'harm reduction' approaches might usefully be employed in the treatment of opiate abusers.

Renewed opiate use occurred in response to specific circumstances. Cognitions, negative moods, and external events were the most common factors associated with lapse. An attempt should be made to identify factors, specific to each individual, which increase the chance of returning to drug use. Intervention can then concentrate on developing ways of coping with these high-risk factors (Marlatt and Gordon 1985). There is evidence of effectiveness of this approach with alcohol abusers (Chaney *et al.* 1978).

Cognitive–behavioural problem-solving training may help those who use drugs as a way of blotting out unpleasant feelings which stem from objective difficulties. Such methods can help former opiate users to remain opiate free (Platt and Metzger 1987). Those who experience dysphoria arising from unrealistic appraisals of themselves or their situations may be helped by other cognitive-behavioural approaches such as Beck's cognitive therapy (Beck and Emery 1977).

Acknowledgements: The work presented here was supported by the UK Department of Health and Social Security. Thanks are due to the staff and patients at the Bethlem-Maudsley Drug Dependence Unit.

References

Beck, A.T. and Emery, G. (1977) *Cognitive Therapy of Substance Abuse*, Philadelphia: Center for Cognitive Therapy.

Bradley, B., Green, L., Phillips, G., and Gossop, M. (1989) 'Circumstances surrounding relapse to opiate addiction', *British Journal of Psychiatry*, in press.

Chaney, E., O'Leary, M., and Marlatt, G.A. (1978) 'Skill training with alcoholics', *Journal of Consulting and Clinical Psychology* 46: 1092–104.

Cooney, N.L., Gillespie, R.A., Baker, L.H., and Kaplan, R.F. (1987) 'Cognitive changes after alcohol cue exposure', *Journal of Consulting and Clinical Psychology* 55: 150–5.

Cummings, C., Gordon, J.R., and Marlatt, G.A. (1980) 'Relapse: prevention and prediction', in W.R. Miller (ed.) *The Addictive Behaviors*, New York: Pergamon.

Gossop, M., Green, L., Phillips, G., and Bradley, B.P. (1987) 'What happens to opiate addicts immediately after treatment: a prospective follow-up study', *British Medical Journal* 294: 1377–80.

Gossop, M., Green, L., Phillips, G., and Bradley, B.P. (1989) 'Lapse, relapse and survival among opiate addicts after treatment: a prospective follow-up study', *British Journal of Psychiatry*, in press.

Hunt, W.A., Barnett, L.W., and Branch, L.G. (1971) 'Relapse rates in addiction programs', *Journal of Clinical Psychology* 27: 455–6.

Litman, G.K., Stapleton, J., Oppenheim, A.N., Peleg, M., and Jackson, P. (1983) 'Situations related to alcoholism relapse', *British Journal of Addiction* 78: 381–9.

McAuliffe, W., Feldman, B., Friedman, R., Launder, E., Magnuson, E., Mahoney, C., Santangelo, S., Ward, W., and Weiss, R. (1986) *Explaining Relapse to Opiate Addiction Following Successful Completion of Treatment*, National Institute on Drug Abuse Monograph Series 72, Rockville, Maryland: Department of Health and Human Services, pp. 136–56.

Marlatt, G.A. (1985) 'Cognitive factors in the relapse process', in G.A. Marlatt and J.R. Gordon (eds) *Relapse Prevention: Maintenance Strategies in the Treatment of Addictive Behaviour*, New York: Guilford Press.

Marlatt, G.A. and Gordon, J.R. (eds) (1985) *Relapse Prevention: Maintenance Strategies in the Treatment of Addictive Behaviour*, New York: Guilford Press.

Platt, J.J. and Metzger, D.S. (1987) 'Cognitive interpersonal problem solving skills and the maintenance of treatment success in heroin addicts', *Psychology of Addictive Behaviours* 1: 5–13.

Wikler, A. (1980) *Opioid Dependence and Treatment*, New York: Plenum.

Chapter Five

Relapse and eating disorders: the recurring illusion

Howard Rankin

The notion of relapse is often inappropriately and misleadingly used when considering eating disorders. This is also true of other ailments, like the addictions covered elsewhere in this volume. I distinguish eating disorders from addictions because I do not believe they are the same. The astute reader will already notice that the writer is in difficulties. Here is a book on relapse in the addictions which is covering disorders that are not addictions and to which the term relapse is often misapplied. Perhaps I should simply write to the editor and suggest that in keeping with the parsimonious times in which we live I have done my bit for Queen and country by slashing my budget from 4,500 to 250 words and simply calling it a day. Another option, however, is to use examples from the area of eating disorders to illustrate the difficulties with the concept of relapse.

Why relapse is a misleading term

I have many concerns about the notion of relapse and the way it has come to be used.

1. The term medicalizes a phenomenon that has little to do with medicine or even clinical psychiatry but everything to do with normal human functioning.
2. As a result of this medicalization, the use of the term relapse often conceals the inadequacy of treatment procedures.
3. This medicalization also misleads people, both 'sufferers' and 'helpers', about the nature of their behaviour and its anticipated course.

The difficulties that are mentioned above can be seen when considering any of the so-called 'addictions' or any of the so-called 'eating disorders'. In this chapter I shall consider three eating-related phenomena: excessive food restriction otherwise known as anorexia, bingeing and purging also known as bulimia, and excessive over-eating known as anything from having a good time to killing yourself. Obesity is intimately related to the three leading causes of death among Americans (heart attack, stroke, and cancer) and directly involved in two other major killers (atherosclerosis and diabetes).

The anorexic

She is brought to your office. Discracefully thin and unprepossessing in appearance, she sits hunched in the corner, uncooperative to the point of rudeness. Her parents are at their wits end. They tell you what a nice girl she is really and how she seems to have become more withdrawn and secretive. They tell you how little she eats and how much she exercises and all the funny food rituals she has developed. The more they talk the more their frustration becomes visible. And the more they talk the more silent their daughter becomes. After about an hour or so of this encounter you are prepared to triumphantly pronounce your verdict: 'Your daughter is anorexic. She's suffering from anorexia nervosa.' And this is your first mistake. I know, I've made it myself many times.

Of course you are technically correct in your diagnosis. But by labelling the girl's behaviour thus, see what you've done. Now parents are thinking about treatment, hospitalization, medication, and asking awkward questions like 'When will Denise recover?' Denise, for her part, is thinking control, coercion, food, fatness, and sheer terror. In short, they are all thinking, as you might be, in terms of a finite illness with a finite course, of the seemingly natural progression of hospitalization–treatment–recovery. Your logic and these concepts may be valid but with them comes the notion of relapse. Now let us suppose that instead of making a sagacious announcement of Denise's condition as anorexia you had said something like this when asked by her parents about the nature of her condition. 'Actually your daughter seems as angry as hell with somebody, probably you. It seems to me as if she is on hunger strike. I'm afraid at this stage I could only guess why she is but hopefully we'll find out in due course.' Now what are the people in the room thinking? Instead of thinking about illnesses and psychiatric conditions, Denise's parents are thinking about anger and emotions. You can relapse from anorexia (because you can recover from it) but you can't relapse from anger. Anger (or any other emotion) is not a relapsing condition – it is a natural, recurring response.

This is not to say that starving yourself to the point of expiration is a natural or normal response that does not require attention.

However, the focus of treatment on *symptoms* can lead to dangerously false perceptions and expectations about what it is that needs to be changed and the process and course of that change.

The treatment

Because the overt manifestations (symptoms) are the most noticeable features of underlying difficulties it is hardly surprising that treatment is focused primarily at them rather than on underlying problems. We don't care too much if Denise is having difficulty expressing her feelings, or thinks she is fat when she is painfully thin but we feel obliged to take notice if her menstruation ceases, ketosis develops, and her condition becomes life threatening. Of course such crisis management is essential but it is only one part of treatment that cannot be divorced from the overall view of her condition.

Let's suppose that Denise is hospitalized. Despite her resistance she begins to eat more. Eventually her weight increases. She manages somehow to overcome her terror of the weight gain. She plays the game well, saying all the right things and not letting on too much about her innermost thoughts. She just wants to gain enough weight to get out of this hospital trap, to regain her control. She still thinks she is fat and has grave doubts about her ability to cope once she has left the secure hospital environment. But, of course, you and your colleagues are skilled therapists. You can see that under the well-guarded facade the body is thin and the defences enormous. In groups and in individual therapy you tackle the major issues of this girl's problems: her anger, her guilt, her perfectionism, her 'thinking style'. You give her coping strategies, skills, tips, and advice. You support, cajole, confront, and encourage. You speak to her parents and her sisters and her friends and her teachers. Eight months have elapsed and it's time for Denise to go home to her parents and her domestic science course.

When her parents come to take Denise home they thank you and despite all your efforts still see this day as somehow marking the end of treatment. 'We never thought it would take as long as eight months to get her right,' her mother says on leaving. The reality of course is that this is not the end of treatment. In fact, treatment has barely begun. It may take eight years rather than eight months and even if Denise lives to be eighty she still may not outgrow these difficulties. It may be extremely difficult for you as the therapist to say, and for them as parents to accept, the reality that this girl will in all probability continue to starve herself, have distorted thoughts about her body, and, if she does manage to eat anything more than a sparrow's diet, will swing violently into bingeing and vomiting. Such a statement would not do much for your credibility. But the plain fact of the matter is that therapy has barely begun and it is the height of arrogance or ignorance to assume that this girl will not have further problems. Only Divine Intervention will limit her life events to those relatively few situations for which treatment has begun to prepare her.

Of course, you continue to see Denise for therapy and to monitor her progress. After about a month of struggling in the real world, Denise, 'has a relapse'. Under pressure from parents or siblings or friends or teachers, Denise adopts her characteristic coping strategy – she stops eating. This should be no surprise. The failure isn't Denise's although *most people including her probably see it that way*. If there is failure at all it is in treatment which has not been intense enough or going on long enough to help the girl deal effectively with this situation. It isn't that this girl has somehow regressed to a prior state, relapsed from being able to deal with the situation to now being incapable of so doing. *She was never able to deal with this situation in the first place.*

The family troop back into your office with an air of despondency and failure. Denise is tearful and fearful. Mother is hurt and forlorn. Father is angry. There follows much talk about failure and square one, resignation and relapse. Eventually you speak to Denise on her own and the whole story is revealed. The first pressure on her was end-of-term exams. Being a perfectionist Denise was determined to do well. To her credit she had moderated this tendency somewhat and had continued on her food plan. In addition there was a boy who had shown interest in her. Just as Denise was coming to terms with the possibility of a relationship she had seen him out with another girl. This too she had dealt with, albeit with difficulty. Finally, following an incident between her father and her maternal grandmother, the level of marital and family tension had skyrocketed. And that was the last straw. Not a good week for Denise. She retreated into the defence and coping style she knew best.

But is it fair to call Denise's retreat a 'relapse'? It is true that she was exhibiting the same problematic eating patterns which might necessitate rehospitalization. However, there is enough evidence that rather than going backwards in the past week Denise has actually *progressed significantly*. She had dealt remarkably well with a variety of difficult situations. She had evidenced some control over her more destructive thinking patterns and she had implemented several coping strategies that she learned in treatment. Despite great temptation to the contrary she had maintained her food plan until the very last. All the indications are that under extreme duress she had indeed shown signs of great improvement right up until the point that the increase in family tension finally overwhelmed her. So how are we to view this turn of events?

Can we really call it a relapse when a client implements our treatment plans as effectively as possible? Can we really call it a relapse when a client is faced with a set of circumstances that would overwhelm anybody? Can we really call it a relapse when a client cannot cope with a situation for which treatment has not prepared her? Can we really call it relapse when it is evident that a client has actually made great progress regardless of her overt symptomatology?

I do not think that the matter is helped any by watering down the term relapse and relabelling it a 'slip'. There clearly is a place for labelling on the basis of the severity of the consequences but the term still implies regression, which may be unjustified. Indeed it seems to me that the term 'slip' was coined in order to minimize the destructive effect on a client's attitude and motivation brought about by a recurrence of symptoms. But it is still reinforcing the notion of regression and failure which simply may be a complete misrepresentation of the facts and a slight against that client's genuine progress.

So, faced with Denise, we can act in three ways. We can agree with her parents that she is back to square one and readmit her to hospital. This course of action is likely to reinforce a sense of failure and hopelessness in everyone. Alternatively, we can minimize the situation, describing it as a 'slip' (thereby implying some sense of failure) and possibly rehospitalizing the girl for a short period to stabilize. Lastly, we can point out not the failure but the success, not the regression but the progress. We can point out that no one could reasonably expect this client to stand up to overwhelming pressures for which she was not prepared. We can point out how well in fact she did cope with mounting pressures, possibly as well as anyone had a right to expect.

Giving things up

Some readers may object that this is a contrived story – a straw man that does not reflect most 'relapses'. But isn't it the case that many 'relapses' are precipitated by similar negative emotional states, whether the behaviour under consideration is alcohol consumption (e.g., Rosenberg 1983), heroin use (e.g., Krueger, 1981) or tobacco smoking (e.g., Gunn 1983). Is not the pattern of relapse remarkably similar regardless of the addiction? Tracking the careers of 'addicts' or 'non-addicts' demonstrates how influential life events are in the ebb and flow of behaviour. The ebb and flow of the 'addict's' behaviour, called recovery and relapse, is no different from the ebb and flow of behaviour in general. In the interest of healthy development and growth we should all be continually challenging ourselves and giving up those aspects of ourselves that are destructive and outdated. Life is about the constant hardship of giving up things that have once been dear and valuable to us but are no longer. Life, if you will, is about the psychology of concession. And in this I must quibble with both popular and scientific writers (my former self included) in that they have considered the psychology of 'giving up' the exclusive domain of addiction. Someone watches too much television – he is addicted. Someone cannot bear to leave their dog – she is addicted. Someone finds it difficult not to put in an extra hour at the office – he is addicted to work. Someone arrives habitually late for work – he is addicted to lying in bed. Someone cannot give up his mistress although he knows the consequences of continuing the liaison will be disastrous – he is addicted to her. A girl cannot stop eating food by the truck load – she is addicted to food. Another girl cannot bring herself to eat anything – she is addicted to starvation. The assumption is that difficulty in giving up behaviours, thoughts, perceptions, attitudes, and personality traits is evidence of addiction. But this concession process is part of normal human functioning. *Life is not a subset of addiction, rather addiction is one subset of life.* The more we understand that life is about constantly giving up these things, about replacing the old with the new, the negative with the positive, the more we shall stop seeing the process as merely part of the addiction affliction. All around there are lessons to be learned about 'relapse' and concession from people and places that have ostensibly nothing to do with addiction.

One of the most insightful and comprehensive accounts of 'relapse' and 'addiction' is contained in a book which at first glance has nothing to do with addiction. I would exhort anyone involved in the addiction field to read Scott Peck's *The Road Less Traveled* (1978). The thrust of this book enables one to focus on the fact that concession is an essential but painful part of healthy functioning. Concession is often so difficult that it is a surprise that it ever happens at all. It seems to me that the emphasis in treatment is often wrong. We should not be at all surprised if, despite great effort, our clients move hesitatingly and painfully slowly along the road of change. We should be more surprised than we typically are when our clients are able to throw off old crutches and supports and walk without them.

Relapse and the arrogance of therapy

One of my major concerns about the use of the term relapse is what it implies about therapy. Often the implication is that therapy, of even short duration, has had a sufficient impact to produce and maintain change. But, even where treatment is powerful enough to promote change, it is but one factor in the whole process of concession.

The bulimic

Let's consider the case of Jan, a bulimic. In the course of her two-month treatment you have undertaken a number of therapeutic procedures. Firstly, you were able to reduce and finally eliminate her purging and laxative use. Of course, the moment that you did this Jan reduced her calorie intake to deal with her fear of fatness. You then spent some time exploring the psychological and behavioural dynamics of her bingeing. You even simulated binges to get Jan used to the idea that she could exercise control and could learn to stop herself once she had started. You spent a fair amount of time talking about the repression of feelings and the need for assertiveness. You talked about set-point and ideal weights, calories, and nutrition. During this time Jan was relatively symptom free and as a consequence much happier in her spirits. There was optimism about her return to the community. When she was discharged she 'fell flat on her face' within forty-eight hours. She returned to her pre-admission pattern of behaviour, bingeing and purging relentlessly. What has happened to make this girl relapse?

The answer is that precisely nothing has happened which is why her characteristic bulimic behaviour continues. The notion of relapse only comes to mind if there is the judgement and subsequent expectation that Jan has already made significant and lasting changes in the period of therapy. Of course the therapeutic endeavours may have had some impact. In the safe confines of your office Jan may indeed have been able to resist foods, terminate a binge, express her feelings. But that does not ensure generalization to the outside world. There is a tendency to think that because clients can successfully deal with key issues in the therapeutic milieu they can continue to do the same effectively outside it. That assumption is a dangerous and misleading one. It is also an assumption that raises several questions about 'reinstatement of dependence' and 're-addiction' (Edwards 1977).

The notion of the 're-addiction' implies that clients are de-addicted in the course of treatment. I would be satisfied that a client has been de-addicted if he can now successfully deal with the range of bio-socio-psychological cues that once triggered his dependent behaviour. But most addictive treatment does not deal with this. All too often treatment 'merely' detoxifies and teaches people how to avoid critical cues, rarely does it de-addict. The notion of re-addiction is too often redundant because de-addiction has not taken place. It is hardly surprising, therefore, that clients should continue their addictions in the face of divorce, marriage, death, bankruptcy, kids, parents, success, failure, illness, etc. It is sometimes very difficult to address all these issues in therapy but the fact that therapy is difficult or even impossible does not allow us to expect our clients to cope satisfactorily with all eventualities. For example, Jan may have left your clinic with confidence, determined to binge no more. On arriving home, however, she received an extremely destructive phone call from her mother. This upset Jan terribly but for six hours she resisted the temptation to binge using all the coping strategies that you had taught her. She went to bed at nine o'clock, ostensibly to hide under the sheets from the beckoning food. At one o'clock in the morning she got up and ate everything in the refrigerator.

It is likely that as a therapist you are frustrated by this turn of events. You know you spent hours talking about such a situation and how to deal with it. You outlined all the coping strategies available. Jan even rehearsed eating a small amount and then stopping. The point is that you may have done all you could to prepare your client for this situation but that it simply was not effective. Not her fault, not yours. There simply may have been no way to prepare Jan efficiently for this situation given the time and resources available to you. Given the limitations of therapy it is not surprising that Jan's response should be her characteristic one. I do believe it is crucial to recognize the limitations of therapy and align our expectations (and those those of our clients) accordingly. I think it is important to accept that limited and inadequate therapeutic contact is not going to enable clients instantaneously to abandon entrenched and precious perceptions and behaviours and that, moreover, therapy is just part of the painful process of concession. Concession is a function of, among other things, a person's resources, their circumstances, and life events.

On effort

Within the contemporary context of 'relapse' there are some commendable models (e.g., Saunders and Allsop 1987). However, in all the models that I have come across there seems to be a key element missing.

The obese

At the Hilton Head Health Institute in South Carolina, about 600 people come through our programmes each year. They come in all shapes and sizes; some want to learn effective stress management techniques, others how to lose and maintain weight, others to review their lifestyle completely. All of them leave with a comprehensive plan to achieve their goals. In talking to these people, before, during, and after their stay on the programme, one fact has become abundantly clear. People consistently underestimate the amount of effort required to give up behaviours and make lasting lifestyle changes. Our clients know what their goals are and are eager to meet them. While most of their attention is initially focused on the allure of the goal and what life will be like once it has been achieved, surprisingly little is focused on the degree of effort required actually to achieve and maintain that goal.

At the Institute we stress that change does require great effort, particularly in the weeks that follow the clients' return home. We stress that their programme has to have top priority in order to have a chance to succeed. I believe the reason why so many good intentions do not reach fruition is that people do not recognize the amount of effort typically required to implement change. This is just as applicable to the person in treatment as it is to the person making a New Year resolution.

One of our clients arrives weighing 190 pounds. She wants to lose sixty pounds. She needs to lose sixty pounds. She is motivated enough to pay a considerable sum of money and devote one month out of her life in order to achieve this goal. During the programme she receives education about nutrition, exercise, metabolism, motivation, stress, habits, etc., etc. She is taught methods of good self-management. We ensure that her life is rescheduled to take account of her need to exercise, appropriate food preparation, and good self-management procedures. At the Institute she performs well. She loses fifteen pounds and reports feeling better than ever. She goes home and is able to implement the programme well for a few weeks or even months. After a while she reports that other events are crowding out her programme and it's becoming a struggle to fit everything in. Gradually she omits crucial parts of the programme and after a short while is only doing those aspects of the programme that require the least effort. What happens next will depend on factors such as circumstance and the impact that our follow-up will have on her to name just two.

Concession is a difficult business. I think it is important to recognize this and convey it to our clients. If maintaining the right balance of priorities requires going to AA meetings seven days a week, so be it. If keeping the right focus entails weighing every food eaten, so be it. If establishing the right mental set requires being unbelievably rigid in your exercise schedule, so be it. Logic suggests, and experience shows, that effort is always required to initiate and maintain behaviour change. However, the amount of effort required generally decreases as self-management and mastery skills are developed and incorporated into daily life. Relapse models need to take these factors into account.

Before embarking on this chapter I wrote to several luminaries in the field of eating disorders asking for any comments and reprints relevant to the subject of relapse in the eating disorders. The lack of cited references in this chapter is in part testimony to the fact that little is known about relapse in the eating disorders that is not known about relapse in any other disorder or about the psychology of concession in general.

One distinguished scholar did at least have the good grace and humility (not to mention the cynicism) to suggest that if I was writing about relapse in the eating disorders I must have more optimism and better success than he. After all you can't relapse unless you've recovered in the first place – can you?

Acknowledgement: I wish to thank Liz Yard for her valuable comments.

References

Edwards, G. (1977) 'The Alcoholism Dependence Syndrome: the usefulness of an idea', in G. Edwards and M. Grant (eds) *Alcoholism, Medicine and Psychiatry: New Knowledge and Responses*, London: Croom Helm.

Gunn, R. (1983) 'Smoking clinic failures and recent life stress', *Addictive Behaviors* 8: 83–7.

Krueger, D.W. (1981) 'Stressful life events and the return to heroin use', *Human Stress* 7: 3–8.

Peck, M.S. (1978) *The Road Less Traveled*, New York: Simon & Schuster.

Rosenberg, H. (1983) 'Relapsed versus non-relapsed alcohol abusers: coping skills, life events and social support', *Addictive Behaviors* 8: 183–6.

Saunders, W. and Allsop, S. (1987) 'Relapse: a psychological perspective', *British Journal of Addiction* 82: 417–29.

Chapter Six

Understanding and preventing relapse in sex offenders

Janice K. Marques and Craig Nelson

There are few problem behaviours in which a relapse episode is as devastating as it is in the case of child molesting and rape. A treatment failure in a sex offender programme means not only that the problem persists for the client, but that at least one innocent victim has been harmed. This grim consequence, along with the often discouraging evidence regarding the frequency of recidivism among these offenders, makes the prevention of relapse in this population an important goal. In this chapter, we will describe the problem of relapse among sex offenders, and will discuss how the field of sexual aggression can benefit from concepts and techniques borrowed or adapted from the area of addictive behaviours. We will also present a treatment model which focuses on training sex offenders to anticipate and cope with the problem of relapse.

Relapse rates for sex offenders are difficult to determine, since most assaults are unreported and most recidivism studies are based on unrepresentative samples of offenders (those who have been convicted and incarcerated). The most recent review of this literature indicates that recidivism rates vary from 0–40 per cent in one-year follow-up studies, 10–46 per cent in two-year studies, and 18–55 per cent in three-year follow-ups (Furby *et al.* 1987). Few long-term studies have been done, but the evidence clearly suggests that relapse continues to be a problem even through the second decade of follow-up (Gibbens *et al.* 1981).

Although the literature rarely indicates that offenders who have received treatment cope with relapse better than do untreated ones (Furby *et al.* 1987), this may be due as much to methodological problems (e.g., treatment and control groups which are not matched on key variables) as it is to treatment inefficacy. There is considerable evidence, however, that certain subgroups of offenders are more likely to reoffend. For example, current reviews (Finkelhor 1986; Furby *et al.* 1987; Quinsey 1986) conclude that recidivism rates tend to be higher for rapists and exhibitionists than for child molesters, and that men who molest male children ('homosexual molesters') recidivate more frequently than those who offend against female children ('heterosexual molesters'). Follow-up studies also indicate that men who have a history of sex offences, who select victims outside the family, or who have engaged in multiple deviant acts with a variety of victims are more likely to repeat their crimes (Abel 1988 in press; Quinsey 1986).

Sex offenders are a heterogeneous group, and vary in the extent to which their deviance is a chronic, repetitive pattern as opposed to an impulsive or more circumscribed response pattern. Although there are certainly some individuals who have committed a single, isolated transgression, evidence from confidential interviews indicates that the average number of paraphilic (sexually deviant) acts reported by non-incarcerated sex offenders is over 100 (Abel *et al.* 1987). The 142 exhibitionists interviewed by Abel *et al.* (1987) reported an average of over 500 victims. Among more aggressive offenders (rapists and child molesters), the homosexual child molesters had the most extensive offence histories, with 153 subjects admitting over 43,000 paraphilic acts, or an average of 282 per offender. The average number of victims for these men was 150. For some offenders, sexual deviance is obviously a chronic problem.

Current diagnostic criteria also reflect the repetitive, compulsive nature of many sexual deviations. Paedophilia, for example, is described as 'usually chronic' in course, and a paedophilic diagnosis is limited to those with 'recurrent intense sexual urges and sexually arousing fantasies' involving sexual activity with children (American Psychiatric Association 1980: 285). In extreme cases, compulsive acting out of such sexual obsession may reach a point at which the individual loses control over his behaviour, much as an alcoholic loses control over his drinking behaviour (Carnes 1983).

The similarity between sexual deviance and other addictive behaviours has been noted by a number of treatment authorities (Knopp 1984), some of whom have adapted treatment models or components from substance abuse programmes for use with sex offenders. In some cases (e.g., Carnes 1983), the addictive process is seen as a direct parallel to the disease of alcoholism, and treatment is a straightforward application of traditional programmes for 'recovering' addicts, such as the Twelve Steps of Alcoholics Anonymous. In other cases, addictions treatment approaches are used because there are similar treatment issues and problems presented by addicts and sexual offenders. As in the addictions, the goal of treatment for sex offenders is to achieve and maintain abstinence in regard to a prohibited and harmful behaviour, one which produces short-term pleasures or satisfaction at the expense of longer-term adverse effects. More often than not, treatment does not occur until the sex offender or alcoholic hits rock bottom, that is, has developed a chronic problem which has produced serious life problems, such as arrest. Treatment typically begins under 'detox' conditions (in which abstinence is enforced), and often the most intensive treatment is conducted in a restricted setting in which the problem behaviour cannot occur. After in-treatment goals have been attained, the offender or alcoholic is then released, usually with a strong commitment to abstinence and at least a minimal plan for continuing care. Unfortunately, as relapse rates indicate, long-term maintenance of treatment gains is a very difficult goal to achieve.

In recent years, addictions treatment models have begun to address many of these common problems. For example, prevention and self-control approaches offer an alternative to traditional disease models which propose that treatment is ineffective unless the victim of the disease has hit bottom. Another important development is the growth of interest in and knowledge of the maintenance phase of behaviour change, which has resulted in programmes specifically designed to help clients anticipate and cope with the problem of relapse. One such approach, the Relapse Prevention (RP) programme designed by Marlatt and Gordon (1985), grew out of research which indicated that the determinants and patterns of relapse are quite similar across a variety of addictions. RP proposes that a successful maintenance programme, whether for smokers, alcoholics, or compulsive gamblers, must specifically prepare the client to handle the common behavioural, affective, and cognitive components associated with the relapse process itself.

At this time, our knowledge of the relapse process in sex offenders is quite limited, since follow-up studies typically report only re-arrest figures, and do not analyse the process and events which lead to relapse, or to successful maintenance (continued abstinence). There are, however, interview data and case studies which suggest that the relapse experience for sex offenders often includes components similar to those reported by others with addictive behaviour problems. For example, the experience of an unpleasant emotional state immediately before losing control, the most common precursor found by Marlatt and Gordon (1980) among various substance abusers, is also reported by a majority of sex offenders. The Queen's Bench Foundation (1976) found that nearly 77 per cent of the rapists in their study reported feeling frustrated, depressed, angry, or rejected prior to their attacks; Pithers *et al.* (1983) reported a similar proportion (75 per cent) of sex offenders who experienced a negative emotional state just prior to their crimes.

Pithers *et al.* (1983) also observed that a number of sex offenders described a common sequence of events which led up to their offences. First, the men found themselves in stressful situations with which they were unable to cope effectively. As a result, they began to experience a negative emotional state, such as anger, frustration, or anxiety. They then began to fantasize about performing the deviant sexual act. The fantasies evolved into thoughts or actual plans in the next step of the sequence. Finally, thoughts were manifested in the commission of the offence. This sequence of stressful situation → no coping response → negative effect → fantasy → thought/plan → behaviour, clearly resembles the pattern reported by alcoholics, smokers, and heroin addicts who have relapsed (Marlatt and Gordon (1980). It has been noted, however, that fantasy appears to play a more central role in the relapse process for sex offenders than for substance abusers (Marques *et al.* 1984).

A recent analysis of interviews in which rapists and child molesters were asked to describe in detail the conditions surrounding their crimes yielded some interesting comparisons among offender types (Day *et al.* 1987). In terms of lifestyle, a feeling of not being in control of one's life when the offence occurred was often reported by both rapists and molesters. A criminal lifestyle (defined as one in which the offender's sole source of income was illegal activities, such as drug dealing) was described by nearly half of the rapists and heterosexual child molesters, but not by any of the homosexual or bisexual molests. On the other hand, these latter two groups had fewer non-deviant sexual interests and contacts than did the other offenders. Alcohol or other drug use at the time of the offence was most common for rapists, and rare for the homosexual molesters. Consistent with previous studies, over three-quarters of the rapists reported anger at the time of their crimes, while few of the molesters did so. The child molesters, in contrast, tended to report positive feelings towards their victims, and even to view the victims as willing participants in the offence. Half of the heterosexual, half of the homosexual, and all of the bisexual molesters shared this view, while none of the rapists described their victims as willing participants.

The following two case examples are presented to illustrate how the relapse episodes of a rapist and a child molester can be viewed from a Relapse Prevention (RP) perspective. The first case is of a 30-year-old rapist with an extensive history of antisocial behaviour which included truancy from school, thefts, sporadic employment, repeated assaultive behaviour, sexual promiscuity, and severe substance abuse. Prior to his current offence, this man had served a prison sentence in another state for attempted rape, a conviction which stemmed from a 'date rape' incident and which he felt was unjustified. Shortly after being placed on parole, he fled to California for fear of being returned to prison for violation of parole due to his increasing alcohol abuse. He settled with relatives and obtained a semi-skilled labouring job. Toward early evening on the day of the offence, he became embroiled in an intense argument with the wife of the relative with whom he was living. He withdrew from the house and proceeded to become increasingly inebriated. He recalled the drinking and his ruminations about the argument, but he claimed no recollection of the subsequent events. According to official court records, when he returned to the house late that night, he entered the bedroom of a young woman guest and threatened her with a kitchen knife if she did not have sex with him. Her screams awakened the other members of the household, who immediately summoned the authorities. When this individual requested treatment, he acknowledged severe difficulties with substance abuse which made him do 'crazy and stupid things', and he also hoped to improve his ability to cope with anger. Despite two convictions for attempted rape, he denied any urges or sexual fantasies regarding aggression against women. A phallometric assessment in a laboratory analogue setting (Laws and Osborn 1983; Earls and Marshall 1983) indeed found no evidence of sexual arousal to themes of either rape or physical aggression against women.

The second illustrative case has been previously described elsewhere (Nelson *et al.* in press). This 36-year-old child molester was sexually victimized as a child by several female baby-sitters. As a teenager, he initiated a pattern of sexually molesting younger girls. He received a brief course of out-patient treatment following these incidents. Shortly after his marriage in his early twenties, he was again arrested for molestation and remanded by the court to a residential treatment facility. After approximately two years of treatment, which included marital counselling and social skills training, he was released upon the recommendation of the treatment staff. For the next five years, he maintained a prosocial lifestyle. He and his wife had a child, his career advanced with promotions into supervisory positions, and he actively participated in community, social, and church activities. His marital relationship then began to deteriorate. He viewed his spouse as becoming demanding and domineering. In turn, his self-esteem and sense of self-worth diminished. To compensate, he began to spend increasing amounts of time with his daughter and her childhood friends. He enjoyed their attention and admiration, and he frequently offered to supervise the children when other adults were not present. During one of these occasions, while he was playing with the children in a swimming pool, he became sexually aroused. His arousal led to the interpretation of one of the girl's actions as seductive to him, and this contact subsequently proceeded into a molestation. When seeking treatment, this individual acknowledged sexual interest in female children (an interest also detected in the phallometric assessment of his sexual arousal pattern), and asked for help in controlling this propensity in order not to reoffend.

Although these two cases demonstrate the variety of antecedents and precursors which can promote relapse, the following analysis from an RP perspective (Brownell *et al.* 1986; Marlatt and Gordon 1980, 1985; Marques *et al.* 1984; Nelson *et al.* in press; Pithers *et al.* 1983) reveals that some common processes are represented in the experiences of the two offenders. Both were released into the community from their previous offences in a state of abstinence, having vowed not to be re-arrested. Each offender had a sense of self-control over his sexually illicit behaviour and expected not to reoffend. In the case of the rapist, he denied that he had committed the crime of attempted rape and failed to recognize any need to control his sexual behaviour. The child molester departed treatment with a sense of being 'cured' and, therefore, no longer at risk for committing another molestation. Neither offender reported being troubled by thoughts, fantasies, or urges of sexually deviant behaviour during these periods of abstinence.

In retrospect, both offenders appeared to set the stage for their reoffences by making choices that surreptitiously placed them in high-risk situations for reoffending. These decisions represented Apparently Irrelevant Decisions (AIDs), choices which overtly appeared rational and defensible, but at the same time clearly set the stage for their subsequent crimes. The rapist, for example, continued his substance abuse unabated, despite its prohibition in the conditions of his parole. He was able to justify to himself the wisdom of leaving the state in order to avoid having his parole violated and being incarcerated. In fact, however, it served only to move him toward more serious legal consequences. The molester, on the other hand, began spending considerable amounts of time with his daughter and her playmates when he found his marital relationship unsatisfactory. Was it not justifiable, if not admirable, for a father to take such interest in the activities of his child? Yet, this decision also placed him in increasing jeopardy to violate his abstinence from molestations. From an RP perspective, highlighting such AIDs for the offenders so that they may avoid them in the future serves as a key intervention in the prevention of relapse. The identification of typical AIDs also deprives the offender of their utility in helping him justify placing himself in high-risk situations.

As a result of the AIDs that both offenders made, each found himself in a high-risk situation which threatened his sense of self-control and eventually overwhelmed his ability to refrain from offending. High-risk situations may be conceived as being composed of a variety of factors or elements. The danger inherent in any high-risk situation is directly related to the number, strength, and interaction of the risk factors or elements present. In the rapist example, the high-risk situation represented an argument with a woman and included risk factors of intense anger, social isolation, thoughts of revenge, access to a potential victim, and increasing levels of intoxication to serve as a disinhibitor. In the molestation example, the high-risk situation represented solitary supervision of children with risk elements including low self-esteem, ready access to potential victims, and a propensity to become sexually aroused by young girls.

The degree of peril for relapse posed by any high-risk situation is inversely related to the offender's capacity to cope with the risk elements that comprise a high-risk situation. Thus, risk of reoffence can be diminished through an enhancement of coping skills for the various risk elements. At the most basic level, adequate coping skills for some high-risk situations may consist of simple escape and avoidance strategies. If the rapist had identified the dangers inherent in this high-risk situation, for example, he could have enhanced his chances of preventing his attempted rape by ceasing to drink and by not returning to the house. Clearly, the child molester's avoidance of circumstances which allowed him to be alone with potential victims would have minimized the likelihood of his reoffence. In addition to escape and avoidance, a variety of more complex coping responses to the high-risk elements could be used to sidetrack the relapse patterns. Improved anger management or the development of alternatives to drinking in response to stress may have assisted the rapist in coping with his particular risk elements. In a somewhat different vein, if the child molester had learned how to decrease his deviant sexual arousal through any of a variety of behavioural techniques (Quinsey and Marshall 1983), or had attempted to resolve his marital problems through counselling or separation, the relapse-engendering potential of his high-risk situation may also have been diminished.

As in the addictions, if an offender fails to emit a satisfactory coping response that returns him to a state of abstinence when he encounters a high-risk situation, he is likely to lapse from his vow of abstinence. In the addictions field, a lapse may be defined as the first instance of the undesirable behaviour (e.g., the first drink, the first cigarette, etc.), and a relapse as the return of the behavioural pattern (steady drinking or smoking). In the application of RP to sexual offending, the relapse is the return to the child molestation or rape. The lapse then becomes that behaviour which immediately precedes the reoffence. In this way, the concept of lapse continues to portray the quality of a slip or mistake that can still be corrected. In almost all cases, the lapse involves a deviant sexual urge, thought or fantasy. Although the rapist in the case illustration indicated that he cannot remember the events immediately preceding his crime, he acknowledged that he must have experienced thoughts of raping the victim as a way of venting his rage. The child molester, on the other hand, had been experiencing considerable deviant sexual urges prior to his return to molesting. Prior to his relapse, he even reported having purchased deviant pornography which he used during his masturbatory fantasies.

Whether or not a lapse leads to a full-blown relapse depends on a number of factors, including the Abstinence Violation Effect (AVE). A major source of the AVE is a conflict between the individual's previous self-image as an abstainer and the recent performance of the prohibited behaviour. That is, 'If I'm a cured sex offender, why am I feeling sexually aroused by a child?' One way of resolving the conflict is to act on the fantasy, admitting that one is still a molester. A second source of the AVE is the individual's attribution of the lapse to personal weakness or failure. In addition to feeling unable to control his urges, the child molester above reported experiencing feelings of guilt, shame, and depression. To the extent that the offender attributes a lapse to personal failure, his expectancy of continued failure will increase, and the chances of relapse also increase.

In the RP programme, individuals are taught to prepare for the occurrence of a lapse, and to counteract the negative self-evaluation and dissonance attendant on the AVE. Had the offenders in the above illustrations recognized that they could continue to maintain control over their behaviour, since it was only their perception of control which had been diminished, they may have been able to avert their crimes. By viewing the lapse as a predictable aspect of the abstinence process, the offender is empowered actively to combat the AVE. Such self-statements as 'I may experience a return of deviant urges from time to time, but I don't have to act on them', or 'the urge I'm experiencing will dissipate whether I act on it or not', may serve as coping responses during this late stage of the cognitive-behavioural chain leading to reoffence.

Although sex offenders represent a heterogeneous population, and describe a wide variety of antecedents to relapse, the commonality of the relapse process itself suggests a unified approach to treatment may be warranted. From an RP perspective, it is assumed that sex offenders must learn to recognize the individual sequence or chain of events that precipitates relapse, and develop coping skills geared to interrupt the chain and avoid reoffending. Sex offences are clearly not isolated or discrete events. Rather, they represent the end points of a long series or chain of events that foster the reoffence. Some points in this chain are external (e.g., access to a potential victim, interpersonal conflict etc.), while others are internal (e.g., inadequate affect management, distorted cognitions and justifications). Once this pattern is delineated, the offender can be taught to plan, develop, and practise strategies for intervening in his idiosyncratic pattern in order to minimize the risks of his reoffence.

As was noted previously, the use of addictions concepts and models with sex offenders has become increasingly popular in recent years, and a number of programmes are currently using techniques specifically designed to help offenders maintain abstinence (Knopp 1984). The utility of such programmes has not yet been demonstrated, but outcome studies are underway. For example our programme, the Sex Offender Treatment and Evaluation Project at Atascadero State Hospital, is a six-year clinical research project designed to test the effectiveness of an intensive RP programme in reducing recidivism among rapists and child molesters who volunteer for treatment during the last two years of their prison terms. Volunteers for the programme are randomly assigned to treatment (the state hospital RP programme) or control (prison time only) conditions, and the reoffence rates of treated and untreated offenders will be compared for five years following their release. At this time, the project has been operating only two years, and the first participants have just recently been released to the community. While it is encouraging to note that these first treated subjects believe that the RP model is useful for sex offenders and will help them avoid reoffending, we do not yet have follow-up data to confirm this.

It is clear that further research is needed to develop, test, and refine long-term maintenance strategies for sexually aggressive individuals. In addition to treatment outcome studies and analyses of relapse episodes, research is needed on offenders who succeed in breaking the pattern of deviance. Given the chronicity of sexual offending for many individuals, an analysis of the methods used by those who have successfully avoided relapse could be most instructive in this field.

References

Abel, G.G., Becker, J.V., Mittelman, M., Cunningham-Rathner, J., Rouleau, J.L., and Murphy, W.D. (1987) 'Self-reported sex crimes of non-incarcerated paraphiliacs', *Journal of Interpersonal Violence* 2(6): 3–25.

Abel, G.G., Mittelman, M., Becker, J.V., Rathner, J., and Rouleau, J.L. (1988) 'Predicting treatment outcome for child molesters', *Annals of the New York Academy of Sciences* 528: 223–34.

American Psychiatric Association (1980) *Diagnostic and Statistical Manual of Mental Disorders*, 3rd edn, Washington, DC: APA.

Brownell, K.D., Marlatt, G.A., Lichtenstein, E., and Wilson, G.T. (1986) 'Understanding and preventing relapse', *American Psychologist* 41: 765–82.

Carnes, P. (1983) *Out of the Shadows: Understanding Sexual Addiction*, Minneapolis: CompCare.

Day, D.M., Miner, M.H., Nafpaktitis, M.K., and Murphy, J.F. (1987) 'Development of a situational competency test for sex offenders', unpublished manuscript.

Earls, C.M. and Marshall, W.L. (1983) 'The current state of the technology in the laboratory assessment of sexual arousal patterns', in J.G. Greer and I.R. Stuart (eds) *The Sexual Aggressor: Current Perspectives on Treatment*, New York: Van Nostrand Reinhold, pp. 336–62.

Finkelhor, D. (1986) 'Abusers: special topics', in D. Finkelhor (ed.) *A Sourcebook on Child Sexual Abuse*, Beverly Hills, California: Sage Publications.

Furby, L., Weinrott, M.R., and Blackshaw, L. (1987) 'Sex offender recidivism: a review', manuscript submitted for publication.

Gibbens, T.C.N., Soothill, K.L., and Way, C.K. (1981) 'Sex offences against young girls: a long-term record study', *Psychological Medicine* 11: 351–7.

Knopp, F.H. (1984) *Retraining Adult Sex Offenders: Methods and Models*, Syracuse, NY: Safer Society Press.

Laws, D.R. and Osborn, C.A. (1983) 'How to build and operate a behavioral laboratory to evaluate and treat sexual deviance', in J.G. Greer and I.R. Stuart (eds) *The Sexual Aggressor: Current Perspectives on Treatment*, New York: Van Nostrand Reinhold, pp. 293–335.

Marlatt, G.A. and Gordon, J.R. (1980) 'Determinants of relapse: implications for the maintenance of behavior change', in P. Davidson and S. Davidson (eds) *Behavioural Medicine: Changing Health Lifestyles*, New York: Brunner/Mazel.

Marlatt, G.A. and Gordon, J.R. (eds) (1985) *Relapse Prevention: Maintenance Strategies in the Treatment of Addictive Behaviors*, New York: Guilford Press.

Marques, J.K. (1985) *Sex Offender Treatment and Evaluation Project: First Report to the Legislature in Response to PC 1365* Sacramento: California Department of Mental Health.

Marques, J.K. (1988) 'The sex offender treatment and evaluation project: California's new outcome study', *Annals of the New York Academy of Sciences* 528: 235–43.

Marques, J.K., Pithers, W.D., and Marlatt, G.A. (1984) *Relapse Prevention: A Self-Control Program for Sex Offenders*, appendix to J.K. Marques *An Innovative Treatment Program for Sex Offenders: Report to the Legislature*, Sacramento: California Department of Mental Health.

Nelson, C., Miner, M., Marques, J., Russell, K., and Achterkirchen, J. (1989) 'Relapse prevention: a cognitive-behavioral model for treatment of the rapist and child molester', *Journal of Social Work and Human Sexuality*, in press.

Pithers, W.D., Marques, J.K., Gibat, C.C., and Marlatt, G.A. (1983) 'Relapse prevention with sexual aggressives: a self-control model of treatment and maintenance of change', in J.G. Greer and I.R. Stuart (eds) *The Sexual Aggressor: Current Perspectives on Treatment*, New York: Van Nostrand Reinhold, pp. 214–39.

Queen's Bench Foundation (1976) *Rape: Prevention and Resistance*, San Francisco: Queen's Bench Foundation.

Quinsey, V.L. (1986) 'Men who have sex with children', in D. Weisstub (ed.) *Law and Mental Health: International Perspectives, vol. 2*, New York: Pergamon.

Quinsey, V.L. and Marshall, W.L. (1983) 'Procedures for reducing inappropriate sexual arousal: an evaluation review', in J.G. Greer and I.R. Stuart (eds) *The Sexual Aggressor: Current Perspectives on Treatment*, New York: Van Nostrand Reinhold, pp. 267–89.

Chapter Seven

Relapses from a gambling perspective

R. Iain F. Brown

Papers have appeared at rare intervals in learned journals of psychoanalysis, psychiatry, psychology, and social work at least since Freud wrote about the gambling problems of Dostoevsky in 1929, and Gamblers Anonymous has been spreading through North America, Britain, Australia, and Europe since the mid-1950s. Earliest systematic estimates of the prevalence of gambling problems (Commission on Review of National Policies towards Gambling in America 1976) indicated that the problem was far from negligible, but it is only relatively recently that gambling addictions have achieved the dubious honour of recognition by the medical establishment as a 'disorder of impulse control' in both DSM-III (American Psychiatric Association 1980) and ICD-9 (WHO 1980) and then as an addiction (American Psychiatric Association 1987) in DSM-IIIR. It now has a regular honourable mention in general books on the addictions with a basis in behavioural psychology (Hodgson and Miller 1982; Orford 1985). More recently still a comprehensive and critical review of theories and empirical work in the field before 1980 became available (Dickerson 1984) and in 1985 the subject gained a scientific journal of its own, the *Journal of Gambling Behaviour*.

It cannot, then, be surprising that systematic empirical studies of relapses in gambling addictions are scarce. Kramer (1987) summarizes some clinical observations. Only Cummings *et al.* (1980) have collected a sample of relapses among gamblers which is comparable with samples of relapses in other addictions in both method of collection and size, and only Marlatt in his well-known illustrative anecdote of the gambler's relapse-road-map gives prominence in his writings to a gambling relapse (Marlatt 1985).

Some indirect indication that relapses in gambling occur at about the same rate as for alcohol problems comes from Brown's studies in dropouts and outcome rates in Gamblers Anonymous (Brown 1986b, 1987a,b,c,d,e, 1988a, in press). Total abstinence after two years among all comers to GA at about 7 per cent is directly comparable

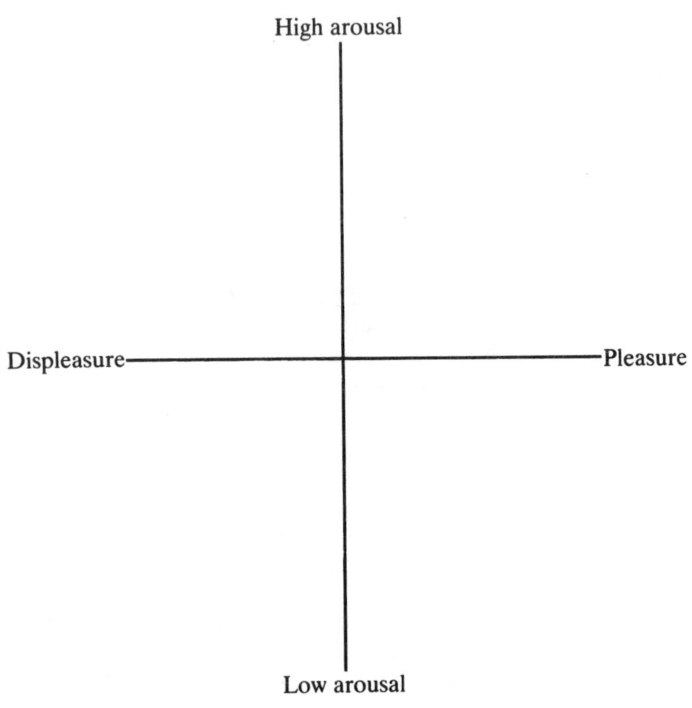

Figure 7.1 The two-dimensional space formed by Russell and Mehrabian's factors of emotional experience

with rates for total abstinence programmes in alcohol problems found in the Rand Report (Armor *et al.* 1978). But dropouts from a self-help group are not necessarily relapses.

Even Cummings *et al.*'s unique sample of gambling relapses is very small and, because generalization from such a sample size may be risky, it would be unwise to put much importance on their findings that more than three-quarters of the relapses were classifiable as *intra*personal as opposed to *inter*personal (79 per cent and 21 per cent respectively); that no gamblers reported relapses associated with positive emotional states (when the rate for all addictions together was 12 per cent); or that gamblers reported the highest relapse rates associated with negative emotional states (47 per cent compared with an overall rate for the addictions of 35 per cent) and the highest rates associated with attempts to test their own personal control by re-entering tempting situations (16 per cent compared with the general rate of 5 per cent). With sample size of only nineteen, even a percentage figure as high as seventy-nine translates into only fifteen relapses and 16 per cent translates into three relapses studied. Nevertheless, there might be some justification for concluding that the general picture for all addictions – suggesting the importance of negative emotional states as associates of relapses – is intensified in this sample of gambling relapses.

It is this importance of affect, negative hedonic tone, and particularly of arousal which the study of gambling addictions highlights within the study of addictions in general and relapses in particular. Two basic dimensions in all affective experience have emerged from extensive factor analyses of self-report data by Thayer (1978a, 1978b) and by Russell and Mehrabian (1977) and these have been well related to psychophysiological measurements of arousal. Russell (1979) found that almost all the reliable variance in this area is accounted for by two orthogonal dimensions of high/low arousal and pleasure/displeasure (figure 7.1). The emotional states associated with relapse, then, are predominantly those of pleasure and especially displeasure surrounding very high and very low states of arousal.

Arousal in normal and addictive gambling

Experimental evidence now appears to show that (1) gambling is very exciting (one individual's heart rate increased by 81 b.p.m. at the blackjack table), (2) some form of arousal or excitement is a major, and possibly the major, reinforcer of gambling behaviour for regular gamblers, and (3) individual differences in sensation seeking are involved, as one of a number of determinants, in the behaviour of more than 60 per cent of regular gamblers (Anderson and Brown 1984). More recently, Leary and Dickerson (1985) have reported supporting experimental data from poker-machine players in Australia, showing significant albeit more modest heart rate increases. The data and tentative conclusions presented in those papers justified some attempts at theoretical reorientations in the explanation of gambling and gambling addictions (Brown 1986a; Anderson and Brown 1987; Brown 1987a, 1987b).

Previous to this, operant Skinnerian models of variable interval and fixed interval reinforcement schedules had been used to account for why individuals, once started on episodes of betting, continued to bet again and again (Dickerson 1977, 1979, 1984; Frank 1979) but they failed to account for the long-term reinstatement phenomenon whereby, after an episode of gambling ceases and the chain of reinforcement is broken, then, sometimes as soon as possible but also sometimes after years without gambling, the whole situation is sought out again and a new episode begun. A classical model in which the autonomic nervous system plays an important role in the conditioning process more easily accounts for the reinstatement phenomena of both ordinary gambling and gambling addictions and allows for the maintenance of the behaviour by internal mood/state/arousal cues in addition to the external situational cues identified in orthodox models of the maintenance of alcohol addiction.

In this model (Brown 1986a), the central phenomenon of normal gambling is a personal experience and an objectively verifiable state of arousal, not sexual but probably autonomic and/or cortical. Irregular reinforcement schedules are only a means of producing this desired phenomenon which is sought repeatedly, even after each reinforcement schedule has been broken by a long time interval, for other reasons than merely because of the addictive properties of the reinforcement schedule alone. Individual differences in sensation seeking (Zuckerman 1979) are expected to be involved both in the repeated seeking of the state and in the capacity to experience it. This arousal component of normal gambling is open to two explanatory models, each with a physiological emphasis, both to optimal level of stimulation and to biological hedonism explanations, and can easily be absorbed into a general model of the development and maintenance of gambling addictions.

Reversal theory and the phenomenology of arousal

Probably of more importance for the psychology of relapses, however, is the assumption that what the gambler was striving for was not so much to win a fortune as to reach and maintain a subjective phenomenological state of excitement and/or escape. This assumption was based from the beginning on empirical data (Anderson and Brown 1984; Commission on the Review of National Policy towards Gambling in America 1976). We know, in addition, from many other studies in psychophysiology, that there is a significant correspondence between the arousal the subject feels and reports and the arousal that is so-called 'objectively' measured. It is this aspect of self-reported arousal, the phenomenology of arousal, that is equally as important as the psychophysiology and is opening up new developments.

The conceptual framework for the study of affective states outlined by Russell (figure 7.1) is particularly useful for the study of arousal phenomena and the positive and negative hedonic tones associated with them because, not only does it provide the framework for the visualization of optimal arousal and optimal level of stimulation accounts of gamblers striving to maintain themselves at the zenith of the inverted 'U' curved of arousal, but it is also the framework for the visualization of a part of a new structured phenomenology, called Reversal Theory, within which a much more sophisticated system for the explanation of the interactions of arousal and negative hedonic tone can be developed.

Reversal theory (Apter 1982) provides a conceptual framework for the study and explanation of homeostatic psychological systems with multiple points of stability. For example, in prolonged fixation of a figure such as the Necker Cube several rapid perceptual switches or 'reversals' may take place between the two relatively stable perceptions of the cube. Apter has given particular attention to bistable systems of metamotivational states, especially to switches of an individual's conscious experience and behaviour between the two specific states he has defined as 'Telic' and 'Paratelic'. A telic state is defined as one in which the individual is primarily oriented towards some essential goal or goals. A paratelic state, in contrast, is defined as one in which the individual is primarily oriented towards some aspect of his continuing behaviour and its related sensations.

In telic states people are future-oriented, planful, concentrating on foci outside themselves, enjoying the pleasure of goal anticipation, meaningfully employed, and prefer to remain in a state of low intensity and low arousal. In paratelic states people are present-oriented, spontaneous, sufficient unto themselves, enjoying the pleasure of immediate sensation, and prefer states of high intensity and high arousal.

By contrast with the inverted 'U' curve assumed by optimal level of arousal theories (Zuckerman 1979), reversal theory (Apter 1982: chapter 4) suggests that there are two separate metamotivational systems, each associated with one or other of the telic and paratelic states and each having its own different optimum level of arousal. The individual switches quite rapidly from one to the other, thus experiencing rapid changes of hedonic tone from time to time in the same situation. The name given by Apter to these switches or changes is 'reversals' from which the theory takes its name.

The relationship between arousal and hedonic tone, pleasure, or

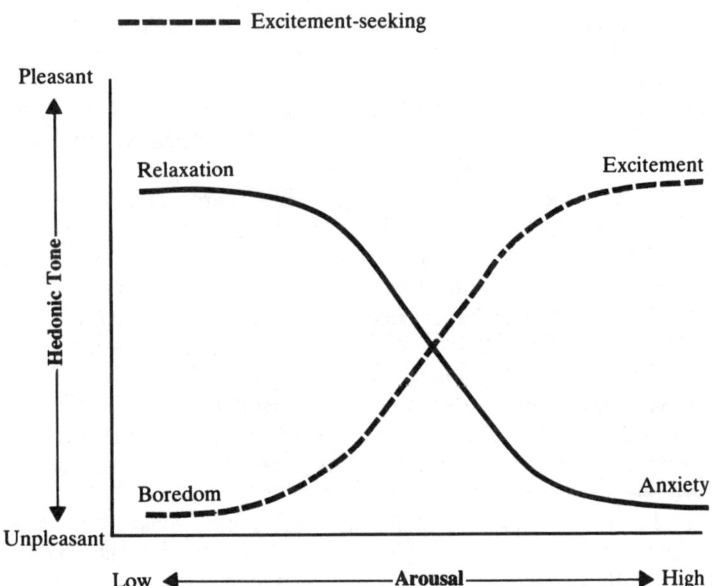

Source: Apter (1982), Figure 4.1, p.84

Figure 7.2 The hypothesized relationship between arousal and Hedonic Tone for the anxiety-avoidance and the excitement-seeking systems

maximum reinforcement is delineated in reversal theory by an 'X' curve (see figure 7.2). Low arousal, pleasurably experienced as relaxation in the anxiety-avoiding telic state, is rapidly reinterpreted and experienced unpleasantly as boredom when a reversal takes place to the excitement-seeking paratelic state. High arousal, unpleasantly experienced as anxiety in the anxiety-avoiding telic state, is, by contrast, rapidly reinterpreted and experienced as pleasurable excitement in the excitement-seeking paratelic state when a reversal takes place again. Because there are two metamotivational systems, telic and paratelic, each with its own preferred or optimum level of arousal the variable of general arousal is now conceived of as bistable.

The habitual preference for one or other of these two states, telic or paratelic, has been reliably measured by the Telic Dominance Scale (TDS) (Murgatroyd *et al.* 1978), consisting of the summation of subscales entitled Serious Mindedness, Planning Orientation, and Arousal Avoidance, which Apter contends measures predispositions to *experience* the world in certain metamotivational states.

Anderson and Brown (1987) found a significant correlation between the Telic Domination Scale and Zuckerman's Sensation Seeking Scale and went on to apply a reversal theory analysis to certain aspects of normal and problem gambling. Brown (1987c) has used reversal theory concepts in his analysis of operant and classical paradigms in the clinical management of gambling problems and Brown (1988b) has developed a systematic theoretical framework for a phenomenology of all addictions which draws on reversal theory concepts. The application of reversal theory specifically to the analysis of relapses might usefully begin with the study of those addicts who became involuntarily fixed in one or the other of the telic or paratelic states and may use their addictive activity as an attempt to change it. O'Connell (1988) has made a reversal theory analysis of smoking cessation and relapses.

Changing the perspective from a passive cognitive–behavioural view of relapses to an active, purposive, and affective/decision-making view of relapses

The recent conceptual frameworks developing from the study of gambling addictions tend towards an emphasis on the importance of arousal, and therefore of affect and subjective experience, in the development and maintenance of addictions. The pioneers in the study of relapses have not always seen them from that perspective.

Marlatt's earlier account of relapse (Marlatt 1978; Marlatt and Gordon 1980) is a two-stage one and contains two models, not often clearly related to each other, a behavioural one and a cognitive one. The dominant and most widely researched one is the behavioural one, focusing in the first stage on relapse-provoking situations, coping responses to them, and violation effects. The kinds of relapse-provoking situations which Marlatt originally described and studied were predominantly classified in relation to some external event (73 per cent), usually in interpersonal relations (which produced frustration and anger) or in social pressure or in an external temptation such as passing a bar. Only a relatively small percentage of the provoking situations seemed to be classified as clearly internal, i.e., negative mood states and euphoria. The major concession at the first stage to the existence of cognitive factors in this model is the idea of 'apparently irrelevant decisions' but whether there is any purposive thinking behind these is not made clear and it is often implied that they are without full conscious awareness or in some kind of borderline twilight between the full realization of their import and some kind of automatism. The assumption, consonant with the behavioural emphasis of the model, seems to have been that the abstaining/controlled drinking organism is passively invaded by stimuli from a relapse-provoking situation and it subsequently makes or fails to make an effective response. Research and clinical practice have tended to focus on this model.

The cognitive stream of Marlatt's thinking, on the other hand, focuses on the concept of cognitive expectancies which are seen as arising from a history of reinforcements from drinking and can be fitted into already familiar general theories of social learning. The relationship between the cognitive and the behavioural streams is not elaborated for the stage in the relapse before the first drink has occurred but one must presume that cognitive expectancies of the effects of the first drink and of a reversion to former patterns of drinking behaviour are always present, although no attempt is made to explain fluctuations in the strength of these expectations and these fluctuations are not implied even in the idea of the programmed relapse.

The behavioural and cognitive models are more explicitly combined in Marlatt's treatment of what he sees as the second distinct stage of the relapse, the violation effect. Here expectancies are seen clearly as determining behaviour, especially the belief that 'one drink = one drunk' promulgated by Alcoholics Anonymous.

This account of relapse has never accorded fully with practical experience in helping gamblers and drinkers. Some clients appear to build up to relapse over weeks. Their fellow attenders at Gamblers Anonymous or at therapeutic groups and their experienced spouses claim, often rightly, to see it coming. Then a situation is provoked by the client and he appears to hang a relapse on it. Or a drinking client who had formerly been depressed, surly, and uncooperative, one day appears relaxed and even friendly. The practitioner thinks that at last the client is pulling through but days later learns that he has been drunk almost since he left the agency last. The obvious conclusion is that when the practitioner last saw him he had finally decided to treat himself to a relapse and he certainly was not going to let any counsellor intervene to disappoint him.

Kramer (1987) made a series of clinical enquiries of relapses among compulsive gamblers well known to him over an extended period of time as out-patients receiving regular treatment primarily but not exclusively for a gambling problem at a Veterans Administration Medical Centre in Brooklyn. He found 'there is much in common when elicited from several clients independently. Often the carefully schemed deception could be targeted many days or weeks ahead of an occasion when the relapsing gambler would not be missed.'

> From a number of our gambling clients in treatment for three or more years they insist that the relapse phenomenon is never a spontaneous impulsive act, never the result of bitter disappointment or the result of misfortune or failure. Rather it is the result of deception first to the gambler, a carefully planned or schemed relapse appointment headed for some exciting 'action'.
>
> (Kramer 1987)

This kind of critique of orthodox theories receives significant support from a study by O'Donnell (1984). Examining evidence from Heather *et al.* (1982) that relapsers who accepted the self-fulfilling prophesy 'one drink = one drunk' as measured by high scores on Schaeffer's questionnaire (Schaeffer 1971) were more likely to return to problem drinking than to harm-free drinking, O'Donnell rejected their argument that this was any more than circumstantial evidence for the Abstinence Violation Effect. On the contrary, the results of a discriminant function analysis of the factors associated with the outcome of relapses in eighty-two male out-patients at a Glasgow alcohol-recovery centre appeared to demonstrate that the relapses of individuals who recovered as opposed to those who had a slip and returned to problem drinking were characterized by the presence of euphoric or dysphoric mood, by type of familiar surroundings, type of company, time of day, and number of drinks taken on that occasion, *not* by scores on the Schaeffer questionnaire ($p < 0.001$ and 88.5 per cent predictive efficiency). The tendency was for multiple relapsers to have their relapse in familiar surroundings, in familiar company, before the evening, and to enter immediately into a prolonged drinking bout.

O'Donnell comments that these findings could be interpreted as indicating an element of intentionality in the multiple relapser's first slip, although there are, of course, other possible interpretations, e.g., that multiple relapsers are simply more careless. By contrast, O'Donnell found that the relapser who will later become abstinent will have his relapse in unfamiliar surroundings with people who are not his usual drinking companions and is more likely to stop himself after one drink. This would be consistent with the work of Litman (Litman *et al.* 1979) who found that abstinent alcoholics employed effective cognitive-vigilance strategies.

What is under attack here is the whole concept of a two-stage relapse model as being appropriate to any more than a particular subsection of the population of relapsing alcoholics, i.e., those who will later recover. Further, the suggestion is that for many addicts the relapse is an intentional phenomenon, chosen, perhaps after deliberation, pursued as a goal, planned and carried through with thoroughness and efficiency – a long way from being a 'failure of resolve' or a 'resolution breakdown', both terms appropriate to a moral model of addictions. A much better substitute term for 'relapse' is 'reversion' because what we are referring to is a return or reversion to a formerly well-established behaviour pattern of alcohol intake or addictive behaviour. Using this term, the reversions of the multiple relapsers in O'Donnell's study are full reversions and the reversions of the abstainers who later established a pattern of controlled drinking or total abstinence were only partial reversions.

Litman *et al.* are, perhaps wisely at this stage of our knowledge, less explicit about an explanatory model of relapse than Marlatt. The outcome of the factor analysis of danger situations (Litman *et al.* 1977; Litman *et al.* 1983) seems to indicate a quite different emphasis from Marlatt's – on internal states as precipitant factors rather than external events which only feature in the most recent analysis as a part share of the factor labelled 'External Events and Euphoria'. Affective components figure much more largely in the Litman *et al.* analysis than in Marlatt's, with two of the three factors referring to them and the first or principal component being a wholly affective one, namely 'Unpleasant Mood States'.

It is the contention in this chapter that the phenomenological, affective, motivational, and decision-making components of relapse have been underestimated in importance, not to say neglected, by the cognitive–behavioural orthodoxy which has also missed the intentional planned and purposive subjective functions of relapse. If, then, the cognitive–behavioural model of reversions is unsatisfactory, what needs to be added to it? Again, a perspective from the study of gambling addictions may provide a useful starting point.

Operant and classical conditioning analyses of the role of arousal in the maintenance and reinstatement of excessive gambling behaviour

Brown has argued (1987a) that if the core of the gambling experience is indeed the experience of very high states of arousal, it, and its anticipation, may be expected, on an operant analysis, to produce (1) physical alterations in adrenalin or endorphin output, both tonic and phasic (Blasczynski *et al.* 1985) and (2) massive temporary increases in sustained high hedonic tone. These can be seen as the reinforcers of the operant behaviour of gambling.

The constant repetition of states of very high arousal may further be expected in addition to produce several classical conditioning effects.

(1) Opponent processes similar to those proposed by Solomon (1977) may be expected, if the gambling episodes are spaced together with the critical frequency, to result in the slow build-up of tendencies to the opposite of the short bursts of high arousal, namely to long periods of depressed arousal when not gambling (figure 7.3). If some form of arousal is indeed a major reinforcer of gambling, then this depressed arousal will be experienced not as pleasant relaxation but rather as extreme boredom and apathy – leading in turn to an even greater need than previously to gamble to relieve the boredom and apathy alone, even when there is no need to gamble in order to chase losses.

(2) There will be an adaptational effect such as is described and documented by Siegel (1977) in his analysis of the psychological components of drug tolerance and greater and greater risks will be required to produce the same hedonic effects.

(3) Following Wikler (1973), there will be many conditioned stimuli, not only around the situations of former gambling, the people and the actions associated with former gambling, but also from the internal mood states which formerly preceded gambling and even from the former cognitive efforts associated with preparations for gambling. Each of these widely generalized conditioned stimuli can be expected to provoke thoughts of gambling and the conditioned emotional effects which accompany them. Such conditioned emotional effects are known in connection with alcohol (Pomerleau *et al.* 1983) and may be expected, possibly to an even greater degree in an activity which produces such powerful arousal effects, in connection with the anticipation of being about to gamble.

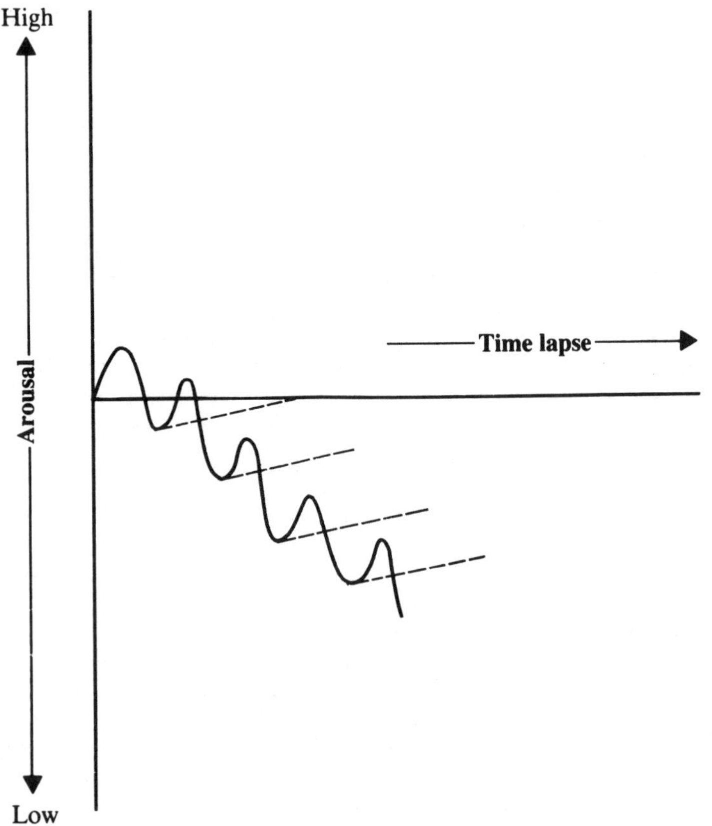

Note: Broken lines show expected returns to baseline if the opponent process was completed without being interrupted by a fresh increase in arousal timed at the critical point.

Source: Brown (1987b)

Figure 7.3 Predicted cumulative effects of frequent repetition of arousal experiences interrupting the opponent process before recovery from the rebound phase

Analysis of relapses

In a limited model of relapses of an opponent process type, Brown suggested (1987b) that each of these conditioned stimuli produced in the addict gambler an association with being about to gamble and all the attendant autonomic reactions and affective states connected with the anticipation, both pleasurable increases in arousal and the aversive resulting opponent process of lowered arousal associated with the rebound from that.

Donovan and Chaney (1985) use an opponent process model mainly to account for changes in drinking effects following long-term repeated exposure but the same processes are operative in the anticipation of a drink and in a drinking episode. Both stimuli for what Solomon (1977, 1980) calls the *A* state (eliciting pleasurable reinforcers) and stimuli for what Solomon calls the *B* state (eliciting aversive reinforcers) can add to the total effect. Donovan and Chaney suggest that stimuli associated with the pleasurable A state, such as handling a bottle of one's favourite beverage, can come to evoke an increment of the *a* process and so be opposed by the opponent process which lasts longer. The gambling equivalent might be the study of form in one's favourite bar which would be a pleasure, followed by a wave of boredom and apathy when the gambler realizes he has no money with which to place a bet. The cumulative *B* state from some strong *A* stimuli may, Donovan and Chaney suggest, become so anhedonic for the experienced alcoholic drinker as to require resumption of drinking for relief and a similar process may be expected to affect the gambler and any other addict – to heroin, etc. In addition, stimuli associated with withdrawal may be expected to directly provoke the *B* state. A powerful *B* state can easily be interpreted and reacted to as a subclinical withdrawal state as suggested by Ludwig and Stark (1974) or even as a bereavement pang, if a major activity formerly central to life is being given up (McAughtrie and Brown 1988). According to opponent process models, however, it is not just withdrawal associations which are dangerous for the maintenance of the treatment programme but pleasurable *A* state associations too.

According to the extension of the opponent process model in the affective/decision-making analysis of relapses (Brown 1987b), once the cognitive expectation is entertained and the attendance affective reactions experienced, the addict enters a process conditioned by his previous patterns of behaviour which, unless he makes courageous efforts to escape, will deliver him up to a relapse or behavioural reversion. This process could also be seen as a form of inner conflict in which the build-in bias towards a particular outcome becomes stronger the longer the conflict continues without a resolution.

The affective/decision-making analysis of the build-up to a relapse

To use the example of gambling, this first cognitive and affective anticipation produces in the subject differing effects depending upon

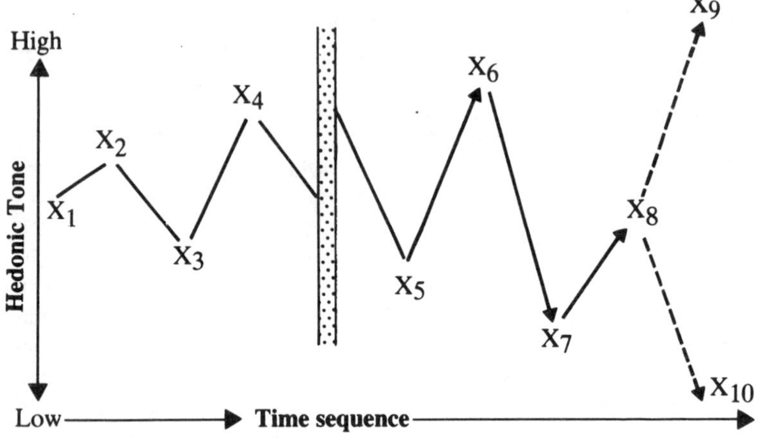

Notes:

X. Internal events, 1 to *n*

1. First entertainment of reversion
2. First decision to reject reversion
3. Second entertainment of reversion
4. Second decision to reject reversion
5. *n*th to 1 entertainment of reversion (with maximum affective relief)
6. *n*th to 1 decision to reject reversion
7. *n*th entertainment of reversion (with declining affective relief)
8. Critical decision
9. Affective consequences of decision at *n* to revert to previous addictive pattern of behaviour
10. Affective consequences of decision at *n* to maintain programme of behaviou change (and block fantasies?)

=*Affective consequences of each preceeding internal event*

Source: Brown (1987b)

Figure 7.4 Affective/decision-making analysis of reversions to previous patterns of addictive behaviour or relapses

whether gambling can continue to be anticipated or not (figure 7.4). If the individual is expecting to gamble and continues to expect to gamble, then these cues will produce an *A* state of temporary arousal and relief from boredom into a state of pleasant arousal (like the *A* state in the opponent process), rewarding the gambler for thinking about gambling, preparing for gambling, and eventually for doing it.

If, on the other hand, a commitment has been made not to gamble or not to gamble to an extent uncontrolled enough to bring real satisfaction, and real gambling cannot be anticipated, these same conditioned stimuli will produce a contrasting rebound effect. This rebound opponent-process-like effect may, if the timing is right, be exacerbated and potentiated by the *B* state resulting from the opponent process arising from the original *A* state caused by the anticipation of gambling, and it will lead to plunges in arousal which will be experienced by the abstinent gambler as deepened boredom, apathy, and restlessness, all highly unpleasant, thus punishing the individual for deciding *not* to gamble. Each change of decision backwards and forwards can be predicted to have cognitive and affective effects. The punishment will increase in proportion to the amount of anticipatory arousal the individual may have previously generated by dallying with the thought of gambling up to the point at which he made the decision to 'disappoint himself'.

Thus, the individual is rewarded by his own conditioned affective responses for every step he takes *towards* relapse and punished for every one he refuses to take and this punishment increases in proportion to the extent to which he has entertained the idea of gambling and been rewarded with anticipatory arousal.

No individual who embarks upon a committed programme of behaviour change can escape coping with the first stages of this punishment at least at *some* time, probably almost as soon as the commitment is made. But, in addition, for long after the fever of particular gambling episodes has died down and perhaps after years of total abstinence, the unexpected revisitation of a long-forgotten set of conditioned stimuli (Wikler 1973), even just the memory of the 'peak experience of the first big win', can trigger a sudden reinstatement of the old pattern of behaviour in an individual who no longer has, even if he once had, adequate coping strategies readily available for the arousal and especially for the anhedonic effects.

It is not claimed that there are never relapses or reversions to the old pattern which arise directly from a sudden impulse which, contingent upon an external stimulus, overwhelms the coping defences and produces a slip of the kind which the Marlatt model is especially able to explain. What *is* claimed, however, is that individuals very rarely revert to a previous, perhaps destructive, pattern, of behaviour in this way at the first surprise attack. On the contrary, they usually resist it successfully, but, for a large proportion, the entertaining of the thought of gambling with its attendant affective reactions sets off a long train of conflict, sometimes extending over many months, in which the decisions change to and fro.

Sometimes the fantasy of gambling again is entertained for a moment or two and the temporary rewards are reaped and then again the commitment to desist is mobilized and the punishment is undergone, to and fro, with increasing intensity of affect, until a critical point is reached. Just before this point the gambler cannot any longer afford to disappoint himself because, having done so so often, even the promise of the fantasy begins to seem a false and an unreal one and no longer produces even the same temporary relief of anticipation as formerly. Soon after this turning point from increasing affect to decreasing affect, the gambler either has to gamble in reality in a full-scale behavioural reversion or give up even the fantasy dalliance and face the inevitable dysphoria without any of his former escapes.

Extension of the analysis to heroin and other 'downers'

The foregoing analysis focused on the example of gambling is applicable to other 'upper' activities and to the ingestion of 'upper' substances such as cocaine but the same analysis can be applied with only a simple inversion to 'downer' or tension-reducing activities and substances (Brown 1987b). Some substances such as alcohol and tobacco can be used as either 'uppers' or 'downers' by skilful manipulation of both timing and strength of succeeding doses and of contextual cues and either one of the above analyses may be applicable to their use, depending on circumstances. This analysis can be extended further to many processes of inner conflict normally thought to be unconnected to any problems of behaviour which might be labelled 'addictive', e.g., guilt-induced conflict over masturbation, and is easily seen as a miniature conflict model of the kind used so centrally by Orford (1985) in the psychological explanation of addictions in general.

Possible reinterpretations of some of the phenomena of relapse

Many of the external contingencies which accompany relapses or reversions can be seen as sought out in a motivated way or provoked by addicts who are on this royal and fantastic road to a relapse. Additionally, if an individual who is already being driven towards a behavioural reversion by his affective conditioned responses as in this analysis meets with a powerful external stimulus, he or she is likely to be much less motivated or less able to mobilize his or her normal defence strategies. So many of the relapses which may appear to be stimulus-contingent may actually, on closer analysis, turn out to be internally generated.

The dalliance is all the more likely and the relief which accompanies it will be all the stronger when the individual who decides to maintain his programme of behaviour change has to contrast his fantasy of biased cognitive expectancies and their affective accompaniments with a grim and unrewarding present reality. It follows, then, that, as Litman found in her factor analyses and as was found in community reinforcement studies (Hunt and Azrin 1973; Azrin 1976), a background of general life satisfaction since behaviour change and what Litman calls the strategy of 'Positive Thinking' (Litman *et al.* 1977) would be expected to be a sound protection against such a build-up towards relapse.

It follows equally clearly that what Litman *et al.* call the strategy of 'Cognitive Vigilance' is likely to be the defence *par excellence* until these favourable background conditions have been built up. Indeed the logical implication of this analysis is that the gambler should be taught thought stopping (Rimm 1973) as an immediate emergency relapse prevention drill because with every moment he goes on thinking about a relapse the more difficult it becomes for him to stop.

Affective/decision-making analyses and cognitive behavioural analyses

There is nothing in the foregoing analysis which contradicts the cognitive–behavioural analysis but rather it can complement it and increase its powers to predict and intervene. There may now be some benefit from a revision of the classification of relapses or reversions into four types:

1. Contingent relapses – arising almost purely from unexpected external stimuli and producing overwhelming automatic or impulsive responses probably with a violation effect.
2. Intrapersonal relapses – arising from a slow build-up of fantasy and of conflict surrounding it, probably with little or no violation effect.
3. Mixed external/internal relapses – arising from a near-equal interaction of contingent and intrapersonal processes.
4. Cue-exposure relapses – arising from unsupervised and undirected attempts at self-treatment by the client by the method of cue exposure (Rankin *et al.* 1983).

According to this classification most reversions would come under the 'mixed' category and, if this were so, it would follow that the interactions between cognitive and affective internal states of readiness and external contingencies in the decision-making process would most repay further attention.

Relapses as purposeful and functional

If, as appeared from O'Donnell's studies in relapsing Glasgow drinkers and from Kramer's clinical impressions of relapsing gamblers, many relapses are planned and executed with efficiency, this would fit with Brown's view of the phenomenology of addictions as being about the learning of an acquired drive to maintain hedonic tone in the short term at the expense of the medium and long term (Brown 1987a, 1988b) and it would suggest that Marlatt's description of the state of perceived control (Marlatt 1985) is mainly descriptive of repressors as opposed to sensitizers (Byrne 1964). For many individuals there will be long-running and recurring entertainment of possibilities of relapse and for others full-scale running fantasies which can be accepted, taken up, and put into operation in a purposive way at any time. These 'relapses' are not 'failures' in any sense of the word and do not necessarily involve any loss of self-efficacy; rather they appear to the individual as freely chosen *reversions to a former pattern of behaviour*.

It has long been acknowledged among both professionals and laymen seeking to promote behaviour change that there is much to be learned from such reversions or relapses when they occur which will aid the individual client in the identification of situations of difficulty of temptation which are particularly threatening to the maintenance of the desired pattern of behaviour change. But other positive functions for the client of such reversions or relapses have not received much discussion and the intention here is to review three possibly major positive functions which clients may seek and find in such reversions.

Behavioural reversions or 'relapses' as attempts at goal review

In this kind of reversion the individual committed to a behaviour change has become increasingly uncertain that the balance of costs and benefits associated with the new pattern of behaviour shows a net gain in hedonic tone, either for the present or for the future or for both. The reversion itself is often triggered off by some external event (Marlatt and Gordon 1985) or by significant mood changes (Litman *et al.* 1983) but the threshold for triggering has previously been considerably lowered either by the build-up of anticipatory changes in arousal consequent upon intermittent fantasizing about it or by the kind of review of the costs and benefits of the programme of behaviour change to be examined here.

It is one of the major tasks of the first stage in the management of any addiction problem to promote a searching review of the benefits and especially the costs of the behaviour suspected of being excessive. Coming at the beginning of the behaviour change process, a clear picture of the balance of costs and benefits usually leads naturally to a commitment to a programme of change and plays an important part in mobilizing the motivation that will maintain the change after the initial steps. Occasional reminders of that first cost-benefit analysis are useful in maintaining behaviour change and avoiding 'relapse' or reversion to the old pattern.

Both tonic and phasic changes in the subjectively perceived balance of costs and benefits must be expected. In the course of any twenty-four period it is sometimes reported that the subjectively perceived balance of costs and benefits can fluctuate quite wildly, especially in the initial stages of establishing the new pattern. Tonic changes occurring as drifts over a longer time base are also possible and even likely, resulting in a shift of the base around which the short-term fluctuations vary, perhaps towards the perception that the costs of change are too great relative to the benefits. Most usually the tonic changes are brought about by such factors as the slow realization that the quality of life has not improved as much as was hoped for when the behaviour change was initiated and the phasic changes are provoked by the presence of strong stimuli previously associated with drinking.

Most often what happens appears to be that the individual, usually having pursued a programme of change for some time, (1) has examined the costs and benefits so often and is aware of having come to so many different conclusions about the balance at different times, (2) has toyed with the idea of returning to the old behaviour pattern and does not trust either the rosy anticipation with which a return to the old behaviour is sometimes viewed or the perhaps exaggerated memories of the painful consequences, and so (3) in general feel that they have lost sight of the truth about whether they need to change their behaviour pattern or not. There is then a need to re-experience the whole old pattern again and so confirm and clarify afresh their picture of its costs and benefits. Sometimes (4) the individual has additionally begun to think that they have identified what they previously did wrong and so know better how to handle themselves now. All of these are reasons for reviewing the previously accepted goal of maintaining a changed pattern of behaviour by returning temporarily to the old pattern for a realistic reassessment of costs and benefits.

Such *goal review* reversions usually appear to result in a powerful and vivid confirmation of those previous cost-benefit analyses which had been in favour of behaviour change and the individual's commitment to the new pattern of behaviour is increased.

Behavioural reversions or 'relapses' as 'away breaks' from an unendurable situation

In this kind of reversion the individual committed to the behaviour change is experiencing extreme dysphoria over long periods. Often the old behaviour pattern has been masking an underlying problem of depression or anxiety which potentiates a depressive or anxious reaction to the behaviour change itself. There is not necessarily any abandonment of the commitment to a goal of behaviour change, only a temporary withdrawal as the individual seeks immediate relief for what may even be a consciously limited period of time.

The usual outcome is remorse, reduced feelings of personal effectiveness, and an intensification of the underlying anxiety or depressive state. If these outcomes are clearly seen then they may result in an intensified commitment to endure the intolerable in the hope of winning through to better times. It can also give increased hope of this if the underlying state is recognized and some programme of relief for it is entered into.

Behavioural reversion of 'relapses' as acts of defiant self-assertion

This kind of reversion most often occurs in individuals who have been subjected to heavy external pressure to seek help and have been more actively directed towards behaviour change. Relatives, figures at the workplace, or even some helping agency are experienced as overbearing, overconcerned, and overcontrolling, so that the individual, who may not disagree with them that behaviour change is necessary, comes to feel that maintenance of the desired behaviour change is being seen as an act of compliance or even submission and that any success with which they continue to sustain it will be shared with or perhaps even be wholly claimed by one or more people.

The behavioural reversion does not represent any revision of a cost-benefit analysis or even a temporary inability to continue with a programme of change. It is more obviously an act of self-assertion, albeit of a rather negativistic kind. It is a warning to all the sources of pressure that this pressure in itself will not be successful in bringing about behaviour change in the individual. If these external sources of pressure are sufficiently demoralized by several such reversions then the individual may only then be free to initiate and successfully execute his/her own self-generated and self-motivated programme of behaviour change which in turn often emerges as being indistinguishable in all significant respects from the very programme from which the original series of reversions took place.

A self-assertion reversion can also, possibly more often, arise from low self-esteem and negative feelings alone with no implication that there is any self-motivated programme of change which the relaxation of any external pressure will make room for.

Sometimes the external pressures can be called off or at least significantly reduced or the individual may become more aware of how his/her need for self-assertion is blocking necessary progress with behaviour change. Alternative ways of making the necessary assertions in other ways can be developed.

In all instances it is important to do whatever can be done to improve the self-esteem of the individual.

The further study of the positive functions of reversions

This classification into *goal review reversions*, *away break reversions*, and *self-assertion reversions* does not make any claim to be exhaustive and does not assume that these will always be found in their pure form entirely distinguishable from one another. Many reversions will have elements or features of all three kinds of positive function described here. This makes the systematic empirical study of such reversions particularly difficult both because clear behavioural criteria for the identification of the presence of even each of the three forms described here and for their distinction from each other are lacking and because so much of the indentification depends upon the individual's self-report or even upon the clinical judgement or imaginative deduction or intuition of the observer. Without such clear criteria for identification the desirable studies of the outcomes of different ways of coping with different kinds of reversion cannot yield worthwhile or reliable results.

An illustrative case study (and the world's first computerized programmed relapse)

Donald McDonald had a gambling problem, a drinking problem, and depressive problem when he first came to see me in my role as a voluntary counsellor at Glasgow Council on Alcohol. He had been struggling on through relapse after relapse over several years' attendance at Gamblers Anonymous. I concluded the first time I saw him that he had been suffering from a chronic low-grade depression and I sent him to his GP with clear instructions on how to present himself so that no GP could possibly mistake his real condition as I saw it. The GP sent him to psychiatry who did not think there was a depressive problem and he did not return to me at that time. A year later his friends in GA sought out my help because he had made a determined attempt on his life and simultaneously a note reached me from psychiatry asking me to take him on for his gambling problem.

Immediately I took him on, before I had even seen him again. Donald had a gambling relapse which I interpreted as a 'self-assertion reversion' to demonstrate to GA, to his spouse, and to me that he was feeling pressured and was not going to give in. My first move was to do nothing about the gambling itself but to eliminate the heavy drinking which was acting as a gateway to gambling. I wrote to the GP explaining that Donald had a drink-related problem, i.e. that every time he drank he got into trouble through gambling, and I explained to Donald that, although I certainly did not think he was 'an alcoholic', his drinking was complicating things in this way. Since I had no intention of wasting time battling it out with a drinking problem over many months when there were two other major problems to be tackled simultaneously, I suggested that he go on Antabuse. Fortunately, Donald had been thinking of it himself already and the GP agreed with me. Over several months we worked with the aftermath of the suicide attempt along with Donald's wife Katriona, in separate individual sessions and as a couple. Donald stayed off gambling but his mood declined.

At first the relapses were of the 'goal review' kind and he soon returned after each one to his total abstinence programme, but, as the depression deepened again, they became more and more frequent and of the 'away break' variety. When he could stand the boring routine of his job no longer, he would just drive his taxi out of town to a place where he had recently enjoyed a good holiday and gamble.

I wrote, with his agreement, to his GP again and suggested that we might try some anti-depressants. This was done and Donald stopped coming to see me. However, Katriona still attended regularly and I began to receive alarming reports which led me to prepare her and her adolescent son to move out in an emergency. Still Donald did not appear and I had nothing but Katriona's report to go on until one Friday he walked in with her 'singing like a linty'. That night he attacked his son in a manic rage, the family fled as prepared and he phoned me to tell me what had happened. I mobilized the ever co-operative GP and the psychiatric hospital accepted him this time round as having an affective disorder, a feature common among gambling addicts (McCormick *et al.* 1984). He is now partially stabilized on lithium salts and, after twenty years of chronic low-grade depression, looks forward eagerly to his regular upward mood swings.

Donald still insisted that in order to stay sane while he waited around in slack periods in his taxi, he had to play with systems for gambling. Although doubtful, I went along with this since I have known a compulsive gambler who would spend a Saturday afternoon sitting by the television set phoning imaginary bets to his bookmaker and total it all up at the end of the day confirming for himself what a fool he would have been to actually gamble it. This man survived in this way for many years as a mainstay of GA.

Donald's next hypomanic episode first became evident when he began sitting up all night working on his systems. Astonishingly, having seldom if ever entered a casino in his life (he was a horsy–doggy man), he began spending his days and nights working on a system for blackjack. He did not even know the rules of the local casino but visits were made to check on them and the system developed. It was no longer gambling, it was an absolute certainty and not only was he going to make his family's fortune, he was going to make mine as well. It just needed another few hundred hours of trial with his cards at home before he had thoroughly tested it and could put it into action. He knew he was not supposed to gamble but the grandiose fantasy never left him alone for long and he moved closer and closer to executing it, showing all the miniature swings of the affective/decision-making model of build-up to release as he discussed it openly with his wife and me.

Finally I brought in my computer and a programme designed to teach the optimum strategy for blackjack and set him up on it to test out his system before he sold his taxi and spent the capital in the real casino. The world's first computer-aided programmed relapse was an utter disaster for the system and for my fortune but a complete success for science.

References

American Psychiatric Association (1980) *Diagnostic and Statistical Manual of Mental Disorders*, 3rd edn, Washington, DC.

American Psychiatric Association (1987) *Diagnostic and Statistical Manual of Mental Disorders*, 3rd edn, revised, Washington, DC.

Anderson, G. and Brown, R.I.F. (1984) 'Real and laboratory gambling, sensation seeking and arousal', *British Journal of Psychology* 75: 401–10.

Anderson, G. and Brown, R.I.F. (1987) 'Some applications of reversal theory to the explanation of gambling and gambling addictions', *Journal of Gambling Behavior* 3: 179–89.

Apter, M.J. (1982) *The Experience of Motivation: The Theory of Psychological Reversals*, London: Academic Press.

Armor, D.J., Polich, J.M., and Stamboul, H.B. (1978) *Alcoholism and Treatment*, New York: Wiley.

Azrin, N.H. (1976) 'Improvements in the community reinforcement approach to alcoholism', *Behavior Research and Therapy* 14: 339–48.

Blasczynski, A., Winter, W., and McConachy, N. (1985) 'Plasma endorphin levels in pathological gambling', in W.R. Eadington (ed.) *The Gambling Studies: Proceedings of the Sixth National Conference on Gambling and Risk Taking*, Bureau of Business and Economic Research, College of Business Administration, University of Nevada, Reno.

Brown, R.I.F. (1986a) 'Arousal and sensation seeking components in the general explanation of gambling and gambling addictions', *International Journal of the Addictions* 21: 1001–16.

Brown, R.I.F. (1986b) 'Dropouts and continuers in Gamblers Anonymous. 1. life-context and other factors', *Journal of Gambling Behavior* 2: 130–40.

Brown, R.I.F. (1987a) 'Classical and operant paradigms in the management of compulsive gamblers', *Behavioural Psychotherapy* 15: 111–22.

Brown, R.I.F. (1987b) 'Gambling addictions, arousal and an affective/decision-making explanation of behavioural reversions or relapses', *International Journal of the Addictions* 22: 1053–67.

Brown, R.I.F. (1987c) 'Dropouts and continuers in Gamblers Anonymous. 2. analysis of free-style accounts of experiences with GA', *Journal of Gambling Behavior* 3: 68–79.

Brown, R.I.F. (1987d) 'Dropouts and continuers in Gamblers Anonymous. 3. some possible specific reasons for dropout', *Journal of Gambling Behaviour* 3: 137–51.

Brown, R.I.F. (1987e) 'Dropouts and continuers in Gamblers Anonymous. 4. evaluation and summary', *Journal of Gambling Behaviour* 3: 202–10.

Brown, R.I.F. (1988a) 'An outcome study of Gamblers Anonymous', *British Journal of Psychiatry*, 152: 284–8.

Brown, R.I.F. (1988b) 'Reversal theory, subjective experience in the explanation of addiction and relapse', in M.J. Apter, J.H. Kerr, and M.P. Cowles (eds) *Progress in Reversal Theory*, Amsterdam: Elsevier.

Byrne, D. (1964) 'Repression-sensitisation as a dimension of personality', in B.A. Maher (ed.) *Progress in Experimental Personality Research, Vol. 1*, New York: Academic Press.

Commission on the Review of National Policy Towards Gambling in America (1976) Washington, DC: United States Government Printing Office (Stock No. 052-003-00243-4).

Cummings, C., Gordon, J.R., and Marlatt, G.A. (1980) 'Relapse: prevention and prediction', in W.R. Miller (ed.) *The Addictive Behaviors*, New York: Pergamon.

Dickerson, M.G. (1977) 'The role of the betting shop environment in the training of compulsive gamblers', *Behavioural Psychotherapy* 1: 24–79.

Dickerson, M.G. (1979) 'FI schedules and persistence at gambling in the UK betting office', *Journal of Applied Behaviour Analysis* 12: 315–23.
Dickerson, M.G. (1984) *Compulsive Gamblers*, London: Longman.
Donovan, D.M. and Chaney, E.F. (1985) 'Alcoholic relapse prevention and intervention: models and methods', in G.A. Marlatt and J.R. Gordon (eds) *Relapse Prevention: Maintenance Strategies in the Treatment of Addictive Behaviors*, New York: Guilford Press.
Frank, M.L. (1979) 'Why people gamble: a behavioural perspective', in Lester, D. (ed.) *Gambling Today*, Springfield, Illinois: C.C. Thomas.
Heather, N., Winton, M., and Rollnick, S. (1982) 'An empirical test of "a cultural delusion of alcoholics"', *Psychological Reports* 50: 379–82.
Hodgson, R.J. and Miller, P.M. (1982) *Self-Watching: Addictions, Habits and Compulsions* New York: Facts on File.
Hunt, G.M. and Azrin, N.H. (1973) 'A community-reinforcement approach to alcoholism', *Behavior Research and Therapy* 11: 91–104.
Kramer, A.S. (1987) *A Preliminary Report on the Relapse Phenomenon Among Pathological Gamblers*, paper presented at the Seventh International Conference on Gambling and Risk Taking, Reno, Nevada.
Leary, K. and Dickerson, M.G. (1985) 'Levels of arousal in high- and low-frequency gamblers', *Behavior Research and Therapy* 23: 635–40.
Litman, G.K., Eiser, J.R., Rawson, N.S.B., and Oppenheim, A.N. (1977) 'Towards a typology of relapse: a preliminary report', *Drug and Alcohol Dependence* 2: 157–62.
Litman, G.K., Eiser, J.R., Rawson, N.S.B., and Oppenheim, A.N. (1979) 'Differences in relapse precipitants and coping behaviour between alcohol relapsers and survivors', *Behavior Research and Therapy* 17: 89–94.
Litman, G.K., Stapleton, J., Oppenheim, A.N., Peleg, M., and Jackson, P. (1983) 'Situations related to alcoholism relapse', *British Journal of Addiction* 78: 381–9.
Ludwig, A.M. and Stark, L.H. (1974) 'Alcohol craving: subjective and situational aspects', *Quarterly Journal of Alcohol Studies* 35: 899–905.
McAughtrie, L. and Brown, R.I.F. (1988) *Addiction Recovery in Gamblers Anonymous as a Loss–Recovery Process: An Empirical Investigation in Gambling Research: Proceedings of the Seventh International Conference of Gambling and Risk Taking*, vol. 5, Reno, Nev.: Bureau of Business and Economic Research, College of Business Administration, University of Nevada.
McCormick, R.A., Russo, A.M., Ramirez, L.F., and Taber, J.I. (1984) 'Affective disorders among pathological gamblers seeking treatment', *American Journal of Psychiatry* 141: 215–18.
Marlatt, G.A. (1978) 'Craving for alcohol, loss of control and relapse: a cognitive-behavioral analysis', in P.E. Nathan, G.A. Marlatt and T. Loberg (eds) *Alcoholism: New Directions in Behavioral Research and Treatment*, New York: Plenum.
Marlatt, G.A. (1985) 'Relapse prevention: theoretical rationale and overview of the model', in G.A. Marlatt and J.R. Gordon (eds) *Relapse Prevention: Maintenance Strategies in the Treatment of Addictive Behaviors*, New York: Guilford Press.
Marlatt, G.A. and Gordon, J.R. (1980) 'Determinants of relapse:

implications for the maintenance of behaviour change', in P. Davidson (ed.) *Behavioral Medicine: Changing Health Lifestyles*, New York: Brunner/Mazel.

Marlatt, G.A. and Gordon, J.R. (eds) (1985) *Relapse Prevention: Maintenance Strategies in the Treatment of Addictive Behaviours*, New York: Guilford Press.

Murgatroyd, S., Rushton, C., Apter, M.J., and Ray, C. (1978) 'The development of the telic dominance scale', *Journal of Personality Assessment* 42: 519–28.

O'Connell, K.A. (1988) 'Reversal theory and smoking cessation', in M.J. Apter, J.H. Kerr, and M.P. Cowles (eds) *Progress in Reversal Theory*, Amsterdam: Elsevier.

O'Donnell, P.J. (1984) 'The Abstinence Violation Effect and circumstances surrounding relapse as predictors of outcome status in male alcoholic patients', *Journal of Psychology* 117: 257–62.

Orford, J. (1985) *Excessive Appetites: A Psychological View of Addiction*, Chichester: Wiley.

Pomerleau, O.F., Fertig, J., Baker, L., and Cooney, N. (1983) 'Reactivity to alcohol cues in alcoholics and non-alcoholics: implications for a stimulus control theory of drinking', *Addictive Behaviors* 8: 1–10.

Rankin, H., Hodgson, R., and Stockwell, T. (1983) 'Cue exposure and response prevention with alcoholics: a controlled trial', *Behavior Research and Therapy* 21: 435–46.

Rimm, D.C. (1973) 'Thought stopping and covert assertion in the treatment of phobias', *Journal of Consulting and Clinical Psychology* 41: 466–7.

Russell, J.A. (1979) 'Affective space is bipolar', *Journal of Personality and Social Psychiatry* 37: 345–56.

Russell, J.A. and Mehrabian, A. (1977) 'Evidence for a three factor theory of emotion', *Journal of Research in Personality* 11: 273–94.

Schaeffer, H.H. (1971) 'A cultural delusion of alcoholics', *Psychological Reports* 29: 587–9.

Siegel, S. (1977) 'The role of conditioning in drug tolerance and addiction', in J.D. Keehn (ed.) *Psychopathology in Animals*, New York: Academic Press.

Solomon, R.L. (1977) 'An opponent-process theory of acquired motivation: the affective dynamics of addiction', in J.D. Maser and M.E.P. Seligman (eds) *Psychopathology: experimental models*, San Francisco: W.H. Freeman.

Solomon, R.L. (1980) 'The opponent process theory of acquired motivations: the costs of pleasure and the benefits of pain', *American Psychologist* 35: 691–712.

Thayer, R.E. (1978a) 'Towards a psychological theory of multidimensional activation (arousal)', *Motivation and Emotion* 2: 1–4.

Thayer, R.E. (1978b) 'Factor analytic and reliability studies on the activation-deactivation adjective check list', *Psychological Reports* 42: 747–56.

Wikler, A. (1973) 'Dynamics of drug dependence', *Archives of General Psychiatry* 28: 611–16.

Zuckerman, M. (1979) *Sensation Seeking: Beyond the Optimal Level of Arousal*, Hillsdale, NJ: Lawrence Erlbaum Associates.

Chapter Eight

Relapse prevention and AIDS among intravenous drug users

Anna Stallard and Nick Heather

Human Immunodeficiency Virus (HIV), the cause of Acquired Immune Deficiency Syndrome (AIDS), is untreatable. At present, AIDS cannot be cured. Although symptomatic treatment is available, there is little else that medicine can offer to those who have caught the virus.

The only effective way to combat the AIDS and HIV is prevention; those who have escaped infection need to change their behaviour by avoiding dangerous sexual and drug-taking practices (DHSS 1988). Those people already affected are encouraged to alter their lifestyle towards healthier living in the hope that this will limit the progress of the virus. Therefore, until effective medical treatment and vaccines are available AIDS is a *behavioural* problem.

Solutions to this problem are usually proposed in terms of both broad-based and specifically targeted education campaigns. Unfortunately, information about AIDS, though necessary, may not be a sufficient basis for behaviour change and maintenance of this change. The paradox of widespread knowledge being accompanied by continued indulgence in dangerous behaviour is well illustrated by smoking; education often serves only to produce wiser and guiltier smokers! Despite the limitations of education campaigns, behavioural methods have not been widely adopted to promote or maintain behaviour changes in relation to AIDS.

In this chapter, two examples of ways in which relapse prevention techniques might be used to address the problem of HIV are described. These examples are based on our experience with intravenous drug users in Scotland where there is an urgent need to limit the spread of HIV in this group.

Existing efforts to initiate behaviour change among intravenous drug abusers (IVDAs)

Since AIDS was first identified, efforts have been made to initiate behaviour change using education and information campaigns. Health education among drug users presents particular difficulties since this group have their own values and norms which may reduce the efficacy and salience of interventions developed by those outside the drug-using subculture. It would be absurd to suggest that such an approach should be abandoned; indeed, the education campaigns have achieved a great deal as illustrated by the work described below. In the gay community, information campaigns achieved dramatic behaviour change (Silverman 1986), and there is some evidence that drug users have also made some changes to their injecting practices (Des Jarlais *et al.* 1985). The initial impact of new information on behaviour has almost reached its limits: the facts are available for everyone to act upon, but clearly more effective intervention is required to improve compliance.

In New Jersey, two surveys of AIDS knowledge were conducted in 1984 (n = 1,000) and 1985 (n = 577) among drug users in treatment (Ginzburg *et al.* 1986). Nearly all of these subjects (over 90 per cent) were familiar with essential information (e.g., that HIV could be spread by sharing injecting equipment), although myths were common (e.g., the belief that people infected with HIV looked ill). Many of the subjects had obtained information from television, radio, and newspapers. Ginzburg *et al.* described the use of former drug addicts to communicate information to current users at 'shooting galleries' on the availability of treatment, the need to stop sharing injecting equipment, and methods of cleaning needles and syringes. There was indirect evidence that the drug users had changed their behaviour – for example, an increase in black market demand for sterile needles and syringes. Ginzburg and colleagues point out that 'what is required is a means of ensuring that what is learned is put into practice' (Ginzburg *et al.* 1986: 380) but do not suggest specific ways of achieving this, other than providing more sources of information.

In New York, two surveys of AIDS knowledge and risk behaviour produced similar results (Friedman *et al.* 1986; Selwyn *et al.* 1985). Interviews were conducted among IVDAs from methadone programmes (Friedman *et al.* n = 59; Selwyn *et al.* n= 146), and among incarcerated drug users (Selwyn *et al.* n = 115). Nearly all of the subjects knew essential information (along with some myths), while 50 per cent to 60 per cent reported that they had made changes such as reducing sharing, increasing the use of clean injecting equipment and adopting safer sex practices. Friedman and his colleagues recommend the use of drug takers as educators to reach those who require information, to reinforce existing knowledge, and to introduce new information in a way which is culturally acceptable.

They suggest that a network of education and support similar to that which developed with such successful results among gay communities (Silverman 1986) could be promoted among drug users.

In Wellington, New Zealand, where the rate of HIV infection among drug users is low, surveys conducted among IVDAs in methadone treatment in 1985 (n = 75) and 1986 (n = 60) showed high levels of AIDS knowledge (Robinson *et al.* 1987). Many drug users (63 per cent) reported that they had reduced sharing injecting equipment. Thus, information was obtained and some behaviour change took place even though all drug users were sero-negative for HIV.

In all three studies, IVDAs showed high levels of knowledge of essential information accompanied by some behaviour change even in geographical areas with low numbers of HIV positive drug users. All the samples were drawn from drug users in treatment, though similar results were found among a small sample of drug users who were not receiving any treatment (Des Jarlais *et al.* 1985). These subjects were recruited from a research 'storefront'; and had no contact with treatment agencies. It is clear that despite their knowledge many drug users are not making necessary behaviour changes, although it is very encouraging that some change is taking place. While acknowledging this problem, the three studies suggest improved education rather than focusing on new strategies such as behavioural techniques. The rest of the chapter will describe our approach to developing such techniques but, before doing so, it would be useful to describe the context in which we were working and the developments in Scotland which led to our addressing the problem of HIV.

AIDS in Scotland

The spread of HIV in Scotland has been quite different from that in the rest of the UK, affecting intravenous drug users rather than gay men. For example, in January 1988, there were 792 known HIV positive IVDAs in Scotland compared with 206 HIV positive gay or bisexual men (CDSU 1988). Another surprising feature about HIV among Scottish IVDAs is the much higher prevalence of HIV in Edinburgh and Dundee on the east than in Glasgow on the west. One possible explanation for this pattern is different policing practice: in Edinburgh and Dundee, drug users were more likely to be searched and have their equipment confiscated (SHHD 1986).

The problem of HIV in this population led to the formation of a government committee chaired by D.B.L. McLelland (SHHD 1986). This committee considered AIDS to be a more serious problem than drug abuse and therefore supported harm reduction strategies, even though this might mean abandoning attempts to help IVDAs to become abstinent. They suggested introducing substitute prescribing in an effort to reduce injecting and to attract clients into counselling. Providing clean injecting equipment was also recommended and an emphasis placed on education and counselling for this population. No specific strategies to help clients effect changes in their behaviour were suggested.

Relapse prevention among IVDAs

The effect of the McLelland report in Scotland was the pragmatic redefinition of treatment goals for drug abusers. A hierarchy of goals has emerged which is accepted by many drug treatment agencies as appropriate, both for sero-positive and negative clients. The basic aim is to limit damage to health and the spread of the virus from one drug user to another. The hierarchy can be defined as follows:

Abstinence;
Using drugs but not injecting;
Using drugs but injecting with sterile equipment;
Injecting drugs but not sharing equipment;
Using drugs and still sharing.

A relapse can be defined as any movement down the hierarchy and relapse prevention can be aimed at maintaining the goal selected by the client. For example, if the client wishes to stop sharing needles while continuing to inject drugs, efforts at relapse prevention should be aimed at identifying risk situations pertinent to sharing. Such relapse prevention programmes might include very simple interventions, such as providing lists of twenty-four-hour chemist shops which provide needles and syringes, or more complex interventions such as assertiveness training to help clients refuse offers to share equipment and cognitive strategies to prevent them feeling guilty or unfriendly if they do refuse to share.

Therapists should have little difficulty with such a hierarchy which is easily accommodated by a behavioural model. Indeed, most behavioural treatment (e.g., anxiety management) includes an assessment of problem behaviour followed by selection of practical treatment goals, based on a balance of desired outcome and the probability that the client can achieve the selected goal, even if it means that the problem remains in a modified form. Clients' needs are better served by using the hierarchy, as it helps them to make tangible progress rather than setting impossible goals. In addition, specific strategies are suggested to the client, rather than repeated general statements about what he or she ought to be doing without any information on how it should be done.

Before the McLelland committee reported, we had begun work on a programme aimed at preventing relapse to heroin use, based on an abstinence goal, within a day centre in Dundee. It soon became apparent, however, that many of the IVDAs were infected with HIV, and it was decided to alter the programme to take this into account. The goal chosen was to prevent relapse to any form of injectable drug use, reaching a compromise between the minimum harm reduction goal of stopping sharing and the other extreme of complete abstinence. Clients wishing to achieve abstinence could participate in such a programme, with stopping injecting becoming an interim goal towards future abstinence. On the other hand, lifestyle change, so crucial for abstinence and yet so difficult to achieve, may not be required for the harm reduction goal, which is therefore less demanding for the client.

In adopting this model, it was necessary to take client characteristics into account. There is a high dropout rate from drug treatment agencies and this requires that relapse prevention (RP) be time limited (in our case, six sessions). Drug workers administering the programme have to be prepared to follow up poor attenders, using all available contacts such as the general practitioner, parents, and other drug treatment agencies. Such active intervention is made essential by the existence of HIV and the urgent need to prevent its spread, as well as protecting infected clients from other infections. The programme should be seen as an adjunct to other support, such as help with financial, legal, and housing problems, which are dealt with separately.

The model of RP used is adapted from that of Marlatt and Gordon (1985) described elsewhere in this book. The components of the six-session programme are described below, while an outline of each session is given in table 8.1.

Client workbook

Each client is given a workbook which contains the structure of the programme along with exercises and diary pages. This provides a permanent written record of the work completed during the sessions which is kept when the programme has been completed.

Identifying high-risk situations

The first session focuses on teaching the client to identify situations in which relapses are more likely to occur. Examples and practice exercises are used to demonstrate that relapse is best viewed in terms of the presence or absence of relapse determinants in specific situations. For example, one exercise consists of a list of everyday situations which are identified as high or low risk. Risk factors are noted by the client, who is steered away from the belief that relapses are caused by weak 'will-power' or some permanent personality characteristic about which nothing can be done.

Assessing risk factors

Self-monitoring

A structured diary is used in which slips, near slips, and feelings of craving and their antecedents are noted by clients and used to teach them to identify risk situations. For example, one client had adopted the strategy of remaining at home all day in order to avoid seeing people or places which reminded him of injecting drugs. He was surprised to notice from his diary that periods of strongest desire to inject drugs occurred when he was at home feeling bored and frustrated. He therefore altered his strategy by going out all day accompanied by a family member.

Risk situation test

This test is adapted from that devised by Chaney and Roszell (1985) but looks specifically at desire to inject drugs in a variety of situations. It consists of twenty-two items each describing certain risk situations. These reflect the relapse determinants described by Marlatt and Gordon (1985), such as negative emotional states, social pressure, and temptation. Each item is presented as a verbal prompt and the client attempts to describe the best way to deal with that particular situation. Subjective ratings of the likelihood of relapsing in the situation are then given by the client. The quality and quantity of solutions are assessed by the therapist.

Problem-solving techniques

Problem solving is a method of coping with problems in a systematic and objective way. Based on the method described by D'Zurilla and Goldfried (1971), it involves breaking down, refining, and working on problems in such a way that they cease to be overwhelming. This method helps the client to distance him or herself from the problem, to break it down into manageable pieces, and to increase the quantity and hence the quality of solutions. The client learns to carry out the technique independently and, therefore, coping skills generated using this method can be produced by the client outside the treatment programme.

The problem solving is used as a framework into which skills training can be introduced, drawing on a wide variety of techniques. The steps involved are shown below.

(i) Defining the problem in detail.
(ii) 'Brainstorming' for solutions. Quantity of ideas is required at this stage, rather than quality. No evaluation of ideas is allowed.
(iii) Selecting a solution.
(iv) Planning action. At this point appropriate skills training can be used, e.g., assertiveness training.
(v) Taking action.
(vi) Evaluating outcome and adjusting solution if necessary.

Coping with craving

For the purposes of the RP programme, 'craving' is defined as a strong desire to use drugs, which may be accompanied by withdrawal symptoms or a subjective experience of withdrawal. For some clients, an easy way to eliminate craving is simply to take the drug by an alternative route. For others, the problem is more complex – the situations in which the drugs are usually available might represent the highest risk in terms of returning to injecting drugs. By deciding to use another route in order to obtain drugs, the user may enter the very situation in which he or she is more likely to inject. For some users the experience of using drugs is inextricably linked to injecting. Therefore the setting in which drug use takes place may have to alter.

To help clients cope with the problem of craving, a modified form of cue exposure has been introduced to the programme. This is a technique aimed at gradually desensitizing clients to drug-related cues by showing items such as needles or syringes to induce craving. There is plenty of evidence which suggests that drug-related cues can elicit conditioned withdrawal or craving (O'Brien *et al.* 1986; Siegel *et al.* 1983).

Cue exposure may be effective by extinguishing conditioned craving (Childress *et al.* 1986). It may also operate cognitively by altering the client's beliefs and expectations about craving by demonstrating that the feelings lessen over time and that control can be exercised over them. It is on the latter basis that cue exposure is used in this programme. Nobody could hope to extinguish responses from *every* relevant cue in six or possibly sixty sessions! Teaching ways of coping with such conditioned responses is a more realistic aim. Clients are taught relaxation and self-talk to reduce the subjective experience of craving.

Table 8.1 The relapse prevention programme described session by session

Session	*Content*
1	Motivational issues, identifying high-risk situations, introduction diary, assessment (SCT).
2	An introduction to problem solving. Skills training within a problem-solving context.
3	An introduction to coping with craving using cue exposure, relaxation, and skills training within a problem-solving context.
4/5/6	Coping with craving, skills training within a problem-solving context.

It is our experience that drug users commonly misinterpret other symptoms such as those of anxiety (and in one case, even pregnancy!) as withdrawal. Cue exposure can also be used to correct such misinterpretations. During the procedure, the therapist induces mild to moderate craving using the minimum exposure necessary. The cues are presented in a hierarchy starting with exposure in imagination, then looking at drug-injecting paraphernalia, finally touching and handling this equipment. Subjective measures of 'desire for a hit' and 'difficulty resisting a hit' are taken, along with physiological measures of galvanic skin response and skin temperature. The client is taught to relax and the graded hierarchy is introduced until a state of low to moderate craving is induced. This is followed by self-talk, using images of coping and escape, along with self-statements of control and confidence, such as 'Because I am relaxed, the feelings become easy to control'. Sometimes the client is already in a state of subjective craving before the session begins and in these cases exposure is not necessary.

Of course, relapse prevention can be used for harm reduction goals other than stopping injecting. The next section gives an example of the way in which the model can be integrated into a minimal intervention and self-help manual.

Minimal interventions

Numerous self-help and minimal intervention programmes are available for a wide variety of problem behaviours. There is no space here to provide a detailed review. In the area of problem drinking, there is evidence that providing self-help material can be effective (Heather 1986). Addictive behaviours in general improve more if even minimal therapist contact is available than with self-help materials alone, though Sanchez-Craig (1987) found that inexperienced therapist contact could be worse than no contact at all. She found that intervention consisting of assessment, feedback, and delivery of self-help materials by an experienced therapist was effective.

The need to intervene actively in drug use has never been greater. Formerly, IVDAs themselves sought help with drug problems unless they were placed in compulsory treatment as part of criminal procedures. In these circumstances they posed a costly problem because of increased crime rates and various health problems, but did not present a danger to others. Public health risk now adds yet another dimension to the complex and expensive problem of drug abuse. Therefore, it is justifiable to search for drug users and attempt to persuade them to make behaviour changes. As mentioned above, the focus of such intervention has been education from the media, drug workers, and ex-drug users, teaching IVDAs about drug use along with ways to prevent spread. What is needed is a more active intervention which can be used anywhere, aimed at maintaining behaviour change. Access to IVDAs can be gained in many different settings, for example, GP surgeries, casualty departments, and courts. It is not always possible to maintain contact with clients in these circumstances, and so it is important to make best use of the time available. An additional benefit of using these settings is the improved change of helping IVDAs who might not go for help through conventional drug treatment agencies.

Minimal interventions and self-help materials may meet this need. Although there is no evidence yet that these interventions are effective with risk behaviour, it is reasonable to attempt improvement of educational and counselling interventions with this model. The need to use relatively unskilled counsellors makes a structured programme more attractive, providing a clear focus for good counsellor training.

An example of such a programme is described below. It could be used independently as a self-help manual or be accompanied by one or more sessions of therapist contact. The first part is devoted to self-assessment and feedback, the second to making and maintaining behaviour change.

Assessment and feedback

A simple risk assessment has been devised which examines AIDS knowledge, drug using, and sexual behaviour. The clients can assess themselves under the guidance of a counsellor. Feedback is given using a traffic light system with a green light for safe practice, amber for lower risk, and red for high-risk behaviour. The client then chooses a goal for behaviour change, and is directed towards the appropriate parts of the manual for advice on making these changes. Clients are free to choose 'amber' goals if they feel unable

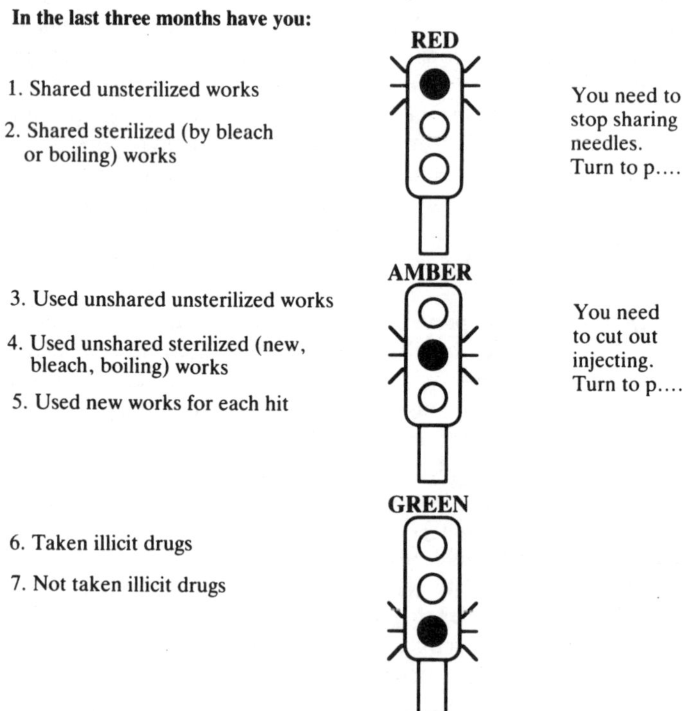

Figure 8.1 An example of a feedback system

to achieve 'green'. An example of the drug-using part of the assessment is given above. The sexual behaviour assessment is similar, having sections on number of partners, use of condoms, and type of partner.

Behaviour change

The assessment is followed by basic information on AIDS and HIV. The remainder of the manual is devoted to relapse prevention, each section dealing with different treatment goals in areas of both sexual and drug-using behaviour. Self-monitoring is used to teach identification of situations in which the client might relapse to risky behaviour. The self-monitoring consists of a structured diary and an analysis of the last four occasions when the client had intended to avoid risky behaviour but failed to do so. Specific strategies are suggested to avoid relapse, depending on the goal chosen. For example, the section on avoiding sharing emphasizes the need to obtain needles before they are required and to resist lending them to others. Problem-solving techniques are introduced similar to those presented in the relapse prevention programme above. In addition, problem areas such as coping with anxiety, avoiding tension, dealing with shyness, and coping with lapses are covered, making use of Marlatt and Gordon's (1985) model of relapse. Finally, up-to-date information on local facilities is appended. This includes addresses of chemists, drug treatment agencies, family planning agencies, needle exchange facilities, and so on, which are prepared to offer help to this client group.

Conclusions

The interventions described above are not novel in content but represent a new style of delivery. Models of relapse prevention can easily be translated to treat drug problems with goals of both modified use and abstinence. Unfortunately, the recipients of such interventions often differ from other groups in their unwillingness to participate consistently in a relapse prevention programme. Those who choose goals of modified use may continue a disorganized drug-using lifestyle which is not compatible with regular attendance for drug treatment. Short-term interventions may be more effective with such clients. Whether or not they will be more effective than education or counselling alone remains to be seen.

Drug abuse is not the only area in which relapse prevention could be used to help people maintain behaviour changes they have made in response to HIV. For example, some gay men attempting to maintain a pattern of safe sexual practice would benefit from learning relapse prevention skills. Risky sexual practices among gay men are more likely to occur along with drug or AIDS use (Stall *et al.* 1986). The RP model has obvious implications for this problem.

Within the heterosexual population, a similar difference between knowledge and behaviour exists as for drug users: most people know what they need to do but do not put this knowledge into practice (DHSS 1987). So far, little has been done to address the problem of maintenance of behaviour change in this population, and RP techniques could provide a useful model for future public education campaigns.

References

Chaney, E.F. and Roszell, D.K. (1985) 'Coping in opiate addicts maintained on methadone', in S. Shiffman and T.A. Wills (eds) *Coping and Substance Abuse*, New York: Academic Press.

Childress, A.R., McLellan, A.T., and O'Brien, C.P. (1986) 'Abstinent opiate abusers exhibit conditioned craving, conditioned withdrawal and reductions in both through extinction', *British Journal of Addiction* 81: 655–60.

Communicable Diseases Scotland Unit (1988) *ANSWER – AIDS News Supplement*, CDS Weekly Report, 16 January.

Department of Health and Social Security (1987) *AIDS: Monitoring Response to the Public Education Campaign, February 1986–February 1987*, London: HMSO.

Department of Health and Social Security (1988) *AIDS and Drug Misuse Part 1: Report By the Advisory Council on the Misuse of Drugs*, London: HMSO.

Des Jarlais, D.C., Friedman, S.R., and Hopkins, W (1985) 'Risk reduction for the Acquired Immune Deficiency Syndrome among intravenous drug users', *Annals of Internal Medicine* 103: 755–9.

Dow, M.G.T. (1983) 'Behavioural bibliography: theoretical and methodological issues in outcome research into self-help programmes', in C. Main (ed.) *Clinical Psychology and Medicine*, London: Plenum.

D'Zurilla, T.J. and Goldfried, M.R. (1971) 'Problem solving and behaviour modification', *Journal of Abnormal Psychology* 78(1): 107–26.

Friedman, S.R., Des Jarlais, D.C., and Sothern, J.L. (1986) 'AIDS health education for intravenous drug users', *Health Education Quarterly* 13(4): 383–93.

Ginzburg, H.M., French, J., Jackson, J., Harstock, P.I., MacDonald, M.G., and Weiss, S.H. (1986) 'Health education and knowledge assessment among intravenous drug users', *Health Education Quarterly* 13(4): 373–82.

Heather, N. (1986) 'Minimal treatment interventions for problem drinkers', in G. Edwards (ed.) *Current Issues in Clinical Psychology Vol. 4*, London: Plenum.

Marlatt, G.A. and Gordon, J. R. (1985) *Relapse Prevention: Maintenance Strategies in the Treatment of Addictive Behaviors*, New York: Guilford Press.

O'Brien, C.P., Ehrman, R.N., and Ternes, J.W. (1986) 'Classical conditioning in human opioid dependence', in S.R. Goldberg and I.P. Stolerman (eds) *Behavioural Analysis of Drug Dependence*, London: Academic Press.

Robinson, G.M., Thornton, N.J., Rout, J., and Mackenzie, N. (1987) 'AIDS – risk behaviours and AIDS knowledge in intravenous drug users', *New Zealand Medical Journal* 100: 209–11.

Sanchez-Craig, M. (1987) *Short Term Treatments: Conceptual and Practical Issues*, paper presented at the Fourth International Conference on Treatment of Addictive Behaviours, Bergen, Norway, August 1987.

Scottish Home and Health Department (1986) *HIV in Scotland: Report of the Scottish Committee on HIV Infection and Intravenous Drug Misuse*, Edinburgh: HMSO.

Selwyn, P.A., Cox, C.P., Feiner, C., Lipshutz, C., and Cohen, R. (1985) *Knowledge About AIDS and High-Risk Behaviour Among Intravenous Drug Abusers in New York City*, presented at the Annual Meeting of the American Public Health Association, Washington DC, 18 November 1985 (cited in Friedman *et al.* 1986).

Siegel, S., Israel, Y., Glaser, F.B., Kalant, H., Popham, R.E., Schmidt, W., and Smart, R.G. (eds) (1983) 'Classical conditioning, drug tolerance, and drug dependence', in R.G. Smart, F.B. Glasser, *et al.* (eds) *Research Advances in Alcohol and Drug Problems Vol. 7*, New York: Plenum.

Silverman, M.F. (1986) 'Introduction: what we have learned', in L. McKusick (ed.) *What to do about AIDS*, California: University of California Press.

Stall, R., McKusick, L. Wiley, J., Coates, T.J., and Ostrow (1986) 'Alcohol and drug use during sexual activity and compliance with safe sex guidelines for AIDS: the AIDS behavioural research project', *Health Education Quarterly* 13(4): 359–71.

Part Two

Chapter Nine

Conceptual issues in the study of relapse

Saul Shiffman

Anatomy of a relapse: the case of Harold

Harold M. had been smoking for twenty years when he decided to quit. His wife and son had been urging him to quit for some time, but it was Jim's sudden death from heart failure that finally boosted his determination. Harold thought about how often he and Jim had smoked together in determined defiance of all the health warnings. Now Jim was dead; he had been two years younger than Harold. Harold had tried to quit four times before; the longest and most recent lasted five months. Nevertheless, Harold felt confident that he would quit this time; he felt more strongly motivated than he ever had before.

Harold bought a book on quitting smoking and completed all the assessments in the book. The results pegged him as a highly dependent smoker. Harold smoked thirty high-nicotine cigarettes per day. He had difficulty in going without smoking even for short periods; when he went to the theatre, he usually had to step out at least once to smoke. He not only smoked first thing on waking, but occasionally woke up in the middle of the night craving a cigarette. The test in the book indicated Harold was a 'negative affect smoker' who increased his smoking under stress. There was no shortage of stress. Harold's small printing business was failing, and he was putting in long hours and much worry in trying to revive it. This was also putting some stress on his marital relationship; he and Mildred fought more often than ever, and, when not fighting, 'walked on eggshells'.

Harold planned his quit effort carefully. He set a quit date, and asked his wife to support him in quitting. He also told his secretary that he would be quitting, knowing that word would get out to the shop floor, where most of his employees smoked. The night before the quit date, Harold threw away his cigarettes and put all his ashtrays and lighters in the basement. He felt frightened, but confident.

The next morning boosted his confidence. Mildred made him a special breakfast and was unusually nice to him. He deliberately did not linger over coffee so as not to get tempted. At work, he put up a 'NO SMOKING' sign in his office, and asked his first appointment not to smoke, explaining that he'd just quit smoking. By the time lunch rolled around, Harold was beginning to believe this would be easy.

The rest of the day was hell. He had lunch with a client, who bullied him into joining him in drinking wine. All through lunch, Harold craved a smoke. It was a physical yearning so strong that he had difficulty concentrating on the client. The craving increased when they'd finished lunch and had to linger to settle on contract terms. Harold felt panicked, and excused himself for a trip to the men's room, where he was able to collect his thoughts and recover his composure. The urge was still there when he returned to the table, but it did not seem so overwhelming.

Returning to his office, Harold found it difficult to concentrate. He had trouble following conversations with clients and suppliers. He also felt incomprehensibly angry; little things bothered him, and he blew up at his secretary and foreman more than once. When he learned that a critical order would be held up because a supplier had failed to deliver inks, Harold could feel the anger welling up in his chest. He found himself unconsciously reaching in his breast pocket for a cigarette to calm himself. He felt shocked at this, and he reminded himself that smoking would probably make him feel worse, not better. He got through the day without smoking, but was exhausted by the effort.

The evening at home was not much better. Although Harold tried to keep his annoyance in check, sparks flew between him and Mildred. Watching TV didn't help; it only reminded him that he used to smoke while watching. Trying to take care of himself, Harold went to bed early, but had trouble sleeping. Twice, he woke up and reached for the cigarettes that were no longer on the night-table. He hoped the next day would be easier.

It wasn't. His concentration failed him; he felt preoccupied. He felt irritable and got angry without knowing why he was angry. His craving for cigarettes seemed to be constantly with him, tugging at him. Once, when he felt on the verge of asking a clerk for a cigarette, he had to retreat to his office, where he could close his eyes and wait for the craving to pass.

The next few days were filled with a constant struggle against the urge to smoke. Only by retreating into his office, relaxing, and reminding himself that he would die if he smoked was Harold able to restrain his urge. He felt ineffective at work; too much energy was going into struggling with his inner turmoil. He drove himself with guilt and threats, but got little done. At home he felt safer from smoking, since no cigarettes were around. But he snapped at his family over little things, and the tension at home was palpably rising. Mildred tried to restrain her anger and be supportive, but the strain showed in the stiff way she held her mouth and the glare in her eyes. Still, Harold was determined not to smoke, and he didn't.

Things improved after about a week. Harold's irritability diminished. He was no longer plagued by constant craving. Craving now came upon him in waves. Sometimes, the source of the craving was clear to him, as when a salesmen he liked lit up while they were touring the shop floor. He'd had to focus his attention on the pounding rhythm of the presses to make those minutes bearable. At other times, cravings struck him out of the blue, even finding him in elevators or in the shower. Although the effort threatened to exhaust him, Harold fought each attack like a skirmish in a critical battle.

On the tenth day, Harold smoked. A friend from across town had come by after work and they'd gone to unwind over a beer or two. At the bar, they bumped into his friend's friends, who smoked almost continuously while they all laughed at each other's jokes. Harold could hardly remember taking the cigarette; it seemed to him almost as if it had been someone else doing it, someone he'd been watching from a long distance. He had smoked two-thirds of it before it penetrated his consciousness. Feeling tense and embarrassed (though no one there knew he was quitting), Harold quickly put the cigarette out and retreated to the men's room, where he discovered he was shaking. His failure to do anything to stop himself from smoking shocked him. He swore not to go back to smoking and, after rinsing his mouth with water, excused himself and went home. Mildred was furious when she smelled smoke on his breath. She had been tolerating his abruptness, trying to wait him out, and now he was smoking again. Their argument spilled over into other issues that had been lingering for months, and they went to bed fuming. For the next few days, a chill descended on them, and they spoke only when they had to.

Smoking that cigarette made Harold aware of how close to the brink he was, and reinvigorated his efforts to avoid smoking. He got an 'I QUIT' pin from the Cancer Society as a reminder to himself and others. The 'NO SMOKING' sign, which he had taken down, was re-mounted in his office. Although he felt suddenly more vulnerable and closer to the brink of relapse, Harold did not smoke. Having 'dodged the bullet', Harold became more confident. This time he had made it, he told himself.

As the weeks wore on, smoking – or rather *not* smoking – faded in importance. Harold experienced occasional urges, sometimes even strong ones, but he was able to dispatch each one as it arose. He tried to keep himself focused; in his mind's eye, he kept seeing himself in Jim's coffin. Other things clamoured for Harold's attention. The business seemed to be doing worse every day. After a disagreement over how to discipline a mechanic, his foreman quit to take a job with a competitor. A major client was moving from town and had cancelled several contracts. Harold had trouble sleeping. He lay awake in a cold sweat thinking about his balance sheet and the balloon payment that was coming due on the second mortgage.

On the fortieth day after he'd quit, Harold smoked. It had been a bad day. He'd had another fight with Mildred as he was leaving the house. At work, he received word that the bank would not lend him any more money or extend his payment schedule. All day, his stomach was tied in a tight knot. As he walked the shop floor, he wished he could smoke. He needed to mobilize himself; he needed to think clearly. The struggle not to smoke seemed to him to have left him exhausted, robbed of the energy he needed to cope with the events that were overtaking him.

That evening, he had dinner with his sales people. After a tense start, they all relaxed as the drinks flowed and the talk turned away from business. When coffee was served, Harold found himself wanting a cigarette. He deserved it. Fred, sitting next to him, objected to Harold's request for a smoke, but Harold glared at him and took the cigarette that was tentatively offered. It hurt his throat, but the scratch in his throat and chest felt comfortably familiar. Harold smoked five cigarettes before going home.

The next morning, Harold felt depressed. Above all, he felt helpless. Despite his best efforts, he had been unable to stay away from cigarettes. Maybe he was just too hooked to beat it. Maybe it would be easier at a later time, when things weren't so hectic. Harold made it to 2 p.m. before smoking. The call was not unexpected. His loan payment was late, and the bank threatened to repossess his presses if he fell more than a month behind. The confrontation left him full of fury and fear, and he went out on to the shop floor looking for a cigarette to calm him. The shipping clerk hesitated, looked at his face, and then handed him a cigarette, drawing his hand back as though Harold might bite it off. Harold was embarrassed; he could only imagine what the clerk saw in his face. He went down to the cafeteria and bought a pack so that he would not have to beg for cigarettes. At the end of the day, Harold threw away the remaining half pack.

For the next few days, Harold struggled with his urges to smoke and with his guilt and shame after each cigarette. He promised himself that each one would be the last, but he didn't throw away the pack he kept in his bottom desk drawer (on top of the 'NO SMOKING' sign). It was a week before Harold brought cigarettes home, and two weeks before he stopped berating himself for smoking. There would be a better time, later, for him to really quit smoking for good.

What caused Harold's relapse? Was it the stressful call from the bank? The accumulated strain of financial and marital difficulties? Harold's nicotine dependence? His withdrawal symptoms? Deficiencies in his coping repertoire? In his ability to sustain motivation? All of these? This case study (a fictionalized composite of several clients' experiences) illustrates the complexity of relapse and its causes. No one single cause can be identified. The final outcome emerges from an entangled gestalt of causes.

Influences on relapse

In order to consider logically the causes of Harold's (or anyone else's) relapse, it is useful to consider three different types of influence on relapse. Variables influencing relapse can be divided into three classes: *enduring personal characteristics*, *background variables*, and *precipitants* (see Shiffman *et al.* 1986). These influences differ in their temporal relation to relapse. Personal characteristics, such as degree of dependence, are presumed to be stable and to influence the probability of relapse in an 'atemporal' fashion. Background variables vary slowly but not precipitously over time, and may 'set the stage' for a relapse episode; cumulative work stress is an example. Finally, precipitants are fast-changing, transient phenomena (such as a sudden stressor) that immediately trigger relapse.

While it should be obvious that no single factor can explain a relapse (consider Harold's complex case), most research designs and most accounts of relapse consider only one class of variables and, implictly, one causal model of relapse. Also, research design decisions sometimes have inadvertent implications for how relapse process is conceptualized. Each of the three kinds of variables is associated with particular research designs and with a particular model of relapse risk. Let us consider each in turn.

Personal characteristics and the constant-risk model

Personal characteristics are variables assumed, implictly or explicitly, to be stable characteristics of the individual. Since the independent variable is expected to be temporally stable, it is typically measured only once, at baseline. In Harold's case, personal characteristics include his degree of dependence, his history of smoking and quitting, etc. Thus, we might say that Harold relapsed because he was a highly dependent smoker. Demographic characteristics, personality factors, and so on, also fall into this category.

But other variables are treated as stable personal characteristics, even if not conceptualized as such. Any variable that is measured only at baseline is implicitly treated as a stable enduring characteristic of the person. Consider motivation for behaviour change. Measuring motivation only once at baseline treats motivation as though it were a stable characteristic, rather than a changeable state. Self-efficacy is similarly treated as though it were a stable personal characteristic. (This is an example of how a research design reflects the operationalization of relapse theory, even if it is not the explictly intended theory.)

A focus on stable personal characteristics also implies a certain interpretation of the question: 'What causes relapse?' Studies emphasizing the role of personal characteristics focus on individual vulnerability; they focus on predicting *who* will relapse, not *when* they will relapse. This, in turn, implies a statement about the importance of time in the relapse process. This approach implies that relapse risk is constant over time, thus giving rise to the *constant* model of relapse proneness.[1] This model's emphasis on individual characteristics makes it incapable of explaining the timing of relapse. Once an individual's die is cast, it is 'only a matter of time' before relapse occurs; the timing of relapse is effectively treated as a random, unexplained variable.

Background factors and the cumulative-risk model

Unlike personal characteristics, background factors relate not to the qualities of the individual per se, but to the person's experiences during the maintenance period. Harold's business and marital difficulties happened to come to a fever pitch during his quit attempt; another time might have been calmer and therefore better for quitting smoking. Unfortunately for Harold, having these stressors in the background made him vulnerable to relapse.

The changeable status of background factors dictates that they be measured repeatedly, and they are usually assessed at regular intervals of weeks or months. The measurement interval reflects their assumed rate of change, which is presumed to be slow and continuous. Most studies of life stress exemplify this model. Since stress is a dynamic factor, it is measured repeatedly, but the change is assumed to be slow and continuous, allowing it to be assessed

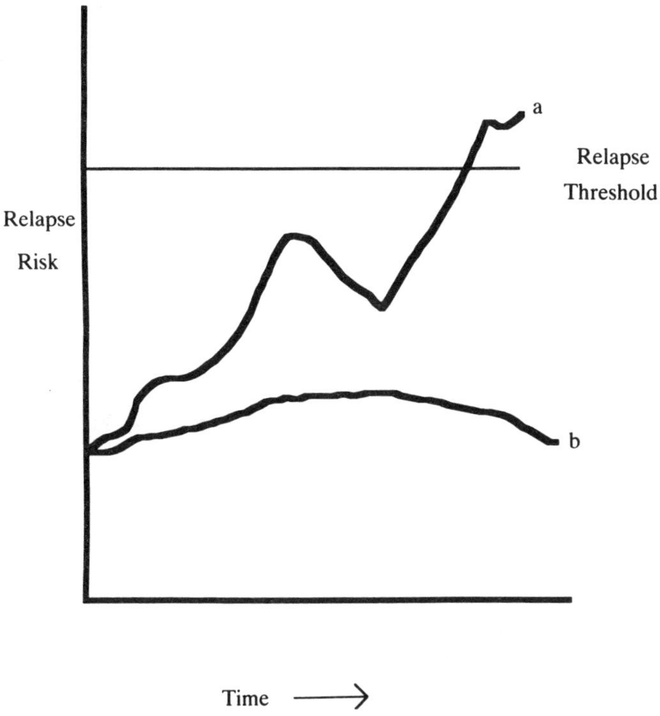

Note: Relapse risk is held to change slowly over time as a function of many risk factors. Different patterns of risk result in different curves (e.g., a and b). Relapse occurs when relapse risk exceeds a threshold value.

Figure 9.1 A cumulative risk model of relapse

with a 'dipstick' approach of periodic measurements.

Studies focusing on background factors *do* aim to explain the timing of relapse, but only within the very broad bounds permitted by the measurement interval: that is, they may explain why a relapse occurred in June (and not April), but not why it occurred on Wednesday (and not Monday). Implicit in this approach is a *cumulative model* of relapse dynamics, which suggests that relapse proneness rises and falls with the accumulation (or diminution) of relevant risk factors such as stress (see figure 9.1). Thus, relapse may be posited to occur when stress (or some other risk) cumulatively reaches some critical level. Background factors provide a backdrop for relapse episodes in the sense that they are thought to

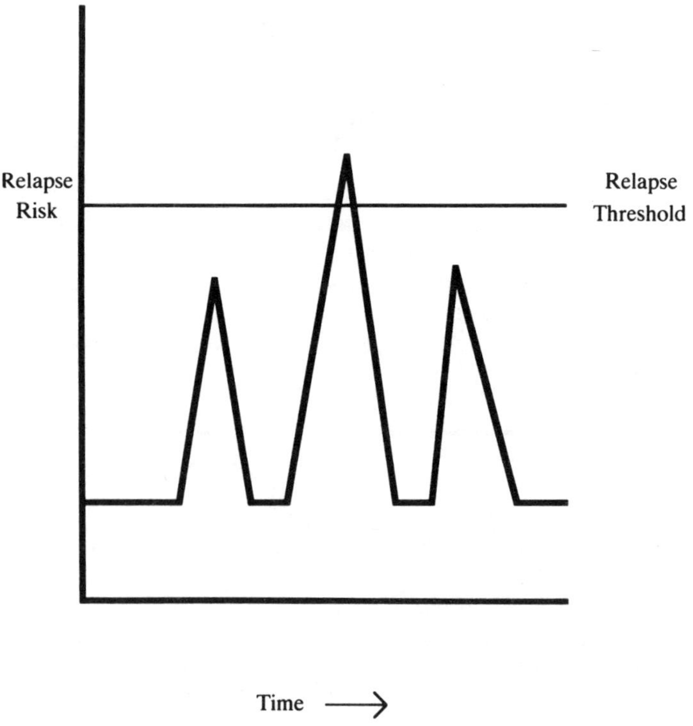

Note: Relapse risk is marked by sudden 'eruptions' of risk during relapse crises, some of which may cross the threshold into relapse. The model implicitly assumes no changes in risk between these episodes.

Figure 9.2 An episodic risk model of relapse

'set the stage' for the episode, without explaining any given episode in particular.

Precipitating factors and the episodic-risk model

Episodic models focus on explaining the specifics of a particular relapse episode. This approach is exemplified by studies of antecedents of particular relapse episodes. These studies focus on fast-changing, transient phenomena, such as momentary shifts in affect or acute exposures to drug cues. In Harold's case, this approach would emphasize the role of alcohol and social cues in Harold's lapses.

The methodologic requirements of studies in this tradition are quite different from the others. Baseline measures are nearly irrelevant. Even regular frequent measurement is not sufficient. Unlike background variables, precipitating variables cannot sensibly be assessed at some regular interval of the investigator's choosing, since they may be uniquely present just at the moment of relapse, rather than as a steady background to the event. Only data about the unique 'moment' are strictly relevant.

Studies of relapse precipitants aim largely to explain the timing of relapse – its occurrence at a particular moment and in particular circumstances. Indeed, they typically make no reference to background factors or personal characteristics. These studies instead focus very heavily on situational determinants of relapse, seemingly implying that the 'right' situation would cause *anyone* to relapse. Thus, they embody an *episodic model* of relapse dynamics, which implies that relapse is precipitous and unpredictable. Graphically (figure 9.2), this approach implies that relapse proneness is subject to sudden 'spikes' that carry the person 'over the brink' into relapse.

The logic of explanation from predispositions and precipitants

I shall argue below that an understanding of relapse requires consideration of factors at all three levels. This is particularly so because of the difference in logic between statements about predispositions and statements about precipitants. Predisposing factors – in this context, personal characteristics and background variables – produce vulnerability to relapse, a potential that can be expressed as a statistical risk. Without other events, such predispositions may never be actualized, remaining a statistical abstraction. Precipitants actualize predispositions, creating actual events from statistical potentials. Although their proximity to the event gives them the appearance of complete causes, their impact depends on pre-existing predispositions.

Explanations from predisposing causes and explanations from precipitating causes are each legitimate and useful. The relative utility of each depends on the circumstances. Often, an explanation from each cause depends on our assumptions about the other cause. Consider a physical analogy, wherein we are trying to explain a broken glass pane: it seems a complete explanation to say that the thrown pebble broke the glass, but only if we know that glass is brittle, i.e., predisposed to break when struck. Consider another case, wherein we explain that the thrown pebble broke the steel plate. Before accepting the explanation, we would require an explanation of the steel plate's peculiar brittleness, i.e., its predisposition to break when struck. Such an explanation would include an account of the steel's peculiar traits or state that rendered it so vulnerable to breakage. (A trait explanation might point to a chemical flaw in the steel; a state explanation might point to the very low ambient temperature.)

Thus predispositions and precipitants are joint partners in explanation. Which one we emphasize depends in part on what we assume about the other influence. To explain events for which there is a known predisposition, we refer to precipitants; to explain events whose precipitants are obvious, we refer to predispositions. (As implied above, we also prefer reference to precipitating factors when we wish to explain the *timing* of an event.) Explanations from predisposition and explanations from precipitation are each legitimate, and each has its own logic. Regardless of which explanation is favoured in a particular instance, a full account of an event must take into account the joint influences of all the factors.

Implications of multiple models of relapse

It should be clear why each of the relapse models outlined above is severely limited. Each only acknowledges a part of the process. The situation is rather like that of the blind men, each of whom had a hold of a part of an elephant, but claimed to know the whole. 'I see. An elephant is rather like a snake', said the one holding the elephant's tail. 'No', said the one holding the leg, 'It is like a tree.' While most relapse investigators acknowledge the need for multiple perspectives, such ecumenism is typically absent from research studies, which tend to emphasize one approach to the exclusion of others.

Failure to take into account all three types of influences on relapse, and to keep clear the distinctions among them, results in substantial confusion in the relapse literature. This is nowhere more evident than in the literature on stress and relapse. It seems clear that stress is related to relapse, but we have made little progress in clarifying its role. Part of the confusion stems from the over-abundance of definitions of stress. But this has been exacerbated by a lack of clear thinking about the multiple roles of stress in relapse. The study of stress is particularly confusing because various stress-relevant variables can appear as individual differences, as background factors, *and* as precipitants.

A striking example of this muddle concerns a study by Pomerleau *et al.* (1978). Pomerleau *et al.* asked smokers enrolled in a cessation clinic about situations where they were likely to smoke, and then followed these smokers one year after they quit smoking. They found that smokers who report smoking when upset or stressed have an elevated risk of relapse. The study contained neither a measure of background stress nor an assessment of stress in relapse episodes. Yet, this study has been cited (e.g., Pomerleau and Rodin 1986) in support of the hypothesis that stress precipitates relapse. This unjustified conclusion requires a leap from the measurement of a personal characteristic to propositions about the role of background and precipitating stressors that may or may not mediate or interact with this personal characteristic.

Making clear distinctions among different kinds of factors can also help interpret apparent inconsistencies in the literature. The literature on the role of tobacco withdrawal symptoms in smoking relapse, for example, is inconsistent. A substantial literature shows that persons who suffer withdrawal symptoms are more vulnerable to relapse (Burns 1969; Manley and Boland 1983; Hirvonen 1983; Gottlieb 1985). This seems to support classical theories of dependence, which hold that all relapse is motivated and reinforced by relief from withdrawal. However, there is also consistent evidence that withdrawal symptoms are not often present during relapse episodes (Shiffman 1982; Cummings *et al.* 1980; O'Connell and Martin 1987).

The inconsistency becomes meaningful when one considers how each set of studies examines the link between withdrawal and relapse. The positive studies treat withdrawal symptoms as background factors; the negative studies treat them as potential precipitants. Thus, the results may not really be inconsistent. They suggest that a severe withdrawal syndrome 'sets the stage' for relapse, but that it does not directly precipitate specific relapse episodes. Perhaps persistent or severe withdrawal symptoms lead, over time, to exhaustion that drains resources for coping. (Note that this implies a *very* different mechanism that invokes reduced capacity to resist temptation to smoke rather than enhanced incentive or temptation to smoke.)

Awareness of these distinctions may also help one spot gaps in research knowledge and effort. It is particularly noticeable that some variables have only been examined at a single level of measurement. Individuals' motivation for behaviour change, as noted above, has been measured almost exclusively at baseline, thus treating it as an enduring individual characteristic. Yet, surely motivation waxes and wanes over time, as is characteristic of background variables. Motivation may also be subject to momentary fluctuations that precipitate acute relapse episodes. This is consistent with Sjoberg and his colleagues' (Sjoberg and Johnson 1978; Sjoberg and Olsson 1981; Sjoberg and Persson 1979) suggestion that relapse episodes are associated with irrational thinking in which judgements about the value of abstinence are distorted. Our failure to consider motivation as a state rather than a trait may have unduly narrowed our understanding of its contribution to maintenance. Research that treats motivation as a dynamic background factor or that examines transient changes in motivation may provide a more accurate picture of its contributions.

The recent wave of work on self-efficacy and relapse has also fallen into a narrow strait by implicitly construing self-efficacy as a stable personal characteristic. An abundance of evidence shows that end-of-treatment assessments of self-efficacy predict subsequent outcomes (DiClemente 1986). By relying on a single measure distant from relapse itself, these studies treat self-efficacy as though it were static. Yet the very same studies show that self-efficacy is changeable: it increases consistently as a result of treatment. Theory and evidence from other domains (Bandura 1977, 1982) also emphasize that self-efficacy judgements are dynamic and are constantly revised in response to experience. Yet, as a result of clinging to a static model of self-efficacy, we have learned little about the week-to-week or moment-to-moment dynamics of self-efficacy. Thus, it is important to match research designs to conceptual models.

Additive and interactive accounts of relapse

At the simplest level, traits, background variables, and precipitants may have additive effects. An additive model acknowledges, for example, that individuals differ in their baseline risk for relapse (as illustrated in the differing origins for the curves in figure 9.3). Thus, an individual with compromised ability to maintain abstinence will more easily be 'pushed over the brink' by background and precipitating factors that would not affect a less vulnerable person. Similarly, the impact of a precipitating event cannot be predicted

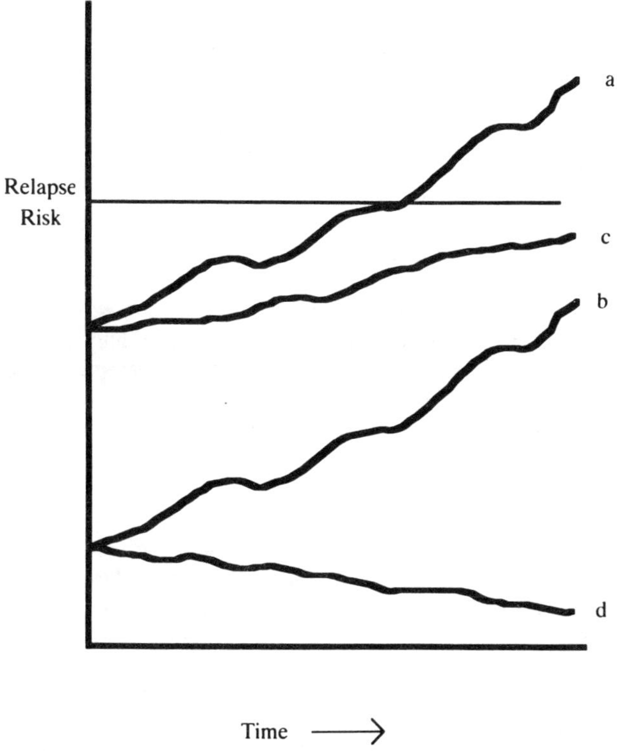

Notes: Trait differences consist of differences evident from the the beginning of the process, and are portrayed as differences in the intercept of each curve. Curves a and b portray addictive effects of trait and background characteristics. In both, background variables lead to identical increases in risk over time. This trend only results in relapse for the person with higher trait-related risk (curve a). (However, a subject with similar traits, but with a different course of background variables might not experience relapse: curve c.) Curves a and d illustrate a statistical interaction, assuming the two curves reflect similar maintenance environments. In this case, trait differences interact with similar experiences to produce different patterns of risk. Although not shown in the figure, one should consider that sudden episodic increases in relapse risk (the 'spikes' shown on figure 9.2) may be superimposed over these curves.

Figure 9.3 The interaction between trait and background variables

without knowledge of the background context, which may elevate or reduce relapse risk. The occurrence of a sudden minor stressor, when it falls against the background of a highly stressful period, might precipitate relapse. Against the background of low stress and high life-satisfaction, even a severe stressor may not result in relapse.

Though more sophisticated than undimensional models, additive models still fail to capture the complexity of relapse. They treat all sources of relapse vulnerability as equal quantities which accumulate like green stamps until the quantity suffices to cause relapse. Additive models fail to account for true *interactions* among variables. Thus, for example, one can easily imagine that stress may only precipitate relapse in those whose drug use was initially tied to stress or stress reduction, while no amount of stress would precipitate relapse in those whose drug use was unrelated to stress.

To explain relapse adequately, interactive models consider all three kinds of factors *and their interrelationships*. These interrelationships take several forms. The most common form of relationship might be called *top-down mediation*, in which the effects of more global and stable processes are mediated by more specific, subsidiary processes. For example, it has been observed that persons who have more smokers in their social network are at enhanced risk for relapse. Yet, this personal characteristic almost certainly acts by making it likely that the person attempts maintenance against a background of chronic exposure to smoking cues, and perhaps by ultimately making it likely that acute cue exposure precipitates a relapse. Similarly, the effects of individual deficits in coping skills are surely mediated by coping failures in specific situations. Thus, the effects of a personal characteristic are mediated by its influence on a background factor that in turn influences a precipitating variable. Mediation implies that all of the effects of the more global process are carried out through its influence on the more specific one. Statistically, this implies that controlling for the effects of the lower-level process would nullify the effects of the global process.

Factors at different levels may also relate to each other through statistical *interaction*, in which the second variable enhances or diminishes the effects of the first. Interactions can occur between two manifestations of the 'same' variable, such as stress, represented at different levels. For example, Harold's being in a stressful period (background stress) made him more vulnerable to the immediate precipitating effects of a momentary stressor (precipitating stress) which might otherwise have been shrugged off without ill effect. The joint effect of the stressors was greater than the sum of the components. This exemplifies a *parallel* interaction between related variables in that 'stress' is involved in both variables: background stress interacting with precipitating stress. (Note that the immediate stressor need not mediate the effects of the background stress; Harold was more vulnerable to the stress of the call from the bank because of the background stress related to marital conflict.) An *orthogonal* interaction involves interaction between two different (unrelated) variables. In Harold's case, chronic stress may have made him more vulnerable to the relapse-promoting effects of acute exposure to smoking cues. Here, the interaction is between two different variables: stress and smoking cues. Orthogonal interactions may even involve seemingly opposite forces: background stress may make one more vulnerable to relapse under *positive* affect (Shiffman 1986a).

Both examples above exemplify *synergistic* interactions, in which both variables work in the same direction (i.e., promoting relapse) and in which each enhances the other's effects. Sometimes, two factors act to mitigate or balance each other's effect, producing a *buffering* interaction. In a buffering interaction, a maintenance-promoting factor (see below for a discussion of factors that promote resistance to relapse) acts to blunt the effect of a relapse-promoting factor. High self-efficacy, for example, might protect one from the impact of an acute stressor. Buffering interactions involve interactions between temptation-promoting and resistance-promoting factors (next section), while synergistic interactions involve sets of variables within each category.

The potential combinations among the variables we have discussed are numerous and complex. As an example of multi-way interactions, consider Harold's second lapse. The situation immediately preceding (and presumably precipitating) the lapse was typical of 'social' relapses (Shiffman 1986a). The setting was rife with cues associated with smoking – alcohol, coffee, and other smokers. Despite Harold's anxious preoccupation, the situation itself was not stressful; indeed, it was relaxing and positive. However, the lapse took place against a background of stress – the growing marital tensions at home, the pressures of Harold's business situation, and, most immediately, the crisis precipitated by the call from his banker.[2] Also relevant is Harold's pre-existing tendency to smoke when stressed and his belief in the calming and reinforcing powers of tobacco, and, perhaps, his severe tobacco dependence. Yet, despite his stressed condition and his predisposition to smoke when stressed, Harold might not have smoked had he not been confronted with immediate smoking cues. Conversely, Harold might have easily fended off the cues were he not feeling so stressed, or were he not a negative affect smoker. Social support from Mildred might also have benefited Harold and buffered him from some of these effects. The lapse is best attributed to the interaction among all these factors, rather than to any single cause.

This account suggests some of the complexity involved in explaining relapse, and the comparative simplicity of models that have implicitly driven research in the area. Although simplifying a phenomenon in order to study it is a productive strategy, research needs increasingly to take account of the multiple influences on relapse and the interactions among them.

Temptation and resistance: relapse-promoting and relapse-protective factors

In most of the foregoing, I have emphasized factors, such as dependence and stress, that make relapse more likely. But relapse cannot be understood without it also considering protective factors that prevent relapse and promote maintenance. Note in Harold's case the several instances where he experienced strong temptation, but actively and successfully resisted it. Maintenance might be viewed as a continuing struggle to resist the temptation to use a drug. Relapse is prevented to the degree that temptations can be minimized or repeatedly resisted as they arise.

It is thus the *balance* between temptation[3] and resistance to temptation that determines whether relapse occurs. This suggests a division of factors influencing relapse into two classes: factors that promote temptation promote relapse; those that promote resistance promote abstinence. By way of example: Harold's exposure to smoking cues promoted temptation to smoke. Conversely, his use of coping in the face of temptation (e.g., his attending to distracting stimuli or his retreat to the safe haven of his office when tempted) increased his ability to resist the temptation. The distinction is not just a matter of the sign on the variable's correlation coefficient. Rather, it implies a difference in the *mechanism* by which each factor affects relapse. Factors associated with increased resistance to temptation don't necessarily make substance use any less appealing; they act to buffer the person's behaviour from the appeal. When we see a person tempted on two occasions, but indulging only once, we cannot conclude that one temptation was stronger than the other. It seems quite sensible to say that the two occasions were equally tempting, but that resistance was stronger on one occasion.

One implication of this model is to predict a buffering interaction between the two factors. Resistance-promoting factors should show their greatest effects when temptation is great. Under conditions of little or no temptation, factors such as coping skills should have little effect.

Just as factors that promote resistance to temptation promote abstinence, factors that *erode* resistance to temptation promote relapse. Consider an example. Evidence suggests that alcohol consumption is associated with relapse to tobacco (Shiffman 1982). This finding can be interpreted to mean that alcohol makes smoking more attractive, as indeed it does (Mintz *et al.* 1985). But alcohol use may also promote smoking relapse through an entirely different mechanism. Drinking appears to interfere with efforts to cope in tempting situations, and thereby to facilitate relapse (Shiffman 1982; Shiffman and Jarvik 1987). The distinction between these mechanisms is made clearer when we consider that the latter will hold even for a smoker who idiosyncratically has no association between drinking and smoking.

I noted earlier that the role of stress in relapse seems particularly important and particularly confusing. One aspect of the stress-relapse link that has not been explored is the possibility that stress elevates relapse risk by decreasing the person's ability to cope with temptation. By taxing coping resources, stress may interfere with coping responses that might otherwise blunt temptation. Social psychological research on stress shows that stress exposure reduces frustration tolerance (Cohen 1980). Also, ex-smokers are less likely to perform coping when they are in a relapse crisis precipitated by stress (Shiffman and Jarvik 1987). Thus, stress might act not only to promote temptation, but also to inhibit resistance to temptation.

In sum, it is important to consider the mechanism by which variables influence relapse or maintenance. Distinguishing between temptation-promoting and resistance-promoting factors may prove theoretically useful, particularly if one can provide a general account of self-control or resistance to temptation. We may learn something about how alcoholics resist drinking from studying how people resist overspending their credit cards or how some persist in exercise even when it is uncomfortable. Distinguishing temptation-promoting and resistance-eroding factors may also have implications for treatment, e.g., treatment should aim to provide both for reduction of temptation and for increased resistance to temptation. Another implication arises out of the buffering interaction between the two types of factors, which suggests that the amount of energy devoted to developing resistance to temptation be predicted on an assessment of a client's likely degree of temptation. Thus, for example, clients who are highly dependent on a substance or who cannot avoid exposure to substance cues might need additional work on resistance to temptation.

Coping

Among factors that contribute to resistance to temptation, coping responses are the most important. Effective coping responses help resist or neutralize temptation. Besides being effective (Shiffman 1984b, 1985, 1987), coping responses are promising targets for intervention. Indeed, most clinical approaches to addictive behaviours emphasize the client's active coping as a key element in successful maintenance. The study of coping may also benefit from introduction of distinctions among types and stages of coping.

Types of coping

A simple but important distinction is between *stress coping* and *temptation coping* (Wills and Shiffman 1985). Most of the 'coping' literature concerns stress coping, which consists of responses intended to blunt the impact of stressors. For some people, drug use itself is a form of stress coping. Temptation coping aims to resist temptation and to prevent drug use. Although these goals might sometimes be abetted by stress coping, the aims of temptation coping are more specific, and it includes many strategies (e.g., concentrating on the negative consequences of drug use) that have nothing to do with stress.

Another major distinction is between behavioural and cognitive coping strategies. Simply put, behavioural coping involves overt action, while cognitive coping involves mental processes only. Lay people, clinicians, and investigators often emphasize behavioural coping, since its more 'active' approach seems more potent. What little data we have (Shiffman 1982, 1984b; Shiffman and Jarvik 1987; Curry and Marlatt 1985; Litman *et al.* 1979) suggests that cognitive coping may actually be more critical to maintenance. Since temptation is inherently bound up with mental processes (craving, expectancies, plans, etc.) cognitive coping may be especially well-suited to combating temptation. In any case, behavioural and cognitive coping may have different properties, and should be consistently distinguished.

There is enormous diversity among coping responses even within these two broad categories. It will be difficult to make meaningful statements about coping without distinguishing among specific coping strategies. Some typical categories of cognitive coping include thinking about the consequences of drug use, applying 'will-power', and using self-commands to control behaviour. Typical behavioural categories include the use of social support, distraction via alternative or incompatible behaviours, and stimulus control. No widely accepted taxonomy of coping is available.

Coping strategies may differ in effectiveness of suitability to particular problems or situations (see, e.g., Shiffman 1984b; Curry and Marlatt 1985), but these differences cannot be detected or described without a meaningful taxonomy. Unfortunately, it is not yet clear which distinctions are most meaningful nor how a taxonomy is to be constructed. Taxonomic distinctions can be made on theoretical grounds or can be developed empirically from analysis of lay or expert ratings. It must also be decided how fine-grained a taxonomy needs to be. Is it useful, for example, to distinguish subtypes of stimulus control (e.g., avoiding situations, forgoing other substances, assuring a supply of alternative substances or behaviours)? One approach might be to develop hierarchical, tree-structured taxonomies that include fine distinctions under higher-order categories. The importance of the fine distinctions might then be put to empirical test (see Shiffman, in press, for an example of an empirically derived hierarchical taxonomy). The contributions of coping to relapse prevention will not be well understood until these basic taxonomic questions are resolved.

Stages of coping

Coping responses also differ in their aims and their timing in relation to relapse crises. Three different kinds or stages of coping can be distinguished (Wills and Shiffman 1985).[4]

Anticipatory coping aims to prevent or minimize temptation. Stimulus control strategies (e.g., Harold's banishing of ashtrays; a dieter keeping salad makings in the refrigerator) are classic examples. These strategies are fundamentally preventive, and are executed planfully and deliberately at a time of the person's choosing, in anticipation of difficulty rather than in response to any current challenge. In this sense, they are fundamentally *strategic*, whereas other coping types (below) are *responsive*. Stimulus control strategies are not the only examples of strategic planning. Making provision for self-rewards or social support is anticipatory coping; so is making a list of reasons for quitting, reading daily 'maintenance messages', taking care to get enough exercise or rest, etc. One property common to many of these strategies is that they involve ongoing activities, rather than single behaviours or cognitions. These tend to be set in motion early in maintenance and to be dropped or become superfluous later (see section on stages of maintenance, below).

Unlike anticipatory coping, *immediate coping* is enacted in response to an immediate threat to abstinence. Immediate coping is performed in the face of temptation, and may be quite specific to the present danger (e.g., Harold's escaping from the shop floor to his office). The timing of the response, and often its character, is dictated by the present circumstances. In contrast to the ongoing activities that mark anticipatory coping, immediate coping is marked by fleeting activities and thoughts. Examples including eating candy to quell an urge, reminding oneself of the consequences of relapsing, or focusing on something else to distract from temptation. Immediate coping activities peak early in maintenance, when temptations are most frequent and intense, but some readiness to respond to relapse crises must be maintained for long periods thereafter.

Finally *restorative coping* involves attempts to recover from breaches of abstinence or from relapse crises. In the case of a lapse or slip, the challenge is to terminate the lapse, restore abstinence, and recover from any psychological harm done by the lapse (e.g., reduced self-efficacy and other Abstinence Violation Effects; Marlatt and Gordon 1985). Even when abstinence is not breached, however, a relapse crisis that brings the person to the brink of relapse may also have demoralizing effects that must be overcome (Shiffman 1984a). Because restorative coping must deal with these psychological sequelae, restorative coping is dominated by cognitive coping responses, such as cognitive restructuring – analysing and explaining the slip, reminding oneself that a slip need not lead to a relapse, etc.

Restorative coping is also often concerned with the prevention of further crises or lapses, and thus frequently involves reinstatement of anticipatory coping strategies. After a lapse, people often try to revitalize their commitment to abstinence, or to reinstitute stimulus control activities that had been dropped (consider Harold's remounting of his 'NO SMOKING' sign). In some special cases, such as dieting, restorative coping includes activities that actually undo the effect of the slip. A dieter who overeats may compensate by eating less or exercising more the next day. Undoing is not possible in most addictive behaviours – smoking, drinking, shooting up, once done, cannot be undone.

Different types of coping have received different amounts of research attention; restorative coping has barely been addressed. Also, most studies of coping have simply not distinguished subtypes of coping, making it impossible to pinpoint what was studied. It is not uncommon for subjects simply to be asked what they did to maintain abstinence, with responses apparently aggregating anticipatory, immediate, and restorative coping (Perri and Richards 1977; Perri *et al.* 1977; Litman *et al.* 1979; Gottlieb *et al.* 1981; Carl 1980). In the absence of finely focused research, we know little about the relative contribution of each stage of coping to successful maintenance.

Stages of maintenance

Thus far, we have dealt with the passage of time only as a moderator of relapse risk. It may be more fruitful to consider maintenance as a developmental process that unfolds and changes over time. Although 'maintenance' has come to be considered a separate phase from 'cessation', there has been little consideration of phases within maintenance itself. It is clinically compelling that 'maintenance' is not a uniform phase: change continues to occur after cessation has been achieved. In mapping the stages of maintenance, it is tempting to specify a particular time at which each transition is expected to occur. This would be misleading. Stages, as conceptualized here, are marked by natural developmental transitions, and cannot be defined by the clock or calendar. Individuals will progress through the stages at different paces. Different substances may also produce systematic differences in the developmental timeline for stages of maintenance. I should emphasize at the outset that the framework presented here is speculative, based more on clinical observation than on conclusive research.

The *acute* stage of maintenance, beginning with cessation, is marked by acute withdrawal symptoms. In many cases, craving is experienced as almost constant, and the person may be quite preoccupied with the forsworn substance. This phase is also often marked by a frenetic flurry of anticipatory and immediate coping activity. Since it follows immediately after cessation and presents a constant challenge, this period is marked by a peak in motivation and in devotion of attention to behaviour change. This phase is also marked by extraordinarily high risk for relapse. (Although the relapse curves published by Hunt and colleagues seem accurate over the long course, they lack information about the early days of maintenance, and are, as a result, quite deceptive. Relapse is often quite rapid: among smokers, as many as 25 per cent may relapse within the first *week*, and up to 50 per cent within two weeks; Shiffman 1988). In many respects, this phase is continuous with cessation. Despite the usefulness of the distinction between cessation and maintenance, any line that is drawn is bound to be arbitrary. The duration of this phase is likely to differ across substances as a function of the duration of the acute withdrawal syndrome.

Relapse risk remains relatively high during the *intermediate* phase of maintenance. While intense craving continues to be experienced, it is now typically experienced as intermittent and episodic. During the acute phase, it is difficult for people to identify relapse crises or high-risk situations ('I crave it all the time'). In the intermediate phase, craving is more episodic, and can more easily be identified with particular situations. Active coping typically continues into this phase, taking two major forms: 'passive' forms of anticipatory coping (e.g., continuing to avoid friends who are users) and bursts of immediate coping in relapse crises.

As the frequency of relapse crises diminishes and abstinence stabilizes, the person may enter a long *protracted* phase of maintenance. In this phase, intense cravings or relapse crises may still occur intermittently, but their frequency drops dramatically. Concomitantly, vigilance and coping activity drop to a minimum. Anticipatory coping activities initiated earlier may be dropped, and readiness to perform immediate coping is reduced. This is dangerous, since the person may be caught unawares by relapse crises that seem to 'come out the blue' and require some coping response. Continued vigilance is necessary, but may be difficult to maintain without constant renewal of motivation.

A final phase, marked by *stable abstinence*, is reached when the person is no longer tempted to use the forsworn substance. Concomitantly, the risk of relapse is quite low. (The existence of a 'safe' end point is controversial: no incontrovertible empirical data have been presented on this issue – Brownell *et al.* 1986; Swan and Denk in press.) The key transition marking entry into this phase may be a cognitive one. Earlier in maintenance, even successful abstainers view themselves as deprived users struggling to remain abstinent. Entry into stable abstinence is marked when the person begins to think of him/herself as a non-user; more often, the person simply does not define him/herself in terms of use/non-use of a substance. Interestingly, Velicer *et al.* (1985) report that ex-smokers' estimations of both the benefits *and* the costs of smoking decline over the course of abstinence. Velicer *et al.*'s interpretation is that smoking progressively becomes less and less an issue for these ex-smokers. In essence, this stage marks the end of behavioural *and* psychological involvement with the forsworn substance. Unfortunately, only a few people reach this stage.

Besides differing in degree of relapse risk, the stages may differ in the dynamics of relapse. For example, withdrawal symptoms may have a much more prominent role in relapse during the acute stage (see, e.g., Cummings *et al.* 1985). During this period, relapse episodes may more closely approximate the image painted by classical theories of addiction, in which relapse was motivated and reinforced by relief from withdrawal symptoms. As this phase passes, other factors, such as stress and environmental cues, may become more prominent. In the protracted phase, relapses are more likely to result from unexpected, surprising events. Major life events or stressors play a larger role here. So do unusual situations that have not yet been successfully mastered. In effect, everyday sources of temptation diminish in importance because they have already been deconditioned, successfully mastered, or succumbed to. The remaining vulnerabilities are related to rare events. A client who experienced a 'late' relapse on a business trip only later realized that she'd not travelled since quitting and had thus not had to learn to cope with the unique demands of that context. The coping demands of this phase are quite different from those encountered earlier. Anticipatory strategies such as stimulus control may become less important, since the source of temptation often cannot be anticipated. Instead, continued vigilance and preparedness to cope immediately with a sudden relapse crisis become critically important. Maintaining motivation is a major challenge during this stage. The newly established pattern of abstinence is often taken for granted and the person may feel literally and psychologically tired of dealing with the problems of quitting. Anticipatory coping activities that serve to bolster and renew motivation may be critical here.

This account suggests that the relative roles of personal characteristics, background variables, and precipitating variables may also shift over the course of maintenance. Precipitating factors may have their greatest influence during the protracted phase of maintenance, when abstinence is relatively well established, but can be disrupted by sudden unexpected challenges. During the acute phase, in contrast, precipitating variables may have a relatively minor role, since temptation seems uniformly high, regardless of the current setting. The influence of personal characteristics may be at its peak in this phase: since their influence remains constant over time (by definition), they will have the greatest impact early on, before the 'high-risk cases' have been weeded out through relapse. Thus, the stages may differ not only in the risk of relapse, but also in the dynamics of relapse. Some contradiction and confusion in the relapse literature may be clarified by distinguishing stages of maintenance.

Lapses and relapses

The discussion thus far has treated 'relapse' as though it were a simple identifiable event. This is in fact true only of a 'lapse'. One of Alan Marlatt's greatest contributions to the study of relapse has been to call attention to the distinction between a *lapse* and a *relapse* (Marlatt and Gordon 1985). A lapse is a single episode in which restraint is violated, whereas a relapse marks the unsuccessful end of the whole behaviour change effort. Thus, a lapse is a specific event, while a relapse is really a psychological construct. It should be immediately clear that this distinction poses definitional difficulties.

When does a lapse become a relapse? Is it a matter of time? Frequency of use? Amount of use? Should the definitions be objectively behavioural (e.g., so many uses over so many days) or subjectively psychological (e.g., the end of efforts to maintain abstinence)? No definition will be entirely satisfactory for all cases or, as discussed below, for all substances.

Though unclear, the distinction between a lapse and a relapse is conceptually important. Earlier theories of addiction had emphasized the inevitability of relapse if abstinence was violated even once. Marlatt pointed out that a relapse is not logically inevitable following a lapse. Marlatt asserts instead that a lapse presents an urgent opportunity for intervention. Since several days often elapse between an initial lapse and subsequent substance use, he argues (Marlatt and Gordon 1980), carefully timed intervention might prevent the next lapse and restore maintenance. Also, Marlatt presents data showing that at least *some* lapses lead to recovery, rather than to relapse. Nevertheless, Marlatt's own data show that relapse is *nearly* inevitable after a lapse – about 90 per cent of all lapses result in relapse (Marlatt and Gordon 1980). In more recent data on smokers, Curry *et al.* (in press) found that almost nobody who lapsed was able to maintain long-term abstinence.

What makes lapses so potent? Several mechanisms could account for their power. Marlatt argues against a simplistic biological theory holding that re-exposure to the addictive substance renews the addiction, resulting in a loss of voluntary control over consumption (Jellinek 1960). Note that, under this theory, lapses act by enhancing temptation to consume the drug, without impinging on resistance to temptation.

Marlatt has suggested a competing theory that attributes the power of lapses to their cognitive sequelae, which makes the person more vulnerable to subsequent temptations. The Abstinence Violation Effect undermines subsequent efforts to resist substance use by lowering self-efficacy and by leading to a self-definition of addiction and failure. The major mechanism proposed is diminished resistance to temptation, although Marlatt also suggests that the AVE may increase temptation itself (via expectancy effects).

Although these are the two leading theories of lapses, other explanations are possible. A contrasting psychological theory emphasizes the 'priming' effects of drugs and food, such that consumption facilitates consumatory behaviour in general (Stewart *et al.* 1984). Thus, lapses act by priming the motivational system so as to make subsequent consumption more rewarding and therefore more likely. Like the re-addiction theory, this theory posits an increase in temptation. In contrast to the re-addiction theory, the priming model posits substance-generic effects: relapse to one substance can be facilitated by consumption of a *different* substance. This may be particularly relevant to relapse among polydrug users.

Lapses may occur in clusters for a simple explanation. The theories above posit that each lapse contributes causally to the next. However, the close temporal association of multiple lapses may not reflect a causal chain, but the operation of an underlying 'third factor'. Perhaps it is not the first lapse itself that promotes further substance use, but rather the persistence of whatever caused the lapse in the first place. Unless the causes of the initial lapse disappear, their continued action should promote repeated lapses, leading to a relapse. (Recovery from a lapse might thus be explained in part by the waning of transient factors that promoted the lapse.) This explanation is compatible with any of the theories cited above.

Despite the conceptual and clinical excitement generated by Marlatt's focus on lapses, very little is known about how lapses lead to relapses. It does seem clear that, despite occasional exceptions, this progression seems nearly universal. While no effective intervention has been reported, there is nevertheless potential for clinical intervention to weaken the link between lapses and relapses.

Comparisons across addictive behaviours

A heartening recent development in the study of relapse has been an increasing tendency to compare relapse patterns across addictive behaviours. Marlatt's work on relapse determinants (Cummings *et al.* 1980; Marlatt and Gordon 1985) has pioneered this approach. Marlatt emphasizes the similarity in precipitants of lapses to drinking, smoking, opiate use, and overeating. While the similarities are, indeed, striking, we should also be sensitive to the differences. For example, both Marlatt's data (Marlatt and Gordon 1985) and my own (Grilo *et al.* 1988) suggest that substance-specific cues and social cues play a greater role in precipitating dieting lapses than they do in other addictive behaviours.

Differences in relapse determinants can reflect fundamental differences in the dynamics of different addictive behaviours. Among the issues worthy of consideration are: the availability of the forsworn substance, the social sanction for its use, and the emphasis on controlled use versus abstinence. The prominence of social and food cues in overeating episodes, for example, probably reflects a combination of these factors: people must continue to eat, and so cannot avoid food cues through total abstinence; eating is socially sanctioned; finally, eating is an important part of social activity. These factors ensure that a dieter will constantly have to struggle with intimate exposure to food cues. In contrast, consider an opiate addict trying to kick an addiction. Opiate abuse is socially forbidden and is not widespread; opiates are not widely available, and their procurement requires considerable effort; with total abstinence, exposure to opiates may be totally avoided. Social cues and pressures may be irrelevant if the opiate use was generally solitary. Thus, the importance of particular influences will vary according to the peculiarities of the particular forsworn substance or behaviour.

Abstinence vs. moderation

Among the factors cited above, the most consequential is the choice or feasibility of abstinence as a goal. One may try to abstain absolutely from alcohol; one cannot abstain from food. The implications of this distinction are enormous. Moderation implies control in the face of constant exposure not only to substance cues, but to consumption itself. When moderation is the goal, monitoring progress is made far more difficult – for the clinician *and* the client. When total abstinence is the goal, any use of the substance stands out as a violation. Definition becomes more difficult when relapse is a matter of degree: how much eating is 'too much'?

When 'violations' are matters of degree, one must decide whether to define lapses objectively (e.g., eating 20 per cent more than some stated goal) or subjectively (e.g., perceived excesses). (Of course, some episodes will meet both criteria.) Neither definition is fully satisfactory. An objective definition does not do justice to the instance where one planned to 'overeat' at a special occasion, wherein the episode is contained within a pattern of moderation. A subjective definition does not account for the person who 'overeats' day after day, regaining lost weight, but claims never to have gone over his/her subjective limit.

Definitional issues must also be confronted when differentiating a limited lapse from a full-blown relapse. Drawing this line is particularly difficult in behaviours which are to be (or must be) maintained in moderation. Many individuals without a weight problem or eating disorder occasionally 'overeat'. Indeed, the ability to self-correct for these fluctuations in eating and weight may be the very hallmark of healthy self-controlled eating habits. At what point does a pattern of overeating depart from normal variation and become a 'relapse'?

Definitions of a lapse also depend on definition of the core behavioural problem. For example, if one is treating an alcoholic, how should one regard the use of anxiolytics? Is it to be considered a 'lapse', if, as some believe, it reflects the same underlying difficulty? Is it 'symptom substitution'? Thornier conceptual dilemmas surround the definition of lapses in compound syndromes such as bulimia. Should one regard overeating as a lapse? Some workers in the field would argue that restraint and overconcern with eating is itself a core symptom of bulimia, so that defining overeating as a lapse only perpetuates these unhealthy attitudes. On this view, only purging episodes should be considered lapses.

Lapses are not always discrete events that can easily be located in time. The timing of the lapse can be hard to define when moderate use is the goal. Consider someone who has a goal of eating 1,500 calories per day, but who consumed 3,000 calories yesterday – 1,000 each at breakfast, lunch and dinner. When exactly did the lapse occur? Halfway through lunch when the 1,501-calorie mark was crossed? When the 1,000 calorie breakfast was eaten? As one might imagine, attempting to isolate a precipitant for such a lapse can be an exercise in futility.[5]

These examples illustrate only some of the possible differences among addictive behaviours. With closer study, other differences will undoubtedly emerge. In sum, there are important commonalities *and* important differences in relapse process among the addictive behaviours. Although many of the same issues and variables are relevant across addictive behaviours, differences among addictions will affect even the very definition of relapse itself. Rather than debate whether the addictive behaviours are similar or different, we ought to identify the dimensions of commonality and difference.

Conclusion

The causes of relapse are complex. The complexity will not yield to understanding without careful analysis. We shall have to consider the influences of personal characteristics, background states, and precipitating events, as well as the interactions among these factors. We shall have to consider not only the influence of individual addiction and tempting environments, but also their dynamic balance with resources for resisting temptation. We shall have to develop models that consider both similarities and differences among addictive behaviours, and an understanding of what underlies these similarities and differences. Finally, we shall have to view maintenance as a changing developmental process, rather than as a static period of waiting for the ultimate outcome.

I began the chapter by telling the story of one relapse and asking 'What caused Harold's relapse?' The chapter aimed not to answer the question, but to analyse it. I have not given a satisfactory account of Harold's relapse, but have suggested the shape such an account must take. The reader is urged to re-read Harold's story to test whether the concepts presented here make Harold's story more comprehensible.

Acknowledgements: Preparation of this chapter was supported in part by grant RO1 HL39234-01 from the Heart, Lung, and Blood Institute, United States Public Health Service. Kathy O'Connell, Peggy Russell, and Rena Wing provided valuable feedback on an earlier draft of the manuscript, and discussions and collaborations with Rena Wing, Thomas Ashby Wills, Sheldon Cohen, and others helped shape the ideas developed here.

Notes

1. No figure is provided to illustrate the constant risk model, since it posits that relapse risk has no relationship with time.
2. An added complication is the reciprocal interaction between smoking cessation, stress, and social support. In Harold's case, his reactions to quitting (e.g., withdrawal symptoms) actually resulted in increased stress and decreased social support. Furthermore, smoking cessation itself is also a stressor; it is not uncommon for ex-smokers to report that smoking cessation is itself almost as stressful as a marital separation (Shiffman *et al.* 1981).
3. The use of the word *temptation* is not meant to evoke connotations of fire and brimstone (though it may remind us that the challenge of maintenance in addictions treatment has much in common with other problems of restraint and impulse control). Temptation is the experience of conflict between long-term benefit (attached to abstinence) and immediate reinforcement (obtained from drug use), which is at the heart of maintenance.
4. Although it is not discussed here because it is not directly germane to maintenance, another form of coping, *preparatory coping*, is involved in efforts to achieve cessation. Preparatory coping activities involve 'gearing up' for the cessation attempt by mustering commitment and resources. (In other words, preparatory coping is most involved in the transition between the 'Contemplation' and 'Action' stages of Prochaska and DiClemente 1986.) Cognitive focus on the negative consequences of drug use and public statements of commitment to quitting are common examples of preparatory coping.
5. Lapses can also be difficult to locate in time when one is concerned with promotion of a positive behaviour. While addictions treatment attempts to decelerate a negative behaviour, a maintenance/relapse analysis is also applicable to the acceleration of a positive behaviour such as exercise. In such cases, lapses are marked by the *absence* of a behaviour, which is much more difficult to localize. The person in

question may have spent two weeks without exercise. At what moment did they lapse from their exercise maintenance?

References

Bandura, A. (1977) 'Self-efficacy: toward a unifying theory of behaviour change', *Psychological Review* 4: 191–215.

Bandura, A. (1982) 'Self-efficacy mechanism in human agency', *American Psychologist* 37: 122–47.

Brownell, K.D., Marlatt, G.A., Lichtenstein, E., and Wilson, G.T. (1986) 'Understanding and preventing relapse', *American Psychologist* 41: 765–82.

Burns, B.H. (1969) 'Chronic chest disease, personality, and success in stopping cigarette smoking', *British Journal of Preventive and Social Medicine* 23: 23–37.

Carl, L.S. (1980) 'Self-planned cessation: a retrospective study of the strategies and resources used by individuals in quitting and remaining quit', *Dissertation Abstracts International* 41: 41, 4576A (University Microfilms No. 81-08, 458).

Cohen, S. (1980) 'After effects of stress on human performance and social behavior: a review of research and theory', *Psychological Bulletin* 88: 82–108.

Cummings, K.M., Giovino, G., Jaen, C.R., and Emrich, L.J. (1985) 'Reports of smoking withdrawal symptoms over a 21 day period of abstinence', *Addictive Behaviors* 10: 373–81.

Cummings, C., Gordon, J.R., and Marlatt, G.A. (1980) 'Relapse: prevention and prediction', in W.R. Miller (ed.) *The Addictive Behaviors*, New York: Pergamon, pp. 291–321.

Curry, S. and Marlatt, G.A. (1985) 'Unaided quitters' strategies for coping with temptations to smoke', in S. Shiffman and T.A. Wills (eds) *Coping and Substance Use*, New York: Academic Press.

Curry, S., Marlatt, G.A., Gordon, J., and Baer, J. (1988) 'A comparison of alternative theoretical approaches to smoking cessation and relapse', *Health Psychology*, in press.

DiClemente, C.C. (1986) 'Self-efficacy and the addictive behaviors', *Journal of Social and Clinical Psychology* 4: 302–15.

DiClemente, C.C. and Prochaska, J.O. (1985) 'Processes and stages of change: coping and competence in smoking behavior change', in S. Shiffman and T.A. Wills (eds) *Coping and Substance Use*, New York: Academic Press.

Gottlieb, A.M. (1985) *The Effects of Nicotine Gum and Expectancy on Smoking Withdrawal Symptoms and Relapse: A Balance Placebo Study*, doctoral dissertation, University of Washington.

Gottlieb, A.M., Friedman, L.F., Cooney, N., Gordon, J., and Marlatt, G.A. (1981) *Quitting Smoking in Self-Help: Relapse and Survival in Unaided Quitters*, paper pesented at the meeting of the Association for the Advancement of Behaviour Therapy, Toronto, Canada.

Grilo, C., Shiffman, S., and Wing, R. (in press) 'Dietary lapses: a

situational analysis', *Journal of Consulting and Clinical Psychology*.
Hirvonen, L. (1983) 'Premises and results of smoking withdrawal', in W.F. Forbes, R.C. Frecker, and D. Nostbakken (eds) *Proceedings of the Fifth World Conference on Smoking and Health*, Winnipeg, Canada: CCSH.
Jellinek, E.M. (1960) *The Disease Concept of Alcoholism*, New Brunswick, NJ: Hill House Press.
Litman, G.K., Eiser, J.R., Rawson, N.S.B., and Oppenheim, A.N. (1979) 'Differences in relapse precipitants and coping behaviour between alcohol relapsers and survivors', *Behaviour Research and Therapy* 17: 89–94.
Manley, R.S. and Boland, F.J. (1983) 'Side-effects and weight gain following a smoking cessation program', *Addictive Behaviors* 8: 375–80.
Marlatt, G.A., and Gordon, J.R. (1980) 'Determinants of relapse: implications for behaviour change', in P. Davidson (ed.) *Behavioral Medicine: Changing Health Lifestyles*, New York: Brunner/Mazel.
Marlatt, G.A. and Gordon, J.R. (eds) (1985) *Relapse Prevention: Maintenance Strategies in the Treatment of Addictive Behavior*, New York: Guilford Press.
Mintz, J., Boyd, G., Rose, J.E., Charuvastra, V.C., and Jarvik, M.E. (1985) 'Alcohol increases cigarette smoking: a laboratory demonstration', *Addictive Behaviors* 10: 203–7.
O'Connell, K.A. and Martin, E.J. (1987) 'Highly tempting situations associated with abstinence, temporary lapse, and relapse among participants in smoking cessation programs', *Journal of Consulting and Clinical Psychology* 55: 367–71.
Perri, M.G. and Richards, C.S. (1977) 'An investigation of naturally-occurring episodes of self-controlled behaviours', *Journal of Counselling Psychology* 24: 178–83.
Perri, M.G., Richards, C.S., and Schultheis, K.R. (1977) 'Behavioral self-control and smoking reduction: a study of self-initiated attempts to reduce smoking', *Behavior Therapy* 8: 360–5.
Pomerleau, O.F., Adkins, D., and Pertschuck, M. (1978) 'Predictors of outcome and recidivism in smoking cessation treatment', *Addictive Behaviors* 3: 65–70.
Pomerleau, O.F. and Rodin, J. (1986) 'Behavioral medicine and health psychology', in S.L. Garfield and A.E. Bergin (eds) *Handbook of Psychotherapy and Behaviour Change (3rd edn)*, New York: Wiley, pp. 483–524.
Prochaska, J.O. and DiClemente, C.C. (1986) 'Toward a comprehensive model of change', in W.R. Miller and N. Heather (eds) *Treating Addictive Behaviors*, New York: Plenum.
Shiffman, S. (1982) 'Relapse following smoking cessation: a situational analysis', *Journal of Consulting and Clinical Psychology* 50: 71–86.
Shiffman, S. (1984a) 'Cognitive antecedents and sequelae of smoking relapse crises', *Journal of Applied Social Psychology* 14: 296–309.
Shiffman, S. (1984b) 'Coping with temptations to smoke', *Journal of Consulting and Clinical Psychology* 52: 261–7.

Shiffman, S. (1985) 'Coping with temptations to smoke', in S. Shiffman and T.A. Willis (eds) *Coping and Substance Use*, New York: Academic Press.

Shiffman, S. (1986a) 'A cluster-analytic typology of smoking relapse episodes', *Addictive Behaviors* 11: 295–307.

Shiffman, S. (1986b) 'Immediate precipitants of relapse', *Health Psychology* 5: 87–8.

Shiffman, S. (1987) 'Maintenance and relapse: coping with temptation', in T.D. Nirenberg (ed.) *Advances in the Treatment of Addictive Behaviors*, Norwood, NJ: Ablex.

Shiffman, S. (1988) 'Smoking behavior: behavioral assessment', in G.A. Marlatt and D.M. Donovan (eds) *Assessment of Addictive Behaviors: Behavioral, Cognitive, and Physiological Procedures*, New York: Guilford Press, in press.

Shiffman, S. and Jarvik, M.E. (1987) 'Situational determinants of coping in smoking relapse crises', *Journal of Applied Social Psychology* 17: 3–15.

Shiffman, S., Read, L., and Jarvik, M.E. (1981) 'The effect of stressful events on relapse in exsmokers', in S. Shiffman (chair) *Stress and Smoking: Effects on Initiation, Maintenance, and Relapse*, symposium conducted at the meeting of the American Psychological Association, Anaheim, California.

Shiffman, S., Shumaker, S.A., Abrams, D.B., Cohen, S., Garvey, A., Grunberg, N.E., and Swan, G.E. (1986) 'Models of smoking relapse', *Health Psychology* 5: 13–27.

Shiffman, S. and Wills, T.A. (1985) *Coping and Substance Use*, New York: Academic Press.

Sjoberg, L. and Johnson, T. (1978) 'Trying to give up smoking: a study of volitional breakdowns', *Addictive Behaviors* 3: 149–64.

Sjoberg, L. and Olsson, G. (1981) 'Volitional problems in carrying through a difficult decision: the case of drug addiction', *Drug and Alcohol Dependence* 7: 177–91.

Sjoberg, L. and Persson, L.O. (1979) 'A study of attempts by obese patients to regulate eating', *Addictive Behaviors* 4: 349–59.

Stewart, J., deWit, H. and Eikelboom, R. (1984) 'The role of conditioned and unconditioned drug effects in the self-administration of opiates and stimulants', *Psychological Review* 91: 251–68.

Swan, G.E. and Denk, C.E. (1988) 'Dynamic models for the maintenance of smoking cessation: event history analysis of late relapse', *Journal of Behavioral Medicine* 10: 527–44.

Velicer, W.F., DiClemente, C.C., Prochaska, J.O., and Brandenburg, N. (1985) 'Decisional balance measure for assessing and predicting smoking status', *Journal of Personality and Social Psychology* 48: 1279–89.

Wills, T.A. and Shiffman, S. (1985) 'Coping behaviour and its relation to substance use: a conceptual framework', in S. Shiffman and T.A. Wills (eds) *Coping and Substance Use*, New York: Academic Press.

Chapter Ten

Does the Marlatt model underestimate the importance of conditioned craving in the relapse process?

Nick Heather and Anna Stallard

Since its first formulation by G. Alan Marlatt and his colleagues in the late 1970s, the concept of relapse prevention, the model of the relapse process associated with it, and the intervention procedures to which it gives rise have generated a great deal of attention in clinical practice and some interesting research. Like any fertile idea in science, one of its chief virtues is that its very popularity has led others to criticize and revise the original formulation (e.g., Saunders and Allsop 1987). It is in this vein that this chapter is written.

The chapter is specifically concerned with the role of craving in the relapse process and how this is handled in the Marlatt model. It is focused on the events leading up to 'the first drink', or the first use of a prohibited substance, and not on the factors bearing on the subsequent course of the relapse. Marlatt's model is concerned equally with events and processes occurring before and after the first use but a critique of the latter part of the model is outside the scope of this chapter. The main aims are to examine the role of craving in the Marlatt account of relapse to first use, and then present some data on relapse determinants among heroin addicts that raise the question of whether the role of substance cues is given sufficient attention in the Marlatt model. We then discuss the way in which the more specific concept of conditioned craving is used by Marlatt and criticize his neglect of the most powerful theory currently available on the manner in which Pavlovian conditioning contributes to alcohol and drug dependence. Finally, we suggest a way in which the social learning and the conditioning views of the relapse process might be reconciled and briefly explore the implications of all this for relapse prevention in practice.

The role of craving in the Marlatt model

It should be remembered that, in its earliest formulations, relapse prevention was described as an alternative to a 'craving' account of relapse, or even in direct opposition to the craving view. In a paper given at an influential conference held in Bergen, Norway, in 1977, Marlatt (1978) contrasted his cognitive-behavioural analysis of relapse with the traditional medical or 'disease' view of the relapse process. Marlatt points out that Keller (1972), in a reformulation of the traditional concept of 'loss of control', placed the main emphasis on the alcoholic's return to the 'first drink' after abstinence rather than loss of control during a drinking bout and attempted to account for the involuntary nature of relapse, as he saw it, by appealing to a crude version of classical conditioning theory.

The craving account of relapse was more precisely developed by Ludwig and his colleagues from the University of Kentucky Medical Center and Marlatt devotes some time in his paper to a critique of this work. Ludwig and Wikler (1974) had elaborated a theory of alcoholic relapse based on the latter's earlier work on conditioned craving in opiate addiction. Wikler (1965) proposed that craving occurring during the addict's withdrawal from opiates becomes conditioned to contiguous cues, such as the physical environment, drug-using associates, and certain emotional states. When these stimuli recur during periods of abstinence, the addict experiences craving for the drug and the probability of relapse is consequently increased. This basic model of relapse is extended by Ludwig and Wikler (1974) to alcohol dependence, although, as Marlatt rightly points out, this is done in a manner which makes the original hypothesis virtually unfalsifiable.

Apart from the detailed critique of Ludwig's work, Marlatt demonstrates that the concept of craving, as formulated by adherents of the disease view of alcoholism, is circular and tautologous; it is superfluous to a scientific explanation of relapse because it has almost no utility in the prediction of behaviour. Marlatt goes so far as to suggest that the concept of craving should be abandoned in the scientific study of alcohol dependence, except as a phenomenological description of the subjective desire for alcohol experienced by alcoholics undergoing withdrawal.

The remainder of the paper is taken up with a presentation of the new, cognitive–behavioural model of relapse, which is now familiar and will not be described in any detail here. Suffice it to say that, in contrast to the disease view which sees relapse as being primarily due to 'internal symptoms such as physical craving for alcohol' (Marlatt 1978: 271), relapse is now seen in terms of an inability on the part of the abstinent alcoholic to cope with high-risk precipitants of drinking. Craving as such forms no part of the model. However, the beginnings of a later version of the concept of craving emerge when Marlatt writes:

> The desire for the anticipated reinforcing effects of drinking is so strong that it is understandable that some alcoholics speak of 'craving' for alcohol – much as someone else might speak of an overwhelming craving for hot fudge sundaes or pecan pie. In this sense, to crave is to desire the anticipated pleasures of consumption; wanting to experience the pleasurable effects of a food or drug is not the same thing as experiencing an internal *need* for the substance itself.
>
> (Marlatt 1978: 196, italics original)

Despite this brief allusion to craving, one of the problems with this early account of the relapse process is that it is difficult to understand precisely *how* a precipitating event is thought to lead to relapse. In other words, what is lacking is a mechanism linking the high-risk situation with the addicted person's subsequent resort to drug taking.

It may have been for this reason that, by the time of the publication of the book *Relapse Prevention* (Marlatt and Gordon 1985), craving had come to occupy a more important role in the relapse model and was now regarded as 'a useful mediational construct' (p. 138). Indeed, 'on the affective side the desire for indulgence may be experienced on a somatic level as an urge or craving for the prohibited substance' (p. 48), both urges and cravings manifesting themselves as nonverbal impulses or emotional-affective states. *Urge* is defined as a relatively sudden impulse to engage in an act, while *craving* is defined as the subjective desire to experience the effects or consequences of a given act. In a later section (p. 134), cravings are said to give rise to urges. Both urges and cravings are assumed

> to be mediated by the anticipated gratification (immediate pleasure or enjoyment) associated with the indulgent act and its affective consequences, and may be the product of both conditioning (e.g. craving as a conditioned response elicited by stimuli associated with past gratification) and cognitive processes (e.g. expectancy for the immediate effects of a particular act or substance). (pp. 48–9)

This last quotation implies that conditioned craving and positive outcome expectancies are not equivalent but are seen as making separate contributions to craving. However, in later sections of the book, craving is defined in a way that makes it equivalent to positive outcome expectancies, irrespective of how the craving is produced. Thus, for example, 'craving is defined here as a subjective state that is mediated by the incentive properties of positive outcome expectancies. In other words, craving is a motivational state associated with a strong desire for an expected positive outcome' (p. 138). And 'exposure to conditioned stimuli associated with prior drug experiences' (p. 138) is one way, among others, in which positive outcome expectancies arise. The extent to which cognitive processes are involved in conditioned craving, and whether or not conditioned craving is a class of positive outcome expectancies or a separate process, is one source of confusion in the description of the model.

It is also stated that craving of the conditioned variety occurs early on in a period of abstinence, in contrast to positive expectancies which subsequently take over as the main danger:

> For those persons who are susceptible to physical withdrawal reactions, the first few days of abstinence may constitute a continual high-risk time period. Physical craving for alcohol may be experienced as a result of either withdrawal (and the desire to alleviate this distress by continued drug use) or exposure to the drug or drug-related cues that elicit conditioned anticipatory reactions. Direct exposure to these cues . . . almost always constitutes a high-risk situation, especially in the early stages of abstinence. Many relapses that occur in the first few days of abstinence may be associated with physical withdrawal symptoms or conditioned anticipatory responses elicited by drug cues.
>
> (p. 75)

Thus, conditioned craving here has a limited role in the relapse process, being practically confined to the early stages of abstinence. Following this initial high-risk period, it is the individual's inability to cope with high-risk situations like frustration or social pressure that is likely to lead to relapse. 'Strong positive expectancies about the drug or activity as a coping strategy' (p. 76) will be more pronounced if the individual has made extensive use of this coping strategy in the past and if the situation faced is especially stressful.

In summary (Marlatt and Gordon 1985: 286), cravings or urges in the Marlatt model derive from the following sources:

1. classical conditioning, in which drug cues or other stimuli previously associated with the addictive behaviour serve as conditioned stimuli that elicit a conditioned craving response;
2. exposure to high-risk situations coupled with low self-efficacy for coping, considered to be the primary source of craving associated with most relapses;
3. physical dependency or withdrawal, which is assumed to play a variable but usually minor role;
4. cultural and personal beliefs about the expected effects of the addictive behaviour;
5. environmental setting.

It seems that cultural and personal beliefs are a further source, besides the individual's own history of using a substance to cope with stressful situations, for positive outcome expectancies relating to drug use. Situational and environmental factors are also said to influence expectancies about the effects of a drug. Thus, ignoring the limited role of physical withdrawal, it seems justifiable to conclude that conditioned craving and positive outcome expectancies are the two main kinds of craving employed in the model, with the former occurring mainly early on during a period of abstinence and the latter occurring later and being of greater significance in the explanation of relapse.

With respect to Marlatt and Gordon's classification of high-risk situations (pp. 77–92), craving is specifically mentioned in Category I-B which is included

> to assess the role of physical withdrawal or craving for a substance to alleviate the unpleasant symptoms associated with withdrawal distress. A subcategory (I-B1) is included specifically for classification of relapse episodes associated primarily with physical withdrawal symptoms . . . . Determinants involving negative physical states other than those associated with withdrawal are included in Subcategory I-B2.
>
> (Marlatt and Gordon 1985: 80; see table 10.1)

Urges or temptations 'that seem to overpower the person' (p. 86) are mentioned in Category I-E, but this is only to be assigned when other situational or intrapersonal factors have been ruled out. There are two situations, however, that appear to trigger valid urges: Subcategory I-E1 applies when an urge is experienced in the presence of substance cues; and Subcategory I-E2 'involves urges that occur in the absence of substance cues – those that seem to come "out of the blue"' (p. 80). This second subcategory was originally included, we are told, to tap into relapses that seem to be the result of an intense subjective desire or 'craving' for a substance, perhaps triggered by an environmental cue or conditioned stimulus previously associated with earlier experiences of withdrawal or craving.

As is now well known, in the analyses of relapse episodes reported by Marlatt and his coworkers (Marlatt and Gordon 1980; Cummings *et al.* 1980), none of the above categories and subcategories featured prominently among the reasons given by alcoholics, heroin addicts, and cigarette smokers for their relapses. Rather, the majority of descriptions fell into Negative Emotional States (Category I-A, see table 10.1), Interpersonal Conflict (Category II-A), and Social Pressure (Category II-B). This provided the empirical justification for the conclusion that craving, as defined in Categories I-B and I-E, was relatively unimportant as a determinant of relapse (Marlatt and Gordon 1980: 141).

A further study of relapse determinants

The corner-stone of the Marlatt model of relapse, and historically the first step in its empirical development, is the analysis of relapse determinants in terms of high-risk situations. The classification system developed by Marlatt and his colleagues for this purpose is shown in table 10.1. In the method used to elicit descriptions of these situations from subjects who have relapsed, they are first asked to give the date and time of the relapse episode, the physical setting in which it occurred, the location, the presence or absence of other people, whether or not the taboo substance was being used, etc. Subjects are then asked the following open-ended questions (Cummings *et al.* 1980: 301, italics original):

1. What would you say was the *main reason* for taking the first drink (cigarette etc.)?
2. Describe any inner thoughts or emotional feelings (things within you as a person) that triggered off your need or desire to take the first drink.
3. Describe any particular circumstances or set of events, things that happened to you in the outside world, that triggered off your need or desire to take the first drink.

Asking someone to give the main reason for a relapse, or the feelings or events which 'triggered it off', can be likened to asking what was the main reason for the start of the First World War. Was it the invasion of Belgium by Germany in August, 1914, the assassination of the Archduke Ferdinand at Sarajevo several weeks earlier, or, more fundamentally, an imbalance of power among the major European nations at the beginning of the twentieth century or the struggle between them for imperial domination? In other words, the question can be asked, and answered, on a number of different levels. No doubt philosophers make clear distinctions between different usages of 'cause' and 'reason' and use different terms to signify them. The point here, however, is that, if alcoholics, heroin addicts, or cigarette smokers are asked to give the main reason for their last relapse to addictive behaviour, the way they reconstruct these past events will depend to a large extent on their interpretation of the kind of 'reason' that is being sought – their general emotional state at the time, their 'inner' motivations, important events that had recently occurred in their lives, the immediate circumstances

Table 10.1 Marlatt and Gordon's relapse categorization system

I Intrapersonal–Environmental Determinants
I-A Coping with Negative Emotional States
I-A1 Frustration and/or Anger
I-A2 Other Negative Emotional States
I-B Coping with Negative Physical–Physiological States
I-BI Physical States Associated with Prior Substance Use
I-B2 Other Negative Physical States
I-C Enhancement of Positive Emotional States
I-D Testing Personal Control
I-E Giving in to Temptations or Urges
I-EI In the Presence of Substance Cues
I-E2 In the Absence of Substance Cues
II Interpersonal Determinants
II-A Coping with Interpersonal Conflict
II-A1 Frustration and/or Anger
II-A2 Other Interpersonal Conflict
II-B Social Pressure
II-B1 Direct Social Pressure
II-B2 Indirect Social Pressure
II-C Enhancement of Positive Emotional States

associated with the relapse, and so on. Further, it is probable that more than one reason might be simultaneously true; indeed, in relation to the First World War example, it is likely that *all* the reasons given above are valid – they are all, in one sense or another, triggers, precipitants, or determinants of 'the war to end all wars'.

Take the following example. A cigarette smoker has been abstinent for a few weeks but is still experiencing episodes of discomfort, irritability, and desire for a cigarette. Perhaps because of the irritability, he has an acrimonious quarrel with his wife about who should be responsible for putting the children to bed. (His wife has been urging him to give up cigarettes for some time and was pleased when he began the current attempt to do so.) He angrily storms out the house and, for lack of anywhere better, goes down to the local pub for a drink. As luck would have it, he meets an old friend there who is an unapologetic heavy smoker and who adopts a 'devil-may-care' attitude to life. Having to watch this person smoke and, generally, being in the smokey pub atmosphere greatly increases his craving for a cigarette. After a while, noticing his obvious discomfort, the friend urges our subject to take a cigarette and scorns his reasons for refusing. Eventually, after a couple of drinks, he gives in and finishes the evening having had half a dozen smokes. When he gets back home, he defiantly tells his wife he's started smoking again.

This, we suggest, is a not atypical story of a relapse. But suppose this subject were asked the reasons for his relapse. One of several could be chosen: the nagging craving for a cigarette in the background; the negative emotional state induced by the interpersonal conflict with the wife; the acute craving resulting from watching others smoke; the social pressure exerted by the so-called friend; the 'disinhibiting' effects of a couple of drinks; an unconscious desire to punish his wife by blaming his relapse on her; and so on.

A model of the events leading up to a relapse which allows more than one kind of event to qualify as a reason is presented in figure 10.1. This model assumes that interpersonal-environmental events, such as having a row or argument, or nonpersonal-environmental events, such as failing an examination or coming out of prison, cannot lead directly to a relapse but must be mediated by an emotional state, either negative or positive. This emotional state in turn leads to a 'craving' for the addictive behaviour either directly or indirectly by means of social pressure or the presence of substance-related cues. Under appropriate circumstances, the craving leads to relapse.

Returning to the example of the relapsed smoker given above, it will be noted that, from inspection of figure 10.1, nearly all the reasons cited could be regarded as valid reasons for the relapse – the quarrel with the wife, the mood of anger, the feeling of relaxation provided by alcohol, the observation of others smoking, the specific social pressure exerted by the friend offering the cigarette, and the severe craving occurring immediately prior to the relapse. (Even the unconscious motivation of wishing to punish the wife could be covered by a somewhat more complex model.) From an objective point of view, who is to say which of these reasons is more 'important' or 'significant' than any other? And from a subjective viewpoint, are we not asking too much of the subject, or of a rater examining the relapse protocol, to choose one of these potential reasons as more important than the rest?

In the Marlatt model, all the events in figure 10.1 are merely described as part of a 'high-risk situation' (see, e.g., figure 1–4 in Marlatt and Gordon 1985: 38). The major part of the model is concerned with events that occur after the high-risk situation has been encountered, notably whether or not the subject possesses skills to cope with the situation and/or positive outcome expectancies for

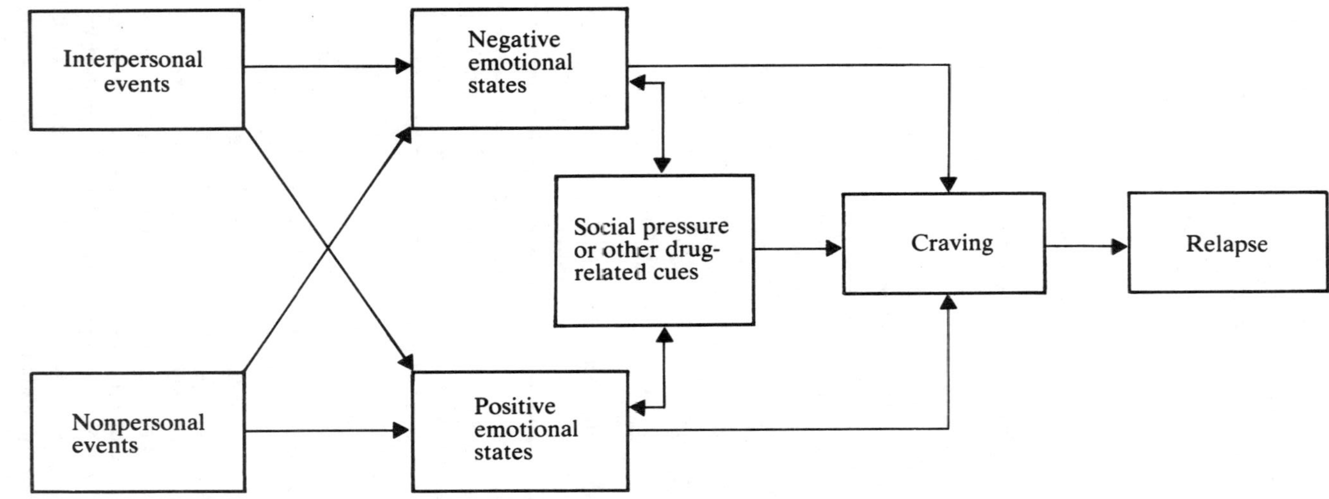

Figure 10.1 A model of relapse determinants in which more than one ‘reason’ for relapse is allowed

the initial use of the substance. Marlatt is concerned to describe the different kinds of high-risk situation that commonly occur and prescribe appropriate methods for dealing with them. But the possibility that more than one kind of reason could be present in a relapse episode or, in other words, that the occurrences of the different types of relapse precipitant described in the model are not mutually exclusive is not considered. Neither is the possibility that different types of precipitant may be temporally and/or causally related to each other (see figure 10.1).

Rationale for the study

As will have been gathered, we had certain criticisms to make of the method used by Marlatt and his colleagues to elicit reasons for relapse from subjects. These criticisms were based partly on the 'scoring rules' described first by Cummings *et al.* as instructions to those scoring the relapse protocols:

> For each relapse episode, only one category can be used for scoring. When multiple categories seem to apply choose the most significant precipitating event for scoring (the event *immediately* preceding the relapse). When it is impossible to decide between two equally likely categories, assign the score on a priority basis: Category I takes precedence over Category II; within each major category, the ordering of categories (A before B, etc.) indicates the priorities.
>
> (Cummings *et al.* 1980; italics original)

Our main objection was to the restriction that only one category could be used for scoring. We therefore wished to know what would be the effect of relaxing this condition and allowing raters to list more than one clear reason that they could identify in the protocol. We further wondered what would be the effect of abandoning the second instruction, i.e., that, in the case of a tie in importance between two categories, the order in which they were described in the categorization system should take precedence. This would obviously tend to favour intrapersonal-environmental determinants (Category I), as opposed to interpersonal determinants (Category II) and, in particular, favour Coping with Negative Emotional States (Category IA) compared with categories later in the sequence. Since, as has been noted, Negative Emotional States was empirically one of the main types of relapse precipitant identified by Cummings *et al.*, we wished to know to what extent this was an artefact of this rule of precedence. It could be added that the advice that Category I-E should only be used when other situational or intrapersonal factors

Table 10.2 Items used to represent relapse categories and subcategories (see table 10.1)

	Item	*Relapse category or subcategory*
A	I felt angry or frustrated, either with myself or because things were not going my way.	I-A1
B	I felt bored.	I-A2
C	I felt anxious or tense.	I-A2
D	When I saw 'works' or heroin I just had to give in.	I-E1
E	I felt sad.	I-A2
F	I felt ill or in pain or uncomfortable because I wanted a hit.	I-B1
G	I was in a good mood and felt like getting high.	I-C
H	I wanted to see what would happen if I just tried one hit.	I-D
I	I just felt tempted to use out of the blue, and went off to get a hit.	I-E2
J	Someone offered me a hit.	II-B1
K	I felt angry or frustrated because of my relationship with someone else.	II-A1
L	I was with others having a good time and we felt like getting high together.	II-C
M	I felt worried or tense about my relationship with someone else.	II-A2
N	I felt ill or in pain but this was not due to withdrawal from opiates.	I-B2
O	I felt others were being critical of me.	II-A2
P	I saw others using.	II-B2

had been ruled out might have a similar biasing effect.

Finally, we were concerned with the more fundamental question of what was the effect of using raters to determine the subject's main reason for relapse, as opposed to allowing the subject to assess directly the relative importance of various factors identified in the literature. We therefore invented a short sentence to represent each of sixteen categories and subcategories in the Cummings *et al.* classification of relapse episodes (see table 10.1). These may be inspected in table 10.2. The subject was asked to rate each of these potential reasons on an eleven-point scale which ranged from 'not at all important' to 'of the greatest possible importance'.

Apart from these aims, we were also concerned to clarify some of the inconsistent results that have been obtained from opiate addicts with respect to major types of relapse precipitant. In the Cummings *et al.* (1980) report, data from two samples are given: 129 subjects recruited from a Washington State treatment programme and sixteen from the Veterans' Administration methadone maintenance programme. Different results were obtained from these two samples, the VA sample showing a much higher percentage for 'negative physical states' (see table 8.1, Cummings *et al.* 1980: 303). This inconsistency was further complicated by the fact that relapse was defined differently in these two samples. Chaney *et al.* (1982) also investigated a VA sample of thirty-eight men on methadone maintenance and found the highest category of precipitants (32 per cent) was for negative physical states not associated with prior substance use (I-B2), whereas 16 per cent involved coping with physiological states that were associated with prior use (I-B1).

Sample and method

A sample of sixty-four subjects forms the basis for the preliminary analysis of data reported here. This included fifty males and fourteen females (mean age = 25 years, s.d. = 5.7). Three treatment settings were used, two in London (17 per cent from an in-patient detoxification and rehabilitation centre, eleven per cent from an out-patient treatment facility) and a drug-free day centre for problem drug users in Dundee (72 per cent). Subjects who had abstained from heroin for two weeks or longer and then relapsed were seen by one of two trained interviewers, each interview lasting about twenty minutes. Descriptions of each relapse were elicited in two ways: (i) open-ended questions regarding times, place, mood, others present, etc., as described by Marlatt and Gordon (1985: 77–93); (ii) a sixteen-item self-completion questionnaire designed to reflect each of Marlatt and Gordon's thirteen subcategories, each item judged by the subject in terms of importance at the time of relapse on a scale of 0 to 10. (In addition, subcategory I-A2 was represented by three separate items and II-A2 by two separate items, see table 10.2.) Demographic data and information regarding dates of relapse and drug use before and after relapse were also collected.

An experienced clinical psychologist, who was unaware of the rationale for the study, categorized each protocol according to Marlatt and Gordon's instructions, identifying a main reason for relapse and, in cases where there was more than one reason of apparently equal importance, assigning priority to the one earlier in the categorization system (see instructions above). Equally important reasons not assigned were noted. The rater was also asked to identify *any* other reasons for relapse present in the protocol. No mention was made of assigning Category I-E only when other categories did not apply.

Results

Figure 10.2 shows the number of occasions in which subjects'

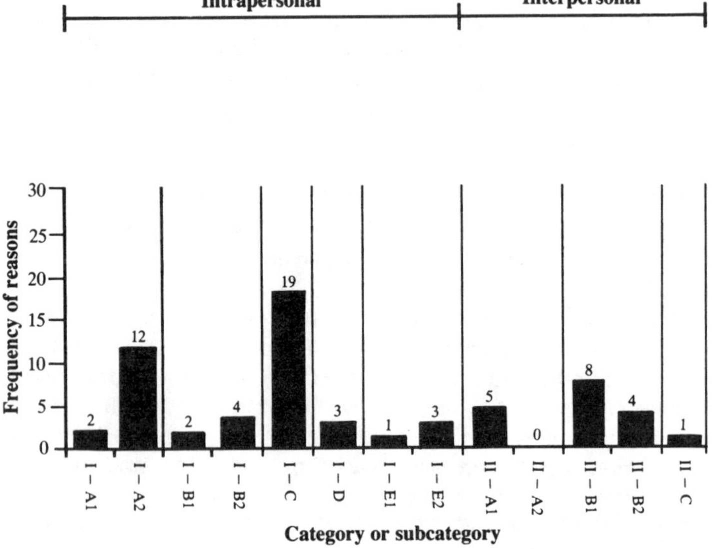

Figure 10.2 The frequency of allocation of Main Reasons to categories and subcategories of the relapse determinant

identified Main Reason fell into each of the relapse categories and subcategories. These results are similar to previous findings in showing relatively high proportions for Negative Emotional States (Categories I-A1 and I-A2 combined: 22 per cent) and for Social Pressure (Categories II-B1 and II-B2 combined: 19 per cent). Interpersonal Conflict (Categories II-A1 and II-A2 combined: 8 per cent) was less prominent in these results. However, the chief way in which these data differ from those reported by Cummings *et al.* (1980) and Chaney *et al.* (1982) is in the greater percentage falling into Category I-C (Intrapersonal–Environmental Enhancement of Positive Emotional States: 30 per cent – e.g., 'I was having a good time and felt like getting high'). This may be connected with the fact that in the present sample, although subjects were contacted at treatment agencies, the majority of relapses described did not occur following treatment and subjects may therefore have been more responsive to the euphoric effects of heroin. When subjects are followed up after treatment and then asked for their reasons for relapse, as in previous work, they may show a greater tendency to see the relapse as evidence of a serious failure on their part and thus interpret the events surrounding it in a more negative light than do subjects who have not recently received treatment. The relatively low mean age of our sample may also be relevant to the difference in results.

The present results for Main Reason also differ from those of Chaney *et al.* (1982) in showing a relatively low proportion in Category I-B2 (Negative Physical/Physiological States not Associated with Prior Substance Use). This difference may be related to the characteristics of the VA samples used in the two previous studies. Our findings are more similar in this particular respect to those reported by Cummings *et al.* (1980) for the sample from a state treatment programme.

No biasing effect was found for the rule of precedence regarding cases where main reasons of equal importance were found, since no such ties were made by the rater. There was also no effect of omitting the instruction that Category I-E was only to be assigned if no other category applied, since this did not result in any increase in the frequency of instances of I-E in the Main Reasons, compared with previous results.

Figure 10.3 shows frequencies for the assignment of Any Reason identified by the rater. It should be noted that, for comparison with the categorization of Main Reasons shown in figure 10.2, the total number of reasons in figure 10.3 adds to more than 64 (= 114) since a single subject could contribute more than one reason. In fact, for 21 subjects (33 per cent) only one reason was identified; for 36 (56 per cent) two reasons were found; and for 7 (11 per cent) three reasons were found to be present. Thus, it is the profile of relative frequencies, rather than absolute frequencies, which is important. The comparison shows that, when more than one reason is allowed, this results in increases to Categories I-A2 (Coping with Other Intrapersonal-Environmental Negative Emotional States – e.g., 'I'd just got out of jail and felt depressed') and Category II-B (Social Pressure), especially II-B2 (Indirect Social Pressure – e.g., 'I went round to see some mates who started fixing').

The results for Any Reason in figure 10.3 suggest that social pressure may act in combination with other types of precipitant in events leading up to a relapse and this is consistent with the process model of relapse antecedents shown in figure 10.1. The frequency of Intrapersonal-Environmental Negative Emotional States also appears to be underestimated in the same way, although this is not as striking in the results. However, this is again consistent with a model of relapse precipitants which insists that more than one type

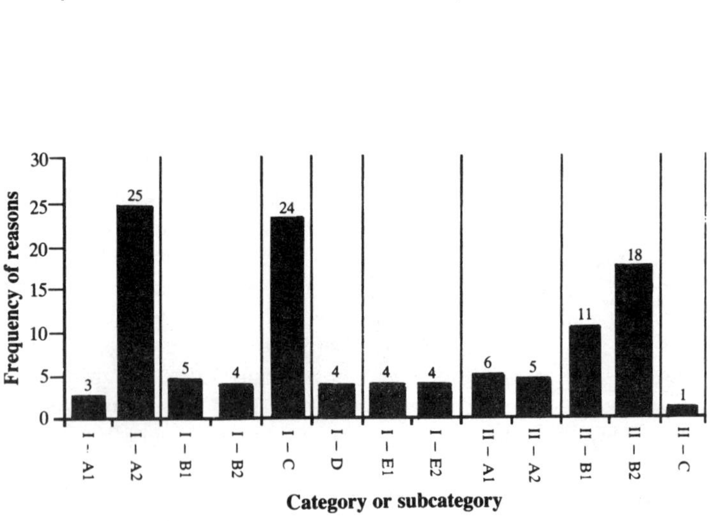

Figure 10.3 The frequency of allocation of Any Reasons to categories and subcategories of the relapse determinant

of determinant may contribute to relapse.

Figure 10.4 gives mean ratings across the total sample for each of Marlatt and Gordon's categories and subcategories (ratings for I-A2 and II-A2 were averaged across the items which represented them). Compared with both categorizations of open-ended descriptions of relapses (i.e., Main Reasons and Any Reasons), the self-rating method results in a marked elevation for Category I-E1 (Giving in to Temptations or Urges in the Presence of Substance Cues – see Item D, 'When I saw works or heroin, I just had to give in'). There is also a less pronounced elevation for Category I-E2 (Giving in to Temptations or Urges in the Absence of Substance Cues). It also confirms the suggestion from the categorization of Any Reasons that the Main Reasons analysis underestimates the importance of Category II-B (Social Pressure). Both types of social pressure show relatively high mean ratings but the greatest increase compared with the Main Reason data is for Indirect Social Pressure (II-B2).

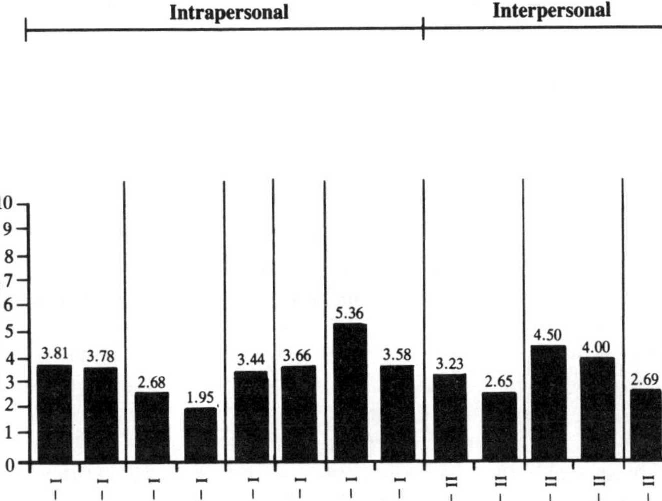

Figure 10.4 Mean subject ratings for categories and subcategories of the relapse determinant

Interpretation of results

The main conclusion we draw from the overall results of this study is that substance cues may be much more important as determinants of relapse than indicated by the Marlatt and Gordon method for the elicitation of relapse determinants. The most striking aspect of the results is the large increase in the significance of 'temptations or urges' when subjects are asked to rate the importance of these factors rather than simply provide verbal descriptions of their relapse. This applies to temptations experienced both in the presence of substance cues (I-E1) and in their absence (I-E2), although the increase was relatively greater for the former than the latter. We also suggest that the increase in the significance of Indirect Social Pressure (II-B2) is consistent with this interpretation, since this category describes relapses in which subjects observed others using prohibited substances. In this case, it would appear that subjects do tend to mention this factor in their open-ended descriptions but that it is less likely than other types of precipitant to be rated as a main reason for relapse.

As a more general conclusion, the results suggest that the way individuals give information about the reasons for their relapse has important effects on the kind of findings obtained. This is reminiscent of data gathered by Ludwig and his colleagues with alcoholics. Ludwig (1972) administered a questionnaire to 176 male in-patient alcoholics who were asked to give their own reasons why they took their first drink after discharge from the hospital and these were then classified by the investigators. The majority of subjects gave a variety of emotional and environmental reasons, including psychological distress, family problems, sociability, and employment problems. Only two gave reasons which could be interpreted as referring to subjective feelings of craving. In a second study, however, Ludwig and Stark (1974) gave sixty male in-patients a structured questionnaire which required subjects to rate items on a scale. On this occasion, craving emerged as a highly important factor in the continuation of drinking during a bout. As Marlatt (1978) points out, these data are not strictly relevant to the issue of the precipitants of the resumption of drinking after abstinence but they do suggest that, when individuals are asked specifically about the importance of craving in their experience of addictive behaviour, its significance tends to increase.

Assuming this analysis to be correct, which of the two versions of their experiences given by alcoholics or heroin addicts are we to place more trust in? It could, of course, be argued that asking subjects about craving is to suggest to them that the investigator thinks it is important and that the results obtained are influenced by the demand characteristics of the research situation. Hence, when subjects are left to their own devices, craving is rarely mentioned. It is at least equally plausible, in our view, that subjects do not mention craving in open-ended interviews because they assume it to be self-evident that it played a part in their relapse. When the researcher asks for the reasons for their relapse, they assume that it is some emotional or situational reason that is being sought. Moreover, it would not be surprising if subjects were found to be inarticulate about a nonverbal impulse or emotional-affective state. Given a model of relapse such as we proposed earlier (figure 10.1), in which more than one 'reason' could be a valid precipitant of a relapse, the underestimation of the importance of craving in the Marlatt and Gordon elicitation method is understandable. Moreover, in our method, subjects were also asked to rate the importance of all the other factors in the Marlatt and Gordon classification scheme, so that these reasons were also 'suggested' to them. The subjects nevertheless showed a tendency to regard craving items as more important than the rest.

An interesting question concerns the length of abstinence shown by subjects giving different reasons for relapse. Marlatt and Gordon would predict that, compared with other categories, those falling into categories I-B and I-E would show a shorter interval between the time of giving up drugs and the time of the first relapse. From the analysis of data on main reasons for relapse, there was some evidence to suggest that this hypothesis may be correct, at least with respect to I-E. However, an analysis of this relationship is still proceeding and will be reported in due course. It should be emphasized, however, that none of the relapses under study occurred during the period immediately following giving up drugs, which was suggested by Marlatt and Gordon as the time when substance cues would be most likely to contribute to relapse.

It should also be emphasized that the results reported here are based on the ratings of only one individual. There is clearly a need to replicate these findings, particularly the changes that take place when different methods of rating are employed, using other blind raters. There is also the issue of inter-rater reliability which was obviously not examined here. If the present findings hold up, it will be necessary to extend the method to other samples of heroin addicts and samples of individuals dependent on other substances or activities. Thus, the findings should be regarded as suggestive only at this stage.

Nevertheless, the important aspect of the results is that a blind rater categorized relapses in much the same way as has been reported in previous work by the Marlatt team but that this picture of the nature of relapse precipitants was significantly altered, in the direction of increased importance for substance cues, when more than one reason for relapse was permitted and when subjects' own ratings were examined. The evidence further suggests that substance cues may be combined with other types of precipitant in the events leading up to a relapse. However, as Cooney *et al.* (1983) point out, in one sense substance cues are the 'final common pathway', by definition, in all relapses.

In support of our findings is a study of relapse among opiate addicts in treatment by Vollmer and Ferstl (1988). The authors used a method similar to that reported here and asked patients to assess the importance of various 'discriminative stimuli' using a nine-point scale. The results showed that the factors mentioned most frequently and also rated highest in importance were contact with people involved with drugs, a desire for the drug, thinking about drugs, and visiting places where drugs were taken. The most important stimuli associated with craving were the sight of intoxicated drug addicts, drugs, and drug equipment.

Marlatt's view of conditioned craving

Although much more work needs to be done on this issue, let us assume that the above findings are valid and that the importance of substance cues in engendering relapse is indeed underestimated in the Marlatt model. On the ground that the relapses in question occurred well after acute physical withdrawal had ceased, this suggests a greater theoretical role for conditioned craving in the explanation of relapse. It may be instructive now to return to the model and examine in more detail Marlatt's view of conditioned craving. This is set out on pages 139 to 142 in Marlatt and Gordon (1985).

In his treatment of this topic, Marlatt concentrates on the Wikler (1965) theory of conditioned withdrawal (see p. 181 above). He first criticizes the application of this concept to relapse among alcoholics made by Ludwig and Wikler (1974) and points out that, if this theory were valid, alcoholics would experience the greatest craving in treatment centres where they have undergone detoxification and withdrawal, whereas experience shows that craving in such situations is very low. Marlatt then cites studies by McAuliffe (1982) and Chaney *et al.* (1982), both of which failed to find evidence of conditioned withdrawal in accounts of relapse by opiate addicts. (It must be pointed out that both these studies are relevant only to the experience of physiological withdrawal as a precipitant of relapse and not to craving as such.)

Nevertheless, Marlatt does see a role for classical conditioning in relapse:

> In our view, classical conditioning does play an important role, but not in the same way posited by Ludwig and Wikler. If a former drug user is exposed to drug-related cues (actual exposure to the drug itself or stimuli associated with prior drug use), it seems likely that this will elicit conditioned positive outcome expectancies of craving . . . . However, the conditioned craving response is not *aversive* in quality (as predicted by the conditioned subclinical withdrawal syndrome model); to the contrary, it is *appetitive* or positive in nature. Exposure to drug cues will elicit positive expectancies and an increased desire for the effects of the drug. It is as though the individual can almost taste and feel the effects of the first drink or injection, much as we assume that dogs anticipate the taste of food when they are

> salivating in response to a conditioned stimulus. Some narcotic addicts will actually give themselves injections of inert substances (e.g. water or saline solutions) when narcotic drugs are unavailable so as to experience a conditioned 'high'. Clearly these 'needle freaks' would not engage in this behaviour if they thought it would elicit the aversive experience of a conditioned withdrawal syndrome.
>
> (Marlatt and Gordon 1985: 140–1, italics original)

There are several points to make about this passage. First, in relation to the reference to 'needle freaks', there is some controversy in the conditioning literature about the significance of 'drug-like', as opposed to 'drug-opposite' conditioned responses (see, e.g., Goudie and Demellweek 1986). An attempt has been made to resolve the controversy by Eikelboom and Stewart (1982). However, the evidence suggests that drug-like responses occur in only a minority of instances and conditions, and that drug-opposite responses are most often observed in experiments on the conditioning of drug effects (MacRae *et al.* 1987). In any event, if conditioned craving really were based on drug-like conditioning of the kind Marlatt describes, we would surely find many more instances of cigarette smokers satisfied by merely holding a cigarette without lighting or smoking it and abstinent alcoholics deriving gratification from being in a bar or holding a glass of beer without drinking it. Common observation suggests that this does not occur.

The most obvious omission in Marlatt's account of the role of conditioning craving is that it ignores what is now the most popular and powerful theory of conditioned craving. This is the compensatory conditioning theory elaborated by Siegel and his colleagues from McMaster University, Ontario (e.g., Siegel 1983), for which a considerable body of experimental and naturalistic evidence now exists (Macrae *et al.* 1987). The theory proposes that both functional tolerance to a drug and withdrawal symptoms are partly learned phenomena, based on conditioned anticipatory responses opposite in nature to a drug's unconditional effects and which compensate for these effects. When drug-related conditional stimuli are presented but no drug is ingested, withdrawal phenomena appear. Unless stimuli associated with drug taking are extinguished, their presentation after a period of abstinence will lead to minimal withdrawal symptoms which may be experienced as craving for the drug and lead to relapse.

Curiously, Marlatt often makes reference to the work of the Siegel group in his published writings but never explores its particular implications for relapse. Instead, he tends to lump Siegel's work together with that of Wikler and others. For instance, in comments on the concept of craving recently published in the *British Journal of Addiction*, Marlatt (1987) refers to Siegel (1979), Ludwig and Wikler (1974), and Solomon (1977) as authors 'who have suggested that craving may be elicited by exposure to conditioned stimuli or cues that previously were associated with withdrawal or "abstinence agony". Craving in the form of conditioned withdrawal has been posited as a determinant of relapse by these theorists' (Marlatt 1987: 42). This is to misrepresent Siegel's theory which is not based on conditioned withdrawal during drug abstinence but on conditioned compensatory responses immediately preceding drug ingestion.

The most obvious relevance of this theory to Marlatt's discussion is that it avoids the criticisms he makes of Wikler's theory. The compensatory conditioning model does not predict that craving would arise in situations associated with prior withdrawal but in those associated with prior drug taking, a prediction which is far more consistent with clinical experience (O'Brien 1976) and self-reports (Mathew *et al.* 1979), and is supported by some experimental evidence (Sideroff and Jarvik 1980; Teasdale 1973). Moreover, since the conditioned craving response is essentially anticipatory in nature, the cognitive component of the response will have the expectant quality that Marlatt rightly demands of drug-related conditioned responses. There is no need to posit a drug-like response to account for this anticipatory quality; a drug-opposite response which is anticipatory in nature is more consistent with the accumulated evidence.

With regard to the emotional tone of the conditioned craving response, Marlatt (1987) uses the analogy of the 'eager anticipation' of sexual foreplay and suggests that craving thus experienced is incompatible with a conditioned response based on withdrawal symptoms. However, since, as we have said, a conditioned craving response in the Siegel theory is an anticipatory response, minimal withdrawal symptoms could be cognitively interpreted by the individual as a pleasurable experience in the manner described by Schachter and Singer (1962). This would probably be more likely to occur during continued drug use and the degree of the positive hedonic tone might increase as the opportunity for the consummatory behaviour approached; during abstinence, when the drug may be physically or psychologically unavailable, craving might be more likely to be experienced as unpleasant. This is admittedly speculative but no less so than Marlatt's observations on the subject. The main advantage in what is being proposed here is that it would relate conditioned craving to a powerful theory of the contribution of Pavlovian processes to drug dependence and relapse. This step would have a further advantage, as we shall see in the next section.

An attempted resolution

In discussions of relapse from outside the Marlatt group, a social learning and conditioning view of relapse are often placed in opposition to each other (e.g., Abrams *et al.* 1986; Wilson 1987). This opposition is related to a wider and more fundamental distinction among theories of addiction identified by Alexander and Hadaway (1982) as the 'exposure' orientation versus the 'adaptive' orientation. Although Alexander and Hadaway are concerned only with opiate addiction in their article, the distinction they identify applies to any substance addiction. The exposure orientation is said to view addiction as a condition engendered by prior drug use, while the adaptive orientation depicts it as a continuing attempt to reduce distress that existed before drug use began. Alexander and Hadaway specifically mention conditioning theories, including Siegel's (1979) theory, as being included within the exposure orientation. On the other hand, the Marlatt relapse prevention model, based as it is on the central notion of addiction as a maladaptive coping response, is clearly part of the adaptive orientation. The school of thought that relates substance use and abuse to coping behaviour in general appears to be increasing in strength (Shiffman and Wills 1985) while the exposure view, as exemplified by conditioning theories of drug dependence, is generating an increasing amount of research.

It is far beyond the scope of this chapter to attempt a full theoretical synthesis of these two fundamental perspectives. Nevertheless, there is one simple and straightforward way in which the two types of account of relapse – the conditioning and the coping view – can be reconciled. This is the notion that internal, dysphoric states are an important class of conditional stimuli leading to compensatory conditioned responses.

This notion was first approximated by Ludwig and Wikler who proposed that any state of neurophysiological arousal, including those induced by 'arguments with spouses, employment difficulties and loneliness' (Ludwig and Wikler 1974: 540) could serve as a cue for a conditioned minimal withdrawal syndrome in a formerly dependent drinker. However, as Marlatt (1978) justly implies, this is to propose a virtually unfalsifiable hypothesis, since it is difficult to imagine any account of relapse which could not be explained by it. The proposition is more precisely and succinctly stated by Poulos *et al.* (1981) who suggest that 'if stress has been reliably associated with abusive drinking for a particular individual, then stress can function as a conditional stimulus for the elicitation of compensatory responses and craving' (Poulos *et al.* 1981: 208). Depression and other negative emotional states are also mentioned by Poulos *et al.* in this connection.

The importance of this simple idea is that it provides a way in which both the coping and the conditioning models of relapse could provide valid accounts. If someone has often used a drug to cope with a negative emotional state, be it depression, anxiety, anger, or frustration, then a conditioned association will be established such that, if the emotional state recurs during a period of abstinence, a conditioned compensatory response will be instigated and interpreted as craving for the drug previously used. This does not propose that 'any state of neurophysiological arousal' can serve as a cue for conditioned craving but only those particular states of arousal, associated with a particular class of environmental events, which apply in the learning history of the individual in question. Thus, the individual nature of the relapse process is not disputed in this proposal.

It should also be made clear that there is nothing incompatible in emphasizing the contribution of Pavlovian processes to relapse following negative emotional states and the important role Marlatt assigns to cognitive expectancies in the relapse process, both efficacy expectancies and, more to the point here, outcome expectancies. This is particularly so if one adopts an explanation of classical conditioning itself founded on the concept of expectancy (Bolles 1972; Mackintosh 1983).

However, it might be asked why there is a need to introduce conditioned craving into the Marlatt model of relapse when it has previously done without such a construct. One reply might be that, without it, the Marlatt view of craving is in danger of becoming 'disembodied', as shown by the following quotation:

> By emphasizing the anticipatory, expectant quality of craving, we are moving the definition away from its physiological or somatic roots. To carry this to its extreme would be to redefine craving purely as a psychological phenomenon, more an addiction of the mind than of the body. Craving, based on this perspective, could be considered as a form of psychological attachment, based on the individual's cognitive capacities to anticipate, expect, and desire the effects of a given activity or substance that has yet to occur.
>
> (Marlatt 1987: 43)

Whether an understanding of craving with little relationship to somatic events is a useful construct, at least in the field of alcohol and drug dependence, must await further theoretical analysis and, hopefully, empirical study.

Implications for treatment

The implications of the view taken in this chapter for treatment interventions are fairly obvious. They imply some increase in the use of methods designed specifically to counteract conditioned craving – notably cue exposure methods. However, the chapter should not be taken simply as a plea for the introduction of cue exposure treatment and the abandonment of the skill training approach associated with the Marlatt relapse prevention model (e.g., Chaney *et al.* 1978). The situation is more complex than that.

Marlatt and Gordon themselves mention cue exposure as a method for modifying cravings and urges and discuss different methods of effecting exposure to alcohol-related cues (Marlatt and Gordon 1985: 243). They also suggest that the 'dry run' technique, in which, after having learned the basic essentials of new coping skills in the treatment setting, clients are taken to a real-life setting to practice their new skills 'as a kind of graduation exercise' (Marlatt and Gordon 1985: 117), could incidentally serve as a cue exposure or flooding experience.

In addition to cue exposure, other methods are mentioned by Marlatt and Gordon (1985) as ways of dealing with conditioned craving. These included stimulus control procedures, detachment, externalizing and labelling, and various cognitive restructuring procedures. Clients are made aware that cravings will eventually subside in intensity and pass away on their own; that the repeated experience of craving after treatment is not a sign that the treatment has failed but is to be expected as a natural part of the recovery process; and that a strong desire for the addictive substance is not due to 'internal' and uncontrollable sources but is related to external factors and coping mechanisms. An advantage claimed for the distinction between 'cravings' and 'urges' is that it is possible to break down the link in the sequence of events leading to the consummatory behaviour and train clients to cope with craving without necessarily indulging in the forbidden substance.

While all these cognitive control procedures undoubtedly have an important part in the modification of conditioned craving and relapse prevention, if it is the case, as suggested here, that substance cues have a more important role throughout the relapse process than envisaged by Marlatt and Gordon (1985), and not merely in the initial stages of abstinence, then this presumably indicates a correspondingly greater use of direct methods of extinction of conditioned craving responses, such as cue exposure. Such methods have been described for alcohol dependence (Cooney *et al.* 1983) and opiate dependence (Childress *et al.* 1986; McLellan *et al.* 1986). Blakey and Baker (1980) described a particular kind of *in vivo* cue exposure method for alcohol abusers, while Rankin *et al.* (1983) have reported on the effectiveness of a priming-dose cue exposure with response prevention technique. The latter clearly has limited relevance to the situation of relapse to the first drink. A type of cue exposure method that has yet to be developed is one where internal mood states are the relevant cues. This method may be especially problematic because internal cues of this kind will be difficult to produce precisely or reliably in treatment. Hypnosis may be one technique of interest here. Meanwhile, extensive research is continuing on the nature of cue reactivity in alcohol dependence (Pomerleau *et al.* 1983; Cooney *et al.* 1984, 1987; Kaplan *et al.* 1985; Laberg 1986; Monti *et al.* 1987, opiate dependence (Sideroff and Jarvik 1980; O'Brien *et al.* 1986), and smoking (Abrams *et al.* 1988; Niaura *et al.* 1988).

However, as far as we are aware, no research has yet carried out a controlled evaluation of a cue exposure treatment programme in comparison with other methods of relapse prevention or other general treatment approaches. Such evaluative research is urgently needed. One obvious target for research is the relative effectiveness of cue exposure and skill training methods in preventing relapse, preferably with samples of clients for whom the most salient class of relapse precipitant has been clearly identified. A study of this kind could include a group that receives both cue exposure and skill training combined, since it can be argued that the two kinds of technique are directed at different aspects of the relapse process and might therefore be additive in their beneficial effects (Cooney *et al.* 1983).

Another important area for research concerns the question of *how* cue exposure methods work when they do – whether by extinction of classically conditioned craving responses, modification of operant responses by decreasing the discriminative stimulus properties of substance cues, or by alteration of cognitive processes, including increases in self-efficacy for coping with feelings of craving without relapse (Wilson 1987). The last possibility is especially important because, if true, it may enable cue exposure treatment programmes to be considerably shortened; if full extinction of conditioned craving responses is necessary, then it would probably take a large number of learning trials to eradicate responses that have been built up over many years of addictive behaviour.

Conclusions

'Conclusions' may be too strong a term for the summary of main points made in this chapter, which should rather be seen as raising some questions, and suggesting some directions for research, regarding the future development of the Marlatt model of relapse prevention. Following a review of the way the concept of craving is used in the model, we presented some preliminary data which could be interpreted as suggesting that the importance of substance cues as precipitants of relapse has been underestimated by the Marlatt group. These data emerged only when a method was employed where more than one 'reason' for a relapse was allowed and when subjects themselves were asked to rate the importance of the various categories of relapse precipitant.

The particular view of conditioned craving taken in the Marlatt model was then criticized, particularly with respect to the adoption of a 'drug-like' conception of conditioned craving responses rather than a 'drug-opposite' conception. The latter would have the advantage of relating the explanation of relapse to the most powerful theory of drug-related conditioned processes currently available, the Siegel theory of conditioned compensatory responses. We then suggested that, by allowing that negative mood states could serve as one important class of conditional stimulus for conditioned compensatory responses, the conditioning and coping views of relapse could largely be reconciled. We finally explored the implications of these arguments for relapse prevention interventions and concluded that more work was needed in the area of the development of cue exposure methods.

Acknowledgements: The authors are very grateful to the following: Shirley McMillan for conducting relapse interviews, Alasdair Murray for rating relapse protocols, Lee Johnston for assistance with preparation of illustrations, Jenny Tebbutt for organizing the references, Janet Greeley and Fred Westbrook for useful comments and suggestions. The research described in the chapter was supported by a research grant from the Scottish Home and Health Department (Chief Scientist Office).

References

Abrams, D.B., Monti, P.M., Corey, K.B., Pinto, R.P., and Jacobus, S.I. (1988) 'Reactivity to smoking cues and relapse: two studies of discriminant validity', *Behaviour Research and Therapy*, in press.

Abrams, D.B., Niaura, R.S., Carey, K.B., Monti, P.M., and Binkoff, J.A. (1986) 'Understanding relapse and recovery in alcohol abuse', *Annals of Behavioural Medicine* 8: 27–32.

Alexander, B.K. and Hadaway, P.F. (1982) 'Opiate addiction: the case for an adaptive orientation', *Psychological Bulletin* 92: 367–81.

Blakey, R. and Baker, R. (1980) 'An exposure approach to alcohol abuse', *Behavior Research and Therapy* 13: 319–26.

Bolles, R.C. (1972) 'Reinforcement, expectancy and learning', *Psychological Review* 79: 394–409.

Chaney, E.F., O'Leary, M.R., and Marlatt, G.A. (1978) 'Skill training with alcoholics', *Journal of Consulting and Clinical Psychology* 46: 1092–104.

Chaney, E.F., Roszell, D.K., and Cummings, C. (1982) 'Relapse in opiate addicts; a behavioural analysis', *Addictive Behaviors* 7: 291-7.

Childress, A.R., McLellan, T., and O'Brien, C.P. (1986) 'Abstinent opiate abusers exhibit conditioned craving, conditioned withdrawal and reduction in both through extinction', *British Journal of Addiction* 81: 655–60.

Cooney, N.L., Baker, L.H., and Pomerleau, O.F. (1983) 'Cue exposure for relapse prevention in alcohol treatment', in R.J. McMahon and K.D. Craig (eds) *Advances in Clinical Behavior Therapy*, New York: Brunner/Mazel, pp. 194–210.

Cooney, N.L., Baker, L.H., Pomerleau, O.F., and Josephy, B. (1984) 'Salivation to drinking cues in alcohol abuse: toward the validation of a physiological measure of craving', *Addictive Behaviors* 9: 91–4.

Cooney, N.L., Gillespie, R.A., Baker, L.H., and Kaplan, R.F. (1987) 'Cognitive changes after alcohol cue exposure', *Journal of Consulting and Clinical Psychology* 55: 150–5.

Cummings, C., Gordon, J.R., and Marlatt, G.A. (1980) 'Relapse: strategies of prevention and prediction', in W.R. Miller (ed.) *The Addictive Behaviors: Treatment of Alcoholism, Drug Abuse, Smoking and Obesity*, Oxford: Pergamon, pp. 291–321.

Eikelboom, R. and Stewart, J. (1982) 'Conditioning of drug-induced physiological responses', *Psychological Review* 89: 507–28.

Goudie, A.J. and Demellweek, C. (1986) 'Conditioning factors in drug tolerance', in S.R. Goldberg and I.P. Stolerman (eds) *Behavioral Analysis of Drug Dependence*, New York: Academic Press, pp. 225–85.

Kaplan, R.F., Cooney, N.L., Baker, L.H., Gillespie, R.A., Meyer, R.E., and Pomerleau, O.F. (1985) 'Reactivity to alcohol-related cues: physiological and subjective responses in alcoholics and non-problem drinkers', *Journal of Studies on Alcohol* 46: 267–72.

Keller, M. (1972) 'On the loss-of-control phenomenon in alcoholism', *British Journal of Addiction* 67: 153–66.

Laberg, J.C. (1986) 'Alcohol and expectancy: subjective, psychophysiological and behavioural responses to alcohol stimuli in severely, moderately and non-dependent drinkers', *British Journal of Addiction* 81: 797–808.

Ludwig, A.M. (1972) 'On and off the wagon: reasons for drinking and

abstaining by alcoholics', *Quarterly Journal of Studies on Alcohol* 33: 91–6.
Ludwig, A.M. and Stark, L.H. (1974) 'Alcohol craving: subjective and situational aspects', *Quarterly Journal of Studies on Alcohol* 35: 899–905.
Ludwig, A.M. and Wikler, A. (1974) 'Craving and relapse to drink', *Quarterly Journal of Studies on Alcohol* 35: 108–30.
McAuliffe, W.E. (1982) 'A test of Wikler's theory of relapse: the frequency of relapse due to conditioned withdrawal sickness', *International Journal of the Addictions* 17: 19–33.
Mackintosh, N.J. (1983) *Conditioning and Associative Learning*, Oxford: Oxford University Press.
McLellan, A.T., Childress, A.R., Ehrman, R., O'Brien, C.P., and Pashko, S. (1986) 'Extinguishing conditioned responses during opiate dependence treatment: turning laboratory findings into clinical procedures;, *Journal of Substance Abuse and Treatment* 3: 33–40.
MacRae, J.R., Scoles, M.T., and Siegel, S. (1987) 'The contribution of Pavlovian conditioning to drug tolerance and dependence', *British Journal of Addiction* 82: 371–80.
Marlatt, G.A. (1978) 'Craving for alcohol, loss of control and relapse: a cognitive behavioural analysis', in P.E. Nathan, G.A. Marlatt, and T. Loberg (eds) *Alcoholism: New Directions in Behavioural Research and Treatment*, New York: Plenum, pp. 271–314.
Marlatt, G.A. (1987) 'Craving notes', *British Journal of Addiction* 82: 43–4.
Marlatt, G.A. and Gordon, J.R. (1980) 'Determinants of relapse: implications for the maintenance of behavior change', in P. Davidson and S. Davidson (eds) *Behavioral Medicine: Changing Health Lifestyles* New York: Brunner/Mazel, pp. 410–57.
Marlatt, G.A. and Gordon, J.R. (1985) *Relapse Prevention: Maintenance Strategies in the Treatment of Addictive Behaviors*, New York: Guilford Press.
Mathew, R.J., Claghorn, J.L., and Largen, J. (1979) 'Craving for alcohol in sober alcoholics', *American Journal of Psychiatry* 136: 603–6.
Monti, P.M., Binkoff, J.A., Abrams, D.B., Zwick, W.R., Nirenberg, T.D., and Liepman, M.R. (1987) 'Reactivity of alcoholics and nonalcoholics to drinking cues', *Journal of Abnormal Psychology* 96: 122–6.
Niaura, R., Abrams, D., and DeMuth, B. (1988) 'Responses to smoking-related stimuli and early relapse to smoking', *Addictive Behaviors*, in press.
O'Brien, C.P. (1976) 'Experimental analysis of conditioning factors in human narcotic addiction', *Pharmacological Review* 27: 533–43.
O'Brien, C.P., Ehrman, R.N., and Ternes, J. W. (1986) 'Classical conditioning in human opioid dependence', in S.R. Goldberg and I.P. Stolerman (eds) *Behavioral Analysis of Drug Dependence*, New York: Academic Press, pp. 329–56.
Pomerleau, O.F., Fertig, J., Baker, L., and Cooney, N. (1983) 'Reactivity

to alcohol cues in alcoholics and nonalcoholics: implications for stimulus control analysis of drinking', *Addictive Behaviors* 8: 1–10.

Poulos, C.X., Hinson, R.E., and Siegel, S. (1981) 'The role of Pavlovian processes in drug tolerance and dependence: implications for treatment', *Addictive Behaviors* 6: 205–11.

Rankin, H., Hodgson, R., and Stockwell, T. (1983) 'Cue exposure and response prevention with alcoholics: a controlled trial', *Behaviour Research and Therapy* 21: 435–46.

Saunders, B. and Allsop, S. (1987) 'Relapse: a psychological perspective', *British Journal of Addiction* 82: 417–29.

Schachter, S. and Singer, J.E. (1962) 'Cognitive, social and psychological determinants of emotional state', *Psychological Review* 69: 379–99.

Shiffman, S. and Wills, T.A. (1985) *Coping and Substance Abuse*, New York: Academic Press.

Sideroff, S. and Jarvik, M.E. (1980) 'Conditioned responses to a videotape showing heroin-related stimuli', *International Journal of the Addictions* 15: 529–36.

Siegel, S. (1979) 'The role of conditioning in drug tolerance and addiction', in J.D. Keehn (ed.) *Psychopathology in Animals: Research and Clinical Applications*, New York: Academic Press, pp. 143–68.

Siegel, S. (1983) 'Classical conditioning, drug tolerance and drug dependence', in Y. Israel, F.B. Glaser, R.E. Popham, W. Schmidt, and R.G. Smart (eds) *Research Advances in Alcohol and Drug Problems*, New York: Plenum, pp. 207–46.

Solomon, R.L. (1977) 'An opponent-process theory of acquired motivation. IV. the affective dynamics of addiction', in J. Maseer and M.E.P. Seligman (eds) *Psychopathology: Experimental Models*, San Francisco: W.H. Freeman, pp. 66–103.

Teasdale, J. (1973) 'Conditioned abstinence in narcotic addicts', *International Journal of the Addictions* 8: 273–92.

Vollmer, H.C. and Ferstl, R. (1988) 'Warum und Wie Werden Drogenabhangige Ruckfallig?', in I. Hand and H.K. Wittchen (eds) *Verhaltenstherapie und Medizin*, Heidelberg: Springer-Verlag, in press.

Wikler, A. (1965) 'Conditioning factors in opiate addiction and relapse', in D.I. Wither and G.G. Kasselbaum (eds) *Narcotics*, New York: McGraw-Hill, pp. 85–100.

Wilson, G.T. (1987) 'Cognitive processes in addiction', *British Journal of Addiction* 82: 343–53.

Chapter Eleven

Attitudes and learning in addiction and relapse

J. Richard Eiser

In this chapter, I shall attempt to bring together two theoretical traditions that have tended to develop rather independently of each other, not simply in the context of addictive behaviour but within psychology as a whole. These are the fields of attitudes and learning. Since both have been considered to greater or lesser extents in other chapters, I shall not attempt to provide a general review of attitudinally or behaviourally oriented research on different addictions. Instead, I shall concentrate on a number of the assumptions implicit in different models and theories. Considered separately, many of these should be reasonably familiar. The issue of their interrelationships, however, has rarely been addressed.

Attitudes and consistency

Before looking at relapse specifically, it may be helpful to remind ourselves of the kinds of issues that have dominated much of attitude research over the last half-century. Once it was conceded that attitudes were susceptible to quantitative measurement (Thurstone 1928), the main concerns were twofold: how can one predict different attitudes from one another, and how can attitudinal measures be used to predict behaviour? Although it is convenient to discuss these concerns in turn, both in fact relate to a common concept – that of 'consistency'. The fundamental premise of many attitude theories is that there is a general drive towards the reduction of inconsistency, both between different kinds of attitudes and beliefs, and between attitudes and behaviour.

Most introductions to attitude theory assign a prominent place to Heider's (1946) 'balance theory' and derived theories of 'cognitive consistency'. Basically, this approach is concerned with distinguishing between different sets of beliefs that may be held by a single individual in terms of how the separate beliefs interrelate. If the separate beliefs are seen to carry similar implications, the structure is said to be balanced or consistent; if they carry contrary implications, the structure is said to be imbalanced. Almost always, the kinds of implications being considered are *evaluative*. Thus, if everything one felt (and believed other liked or respected people to feel) about an object (or issue or person) seemed to point towards that object being 'good', the situation would be experienced as 'balanced'; if some beliefs implied that the object was 'good' and some that it was 'bad', the situation would be more 'imbalanced'. In short, balanced structures are ones that allow for simpler, non-ambivalent evaluations. Such structures, according to Heider and others, would be more predictable, memorable, resistant to change and aesthetically preferable. Balance theory, in other words, posits a drive towards evaluative simplicity.

This is not the place for a general critique of research and theory in this area (see Eiser 1986). However, it is worth pointing out that balance theory is far from being true for all people all of the time. Apart from many difficulties over differences between individuals, issues, and situations, the central problem is this: before any two beliefs can be defined as consistent or inconsistent with each other, they have first to be seen as *related* or relevant to each other. However, this question of relevance is very much an arbitrary or subjective affair. For example, imagine an interview panel confronted by a candidate of rather scruffy appearance but high academic qualifications: would this be experienced as consistency or inconsistency, or neither? A straight application of balance theory would imply that the panel's reactions would be ambivalent, along the lines of 'Scruffy = Bad; Clever = Good; therefore difficult to decide'. However, it is easy to think of many other ways the candidate's attributes could be encoded, according both to the theories and the interests of the interviewers. No (simple) inconsistency would be experienced by an interviewer who subscribed to the view that 'Clever people are often scruffy' (or even the converse!). Furthermore, the importance of either attribute would depend critically on what the candidate was being interviewed *for*: a research and development department would be looking for different qualities than would a public relations agency.

Consistency in attitude organization, therefore, is not an abstract or formal property of people's beliefs. Rather, it is a reflection of the way in which people *select* different attributes of an issue as important and relevant to each other. The major weakness of balance theory and its derivatives is that no account is offered of how this process of selection takes place. This has many implications for the notion that drug users may have 'ambivalent' attitudes towards their own behaviour and towards treatment.

Predicting behaviour from attitudes

The other aspect of the consistency notion is that attitudes should tend to be consistent with behaviour. The intuition that this somehow must be so survived many decades of research where specific acts (e.g., towards members of different ethnic groups) were shown to be only weakly correlated with general measures of attitude. Reactions to such evidence took a number of forms. Within 'cognitive dissonance theory' (Festinger 1957), for example, the basic consistency principle was extended to predict that people should be motivated (under certain conditions) to reconstruct their previous attitudes so as to make them more consistent with subsequent behaviour. Bem (1967) derived predictions along the same lines by hypothesizing that people infer their own attitudes from observing their own behaviour. Both these approaches are interesting in their departure from the (still) dominant view that attitudes and attitude change typically are causally antecedent to behaviour and behaviour change. Another widely cited approach was the 'three-component' model proposed by Rosenberg and Hovland (1960), according to which attitudes consist of three distinct but interrelated components: affect, cognition, and behaviour.

Probably the most significant influence with regard to the area of attitude-behaviour prediction, though, has been that of Fishbein and Ajzen (1975; Ajzen and Fishbein 1977, 1980). They provide a convincing explanation of the negative findings of previous research by arguing that many studies have failed to measure attitudes and behaviour at comparable levels of specificity. To predict specific acts, one needs specific measures of attitude towards performing such acts in specific contexts towards specific targets, not just general measures of like or dislike, say, towards particular groups of whom a target person is a member. Once different kinds of measures are matched for levels of specificity, predictions of behaviour from attitude can become highly reliable.

From such results, Ajzen and Fishbein (1980) develop their 'theory of reasoned action'. The assumptions of this theory are relatively straightforward. The best predictor of behaviour (or at least the best predictor one can incorporate in a psychological model) is *intention*. If behaviour cannot be changed by the exercise of intention (if it is 'beyond volitional control'), the theory is not expected to apply. Intention is in turn dependent on two composite variables: *attitude* and *subjective norm*. Both of these reflect the summated influence of different forms of *belief*. The attitude component depends on beliefs about whether the act in question will lead to particular good or bad consequences. The subjective norm, or normative component, depends on actors' beliefs about how they will be regarded by other people with whose wishes they may wish to comply. Both sets of beliefs, in other words, are forms of *expectancy*.

This model has been successfully applied to the prediction of behaviour in a wide variety of contexts. However, conceptual objections can be raised to its acceptance as a general explanatory theory. First, the high correlations with behavioural criteria are achieved at a price: it is less easy to consider behavioural patterns or syndromes that are more general than a single act, and the manner in which component beliefs are measured is extremely formalized. Departures from the standard measurement format can undermine the model's predictive success (Budd 1987). Second, the implied direction of causal influence is from specific expectancies to overall attitudes and subjective norms, and from these to intention and thence to behaviour. Although behaviour can provide information feedback, beliefs and attitudes essentially 'come first'. However, where habitual behaviours are considered, previous behaviour can provide good predictions of present or future behaviour irrespective of present attitude (Bentler and Speckart 1979). Third, individuals with different overall attitudes can typically attach greater importance or 'salience' to different beliefs and expectancies (Budd 1986; van der Pligt and Eiser 1984). This suggests that component beliefs should not necessarily be considered as causally prior to overall attitudes.

To draw this work together to a preliminary conclusion, it is clear that attitudinal and expectancy variables can show predictable relationships with behaviour. The same, in fact, applies to the prediction of emotional reactions (Leventhal 1980, 1984). However, problems arise when one tries to assert that certain classes of variables (usually it is cognitive variables that have been so considered) are causally antecedent to other classes (such as affective and behavioural responses). To the extent that it makes sense to talk of consistency among different 'components' of attitude, such consistency would seem to reflect some form of cyclical or reciprocal influence. However, such apparent consistency is often dependent on quite narrow situational and methodological constraints. It does not take much departure from these constraints for affect, cognition, and behaviour to seem quite distinct response systems.

Relapse and extinction

By now, probably the best-known conceptualization of relapse is that put forward by Hunt and his colleagues (Hunt *et al.* 1971; Hunt and Matarazzo 1970, 1973). The observation which they made was that the numbers of ex-addicts remaining abstinent at different periods after treatment declined with time, so that the relationship appeared graphically as an inverted-J-shape curve. To the shape of this curve, an almost mystic significance was attached. The finding of similar curves for relapse in different kinds of addictive behaviours invited the conclusion that all addictions were basically 'the same' (something one may wish to argue anyway, but for different reasons). In particular, Hunt was impressed by the similarity of the shape of the curve to *extinction* curves in animal learning, which describe how an animal's strength or frequency of performance of some task declines with time since the termination of a schedule of reinforcement. Put another way, relapse represents a form of '*forgetting*'.

If extinction processes play any part in relapse, this certainly cannot be inferred from data of this kind. Granted the nature of the calculations from which the curves are derived, it is almost inevitable that they will be downward sloping and negatively accelerated, that is, an inverted J. It is absolutely inevitable that the curve can never go up. The reason for this is quite simple. The curves are *cumulative* and represent the proportion of the total population who have, or have not yet, relapsed by the end of a given time period. Anyone who has once relapsed cannot reappear later to swell the number of abstainers or survivors. As Sutton (1979) has pointed out, one can obtain cumulative survival curves of the same shape from contexts that have nothing whatsoever to do with forgetting (e.g., survival and mortality within the first four years of life).

Two other related points may be made. The first concerns the distinction between relapse curves and relapse *rates* (Litman *et al.* 1979). As distinct from cumulative relapse curves, where the percentages are calculated on the basis of the *total* population, a relapse rate represents the probability that someone who was still abstinent at the beginning of a given time period will have relapsed by the end. In other words, relapse rates are calculated on the basis only of those still 'eligible' to relapse at the start of the sampling period. Relapse rates calculated in this way can increase, decrease, or stay constant over time, and this will affect the acceleration of the cumulative relapse curve. However, as shown by Litman *et al.*, quite marked variations in relapse rate can leave the basic form of the relapse curve relatively unaffected. In short, the extinction interpretation would seem to require that relapse rates increase over time, but such an increase cannot be inferred from the negatively accelerated shape of the cumulative curve. In fact, the cumulative curves presented by Hunt *et al.* (1971) disguise relapse rates that *decrease* over time. Thus, for example, a heroin addict who has survived the first three months after treatment without relapsing is quite likely to remain abstinent for the next three months. However, someone who has already been abstinent for six months is even more likely to survive till nine months. This makes good intuitive sense, but is not easily reconciled with an extinction notion.

The second point is also quite basic. As noted by Sidman (1952), there are grave difficulties in attempting to infer the shape of *individual* learning or forgetting curves from the shape of group curves. In fact, the shape of any single individual's response curve will only correspond to the average group curve under very exceptional circumstances (such as when interindividual variation is minimal: a condition that can scarcely be said to apply in this context). Whatever it is that is supposedly 'extinguished' after treatment, therefore, cannot be assumed to extinguish at the same rate for different individuals, or to be read off easily from the group response curve.

These difficulties with the Hunt interpretation arise simply from the nature of cumulative data. They certainly do not preclude the possibility that some form of forgetting takes place after clients leave treatment, but we cannot tell from such relapse curves exactly what is forgotten, by whom, or how quickly. However, an even more basic problem relates to the implicit definition of relapse itself. As many other chapters in this book testify, relapse is rarely (if ever) a simple once-and-for-all affair, yet this is precisely how it is defined for purposes of Hunt's calculations. Once someone has broken abstinence, they are said to 'have relapsed': they are discarded from further calculations, and simply become part of history. However, the fact that people can have a number of longer or shorter 'lapses' on the way to either stable abstinence or incontestable 'relapse' makes nonsense of interpretations based exclusively on group curves.

An alternative empirical approach was taken by Litman *et al.* (1979). The data were based on wives' reports of husbands' drinking patterns over a period of two years following initial consultation for a drinking problem presented by the husband. These data provided records of the month in which the husband first resumed heavy drinking – a measure comparable to standard measures of relapse. In addition, though, the data provided much information on the frequency of heavy drinking, as well as on month-to-month changes in drinking frequency. Litman *et al.* derived a number of independent measures from these records, and factor-analysed them to establish how they related to each other. They found that the more standard measure of relapse (the number of months before heavy drinking was resumed) was only weakly related to most other measures, and did not predict the extent or direction of most month-to-month variation in drinking patterns.

Relapse and conditioning

There have been many models of addictive behaviour based on principles of conditioning, but one of the best formulated is the 'opponent process' model of Solomon (1980). Solomon's model is concerned not simply with behavioural reinforcement, but more with the conditioning of different emotional states that he assumes provide the motivation for continued drug use. The essence of the model is that all unconditioned stimuli give rise both to primary emotional states and to secondary states opposed to the primary ones, the function of which is to dampen or shut off the primary reaction after a certain latency and to bring the person or animal back to a state of emotional homeostasis. One of the features of such opponent processes is that they can cause a temporary 'overshoot' as the effects of the unconditioned stimulus wear off. Thus, excitement or elation can be followed by a brief feeling of flatness or depression, pain or anxiety by a feeling of relief, and so on. Applied to drug use, drugs are seen as constituting an unconditioned stimulus, and overshoot reactions such as just described correspond to withdrawal effects. Solomon further assumes, at least for dependence-producing drugs, that repeated exposure to the unconditioned stimulus (the drug) leads to a weakening of the primary emotional state (this corresponds to the development of tolerance) arising from the opponent process coming into play after a short latency and at increased strength. In other words, with repeated dosing, the drug users will experience weaker positive effects but stronger withdrawal effects.

If this was all there was to the opponent process model, it would provide few advantages over more medical definitions of dependence in terms of tolerance and withdrawal. However, the distinctive feature of the model is that both 'highs' and withdrawal effects are regarded as *acquired* emotional states with motivational properties. In other words, the important questions relate to how these states are *learned*. According to Solomon, they can become conditioned to situational cues. In other words, whether a person will experience the positive effects of a drug or the negative effects of abstinence will depend on the presence or absence of various environmental stimuli. In short, drug use and associated emotional states can represent the products of 'state-dependent learning'.

Different kinds of evidence lend support to this position. Experimentally induced morphine tolerance in rats has been shown to be specific to the particular environment (i.e., cage) in which the drug was administered, such tolerance being much reduced when the animals are moved to a new environment (Siegel 1977). The findings of Robins *et al.* (1974), that a large percentage of American servicemen ceased using opiates after returning from Vietnam, could also be interpreted in these terms. For these men, opiate dependence was acquired in the presence of cues associated with the stress of war: removing these cues removed the dependence.

How then does this model account for dependence and relapse? The answers are related but distinguishable. Dependence reflects mainly the operation of an 'addictive cycle', whereby repeated dosing strengthens the withdrawal effect, which in turn makes repeated dosing (to avoid or terminate withdrawal) even more reinforcing. The strength of the withdrawal effect thus occupies a central place in Solomon's theory. Indeed, it is precisely on this point that he has been challenged by a number of critics (e.g., Alexander and Hadaway 1982), who claim that the presence or absence of withdrawal effects is incidental to the nature of dependence. However, it is important to note a paradox to which Solomon himself pays rather little attention. *Actual* withdrawal is something a dependent drug user with an adequate supply will avoid like the plague. The addictive cycle to which Solomon refers does not, therefore, depend upon the repeated *experience* of withdrawal, but upon the repeated *expectation* of withdrawal. From this point of view, the reinforcing function of repeated dosing arises not from the fact that withdrawal is terminated, but from the fact that it is *avoided*. As is well known, avoidance learning is extremely resistant to extinction. In terms of cognitive learning theory (Tarpy 1982), this reflects the acquisition of an expectancy that failure to perform a response will lead to negative consequences: so long as the animal continues to respond (or the person continues to smoke, or whatever), there will be no feedback that contradicts this expectancy.

The explanation of relapse, according to this model, is somewhat more complex. The great advantage of the Solomon over the Hunt model in this respect is that relapse does not have to be regarded as once and for all; nor even as anything that necessarily has much to do with what may have gone on during treatment (a paradoxical but thought-provoking implication). *Forgetting* is no longer the lynch-pin of relapse since, by and large, avoidance responses are not forgotten. Instead, relapse reflects the *remembering* of previous conditioning (inadequately unlearned, i.e., extinguished, during the course of treatment). The conditioned stimuli can be any environmental cues, people, places, or situations that in the past have been associated with drug use and/or with the emotional states to which drug use has been a learned response. Unless the ex-addict has become adequately habituated or desensitized to all these stimuli (a pretty tall order), the risk of relapse can remain present for a very long time. Habits are not necessarily forgotten just because they have been broken.

Much of the ambiguity in the conditioning approach to relapse relates to what exactly is the form of conditioning that has taken place. Here it must be stressed that Solomon is far from being an out-and-out behaviourist. He is not saying that *all* that gets conditioned is the behaviour, in the sense that the *act* of drinking might be conditioned to the sight of a non-empty bottle or whatever. Such 'automatic' or reflexive drug use may well play a vital part in much relapse, but this does not seem to be the main point of this model. What Solomon tries to explain is the acquired *motivation* to self-inject, drink, smoke, or whatever. For him re-administration of a drug – and hence relapse – is a behavioural response to an acquired motivational state corresponding essentially to what most addiction researchers term 'craving'. Craving, in turn, is the representation in action-related terms of the negative emotions associated with actual or anticipated withdrawal. To put it more simply, craving is the emotional state 'This is or will be awful' combined with the cognition 'I can stop it being awful if I have a drug (or drink, etc.)'.

Once again, Solomon has been criticized for the importance attached to withdrawal effects (Alexander and Hadaway 1982). McAuliffe and Gordon (1974) found only one of a sample of sixty addicts who referred to conditioned withdrawal symptoms as a relapse precipitant (though it is a commonplace that people do not always have insight into the extent to which their own reactions can be conditioned). Treatment aimed at the elimination of conditioned withdrawal symptoms (e.g., Teasdale 1973) provides no exceptional protection against relapse. It may be reasonable, however, to broaden Solomon's approach to allow the conditioned *motivational* state of 'I need a drug (or drink, etc.)' – whether we call this 'craving' is largely a matter of semantics – to be considered as a learned response to conditioned *emotional* states that arise in response to a whole range of environmental cues. These emotional states could include actual or anticipated withdrawal symptoms, as Solomon would maintain, but there is absolutely no reason why they should be restricted to these. 'Personal distress' – the concept on which Alexander and Hadaway (1982), for instance, place so much weight – could extremely plausibly be thought of as just such a category of negative emotional experience. There is even no reason why we should restrict ourselves to negative emotions. Despite the undoubted biases that can operate in the direction of addicts describing relapse in negative terms, *positive* feelings and happy occasions may also sometimes lessen the vigilance of those attempting to remain abstinent (Litman *et al.* 1979).

At this point it is worth pausing to consider where we have arrived at in explanations of relapse derived from the principles of learning. Concepts of conditioning and reinforcement seem to have much to offer, but their application requires attention to subjective factors, such as people's feelings, emotional reactions, and expectations of positive and negative consequences. Such factors might well, in other contexts, be regarded as attitudinal. Can the circle between attitude theory and learning theory be joined?

Attitudes, learning and consistency

Attitudes have been variously considered as forms of motives, feelings, thoughts, perceptions, memories, and reactions. Although it is rarely, if ever, disputed that attitudes are acquired through learning, rather little attention has been paid to the question of *how* such learning takes place. The crux of the problem is this: it is easy enough to hypothesize how principles of reinforcement and association could lead to the conditioning and acquisition of specific forms of attitudinal *responses*, considered separately. Assume any system of social rewards and sanctions for particular forms of attitude expression, and you have assumed the reinforcement contingencies for the shaping of such expression. But how do we get from individual expressive acts to attitudes as structures that are 'more than the sum of their parts', where the meaning of the whole depends on the degree of consistency and interrelatedness between the different component elements? How, in short, can principles of learning help us in any way to understand what is supposedly the fundamental aspect of attitudes, namely their consistent structure?

Traditionally, attitude research has treated consistency as somehow 'natural' and inconsistency as somehow 'deviant' and in need of special explanation. But suppose this tradition has been looking in the wrong direction. Suppose that consistency is a condition attained only imperfectly, fleetingly, and with difficulty. Previous research provides evidence that, under some conditions, people will *try* to achieve consistency. It provides rather little direct evidence that people are 'typically' or 'naturally' consistent across the range of their feelings, beliefs, and behaviour. If we turn the problem on its head, the issue becomes one of how individuals *construct* consistency (if and when they do) from the building blocks of separate thoughts and responses. It is consistency that requires an explanation, not the inconsistency or independence of different response systems.

If we look to the literature on animal learning for guidance or even mere analogy, there is evidence that different kinds of responses to a stimulus can be acquired in such a way that they appear consistent with each other (as when conditioned fear is reflected in escape behaviour). However, there are strict limits on this kind of 'consistency': different kinds of responses (e.g., emotional, motor) must share the same learning history – they must have been acquired contiguously under the same conditions – if they are to covary strongly with each other (Tarpy 1982). This is rarely going to be the case with different kinds of attitudinal responses. A smoker may acquire expectancies to the taste of cigarettes, and may learn about the link between smoking and lung cancer, but most probably these forms of learning will take place in isolation from each other. In short, there is no *a priori* reason to expect reactions or responses of different kinds to co-vary consistently with one another unless they have been acquired together. This applies to human beings as much as to other animals. However, human language provides the opportunity for categorizing very different kinds of objects and situations as relevant to one another. Because of this, we may look for other forms of consistency within the human context that depend upon categorical definitions of individual thoughts, feelings, and behaviour as 'going together'.

The vital point, though, is that such categories, upon which the definition of consistency in this sense depends, are *all* more or less arbitrary. Not just ordinary language but the terminology of addiction research too is replete with examples: 'smoking attitudes', 'drinking motives', 'health-related behaviours', 'coping responses', 'beliefs in self-efficacy', and many others. The usefulness of such concepts is entirely an empirical matter. *Do* different kinds of 'smoking attitudes' (for example) co-vary with each other or not? If not, the implicit assumption that different specific views and beliefs are all indicators of a common underlying 'attitude towards smoking' may be misleading. However, whereas the validity or usefulness of such categories is an empirical question, their origin is *social*. We do not simply acquire isolated responses and expectancies. We learn, from other people and through the use of language, how such isolated responses and expectancies may be interpreted as belonging together in higher-order categories.

These category systems on which so much human communication depends are largely subjective and selective. That is why people so often disagree with each other, and this is especially true with regard to attitudinal disagreements. Political rhetoric consists largely of messages of the form 'See this issue as an example of this broader principle, and as bound up with these other issues to which you are committed, because of who and what you are'. If there were no room for disagreement over how issues should be defined and categorized, there would be no need for rhetoric (Billig 1987). Reality is socially defined in terms of categories, but the nature and application of such categories (and hence the nature of reality) remains constantly open to dispute.

The issue of attitude-behaviour consistency depends likewise on the imposition of subjective and selective category systems implying that particular kinds of attitudes 'should' go together with different kinds of behaviour. A large part of socialization can be seen as training in cross-response consistency: you must be nice to your friends, you must keep your promises, and such like. We learn that we may be *held to account* for what we say we feel in what we do, and *vice versa*. Consistency – the basic principle of so much attitude theory – is thus a *social product* and not necessarily a 'natural' state of mind. Both the definition of consistency and the motivation to be consistent derive from social learning (Eiser 1987). However, we also learn that the social demands to be consistent (in relation to some higher-order category) may be intermittent and situationally dependent. Taking the analogy of bureaucratic decision making, the imperative to 'follow precedent' can be neatly balanced by the imperative to 'consider each case on its merits' (Billig 1985). In short, we learn that it is socially desirable in many situations to act in a manner that is *inconsistent* with a higher-order category.

Attitudes and addictive behaviour

The question of what counts as consistency is particularly relevant when we try to use attitudinal measures to predict and/or explain addictive behaviours. There is a large amount of work within the broad framework of an expectancy-value approach that links people's expectations of benefits and costs with their behaviour. Users of any substance are more likely to say that they expect benefits, and less likely to say that they expect costs, as a result of such substance use than are non-users (e.g., for smoking, Fishbein 1982; Mausner and Platt 1971). From this comparative point of view, then, attitudes and behaviour are consistent. However, the same data can be interpreted in an absolute sense as suggesting that the attitudes and behaviour of drug users are inconsistent, since often the perceived benefits of use are outweighed by the perceived costs. Users may underestimate the damage they are doing to themselves but they may still admit that their behaviour is damaging overall.

Much can be and has been said about the differential importance of short-term benefits and long-term costs, particularly in relation to the uptake of drug use by adolescents. This issue is very relevant to a discussion of addictive behaviour in terms of reinforcements. It also fits in with the view that different expectancies can be acquired independently of each other. The young user must rely on information from other people to appreciate the long-term health hazards of his or her behaviour. Expectations of short-term benefits in terms of mood changes, however, may be confirmed by direct personal experience. There is still the question of how such personal experience is interpreted, however. A case could be made that many young users rely upon expectations acquired from others so as to interpret otherwise ambiguous drug effects as constituting desirable changes in mood (Eiser 1985; Marsh 1984). This would fit in with more general evidence for the 'cognitive labelling' of emotional states (Reisenzein 1983; Schachter and Singer 1962).

Of more direct relevance to the issue of relapse, however, is the problem that many users continue to use drugs, or to relapse after periods of abstinence, even though they know that it is 'bad for them'. Can this be reconciled with an expectancy-value approach to attitudes and behaviour? The answer seems to be broadly 'yes', provided one looks more closely at the nature of the behaviour one is trying to predict. Discrepancies between expected outcomes and behaviour seem to depend on a view of the drug user as having a choice of the form 'To smoke or not to smoke', 'To drink or not to drink', etc. Without getting into metaphysical arguments over whether users *really* have such a choice, in terms both of what one is trying to predict and of how things appear to the person concerned, the immediate decision faced is more of the form 'To try to give up or not to try to give up'. The expected outcomes that should affect this decision are the expected outcomes of *trying* (not necessarily just of continuing to smoke or whatever). In other words, the benefits of stopping have to be weighted by whether the person concerned expects to succeed or fail in any attempt at stopping. If he or she expects to fail there will be little 'rational' point in trying, whatever the hypothetical benefits of success (Eiser and Sutton 1977).

There is good evidence, in the literature on smoking, that people's *confidence* in their own ability to give up relates to whether they will try to do so, and to whether they will succeed if they try (Eiser *et al.* 1985). Furthermore, the effectiveness of persuasive communications can be shown to depend on how much they influence confidence. Just telling smokers that they would be healthier if they stopped smoking has little influence unless combined with a convincing message that cessation or abstinence can in fact be achieved. Confidence, in this sense, is similar to Bandura's (1977) notion of 'self-efficacy', although more specific in terms of its focus on a particular behavioural goal.

But how much is such confidence or expectancy of success acquired? According to Weiner (1985), expectancy of future success depends on how one explains previous experience of success and failure. Essentially, confidence should be higher if previous successes are attributed to causal factors that are stable and likely to persist or recur, and if previous failures are attributed to unstable factors that may not be relevant in the context of future attempts. When it comes to trying to give up an addictive behaviour, it is extremely likely that the person in question has made several unsuccessful attempts before. It therefore becomes crucial how such previous failures are explained. If they are attributed to uncontrollable and unalterable factors, something analogous to a state of 'learned helplessness' (Abramson *et al.* 1978) may result. The person will try less hard because he or she 'knows' that there is little or no chance of success. Such pessimism, in turn, will be confirmed by yet another failure, overlaying the 'addictive cycle' of metabolic change and/or dependence with one of lowered expectations.

An especially interesting feature of the attributional processes that lead to a lack of confidence in one's ability to give up drugs is their close link with a preparedness to see oneself as an 'addict'. Those who describe themselves as addicted anticipate greater difficulty in giving up either drugs (Eiser and Gossop 1979) or cigarettes (Eiser *et al.* 1985; Eiser and van der Pligt 1986). It is worth remembering the McKennell and Thomas (1967) definition of 'dissonant' smokers as those who would like to give up smoking if they could do so easily (but cannot because they are 'addicted'). The concept of addiction has been used by researchers to account for the apparent discrepancy between the attitudes and behaviour of drug users. It is, therefore, not too surprising that it can be similarly employed by the drug users themselves: if they are 'addicts', they cannot really be 'blamed' for continuing to act in ways that they know are bad for them. The health messages can be simultaneously acknowledged and ignored. Drug use can therefore continue alongside beliefs that appear inconsistent with such behaviour. The price paid for this discrepancy in cognitive terms, however, is a self-fulfilling lowering of confidence in one's capacity for behavioural change.

Implications for the prevention of relapse

Many theories of behaviour seem best suited to explaining how people can come to act purposefully and rationally. However, much research can be interpreted as highlighting the apparent contradictions and dissociations among people's different thoughts and actions. There is nothing 'natural' about behavioural or cognitive consistency, and when consistency is found, its definition depends on the frame of reference or context in terms of which different actions and thoughts are considered in relation to one another. This bears directly on the notion of relapse, which is typically regarded as a form of behaviour that is *inconsistent* with previous training/treatment, but likely to be seen as predictive of a *consistent*, i.e., relatively irreversible, shift away from abstinence or even from temperance. Relapse is *not* predicted from the learning experiences of treatment, but *does* supposedly predict subsequent repeated drug use or abuse. According to this more traditional view, too, relapse is something the individual is expected to feel bad about. In other words, it is a form of behaviour that is *inconsistent* with various attitudes and beliefs (some of which may have been acquired during treatment).

There are good grounds for challenging this traditional view. From the conditioning literature, we may infer that, just as addiction is a form of state-dependent learning, so relapse may be a reaction to *specific* situational precipitants (the influence of which doubtless derives from earlier situation-specific conditioning). This implies that relapse in one kind of situation may *not* be necessarily predictive of subsequent resumptions of drug use in other situations. It must be stressed, though, that such a conclusion does not take account of possible 'priming' or 'loss of control' effects, however mediated, postulated by some to lead to a more or less automatic escalation from initial redosing to excessive use. Furthermore, the 'specific' situations in which relapse is likely to occur may in fact be very difficult for the individual to avoid.

Even so, the message is that there are good theoretical grounds – supported by many empirical findings – not to regard relapse as an all-or-none affair. Drug users may return to relatively stable rates of abstinence even after occasional 'lapses'. However, the same theoretical arguments (concerning particularly the situational specificity of addiction and its acquisition) suggest that some of the more optimistic claims regarding the possibility of return to 'controlled' drinking, drug use, etc., should be viewed cautiously. Too often the issue of 'safe' use of alcohol or whatever by the reformed addict is seen as a matter of quantity and frequency. Can someone allow themselves a glass of whisky without feeling compelled to go on to finish a whole bottle? Can someone limit their drinking to once a week? To my mind, these questions cannot be sensibly asked or answered without regard to the context in which such controlled or uncontrolled drinking is likely to occur. Just as relapse in one situation may not always predict relapse in another, so self-control in one situation may not predict self-control in another where other cues and precipitants may be effective. Perhaps controlled drinking (or whatever) is likely to be more easily attained when therapeutic interventions help the individual to differentiate situations where moderate consumption can be risked from situations where it cannot.

So far this interpretation rests heavily on the notion that learning is a process that occurs in the context of specific situations, and may not always generalize to different situations. However, more cognitive factors must also be considered and one of these is how instances of either successful or unsuccessful attempts at resisting temptation are interpreted by the individual. Particular examples of restraint or lapse may be interpreted by the former addict as *general* indicators of success or failure in a way that does not fully acknowledge the situational specificity of either outcome. This may lead to either excessive optimism or excessive pessimism regarding the prospects for long-term abstinence or self-control. The labelling of oneself as a 'success' or 'failure' on the basis of specific outcomes could lead, in other words, to more generalized expectancies of success or failure.

Such expectancies, as I have argued, are likely to be a prime determinant of an addict's motivation to try to give up drugs. Such motivation is likely to be reinforced by particular successes from which the addict may be encouraged to generalize. However, most drug users have a long history of failed attempts at cessation. Furthermore, they are unlikely to succeed in any present attempt without at least an occasional lapse. A central issue therefore remains one of encouraging interpretations of such outcomes that are not so irredeemably negative that confidence is completely undermined. To bolster such confidence, therefore, one needs to encourage generalization from instances of success (while still stressing the importance of vigilance to the specific cues likely to precipitate drug use in particular situations). At the same time one needs to discourage generalization from instances of past or present failure, and to stress that a lapse in one context need not lead automatically to a general relapse – that 'one drink' need not amount to 'one drunk'.

The benefits of bolstering confidence in this way should not be confused with the question of whether controlled or moderate drinking (or other drug use) is a legitimate treatment goal. Despite all the moralistic posturing, in the end it is an empirical question whether moderate consumption is more easily attainable than total abstinence, by whom, and for which substances. I am not necessarily suggesting abandoning abstinence as an eventual goal (at least for some people and some substances). Rather, I am expressing support for more step-by-step approaches, which involve training the client to resist specific cues and temptations in turn. A corollary of such approaches has to be a tolerant, or at least understanding, attitude towards *some* lapses in *some* contexts. It must be accepted that some straying from the straight and narrow is more or less typical of the period between treatment and complete recovery. Indeed, the very use of the term 'treatment' can be misleading if taken to imply that the process of behavioural change, of unlearning and relearning, is complete as soon as the former addict leaves the clinic to face the outside world. One of the weakest parts of the 'extinction' approach (Hunt and Matarazzo 1973) is the notion that relapse depends on the *forgetting* of what has been previously learned (in the clinic), rather than on the incompleteness of the retraining that clinical treatment is likely to involve.

It may be asked how desired behavioural change can be facilitated or reinforced by a change in attitudes. A person's motivation to give up drugs will be influenced by his or her attitudes, but the nature of this influence may be more complex than is often assumed. Many writers have commented on addicts' ambivalent attitudes towards using or giving up drugs. While few addicts completely deny the more obvious costs and dangers of their habit, they also perceive compensatory benefits. Whether drug use is considered as an example of attitude-behaviour discrepancy or of attitude-behaviour consistency depends, therefore, on the relative salience to the individual of such costs and benefits. From this it might seem to follow that the addict's motivation to give up drugs could be increased by persuasive interventions designed to increase the subjective importance of such costs and decrease the subjective importance of such benefits. This, of course, is what has been attempted over and over again. It is the standard fare of media campaigns on all health-related issues. Maybe such campaigns can sometimes help to deter some young people from taking up such habits – maybe. As a means of persuading established users of drugs to give up or reduce their consumption, they must at best be regarded as poor value for money; they may even be counterproductive. But why is this so? Aren't we all motivated to behave consistently with our attitudes?

The answer to the last question is – no, not necessarily. On the one hand, it is almost always possible to find *some* attitude that can bolster resistance to demands for behaviour change. On the other hand, and even more crucially, the very motivation to act consistently with one's attitudes is *socially acquired*. Attitude–behaviour consistency is not an innate, invariant fixed action pattern, but the product of learning. As such it will be acquired patchily and to different extents by different individuals in different contexts. Although there are often social demands for attitude–behaviour consistency, the skill to resist such demands is also socially acquired. Arguably, addicts are experts at such resistance. At any rate, they have had more than their share of being told that they should not be doing what they are doing and that they are acting in ways that will produce bad consequences. However, any 'dissonance' produced by such warnings and demands can be resolved by a denial of free choice. Such self-attribution of addiction (Eiser 1982) not only undermines confidence in one's ability, and hence one's motivation, to give up drugs. It also negates the relevance of the messages about dire consequences that are intended to heighten such motivation. More generally, though, the very repetitiveness of such messages means that drug users are likely to become thoroughly habituated to most of the anxiety that the messages would otherwise be expected to produce. When this is combined with the repetitiveness of the drug use itself (with its concomitant short-term rewards), we are left with an ideal schedule for extinction of attention to warnings of long-term costs as well as to the implied threats of social disapproval if such warnings are not heeded.

'Persuading' drug users to give up drugs is never going to be easy, therefore. The first problem is not the scarcity of good arguments on which any attempt at persuasion can be based, but their familiarity. The second problem is that a change in attitude may not be enough to produce a change in behaviour, especially where people are so well practised at behaving in ways that are inconsistent with the attitudes in question. Overcoming the first problem requires creativity, style, and a sensitivity to the concerns of the individuals one is hoping to persuade. Overcoming the second problem requires a more direct application of psychological theory. Berating drug users for the inconsistency between their attitudes and behaviour is like flogging the proverbial dead horse. It also conveys the counter-productive message 'You do things you know you oughtn't' (from which it is a small step to 'Telling you that you oughtn't do these things won't make any difference'). To get out of this trap, drug users must be retrained to believe that they *can* act (at least some of the time) in ways that are consistent with their attitudes. If such consistency can be seen as attainable, it may come to be seen also as more desirable, and as reinforcing if achieved. Again, this requires a step-by-step approach to the training and learning of specific behaviours in specific contexts.

Concluding remarks

The central point of my argument has been that one should not consider either addiction or relapse as global terms, but should look instead at specific patterns of excessive or moderate drug use and of abstinence and at the specific contexts in which such patterns occur. This emphasis on situation-specific learning is more optimistic in its implications than are the 'sudden death' measures and conceptions of relapse used in some previous research (e.g., Hunt and Matarazzo 1973). A lapse in one situation need not generalize to relapse in all situations.

There are, however, factors that can lead, more pessimistically, to such a generalization. Any lapse contains some risk of a reinstatement of an addictive cycle of negative consequences which the individual attempts to relieve by renewed drug use. Such negative consequences can involve metabolic changes and the reinstatement of conditioned responses, but they can also involve more social costs, for instance in terms of loss of self-esteem and the disruption of relationships at work and at home. In whatever terms one defines such a cycle, the challenge is that of finding ways of preventing the escalation from lapse to relapse. In so far as the main dangers lie in the environment to which the former addict will return on leaving the clinic, there is a need for social change and the provision of safer, drug-free environments in which healthier lifestyles can be reacquired. No one assumes that such social and environmental change be easily or quickly attained. In so far as a person's drug use is a response to general feelings of distress or inability to cope (Alexander and Hadaway 1982), there is a need to deal therapeutically with such emotions and not just with the specific behaviours to which they give rise. In so far as the problem lies with drug users' own pessimism regarding their ability to change their behaviour, the task of the therapist should be to identify *attainable* goals of restraint and abstinence in the context of specific situations. If people *will* generalize from one context to another when they think about their behaviour, then let them at least generalize from success rather than from failure.

References

Abramson, L.Y., Seligman, M.E.P., and Teasdale, J.D. (1978) 'Learned helplessness in humans: critique and reformulation', *Journal of Abnormal Psychology* 87: 49–74.

Ajzen, I. and Fishbein, M. (1977) 'Attitude–behavior relations: a theoretical analysis and a review of empirical research', *Psychological Bulletin* 84: 888–918.

Ajzen, I. and Fishbein, M. (1980) *Understanding Attitudes and Predicting Social Behavior*, Englewood Cliffs, NJ: Prentice-Hall.

Alexander, B.K. and Hadaway, P.F. (1982) 'Opiate addiction: the case for an adaptive orientation', *Psychological Bulletin* 92: 367–81.

Bandura, A. (1977) 'Self-efficacy: toward a unifying theory of behavioral change', *Psychological Review* 84: 191–215.

Bem, D.J. (1967) 'Self-perception: an alternative interpretation of cognitive dissonance phenomena', *Psychological Review* 74: 183–200.

Bentler, P.M. and Speckart, G. (1979) 'Models of attitude-behavior relations', *Psychological Review* 86: 452–64.

Billig, M. (1985) 'Prejudice, categorization and particularization: from a perceptual to a rhetorical approach', *European Journal of Social Psychology* 15: 79–103.

Billig, M. (1987) *Arguing and Thinking: A Rhetorical Approach to Social Psychology*, Cambridge: Cambridge University Press.

Budd, R.J. (1986) 'Predicting cigarette use: the need to incorporate measures of salience in the theory of reasoned action', *Journal of Applied Social Psychology* 16: 663–86.

Budd, R.J. (1987) 'Response bias and theory of reasoned action', *Social Cognition* 5: 95–107.

Eiser, J.R. (1982) 'Addiction as attribution: cognitive processes in giving up smoking', in J.R. Eiser (ed.) *Social Psychology and Behavioral Medicine*, Chichester: Wiley.

Eiser, J.R. (1985) 'Smoking: the social learning of an addiction', *Journal of Social and Clinical Psychology* 3: 446–57.

Eiser, J.R. (1986) *Social Psychology: Attitudes, Cognition and Social Behaviour*, Cambridge: Cambridge University Press.

Eiser, J.R. (1987) *The Expression of Attitude*, New York: Springer-Verlag.

Eiser, J.R. and Gossop, M.R. (1979) '"Hooked" and "sick": addicts' perceptions of their addiction', *Addictive Behaviors* 4: 185–91.

Eiser, J.R. and Sutton, S.R. (1977) 'Smoking as a subjectively rational choice', *Addictive Behaviors* 2: 129–34.

Eiser, J.R. and van der Pligt, J. (1986) 'Smoking cessation and smokers' perceptions of their addiction', *Journal of Social and Clinical Psychology* 4: 60–70.

Eiser, J.R., van der Pligt, J., Raw, M., and Sutton, S.R. (1985) 'Trying to stop smoking: effects of perceived addiction, attributions for failure and expectancy of success', *Journal of Behavioral Medicine* 8: 321–41.

Festinger, L. (1957) *A Theory of Cognitive Dissonance*, Evanston, Illinois: Row, Peterson.

Fishbein, M. (1982) 'Social psychological analysis of smoking behavior', in J.R. Eiser (ed.) *Social Psychology and Behavioral Medicine*, Chichester: Wiley.

Fishbein, M. and Ajzen, I. (1975) *Belief, Attitude, Intention and Behavior: An Introduction to Theory and Research*, Reading, Mass.: Addison-Wesley.

Heider, F. (1946) 'Attitudes and cognitive organization', *Journal of Psychology* 21: 107–12.

Hunt, W.A., Barnett, L.W., and Branch, L.G. (1971) 'Relapse rates in addiction programs', *Journal of Clinical Psychology* 27: 455–6.

Hunt, W.A. and Matarazzo, J.D. (1970) 'Habit mechanisms in smoking', in W.A. Hunt (ed.) *Learning Mechanisms in Smoking*, Chicago: Aldine.

Hunt, W.A. and Matarazzo, J.D. (1973) 'Three years later: recent developments in the experimental modification of smoking behavior', *Journal of Abnormal Psychology* 81: 107–14.

Leventhal, H. (1980) 'Toward a comprehensive theory of emotion', in L. Berkowitz (ed.) *Advances in Experimental Social Psychology Vol. 13*, New York: Academic Press.

Leventhal, H. (1984) 'A perceptual-motor theory of emotion', in L. Berkowitz (ed.) *Advances in Experimental Social Psychology Vol. 17*, New York: Academic Press.

Litman, G.K., Eiser, J.R., Rawson, N.S.B., and Oppenheim, A.N. (1979) 'Differences in relapse precipitants and coping behaviour between alcohol relapsers and survivors', *Behavior Research and Therapy* 17: 89–94.

Litman, G.K., Eiser, J.R., and Taylor, C. (1979) 'Dependence, relapse and extinction: a theoretical critique and a behavioral examination', *Journal of Clinical Psychology* 35: 192–9.

McAuliffe, W.E. and Gordon, R.A. (1974) 'A test of Lindesmith's theory of addiction: the frequency of euphoria among long-term addicts', *American Journal of Sociology* 79: 795–840.

McAuliffe, W.E. and Gordon, R.A. (1980) 'Reinforcement and the combination of effects: summary of a theory of opiate addiction', in D.J. Lettieri, M. Sayers, and H.W. Pearson (eds) *Theories on Drug Abuse*, National Institute on Drug Abuse Research Monograph 30, Washington, DC: US Government Printing Office.

McKennell, A.C. and Thomas, R.K. (1967) *Adults' and Adolescents' Smoking Habits and Attitudes*, Government Social Survey SS353/B, London: HMSO.

Marsh, A. (1984) 'Smoking: habit or choice', *Population Trends* (HMSO) 36: 14–20.

Mausner, B. and Platt, E.S. (1971) *Smoking: a Behavioral Analysis*, New York: Pergamon.

Reisenzein, R. (1983) 'The Schachter theory of emotion: two decades later', *Psychological Bulletin* 94: 239–64.

Robins, L.N., Davis, D.H., and Goodwin, D.W. (1974) 'Drug use by U.S. Army enlisted men in Vietnam: a follow-up on their return home', *American Journal of Epidemiology* 99: 235–49.

Rosenberg, M.J. and Hovland, C.I. (1960) 'Cognitive, affective and behavioral components of attitudes', in C.I. Hovland and M.J. Rosenberg (eds) *Attitude Organization and Change: An Analysis of Consistency among Attitude Components*, New Haven, Connecticut: Yale University Press.

Schachter, S. and Singer, J.E. (1962) 'Cognitive, social and physiological determinants of emotional state', *Psychological Review* 69: 379–99.

Sidman, M. (1952) 'A note on functional relations obtained from group data', *Psychological Bulletin* 49: 263–9.

Siegel, S. (1977) 'Morphine tolerance acquisition as an associative process',

Journal of Experimental Psychology: Animal Behavior Processes 3: 1–13.
Solomon, R.L. (1980), 'The opponent-process theory of acquired motivation: the cost of pleasure and the benefits of pain', *American Psychologist* 35: 691–712.
Sutton, S.R. (1979) 'Interpreting relapse curves', *Journal of Consulting and Clinical Psychology* 47: 96–8.
Tarpy, R.M. (1982) *Principles of Animal Learning and Motivation*, Glenview, Illinois: Scott, Foresman.
Teasdale, J.D. (1973) 'Conditioned abstinence in narcotic addicts', *International Journal of the Addictions* 8: 273–92.
Thurstone, L.L. (1928) 'Attitudes can be measured', *American Journal of Sociology* 33: 529–54.
van der Pligt, J. and Eiser, J.R. (1984) 'Dimensional salience, judgement and attitudes', in J.R. Eiser (ed.) *Attitudinal Judgment*, New York: Springer-Verlag.
Weiner, B. (1985) 'An attributional of achievement motivation and emotion', *Psychological Review* 92: 548–73.

Chapter Twelve

The end of optimism: the prehistory of relapse

Virginia Berridge

Introduction

The concept of relapse and of its prevention has been an area of growth in alcohol and drug research in recent years. Various relapse inventories have been identified and factors singled out which may contribute to relapse – or to survival. Relapse is now a flourishing area of academic and practical discussion (Marlatt and Gordon 1985). In the welter of controversy and the development and evaluation of different strategies, there is an urge to look forward to future developments and progress. But this paper will do the opposite. It intends to look backwards at the historical aspects of treatment and relapse, not as an exercise in nostalgia, or a search for presumed antecedents, or even a prehistory for contemporary controversies. Rather, it will seek to analyse the way in which medical treatment was first established as an appropriate way of responding to both working- and middle-class alcohol and drug use. Despite the pessimism of the hereditary theories which underpinned the process of medicalization, the notion of treatment was initially optimistic about the possibility of cure. But the focus of treatment ideology and practice later changed. The focus on the process of committal and optimism about treatment gave way to greater therapeutic pessimism and to an emphasis on the psychology of addiction. The concept of relapse emerged as part of this new medico-psychological paradigm. Treatment was extended to include relapse.

We might see these developments as examples of progress, with the first tentative understandings of the last century leading inexorably to the presumed greater sophistication of the present. But there are more fundamental issues involved. Ideas about inebriety treatment and relapse, and the ways in which these ideas were expressed, were determined by, and the expression of, the social values and professional goals of inebriety specialists. Treatment and relapse did not operate independently of the social context of the late nineteenth and early twentieth centuries. The following paper will aim to untangle the interactions which structured the emergence of those concepts.

Before treatment

Treatment has not always been an essential part of the reaction to excessive and dangerous use of alcohol and drugs. Around the middle of the nineteenth century the concept of a condition necessitating active intervention of a medical sort was not firmly established. Certainly the bare bones of a theory of disease existed, for alcohol at least. Thomas Trotter's 1804 *Essay on Drunkenness* and, in America, Benjamin Rush's earlier (1797) *Inquiry into the Effects of Spirituous Liquors upon the Human Body* have long been seen as establishing the ground rules for a medical theory of alcoholism. However, as Roy Porter has recently pointed out, such theories were not new in the nineteenth century and there were eighteenth-century antecedents in plenty; what was new was a configuration of social and political forces which gave them importance (Porter 1985). It was likewise for drugs. Although concepts such as tolerance and withdrawal in relation to the use of opium were commonly used by eighteenth-century medical writers, it was only in the late nineteenth century that a fully-fledged medical theory of disease was established (Berridge and Edwards 1987). Treatment for these conditions was another matter. The idea that excessive opium was a bad habit rather than a disease meant that treatment of the condition was not considered essential. The nineteenth-century medical journals contained many an opium-eating case history where the idea of treatment figured little. The doctor was called in to treat disturbing symptoms, not to rid the opium eater of the condition itself. Decisions on the type of medical intervention which was to be made were often the responsibility of the patient and family, rather than the doctor. The question of treatment for an opium overdose – a common occurrence when the drug was available over the counter and frequently of uncertain strength because of adulteration – was far more prominent. Most medical texts had a section on opium poisoning and its treatment. The first standard discussions of treatment often developed out of these sections as they divided in the late nineteenth century into acute and chronic poisoning by opium, chronic poisoning being addiction and its treatment.

For alcohol, the question of treatment was complicated by the existence of the temperance movement. As Brian Harrison has noted, scientific work defining the separate condition of alcoholism tended to take place on the Continent in the nineteenth century rather than in England because of the prominence of temperance as a public issue (Harrison 1971). The prominence of temperance, too, meant that treatment (although not defined as such) was initially based on that movement. The sobriety of the reformed drunkard was reinforced by creating a new framework of life which involved keeping the drunkard out of the pub and providing a range of suitable alternative pursuits – temperance coffee houses, cafés, reading rooms – to keep him away from drink. The possibility of individual back-sliding was ever present and could be prevented by the exertion of individual will-power, reinforced by measures such as the taking of the pledge and the provision of an alternative social life within the temperance movement. The stress on complete abstinence as the aim of treatment reflected the shift from the earlier elite form of the movement to a more popular organization with strong artisan support. The temperance approach to treatment was both a moral and an environmental one, based on a self-helping voluntary approach.

Formal treatment and professional aspirations 1870s–1890s

Treatment in its later medical sense, ideas of cure and of relapse were clearly anachronisms in the temperance movement, where reform and the pledge were paramount. Relapse was a question of moral backsliding rather than a defined process or condition. In the last quarter of the century in England, this situation began to change. A more formal, medically defined ideology of treatment emerged, based on institutional care and with strong parallels with contemporary ideas about the treatment of insanity. The break between 'temperance therapeutics' and medical institutional treatment was not a clear-cut one; and the professionalization of treatment owed much in terms of ideology and of personnel to its temperance forebears. It was around mid-century that demands for a more formal system of control (and treatment) for inebriates was first made. Dr Alexander Peddie of Edinburgh read a paper to the Edinburgh Medico-Chirurgical Society on 'The necessity of some legalised arrangements for the treatment of Dipsomania or the Drinking Insanity' (Peddie 1886). The Scottish Lunacy Commission in its report of 1857 recommended that the government should devise special regulations for control over insanity arising from intemperance. The proposal came to nothing because of the difficulties of including it in a Lunacy Bill. But it led to a considerable amount of discussion of the need for legislation and possible institutionalization in which the medical profession was increasingly prominent. In 1870, additional interest was aroused by the formation of the

American Association for the Cure of Inebriety (Blumberg 1978; Brown 1986). Dr Donald Dalrymple, MP for Bath, organized public meetings, deputations to Parliament, introduced a resolution and then a bill in the Commons. In 1872 the Select Committee on Habitual Drunkards brought the issue of inebriate institutions as a form of treatment to the fore. Dalrymple himself died in 1875, but the Society for Promoting Legislation for the Control and Cure of Habitual Drunkards took up the cause from 1876. In 1879, an Habitual Drunkards Act was passed. It was not one based on the Dalrymple Bills or the report of the 1872 Select Committee. It was shorn of their compulsory clauses and of their intended application to the labouring, pauper, and criminal classes. In practice, institutional care was limited to the voluntary facilities provided by the Homes for Inebriates Association and government-inspected by Home Office inspectors under the Acts (another was passed in 1888) (MacLeod 1967). There were fourteen such homes by 1898. The Dalrymple Home at Rickmansworth, founded in 1884 after a public meeting at the Mansion House in 1882 had set up the Association of the Dalrymple Homes for Inebriates (later the Homes for Inebriates Association), was the most important.

The Homes for Inebriates Association and the Dalrymple Home marked a half-way stage in the move towards defined professional concepts of treatment and cure. The intellectual underpinning for medical treatment was provided by theories of disease. In Britain, these developed most notably through the Society for the Study and Cure of Inebriety, also founded in 1884. The Society, composed of medical members and lay associates, from the start promoted a strongly physical concept of disease. Norman Kerr, President of the Society, speaking at the Society's inaugural meeting in 1884, expressed it thus:

> I have not attempted to dogmatize on disputed points as to whether inebriety is a sin, a vice, a crime, or a disease. In my humble judgement, it is sometimes all four, but oftener a disease than anything else, and even when anything else, generally a disease as well . . . the drinker who is either driven by an ungovernable impulse, or is pursued by a constant desire to fly to intoxicating liquors, is in a disease state; in all indulgence in intoxicants there is a physical influence in operation, a physiological neurotic effect, the tendency of which is to create an appetite for more of the intoxicating agent.
>
> (Kerr 1884)

Disease was seen as based, not in the mind, but in the brain and the nervous system. Such theories retained a strong moral element, expressed most clearly in the concept of 'disease of the will'. But physiological theories of mental functioning, the belief that inebriety, like other mental diseases, had its source in localized brain lesions, and that both mental and moral characteristics resulted from physical defects in the nervous system, helped the inebriety specialists bridge the gap between mental and moral approaches. Kerr expressed this approach in a Presidential address in 1887.

> Whether inherited or acquired, this want of tone in the brain and nerve centres, with its accompanying defective inhibitory power, is usually preceded by a neurasthenic condition or state of nervous exhaustion. This is a well-marked pathological lesion which can in most cases be recognised by the skilled and intelligent physician. In this inchoate stage of the disease, there is a real departure from health, a truly diseased condition of the higher, if not the lower, nerve centres. Inebriety, once developed, pursues its course influenced by environment, by meteorological and climatic conditions, and by other modifying forces which affect the nervous fluids.
>
> (Kerr 1887)

The overriding tendency in the Society and among medical inebriety specialists in these early years was belief in a hereditary aetiology. Degeneration, as Samuel Shortt has noted, was the 'dominant etiological notion of late nineteenth-century somatic psychiatry' (Shortt 1986). This marked a change from the first half of the century. Psychological causes were then considered more important, although still resulting in discernible changes in brain structure. This emphasis had changed by the time that inebriety specialists were forming ideas about disease and treatment. The concept of hereditary degeneration was associated in particular with mid-nineteenth-century French psychiatrists. In the thought of the most widely known of these, Benedict Morel, there was an emphasis on Lamarckian transmission of acquired characteristics and a belief that inherited diseases could change to different forms in later generations (Bynum 1968, 1984). Ideas of hereditary degeneration were widespread, as for instance in Krafft-Ebing's work on sexual pathology, Lombroso on criminality, and Havelock Ellis on homosexuality. For psychiatry, Henry Maudsley was the principal exponent of hereditary views, expressed in his *Physiology and Pathology of Mind* (1867) and *Responsibility in Mental Disease* (1874). The degenerationist school of thought also dominated views of inebriety, in various forms, until the First World War. Dr George Harley, speaking in a discussion at a Society for the Study of Inebriety meeting in 1884, considered that:

> Hereditary insanity is due to the transmission from parent to child – not of abnormal thoughts, but of the morbid brain tissue itself in which the thoughts originate. In like manner, the drunkard does not transmit to his offspring the craving for alcohol, but the abnormal organic bodily tissue which gives rise to the craving.
>
> (Harley 1884)

The application of degeneration theory to drunkenness provided an optimistic epistemology whereby science and medicine justified a claim to authority in a field which, like insanity, encompassed both natural and social causation. The newly defined specialism of inebriety and the specialists involved closely allied themselves with contemporary views about the causation of insanity. Like Victorian alienists, their primary focus in the 1870s and 1880s was on the custodial treatment of the poor, in this case the drunken poor. Like alienists, the inebriety specialists hoped to find social and professional authority through theories of individual pathology which implicitly justified the class relationships of the time.

Despite their pessimism about aetiology, the inebriety specialists retained (at least in the early years of the Society for the Study of Inebriety) an optimistic outlook. Their activities were dominated by a belief in the role of the state in securing an adequate institutional structure for treatment and for the conditions within treatment which were most likely to lead to cure. For much of the period before the First World War then, in particular from the 1870s to the 1900s, inebriety specialists pressed for forms of state funding and inspection of a range of inebriates' homes and inebriates' reformatories. Within these institutions, they sought legal compulsory treatment. Because of this concentration, there was little acknowledgement of any medical concept of relapse. The focus was on establishing inebriety as a disease and on the process of committal for treatment of the large number of drunkards who currently went to prison. The necessary optimism about the possibilities of medical custodial treatment denied any notion of a medical concept of relapse. The aims of the medical campaign for the Inebriates Acts were broad, but the legislative and practical success they achieved was limited. Although the aims focused on the working-class drinker, there was also a concern for the custodial treatment of middle-class drunkards. The distinction established between criminal and non-criminal inebriates in proposed and actual legislation mirrored the difference in approach. The story of these acts is well known. (MacLeod 1967). The permissive and temporary legislation of the Habitual Drunkards Act of 1879 was made permanent (after pressure from the Society for the Study of Inebriety and British Medical Association) by the Inebriates Act of 1888. But the government-licensed and inspected retreats established were accessible only to those who could afford private care and not to the poor. It was not until ten years later, with the passing of the 1898 Inebriates Act, that some provision for the pauper drunkard was possible. Limited powers were established to commit criminal habitual drunkards to a system of reformatories. Non-criminal inebriates were dealt with separately through the system of retreats. But the establishment of reformatories was left as a matter for the local authorities. Continuing battles with the Home Office about the financing of reformatories and the indifference of magistrates, who saw drunkards as criminals first and medicalized inebriates a very poor second, ensured that few such reformatories were established, catering only for a very small minority of the large population of excessive drinkers. Only twelve certified reformatories were built, dealing with only 4,590 inmates in total over roughly a twenty-year period. This compares with prison committal rates of 250,000 a year for drunkenness during the same period (Radzinowicz and Hood 1986). The institutional treatment system never developed into a viable counterpart to the system of state lunatic asylums. Although further amending bills were regularly introduced every year in the early years of the twentieth century, none passed into law. When a bill was planned in 1914, the outbreak of war prevented action; the First World War really marked the end of the use of the Inebriates Acts as a state-funded and licensed treatment system (Baumohl and Room 1987).

The issue on which most of these efforts foundered (leaving finance aside) was that of compulsion. The temperance and medical reformers had as a primary aim, at least since the time of Donald Dalrymple in the 1870s, the compulsory detention of voluntary patients and of criminal drunkards for a period long enough to cure. This objective was never fully realized even for the latter, and certainly not for the former. Yet there was an unwavering concentration on it over a forty-year period, accompanied by a necessary optimism about the possibilities of cure were compulsion to be achieved. On 19 September 1885, a special train from Euston carried a mixed group of medical men, clergymen, abstainers, and prohibitionists to the Dalrymple House for a reception for Dr Joseph Parrish, President of the American Association for the Cure of Inebriety. The resolution passed at this gathering demonstrated the admiration for American example: the US had established a state-financed system of treatment. It also underlined the desirability both of compulsion and of medical treatment:

> this meeting rejoices at the fair amount of success which has followed the treatment of inebriety as a disease; and trusts that this visit of Dr. Parrish will aid in the removal of all the existing impediments to the simple and prompt admission of voluntary patients in England under the compulsory detention provisions of the Habitual Drunkards Act, and will stimulate a popular demand for permanent legislation, and for more effectual legislative measures for powers of committal in certain cases of confirmed inebriety.
>
> (Proceedings 1885)

The meeting, while welcoming temperance action, placed its faith in 'enlightened medical treatment . . . a united and sustained attempt at the rescue, reformation and cure of the pitiful victims of alcoholic indulgence'. In the early 1900s, the Society was still calling for compulsory control. The theme of compulsion had an enduring tendency; it was to arise again in doctors' discussion of the treatment of drug addiction in the late 1930s and was one of the recommendations of the Second Brain Committee in 1965. In the late nineteenth century it derived from the temperance and prohibitionist antecedents of much of the medical ideology of the inebriety specialist, and was at one with their stress on total abstinence as the goal of treatment. It was also at one with the contemporary treatment of insanity. The focus on inebriety as a physical form of disease also meant that doctors were advocating the forms of control established in the public health sphere at this time for infectious diseases. The Compulsory Notification of Infectious Disease Act of 1889 established such procedures and isolation hospitals for smallpox, diphtheria, scarlet fever and typhoid (Wohl 1983). Although notification was not adopted in Britain (in the case of drugs) until the late 1960s, the analogy of infectious disease and quarantine ensured the continuance of the idea of compulsion.

The desire to achieve a state-funded institutional system of treatment and compulsory detention for a long period within it necessarily meant that the idea of failure rarely entered centrally into discussions of inebriety, in particular in the 1880s. Surgeon-Major G.K. Poole, talking to the Society for the Study of Inebriety in 1888 on the subject of 'Is Inebriety Curable?', urged the collection of statistics to prove the point that inebriety was indeed curable. The popular idea was that there was no cure – but the few statistics for inebriates' homes available showed, according to Poole, that the greater number of cases were curable when taken in hand at an early stage. His view was 'that only such cases are cured as are under a prolonged system of careful supervision and treatment' and 'that cases are only complete that are treated on sound scientific principles based upon religious influences' (Poole 1888). Arguments of this type, necessarily focused on the origins of disease, on committal and cure, meant that there was little discussion of failure and of relapse. The optimism about medical cure meant that no medical notion of relapse was developed at this stage. The professional interests of inebriety specialists were adequately satisfied in the 1880s by demonstrations of the nature of disease and by legislative action. There was little consideration of what lay beyond these initial stages. Where relapse was discussed, it was still in the language of moral failing, as a continuation of the temperance interests earlier in the century. In a discussion on the need for inebriates' homes in 1887, Mr John Hilton claimed:

> In his own experience it was comparatively easy to reclaim a drunkard. The difficulty was to keep the reclaimed inebriate firm. He had often found restored inebriates go on for a long time, and then suddenly break down . . . . One told him he was walking on the street, when a sudden overpowering desire to take a glass of strong drink came over him. He tried to repress it, but failed. The old want of drink persisted, and he had to run down the street as hard as he could, get home, and lock himself in his bedroom, where he spent some time praying and agonising before this fierce craving ceased.
>
> (Trevor 1887)

The assurance conveyed by degeneration theory and optimism about the possibilities of compulsory confinement ensured that relapse was at this stage still a question of morality rather than part of the medical concept of inebriety.

The nature of treatment 1870s–1890s

The way in which treatment actually operated underlines the initial emphasis on committal and cure. Once the inebriate was confined, there appears to have been little actual treatment at all. Shortt has commented that 'In most Anglo-American asylums incarceration became an exercise in environmental management rather than active treatment' (Shortt 1986). This certainly seems to have been the case in the inebriates' homes and retreats established under the Acts of 1879 and 1888. Although the notion of disease was essentially a physiological one, the means employed to bring about the treatment goal of total abstinence were largely moral. The inebriety specialists claimed to be pioneers in a paradigm shift away from a moral view of drunkenness, but the treatment which they advocated was almost entirely directed at the restoration of general health and the bolstering of the will. Dr E.J. Gray, superintendent of Old Park Hall Retreat in Walsall, Staffordshire, gave a good résumé of this combination of passive therapeutics and moral treatment in 1888. Gray took in two classes of inebriate, the second-class patients having 'to render services about the grounds morning and afternoon, or in the workshop'. The general restoration of bodily health was attained by activities such as a weekly cricket match, gardening, and mowing the lawns. The rest of the treatment regime combined an attention to physical and moral well-being.

> We begin the day with prayers read from the Book of Common Prayer, and finish the day with prayers. Breakfast at nine o'clock, which consists of porridge (to which I attach a great importance), bacon and dried fish, varied with eggs, sausages, bread, butter, jam and marmalade. Luncheon at 1.30 – soup, pastry and cheese. Dinner at six –soup or fish, a joint varied with rabbit, poultry, etc., pudding and cheese. Tea at 8.30 – tea, bread and butter. I allow each patient two ounces of tobacco a week. The evenings are generally spent at a game of whist or billiards with occasional evenings of music and singing with the family. Daily papers. Patients are allowed an order for Church on Sunday mornings, and in the evenings in the Summer, but not in winter evenings unless with some part of the family. The great difficulty is to get them to take sufficient manual exercise, having got into lazy, irregular and indolent habits, it naturally is hard for them to commence the active life, those who do, make very fast progress.
>
> I try to impress upon them the necessity of looking to Him who is the author and giver of all good things for help, to try to walk side by side with Him.
>
> (Gray 1888)

The combination of food, work, and religion sought to put the inebriate's physical system and his (or her) moral sense on the best possible basis, replacing external restraint by internalized self-control based on acceptable moral and social values.

Absent from most of these discussions, based as they were on the idea of detention (eventually to be compulsory) for periods of twelve months to two years, was any factual information that this type of control had definite advantages. Few follow-up records were kept and there was generally little concept of the need for after-care. Statistics from the Dalrymple Home were regularly published in the *Proceedings* of the Society for the Study of Inebriety from 1886, and these appeared to show a 'cure' rate of 33 per cent. This figure was generally accepted in discussions of the validity of treatment. Yet it seems to have been based on shaky foundations. A two-page summary of 115 cases treated in the Dalrymple Home since its opening devoted only six lines to 'After History' (Dalrymple Home 1888). The tally was as follows:

Doing well	52
Improved	4
Not improved	36
Insane	1
Dead	4
Not heard from	18
	115

There was no criteria for the category of 'doing well', yet the optimism about cure continued. 'Gather these men into hospitals and asylums,' said Dr Thomas Crothers, superintendent of the Walnut Lodge asylum in the US in 1886, 'over thirty per cent of them can be permanently cured. The remainder can be made self-sustaining' (Crothers 1886). Norman Kerr thought that this cure rate could be vastly improved upon given compulsion and earlier treatment (Kesteven 1896). It was not until the late 1890s that any question of after-care was even considered. R.W. Branthwaite, then medical superintendent at the Dalrymple Home, noted that treatment should be divided into two parts – management of the acute condition and subsequent treatment (Branthwaite 1898).

Psychological theory, treatment and relapse 1890s–1920s

This greater consciousness of the need for after-care was part of the development of ideas about treatment – and about the possibility of relapse – in the period prior to the First World War. The notions of compulsory institutional treatment, in particular of the working-class drunkard, were not dropped, but they became less central to the concerns of inebriety specialists. Changes in the treatment and concept of inebriety were again congruent with shifts in the conceptualization and treatment of insanity. For the latter, the doctrine of institutionalization had brought with it unwelcome professional consequences, not least the marginalization of alienists within the Victorian medical profession. In the early twentieth century, theories about the aetiology of insanity and ideas about its treatment were moving in a number of directions in order to escape the narrow confines of institutional treatment. The theory and practice of inebriety treatment followed in some of these. Two tendencies were particularly noticeable. The question of working-class drunkenness became bound up in discussions of the threat of the feeble-minded in the wake of the revelations of physical unfitness during the Boer War and of the Inter-Departmental Committee on Physical Deterioration of 1904. From this came an emphasis on prevention of alcohol consumption, as part of the mental hygiene movement. It was the development of theories applicable to middle-class drinking which was particularly pertinent to the medicalization of relapse. There was a move away from the early, narrowly physicalist concept of disease towards an incorporation of a notion of the dynamic unconscious, based on Freudian theory. This change in theory had the social function of reaching out to a new middle-class clientele beyond the confines of an institution or an inebriate asylum, and was to develop more fully in the 1920s and 1930s. It had a notable effect on treatment methods and on the earlier optimism about cure.

For working-class drunkards, the main outlines of the argument were clear. Alcohol was centrally important to concerns about the future of the race. The clearest statement of this tenet came in the Report of the Inter-Departmental Committee on Physical Deterioration in 1904. 'The Committee,' it concluded, 'are convinced that the abuse of alcoholic stimulants is a most potent and deadly agent of physical deterioration' (Inter-Departmental Committee 1904). This statement arose largely out of medical evidence to the committee, and in the early years of the twentieth century the full range of medical arguments about alcohol and the threat of racial degeneration emerged. The focus was on the individual failings of women as mothers (Gutzke 1984). Dr William Sullivan, speaking in 1900 on 'The Children of the Female Drunkard', stressed 'the important role which the alcoholism of women may play in racial deterioration' (Sullivan 1900). He compared death rates of the children of women in Liverpool Prison, where the death rates of children of inebriate mothers was two-and-a-half times that of the others (Sullivan did not emphasize the fact that even the sober mothers lost 25 per cent of their children before they were two). His conclusions for the future of the race were pessimistic – 'The socially unadapted classes of humanity – the criminal degenerate, the prostitute, the vagrant – are recruited in no inconsiderable proportion from the offspring of the alcoholic .' The question of race was considered to be important – the greater susceptibility to alcohol of native races as opposed to English or Scottish, for example, or the temperate habits of Jewish working-class mothers by comparison with their English counterparts. Particular attention was paid to the way in which mechanisms of transmission worked. The Lamarckian position of the inheritability of acquired (and environmentally based) characteristics came under attack from a biological direction. Selection, it was argued, could operate only on natural variations; these were due not to environmental influences, but to the innate developmental tendency of the fertilized ovum. The role of the mother was thus biologically central. Other arguments stressed the importance of alcohol in its effect on breast feeding and in the potential nutritional capabilities of breast milk.

The role of motherhood was central to concerns about the future of the race which fuelled much of the Edwardian liberal social legislation and underpinned the welfare liberalism of the pre-war years (Davin 1978; Lewis 1980; Dyhouse 1978). The debate on alcohol took place within this overall political and cultural environment, but the role envisaged in medical circles for the state in this area was slight, and rested largely on education of the individual. Prevention made its way on to the medical agenda for alcohol. Positive and negative eugenists differed in their reactions to state action, the latter opposing any state intervention in terms of wider compulsory education, free milk, school meals, as tending to interfere with the process of natural selection and further enfeeble the race. These debates found their echo in the alcohol field where some medical men took the line that families inheriting a tendency to drink would eventually be eliminated, while fitter families would survive. But even the intervention proposed by medical supporters of a more positive line was relatively slight. Education and preventive activity were seen as primary means of teaching working-class women and reducing drinking. In 1903–4 many doctors supported an appeal to the Department of Education to ensure instruction in 'scientific knowledge on temperance' in public elementary schools. In November 1904, a committee of the medical profession issued a circular suggesting that hygiene and temperance be entered in the official code of instruction (the time was to be found by giving less attention to geography and history). A handbook of such instruction was issued, but its use, while permitted, was never officially enforced (Claude Taylor 1905). The issue of temperance education posters under local authority auspices had likewise declined by the outbreak of war.

The desire for national efficiency and fear of racial decline thus saw prevention and health education enter into the sphere of medical interest in the treatment of working-class inebriety. There was also another strand in the development of ideas about treatment in these years which had its particular application to the middle-class inebriate. This was the beginnings of a move away from a strictly deterministic hereditary approach to disease towards an exploration of the subconscious. Its practical effect, realized most fully in the 1920s and 1930s, was to lead inebriety treatment out of an institutional context, towards a focus on shorter treatments and towards the use of treatments based on drugs. The focus of inebriety treatment expanded beyond a concern for the chronic, mostly working-class inebriate who could be compulsorily confined in state-funded institutions. It encompassed a middle-class clientele broader than the limited number of drinkers who had been willing voluntarily to enter inebriates' homes. Just as the psychiatric gaze was widening to encompass middle-class citizens in the community, so was that of inebriety specialists (or specialists in alcoholism, a term beginning to be used just before the First World War). Although the inebriety specialists continued to support an extension of the inebriety acts and the expansion of compulsory committal, increasingly this was part of a broader concept of treatment. As the *British Journal of Inebriety* put it in 1906,

> it is not the object of the Society to engage in a propaganda dealing with constructive or restrictive policies. It seeks, rather, the elucidation of the physiological, psychological and pathological conditions which form, as it were, the biological basis on the recognition of which all rational reform must depend.
>
> (Society for the Study of Inebriety 1906)

Treatment methods although still set within an overall institutional context and predicated on the idea of absolute withdrawal and total abstinence as a goal began gradually to change. The increased emphasis on psychological factors and the role of the unconscious meant that hypnotism appeared as a form of treatment. Drug treatments also appear to have become more common. The medical attitude to these was divided. Where the drug treatment was part of a commercial package, like the Keeley Cure, opposition was strong, and was part of the move against secret 'cures' and patent medicines of the early 1900s. But drug treatment in a medical context offered clear advantages to a medical profession faced with a middle-class clientele reluctant to enter institutions for lengthy periods. They offered to intending patients the advantages of a shorter period of detention and an apparently less onerous course of treatment. Dr Mary Gordon thought that four-week courses of drug-aided detoxification had some advantage:

> it is worth while to sober a patient, because he may never break down again. Many persons cannot leave their work for long treatment, and must get what they can. It is something if they are kept sober for a few months at a time. If only a few are improved, treatment is good.
>
> (Gordon 1906)

Specialists took care to emphasize that this new attitude to treatment did not simply involve medical purveying of drink or drugs – the patient was to be seen through and supported through a crisis by something other than his usual drink or drug. The sick role and the relationship between patient and doctor was crucial.

The role of drug addiction in the overall shift of theories of disease and in the forms of treatment offered was significant. The population of drug addicts who came to medical attention (largely through the use of medically prescribed hypodermic morphine) had always been preponderantly middle class (Berridge and Edwards 1987). The working-class opium eater or chlorodyne drinker had never figured so largely in medical disease concerns as had the working-class drunkard. Psychological theories had a greater appeal when applied to the middle-class morphinist; and drug treatment for this class and type of patient also appears to have had greater legitimacy. Francis Hare, medical superintendent of the Norwood Sanatorium, noted, in 1910, that the morphine habit was nearly always continuous, or chronic. This meant that withdrawal had to be gradual rather than sudden as in the case of paroxysmal drinking, or dipsomania. The morphine could be reduced very quickly at first, but morphine, he argued, differed from alcohol in that the smaller amounts of the drug were difficult to drop completely (Hare 1910). Here was medical justification for an extensive policy of maintenance prescribing of drugs for middle-class patients which gained official legitimacy in the Rolleston Report of 1926.

Implicit in both the preventive and treatment reactions, but in particular in the latter, was the end of optimism about the possibilities of treatment and the incorporation of the idea of relapse as a medical rather than a moral concept. J.W. Astley Cooper, superintendent of Ghyllwoods Sanatorium, in a paper read to the psycho-medical society at Liverpool in 1910, demonstrated the transmutation of the moral into the medical. One of the aims of treatment, as he saw it, was to 're-educate, or awaken, a weak or dormant self-control, self-respect and ambition.' But the language of morality was transmuted when he moved to a more specific discussion of treatment.

> The psychic treatment of inebriety should consist of the frequent suggestion of normal and reasonable ideas on the use of alcohol, the necessity for abstinence, and the reasons for such necessity during the whole course of treatment and afterwards, with the object of replacing with such normal and reasonable ideas the erroneous ideas and auto-suggestions already existing and impelling the patient, consciously or unconsciously, towards relapse.
>
> (Astley Cooper 1911)

The medicalization of relapse and its incorporation within the psychological model brought with it a greater emphasis on after-care and on the compilation of more effective treatment statistics indicating success of treatment in relation to other factors. On the eve of war, much of this was still rudimentary. Dr F.S.D. Hogg, medical superintendent of the Dalrymple Home in 1915, compiled statistics based on a group of over a thousand patients who had passed through the Home, relating characteristics such as age, marital status, and, interestingly, temperament to length and success of treatment. But Hogg's management of after-care and the prevention of relapse appears to have been based on three factors; the development of hobbies, no drinking at all, and an absolute ban on any reference by wives to a husband's past drinking habits (Hogg 1915). None the less, investigations of this type underlined the extension of the concept of treatment to incorporate the idea of relapse.

Conclusion

The medical concept of relapse emerged out of the end of therapeutic optimism. Late nineteenth-century psychiatry, as Samuel Shortt has noted, was possessed of few cures but a great deal of weighty theory. The inebriety specialists' initial focus on the goal of compulsory treatment, primarily for a working-class clientele, denied the possibility that treatment, even if compulsory, might not lead to cure. With few statistics and no after-care, there was no reason to doubt the efficacy of cure. Relapse remained a moral not a medical concept. But changes in the perceived role of inebriety specialists and in their professional goals, together with the social and class relationships in Edwardian Britain, brought a change of focus in the ideology of disease and treatment. Inebriety specialists, like psychiatrists, began to move away from the institutional context and towards a wider clientele in the community. The earlier focus on the origins of disease, on committal and cure broadened to encompass, for the working-class drinker, prevention, and for a middle-class clientele, after-care and relapse.

Acknowledgements: I am grateful to the Society for the Study of Addiction for financial support. My thanks are also due to Liz Dillon and Carol Dixon for secretarial assistance.

References

Astley Cooper, J.W. (1911) 'The treatment of alcohol inebriety by psychotherapy', *British Journal of Inebriety* 8: 135–42.

Baumohl, J. and Room, R. (1987) 'Inebriety, doctors and the state: alcoholism treatment institutions before 1940', in M. Galanter (ed.) *Recent Developments in Alcoholism, Vol. 5*, New York: Plenum, pp. 135–74.

Berridge, V. and Edwards, G. (1987) *Opium and the People: Opiate Use in Nineteenth Century England*, London: Yale University Press.

Blumberg, L. (1978) 'The American Association for the Study and Cure of Inebriety', *Alcoholism: Clinical and Experimental Research* 2: 235–40.

Branthwaite, R.W. (1898) 'Some clinical experiences in the treatment of inebriety', *Proceedings of the Society for the Study of Inebriety* 56: 1–14.

Brown, E. (1986) 'English interest in the treatment of alcoholism in the United States during the early 1870s', *British Journal of Addiction* 81: 545–51.

Bynum, W.F. (1968) 'Chronic alcoholism in the first half of the nineteenth century', *Bulletin of the History of Medicine* 42: 160–85.

Bynum, W.F. (1984) 'Alcoholism and degeneration in 19th century European medicine and psychiatry', *British Journal of Addiction* 79: 59–70.

Crothers, T.D. (1886) 'The sanitary relations of inebriety', *Proceedings of the Society of the Study and Cure of Inebriety* 9: 1–7.

Dalrymple Home (1888) 'Summary of the one hundred and fifteen cases discharged since the opening of the Dalrymple Home', *Proceedings of the Society for the Study of Inebriety* 16: 15–16.

Davin, A. (1978) 'Imperialism and motherhood', *History Workshop* 5: 9–65.

Dyhouse, C. (1978) 'Working class mothers and infant mortality in England, 1895–1914', *Journal of Social History* 12: 248–67.

Gordon, M. (1906) 'The drug treatment of inebriety', *British Journal of Inebriety* 4: 137–53.

Gray, F.J. (1888) 'The classes of inebriates and their treatment', *Proceedings of the Society for the Study of Inebriety* 18: 1–11.

Gutzke, D. (1984) 'The Cry of the Children: the Edwardian medical campaign against maternal drinking', *British Journal of Addiction* 79: 71–84.

Hare, F. (1910) 'The withdrawal of narcotics from habitués', *British Journal of Inebriety* 8: 86–90.

Harley, G. (1884) 'Discussion on Inebriety and Volition', *Proceedings of the Society for the Study and Cure of Inebriety* 1: 38.

Harrison, B. (1971) *Drink and the Victorians*, London: Faber.

Hogg, F.S.D. (1915) 'The after history and care of inebriates', *British Journal of Inebriety* 12: 195–203.

Inter-Departmental Committee (1904) *Report of the Inter-Departmental Committee on Physical Deterioration*.

Kerr, N. (1884) 'President's Inaugural Address', *Proceedings of the Society*

for the Study and Cure of Inebriety 1: 1–16.
Kerr, N. (1887) 'The pathology of inebriety', *Proceedings of the Society for the Study and Cure of Inebriety* 12: 1–12.
Kesteven, W.H. (1896) 'The method of dealing with habitual drunkards', *Proceedings of Society for Study of Inebriety* 47: 1–11 (contribution to discussion by Norman Kerr).
Lewis, J. (1980) *The Politics of Motherhood*, London: Croom Helm.
MacLeod, R. (1967) 'The edge of hope: social policy and chronic alcoholism, 1870–1900', *Journal of the History of Medicine and Allied Sciences* 22: 215–45.
Marlatt, G.A. and Gordon, J.R. (1985) *Relapse Prevention: Maintenance Strategies in the Treatment of Addictive Behaviors*, New York : Guilford Press.
Peddie, A. (1886) 'The Habitual Drunkards Act, 1879, inefficient and not adequate to accomplish the important objects desirable', *Proceedings of the Society for the Study and Cure of Inebriety* 7: 3–16.
Poole, G.K. (1888) 'Is inebriety curable?', *Proceedings of the Society for the Study of Inebriety* 17: 1–9.
Porter, R. (1985) 'The drinking man's disease: the "pre-history" of alcoholism in Georgian Britain', *British Journal of Addiction* 80: 385–96.
Proceedings of the Society for the Study and Cure of Inebriety (1885) 'Special train from Euston to Rickmansworth . . .' 6: 1.
Radzinowicz, L. and Hood (1986) *A History of English Criminal Law and its Administration from 1750, Vol. 5: The Emergence of Penal Policy*, London: Stevens & Sons.
Shortt, S.E.D. (1986) *Victorian Lunacy: Richard M. Bucke and the Practice of Late Nineteenth Century Psychiatry*, Cambridge: Cambridge University Press.
Society for the Study of Inebriety (1906) 'The Work of the Society for the Study of Inebriety', *British Journal of Inebriety* 3: 153–5.
Sullivan, W.C. (1900) 'The children of the female drunkard', *Proceedings of the Society for the Study of Inebriety* 63.
Taylor, E. Claude (1905) 'The teaching of temperance in elementary schools', *British Journal of Inebriety* 3: 36–9.
Trevor, T. (1887) 'The prevailing indifference to inebriety', *Proceedings of the Society for the Study and Cure of Inebriety* 11: 13.
Wohl, A. (1983) *Endangered Lives: Public Health in Victorian Britain*, London: Dent.

Chapter Thirteen

Relapse: a critique

Bill Saunders and Steven Allsop

Some opening remarks

The invitation to write this critique on 'relapse' was accepted with alacrity and pleasure. Here suddenly was an opportunity to speculate on a most interesting topic, to consider with some rigour the vexed issue of 'relapse' and to pose a few conundrums about 'why do clients do it?' Such an invitation also permitted the grinding of the odd axe and perhaps the venting of a little prejudice. Now, after the statutory library searches have been completed, some papers read, and arguments enjoyed, the difficulty of our task has been well and truly realized. We must at the beginning acknowledge that we have difficulty in even answering the basic question of where the subject of 'relapse' begins and ends.

This difficulty is perhaps best illustrated by reference to the work of two colleagues in the Addiction Research Unit in London. Their views on 'relapse' are interestingly disparate. The importance of investigating 'relapse' in relation to alcohol problems was originally stated by Gloria Litman, who beguilingly noted that if only 'relapse' could be prevented or minimized then our inadequate and relatively ineffective treatments would be improved. What we needed, she proposed, was not more alcoholism treatment but some 'relapse' prevention. She contended that our clinical focus was misdirected and was not addressed to the essential target – that of helping people not start up again once they had stopped (Litman *et al.* 1977; Litman 1980).

Recently however, Professor Edwards of the same Institute has commented that:

> The phrase 'relapse prevention' may usefully stimulate thought, break old moulds, get the adrenalin flowing, give the title to a book, but at the end of the day it can be an invitation to an artificial segmentation of the interacting, total and fluctuating process of change.
>
> (Edwards 1987: 319)

Should, therefore, emphasis of our clinical and research endeavours in the management of drug-use problems be on 'relapse'? Or does such a focus represent an 'artificial segmentation', a splitting-off of one aspect of behaviour change to the detriment of our total understanding? It is possible that the close scrutiny of 'relapse' may distract researchers, and the field in general, from a broader focus on the major issue – that of giving up or getting out of addiction behaviours. The study of 'relapse' is after all the investigation of those who only give up temporarily. Perhaps focusing on the 'succeeders', or those who make the break, would be more informative. In which case this very book should be concerned with giving up, not giving in.

A further comment from workers in the Addiction Research Unit also comes to mind. Writing about the outcome of people who ten years earlier had been treated for their alcohol-related problems, Taylor *et al.* noted: 'Rather than making simple comparisons of pre and post treatment states, looking for the often puny effects of treatment, the aim is instead to chart the larger, natural effects of ten years of life' (Taylor *et al.* 1986: 96).

Is the detailed investigation of 'relapse', and the subsequent development of individually tailored 'relapse' prevention and management strategies another exercise in teasing out 'puny effects', with the cost being that opportunities to examine the larger, more important factors of why people succeed or fail – those relating to everyday life – are ignored?

We are tempted to say yes, that clinical enthusiasm, and the need to boost our inadequate and ineffective treatments, may have overrun our latent appreciation that many people mend their ways without recourse to counselling and without any real appreciation of 'relapse' management and prevention strategies. There already exists a glossary of terms relating to 'relapse', of which outcome expectancies, self-efficacy, abstinence-violation effect, robust resolutions, cognitive vigilance, contemplation, reinstatement after abstinence, relapse proneness, and apparently irrelevant decisions are but a few. Is 'relapse' a separate issue with a need for different and distinct explanation, or is it part and parcel of everyday, ordinary human behaviour and thus understandable by us all?

A grapple with terminology

Before we attempt to put 'relapse' in what we believe is a proper context, it is necessary to step back and clarify a related issue. Already in this paper the term 'relapse' has been used eighteen times, without any attempt at definition, though on each occasion we have been careful to 'anoint' the word with inverted commas. Such an act is a marker of our dissatisfaction with the word, a dissatisfaction which has been well noted by others. For example, Grabowski has recently posted the following warning as to the inadequacy of the term.

> It connotes, coincident with its origins in a medical model, a dichotomous state. One 'has' the 'disease' of drug abuse or one does not. The conceptual error in it is evident in the phasing. One 'has' the disease or condition of diabetes, cholera, trisomy 21, or hepatitis, but one engages in the behaviour of drug abuse. Behavioural factors of drug abuse generate physiological consequences that a patient 'has' and they must be medically treated. However it is well documented that these treatments do not ameliorate the original behavioural disorder. Thus one can relapse to illness, but relapse to drug abuse is an inept articulation of the problem.
>
> (Grabowski 1986: 42)

Grabowski is posing a problem here – how to articulate more aptly the situation whereby an individual goes back to drug use after attempting to stop or curtail use. What is required is a more appropriate term, and one way to succeed in this labelling task is to describe precisely the phenomenon that we are trying to catch and tag with terminology. This does not at first sight appear to be a very difficult task. After all, we all know what 'relapses' are, since even very limited clinical experience brings one into contact with 'relapses' and 'relapsers'. Yet the difficulty is that as soon as one moves beyond simple description – of the starting up after stopping type – ideological boundaries are breached.

As noted above, 'relapse' belongs in a context and, in this analysis at least, its parent condition is addiction behaviour. How one construes addiction behaviour influences the terminology and definition of 'relapse'. Take for example the definition of 'relapse' that we have favoured. 'Relapse' is 'a change, either temporary or permanent in a resolution to change' (Saunders and Allsop 1987). This definition, while pithy, is prejudiced. Contained within the definition is the notion of individuals resolving to make changes, and then reconsidering their initial decision. Such a definition of relapse is unashamedly a cognitive-behavioural one, in which decision making is a central feature. Such a notion is at odds with the much cherished and well-established belief that addiction is a disease. One cannot choose to stop having measles, multiple sclerosis, or mumps. Even if addiction is not determined as being that type of disease, but rather a disease of the diabetes or syndrome kind, one still cannot decide the course of the condition.

Here then is the difficulty. As soon as one attempts to use a new term to encapsulate what was formerly known as 'relapse', one is crossing that old, but still very conflicted rubicon of disease vs. non-disease. Those of us in the non-disease camp, and this book is a product of that stable, should immediately and for ever reject the use of the word 'relapse', because it perpetuates disease model notions and rhetoric. Grabowski is correct. One cannot relapse to drug use. Changing one's mind is not a disease, nor a symptom of one, but a choice, even if on some occasions it is a choice that results in personal humiliation or harm. Re-experiencing the physiological consequences of a decision to resume drug use – such as a new bout of withdrawal symptoms – *may* be termed relapse since in the accepted medical sense relapse is the reinstatement of pre-treatment symptomatology. However, drug use itself is a behaviour undertaken by people who have choices and make them.

As Brandon *et al.* have noted of smokers' resumption of tobacco use, 'in nearly all cases subjects acquired their relapse cigarette through deliberate action . . . only 1.9 per cent of the subjects were offered the first cigarette smoked' (Brandon *et al.* 1986: 109). They continued to note that 'in the majority of cases relapse to regular smoking does not occur precipitously. In fact over half of all subjects waited more than 24 hours before having a second cigarette' (Brandon *et al.* 1986: 115).

Here then is the 'relapser' as a deliberate actor, a decision maker whose choices may at times be inconvenient, impulsive, inchoate, but a decision maker none the less. The word 'relapse' fails to do justice to this process. But what term should replace relapse?

Grabowski (1986) has favoured 'reinitiation' or 'reacquisition', and the current authors have toyed with the terms 'reversal' and 'reflection'. In the cycle of change model proposed by Prochaska and DiClemente (1983), in which people move through various stages of change, it is possible to propose that 're-cyclers' is an appropriate term. Unfortunately, all these terms suffer from the difficulty introduced by the use of the 're' prefix. By its use it is implied that individuals somehow go back to where they were, and then carry on in their problematic drug use as though nothing had happened. This is not true. People who attempt to make a break from drug use, or any other addiction behaviour, but who after succeeding for a while go back to their addiction behaviour are not the same as people who have made no such attempt. Giving up, even for a little time, gives indication of the user's dissatisfaction with their drug use, and is an acknowledgement of the desire for change, even if such dissatisfaction and desire are only temporary.

The outcome of returning to use is also indicative that changing an established behaviour is difficult. For some individuals the re-use of drugs, while not necessarily an optimum device, has been deemed preferable to the discomfort inherent in being abstinent. We would argue that a term like reversal, or reacquisition, does not do justice to the experience of attempting to give up and then resuming use of a drug.

A central issue here is whether attempting to give up and then going back to use is a step towards successful resolution of the problem, or is it a step toward perdition? Much of the traditional clinical literature is resonant with suggestion that all returns to use are inimical. The pall of irreversibility and decline hangs heavily over those found to have taken up again some of their old ways. But in the process of giving up it may well be that a failed attempt, or attempts, are forerunners to more successful initiatives. Our clinical experience is that very, very few individuals make the break at the first attempt.

This belief is well supported by research, especially that from the smoking arena. Lichtenstein and Weiss, in an analysis of people who had attempted to quit smoking as compared to non-attempters, noted that those who had made an attempt:

> show important increases in self-efficacy, decreases in temptation to smoke, and increases in the use of particular change processes such as helping relationships. Positive gains occur even though those individuals return to regular smoking. In traditional smoking-cessation treatment programmes, these individuals would be counted as failures, even though they were better prepared for future action after relapse than before attempting cessation.
>
> (Lichtenstein and Weiss 1986: 37)

Prochaska and DiClemente (1986) have suggested that on average three major attempts to give up nicotine addiction occur before non-smoking status is achieved. This is not to say that 'relapses' are inherently good for people. We all know individuals whose multiple attempts at stopping drug use and multiple failures have induced a sense of hopelessness, helplessness, and harmful apathy. But a 'relapse' can be used as a marker of progress so far achieved, be an indication of the value of different coping strategies, and highlight the need to monitor circumstances, mood, or motivation.

Unfortunately the word 'relapse' is indicative of a going backwards. In one thesaurus the word relapse is catalogued with such words as backsliding, degeneration, recrudescence, retrogression, recidivism, fall from grace, falling back, and a turn for the worse. These words do not suggest that a return to drug use may in fact be part of the pathway out of problematic drug use and may thus constitute a sign of progress rather than decline. After all, it is only people who have stopped and then resumed drug use who become labelled 'relapsers' – those who do not initiate change are merely problem drinkers, 'alcoholics', or 'drug addicts'. It seems unfair to doubly damn those who have made some break, with the terms 'relapsed alcoholic' or 'relapsed addict'.

What of course we should now do is unveil a word which captures the essential essence of the above considerations. The word needs to encompass a sense of movement, of deciding to change a troublesome behaviour, and of succeeding with this resolution for a while, but then being hailed back and re-adopting – either entirely or to some extent – the previous pattern of behaviour. A sense of some gain, of learning from the experience may or may not be present. Self-esteem may be increased or lowered, the coping skill repertoire extended or depleted, confidence enhanced or eroded. What word is to be used? We have deliberated and argued, thumbed thesauruses, consulted practitioners, students, colleagues, and friends. The improbable 'tergiversatizer' was suggested, as was 'reverser', 'resumer', 'processor', and the interesting 'apostalizer' – the individual who has renounced her/his vows. We toyed with 'reflecter' – at least it conjured up some image of contemplation, of looking back on one's experiences, but it also held notions of mirror-image and going backwards. In desperation 'spirallers', 'irresolutes', 're-contemplators', 'reprobates' (sorry!), and 'progressors' were considered, and quite quickly (and appropriately) rejected.

At this stage we recalled a symposium on relapse, held by the Society for the Study of Addiction in Scotland in 1985, in which a group of addiction workers debated this very issue for some hours. The conclusion was that no adequate term existed which would convey the range and complexity of issues currently subsumed under the term 'relapse'. A new term would need to be coined to embrace the processes under consideration. We needed a name, and one wag suggested 'George' – it was after all his name and as names went he felt it had served him well, so why not the addiction field? We doubt that this term will be grasped to the bosom of the addictions field, but at least our use of 'George' is a marker, however facetious, of our dissatisfaction with the terms 'relapse' and 'relapsers'. Our comments may even be a prompt to the creativity of others. A more appropriate term than 'relapse' is desperately needed, but we suspect that a single term cannot be found. The issues to be covered by this word are too complex and too wide ranging.

On the making of resolutions

Having been critical of the terminology usually employed to encapsulate the activity of stopping drug use and then restarting, it is relevant to examine closely this very process whereby people attempt to change their ways but do not succeed in carrying out their intentions. Much has been written in the alcohol literature which suggests that the taking up again of drinking or other drug taking is a behaviour which is peculiar to problem drinkers or problem drug users. At this stage we would like to strongly emphasize that in our view becoming a 'relapser' is a process which is no different in kind for the problem drug user or any person who attempts to alter any established pattern of behaviour. In this belief we are consistent with Marlatt and Gordon (1985) who have defined relapse as 'a breakdown or failure in a person's attempt to change or modify any target behaviour'. Thus, one can 'relapse' from an exercise programme, a savings plan, a diet, or resolutions to give up the horses, a relationship, or cigarettes. The point here of course is that making a resolution to change is a common process, undertaken by us all from time to time, and usually with only short-term impact. The trouble with much of the thinking in the addiction field is that it becomes so ensnared with the alcohol or the other drugs that it becomes divorced from general principles. Entities which pertain only to alcohol or drugs are then created and a specialist but biased perspective developed.

What we contend is that we need not the tighter and closer inspection of why 'alcoholics' 'relapse', but greater investigation and cognizance of why you and I do not keep our resolutions. Being a 'relapser' really is a common process, the understanding of which will be better served by investigating non-pathological conditions, in normal rather than clinical samples using established psychological models.

In this regard the work of Sutton (1986, 1987) warrants mention. In a series of studies he has attempted to apply mainstream decision-making theory to the giving up of cigarette use. Sutton has recently outlined the problem facing those of us who attempt change:

> The key decision is seen as one of whether or not to try to change one's behaviour . . . . Once the person has embarked on such an attempt he or she will be faced repeatedly with another decision, namely whether to persevere with the attempt, often in spite of unpleasant withdrawal symptoms, or whether to abandon it. It is an unfortunate fact that the decision to try to change can always be deferred and when acted on can be revoked at any time.
>
> (Sutton 1986: 109)

In his investigation of why people give up smoking Sutton has employed Subjective Expected Utility theory, a decision-making model based on the premise that individuals act *as if* they were weighing up the pros and cons of any behaviour in terms of its expected benefits and costs. In one study involving smokers who had responded to a TV programme offering a self-help quit kit, 2,000 respondents completed questions as to their anticipated outcomes if they were to continue or to stop smoking. Respondents reported whether they thought stopping or continuing to smoke would reduce/increase the likelihood of various outcomes – for example, developing heart disease, lung cancer, being irritable, experiencing withdrawal symptoms, or putting on weight. In his study Sutton discovered that respondents did evaluate the various suggested possible outcomes differently, and that these could be added up to produce an overall value score which indicated whether the individual perceived stopping as being more desirable than continuing or vice versa. Those who placed greater value on stopping rather than continuing were more likely to indicate that they would attempt to stop in the future, and on three-month follow-up were also more likely to have made an attempt to stop. The value of perceiving addiction behaviour in this way is that it allows individuals to have reasons for stopping and reasons for continuing to use simultaneously. The eventual outcome depends on the overall balance of these conflicting expectations. This approach is consistent with Stimson and Oppenheimer's view, adroitly expressed in their report of a ten-year follow-up of 128 heroin users, that:

> at any time there are some advantages in continuing as an addict and some in ceasing. The conflict between reasons for continuing and reasons for stopping is a source of tension. In retrospectively assessing their lives, many [addicts] saw a shift in the balance between advantages and disadvantages as having led them to make a decision to stop using drugs.
>
> (Stimson and Oppenheimer 1982: 160)

Prochaska and DiClemente (1986), in writing about the transition from being a pre-contemplator (i.e., a happy user) to being a contemplator (or in a stage of feeling two ways about one's drug use) and then an actioner, having acknowledged that, while the path from one to the other is poorly understood,

> decisional-balance variables are associated . . . with movement from pre-contemplation to contemplation . . . . The pros of smoking clearly outweigh the cons until subjects move into the contemplation stage. During this stage however the cons begin

> to surpass the pros even though both are important for the smoker.
>
> (Prochaska and DiClemente 1986: 16)

These and similar studies have several implications for our understanding of 'relapse'. The first is that people who attempt to change are not all the same. The task of giving up smoking, for example, is approached with different levels of inclination or perceived value. How worthwhile one considers an activity will influence the amount of time, effort, and costs one is prepared to expend to reach the set goal. An important implication of Sutton's work is that any investigation of why people make and then break a resolution requires an understanding of the overall value placed on the attempt by the individual. Examination of, for example, common immediate precipitants of 'relapse' is severely flawed if in such investigation it is assumed that all people start equally and hence are similarly influenced by a given event. An individual who is only just convinced of the value of giving up smoking is more likely to be challenged by an offer of a cigarette after dinner than is an individual who places high value on stopping.

High-risk situations are only high risk because the individual perceives them as such, which is a function of the individual rather than a specific event. It is possible that relapses occur because the individual embarks on behaviour change while the balance between the costs and benefits of continuing or stopping to use drugs is still tipped toward continued use.

If a literary example is allowed, Iris Murdoch's description of the separation of the two central characters in *Nuns and Soldiers* is most apposite. Murdoch wrote:

> The resolution taken by Tim and Gertrude to make an end of their love had proved a weak one. As they a hundred times said later, they came together again because they could not do without each other. The illness was too extreme, the affinity too deep, the need too violent, the destiny too relentless. They employed many words, smiling at each other and holding hands. Tim had only managed to depart on that night, and Gertrude to tolerate, to survive his departure, because a secret voice in each of them said: 'this is not the end'.
>
> (Murdoch 1981: 279)

How many of us, when making a resolution to give up something, some person, or some activity, are aware, even as we espouse the need for change and embark on action that this is not really the end of things?

Resolutions to change vary in their quality, robustness, and necessity. The very making of them, in terms of weighing up the pros and cons of a behaviour, can influence the eventual outcome. This has been well described by Stewart in her graphic autobiographical account of heroin use. She duly weighed up the benefits of quitting. Her list included:

> trips to the ballet and the theatre, holidays abroad, buying new clothes, and getting a new hairstyle. At the bottom of the list, as if it did not matter as much as the rest came the single statement 'change life'. It stuck out like a sore thumb. It was the crux of the matter. A new hairdo could not outweigh the hunger for smack. The command to change seemed ludicrously grave and quite impossible to carry out. Nevertheless I got on with the cure, motivated like many others primarily by impecunity. I waited impatiently for the moment when I could relapse.
>
> (Stewart 1987: 153)

There is a distinct difference between deciding to stop drug use and deciding to change the way one lives. The former is probably not possible without doing the latter. Yet many resolves about drug use are made without the appreciation that lifestyle change is necessary. Just stopping is not enough. Remaining in the same life circumstances ensures continuing challenges to the new way. Even if one appreciates the dangers of continued use, and the fact that the adverse consequences are in the ascendency, it is still possible to continue drug use. Stewart also noted:

> Hunting for a reason to stop that outweighs the drive to stay hooked is the major problem. During one soul-searching session I neatly listed advantages and disadvantages of taking smack. Potential consequences of using heroin including being charged with an offence, starring in a scandal, losing home, job, health, wealth, friends, and credibility of every kind. Advantages were impossible to find. The following statements appeared on the list of reasons not to stop: 'It (Heroin) makes life easy'; 'I'm scared to stop' and 'I don't feel like it'. A moment's thought contradicted the first two and left me confronted by the third. I did not 'feel like it'. I did not stop, but logic had not assisted the choice.
>
> (Stewart 1987): 152)

There is a sense here that the understanding that one should stop but does not adds to the user's difficulties. A sense of having handed over control, of almost acting against one's will and against one's best interests is suggested. Orford (1985) has argued that it is just this type of conflict over one's use ('I want to' but 'I shouldn't') which is the hallmark feature of an excessive appetite. Such exasperation with one's own behaviour has also been found by Prochaska and DiClemente (1986) to be a precipitant to deciding to change, and 'self re-evaluation' (will I like myself better as a junkie or non-user?) is an important part of the contemplation stage.

What needs to be emphasized is that in analyses such as Prochaska and DiClemente's (1986) or Sutton's (1987), the objective and detached world of decision-making theory can distance one from an appreciation of the turmoil and emotional nature of the proceedings. This is not to imply that logic and weighing the pros and cons plays no part, but that much decision making is of an harassed, emotionally charged, impulsive, conflicted, and desperate nature. Tam Stewart did eventually decide to quit using heroin – but her account is valuable for its depiction of 'hot' resolution making:

> Last summer I kicked my heroin habit. I did not really decide to stop. The decision was forced upon me. Things had been hotting up for a while: the bank was on my back; I had nothing left to sell; there was no direction, no creativity, no hope. Sanity was being sucked up the tube. I became marginally paranoid. People were following me. Trips to score caused panic, paranoia, actually something close to terror . . . every dawn the door was kicked in by a phantom drug squad and I held my breath listening for their footsteps. I slept with the curtain parted so I would wake at first light to pre-empt their beastly plans . . . . One particular Sunday the paranoia peaked.
>
> We went down around lunchtime to our usual place. The weather was hot. Very hot. There was a party spirit in the streets. Loud music wailed. Rastas hung out of windows in Warwick Street, bare-chested and celebratory, but the scorched grass at the roadside reeked of dog-shit and discontent buzzed through the ghetto with the flies. I waited. He was out. Come back in three-quarters of an hour. We did. Sorry. Come at 3 o'clock. Try later. By now there was a queue . . . . I waited . . . the madness went on. I went home . . . .
>
> Bobby turned up at tea-time. Everything was all right again. Our eyes and our noses were dry once more. We had spent six hours of the day and a lot of anxiety just for that. To say nothing of the sixty pounds. Self disgust was swelling like an over-ripe boil. I had almost had enough. I resolved to get the hell out while I was still sane. I resolved to stop. There were no more mountains to climb this side of September, no job, no

> tasks, no nothing. I phoned a friend in London. I could stay there.
>
> Tuesday was the last of it. At the station I panicked. Twenty pounds had been dispatched at the last moment. But Bobby did not make it back with the supplies and I left on the train, beside myself, nearly stepping off to wait, after all, for as long as it took. In the toilet . . . I whacked off the last of what I had. The journey passed in seconds, the few when I had my eyes open. Getting my bags to the taxi was quite hard. I came off in London. It was not easy. I spent August in Wales, looking for the green countryside for a sense of renewal and well being.
>
> (Stewart 1987: 1–2)

This articulate description of making the break is a marker of the importance of the nature of the resolution to stop. Although 'it was not easy' to remain drug free, one has a sense of a resumption of use being improbable because the power of the resolve and the distress that had engendered it were indelibly etched.

In understanding 'relapse' there is a need for an understanding of how the resolution to change is precipitated and where in the overall context of a drug-use career it fits in. As one participant in a recent seminar on 'giving up addictions' sagely noted, 'People only change when the pain of staying where they are is greater than the pain of changing.' A short, anecdotal phrase, which encapsulates both the notion of weighing up options and the emotion inherent in deciding to alter established behaviours. 'Relapse' cannot be understood without some appreciation or gauge of the robustness and quality of the decision to change. Although it is a truism, only those that have decided to attempt change are open to the label of 'relapser'. The nature of that decision to change needs to be included in any analysis of that individual's 'relapse'.

On the breaking of resolutions

Having embarked on the undertaking of a resolution to change, challenges to that resolution, however robust, rigorous, or reliable, will occur. To date, much of the 'relapse' literature has been concerned with reasoning out the nature of such challenges and whether the individual can cope with them. The essential thrust of this work has been that if an individual can be appropriately trained then she/he will be able to deploy such skills as and when necessary. In a manner of speaking, clients have been made more 'relapse proof', and via instruction their potential for relapse restricted. The question to consider is whether in the study of 'relapse' we have lost sight of the individual drug user as a social actor with a drug-use career and her/his own set of social circumstances, the last of which may dictate to a far greater degree than any psychological process the success or otherwise of one's resolution to change. For example, Polich *et al.* (1980) have shown that the lives of people attempting to make the break from excessive alcohol consumption are less well endowed than those of non-problem drinkers. The impact of bad housing, poor job opportunities, embittered relationships, and dissatisfaction with one's lot in life are variables which have not received sufficient emphasis within the 'relapse' literature.

In reviews of treatment outcome it is consistently reported that client characteristics, in terms of marital status, social stability, and employment record, are predictive of outcome. Individuals whose lives are more intact do better. For example, addictive patterns of drug use are so time consuming that, once stopped, acres of time are available. This is much easier to pass if one has home, family, friends, and employment. Lacking such resources the boredom of giving up can be immense. As one socially impoverished client once remarked, 'in the grey days of abstention my relapses were the fireworks of life'.

Consistent with this anecdotal comment is the work of Billings and Moos (1983) who, in comparison with 'relapsers' and 'survivors', found that respondents who reported high ratings on family and job satisfaction scales tended to do well, while those without such supports reported twice as many adverse life events and high 'relapse' rates. They also reported that the gradual achievement of abstinence prompted the development of more effective ways of coping with everyday existence. There is a need to consider the development of such skills against the background of social supports and quality of everyday life. As Tuchfeld (1981), in his study of some fifty 'spontaneous remitters' from alcohol problems, found, successful resolution was a staged process in which the initial resolution prompted action, which was then maintained by those who had supportive families, good-quality relationships and worthwhile employment. These social factors are also reported by Stall and Biernacki (1986) in their across-the-addictions review of why people give up, and are to be found in Stimson and Oppenheimer's (1982) follow-up of treated heroin addicts and Orford and Edward's (1977) classic alcohol treatment study.

The implications for the study of 'relapse' is clear. The social context in which the decision to change is made is critical in determining outcome. Giving up excessive drinking, or revoking a resolution to do so, is a process that is influenced by the events that precede the decision to stop, as well as those that follow – all set against the background of the individual's social circumstances. The strength of resolution to change is not immutably set at the beginning but is influenced, perhaps daily, by the consequences of undertaking action. The benefits of the action will be influenced by one's social milieu, the response of friends, relatives, and social contacts. The amount of plasticity in one's lifestyle, the opportunity for movement for 'relapse' or survival is a complex one, in which psychological constructs such as subjective expected utility, self-efficacy, and outcome expectancies interact with social variables such as the quality of marital and family relationships, economic considerations, satisfaction with one's lot, life events, and the physiological consequences of being a drug user. Charting 'relapse', or attempting to gauge why 'they do it', will be coloured for each individual by their own particular circumstances – social and psychological. That is not to say that all is incoherent flux but rather that simple schemes or models are insufficient. In the treatment of addiction problems, workers have appreciated for some time that there is no simple prognostic index. Unfortunately, in the study of 'relapse' some of the hard-won lessons in the treatment arena have been ignored in the rush to the new lodestone.

Having made our plea for the social context of individuals to be included in any model of 'relapse', we can now refer to some of the psychological processes that do seem to underpin 'relapse'. While subjective expected utility may be a good indicator of which people initiate change, self-efficacy, or confidence in one's ability to carry out a task successfully, has been found to be an important factor in determining which people sustain their resolutions. In the trial of cognitive-behavioural strategies referred to above we found that self-efficacy after treatment was the single most predictive outcome factor (Allsop *et al.* 1989), a finding also reported by DiClemente (1981), who used a twelve-item confidence-in-resisting-temptations questionnaire to predict which smokers would successfully quit. Interestingly, Sutton (1987) has reported that confidence in stopping is positively associated with the overall level of subjective expected utility of stopping smoking and with levels of intention. In a study of 966 cigarette smokers, those who had positive expectancies for stopping (based on thirty-two possible outcome measures) reported greater confidence in their ability to stop and had greater intention to stop. Over the next six months such respondents made more attempts to stop than their less motivated counterparts. Also of interest, but something of an aside, in Sutton's study those that did attempt to stop smoking were found on initial assessment to have made more attempts to quit in the past. Again, trying to stop and failing to do so is less an example of backsliding or recidivism, more an aspect of the resolution of a problematic behaviour.

The issue of confidence and subjective expected utility has also been well portrayed by Prochaska and DiClemente (1986). In a recent revision of their cycle of change model they used data from a two-year, longitudinal study of 886 individuals who attempted to give up smoking without therapeutic support to chart the influence of confidence over time. What they discovered was that confidence in being able to stop increases during the contemplation stage prior to action, and that for successful quitters, confidence further developed as a consequence of maintaining the change. The work of Litman and her colleagues is also of importance here (Litman *et al.* 1979; Litman 1986). In a study of 'relapsers' and survivors, the 'relapsers', on admission to treatment, reported more situations as being challenges to their sobriety and also doubted their ability to resist temptations. Conversely, the survivors believed they had skills to cope with high-risk situations and would be able to deploy them. Litman has suggested that in clinical work care needs to be taken to tailor responses to clients' needs with either an essentially cognitive or a skills approach being adopted. Thus, self-efficacy, coping skills, and cognitive vigilance, or keeping the original resolution salient, may all be seen as important in maintaining a resolution to change.

However, these individualistic factors need to be assessed in the context of social circumstances. This interactive perspective has been emphasized by Shiffman (1986) who, in a recent review of 'relapse' and smoking, distinguished between background and precipitating factors. This useful distinction is supported by his use of the concept of 'relapse proneness'. The idea is that individuals are susceptible to going back on their resolutions, and that this 'proneness' is determined by a wide range of personal, cognitive, environmental, experiential, and trigger factors. The task for investigators of 'relapses' is to determine the interplay of variables that are important in keeping or giving away a resolution. Thus, it is not a case of assessing high-risk situations but of determining how high-risk situations and overall motivational state interact. Presumably, people with well-thought-out decisions, who value the attempts they are making to change, who are well supported by friends, family, and spouse, and who are also confident in their abilities, are less susceptible to challenges than are less well-committed individuals. However, even well-resolved individuals, who at three weeks into a change of behaviour do not recognize, ignore, or resist challenges, may at three months be severely tested by similar challenges. Social circumstances, cognitive vigilance, and confidence can alter.

This type of challenge analysis is, however, one sided if it is implied that individual decisions to change are eventually eroded by coming into contact with unexpected or strong temptations. To cite the work of Lichtenstein and Weiss (1986), going back on one's vows may be a more deliberate undertaking. In our research and clinical work we have been impressed by the number of reversions to former ways that have been deliberately sought out. Elsewhere we have encapsulated this aspect of human behaviour into the question 'do relapses happen to people or do people make relapses happen?' We believe the answers to be, respectively, sometimes and often. Marlatt and Gordon (1985) have introduced the idea of relapse 'set-ups', in which individuals make mini-decisions that bring them closer and closer to very tempting situations, to which they then succumb. While the individual concerns may then be able to claim that they were overwhelmed by circumstances, in effect they were masters of their own drift to temptation. Similarly, as noted above, Litman *et al.* (1979), in their analysis of 'relapsers' and 'survivors', found that the survivors demonstrated a greater degree of 'cognitive vigilance', or awareness of potential challenges, and the high costs of resuming the old behaviour. 'Relapsers' also perceived more events as being of potential threat. However, as a speculation, it is possible that the number of perceived high-risk situations is a function of the quality of one's lifestyle, with the less well-supported or endowed being more susceptible and vulnerable to adverse experiences. A concept such as 'relapse proneness', or some type of overall gauge of the interaction of social and psychological variables, gives emphasis to the complex process of attempting to give up an established behaviour.

An aside

The use and implications of a term like 'relapse proneness' raise another strand of debate. It is traditional in the drug arena to consider the 'relapse' process as being two staged. In disease thinking 'craving' and 'loss of control' were responsible for 'relapse', while in Marlatt's and Gordon's (1985) model, 'high-risk situations' and the 'abstinence violation effect' were deemed the two components of the process whereby individuals moved from abstinence to some use, and then on to problematic use. As may be appreciated if one acknowledges social factors and psychological concepts, such as subjective expected utility and self-efficacy, as being important variables in the decision to resume use, then continued use may be a consequence of these factors, and not some after-the-first-use type of variable. If, after some abstinence, one is still confronted with unemployment, a hostile marital relationship, poor housing, and little expectation that much will alter, then to orchestrate a situation of being tempted – to which one gives in – may not be a precursor to a single episode of use, but rather a marker of the resumption of the past behaviour. Thus even the shift from re-use to problematic use may not be caused by a psychological reaction to the initial resumption but be due to dissatisfaction with one's lot in life and the ongoing waning of the initial resolution to quit.

Furthermore, if 'relapse' is a process that can be understood via social-psychological principles, is the field well served by the packaging of such concepts as cognitive dissonance and attribution theory into 'The Abstinence Violation Effect'? (Marlatt and Gordon 1985). This has the potential of being misconstrued as an addiction-specific entity, divorced from the experience of ordinary, non-addicted people. Such marketing of psychological concepts can have the effect of mystifying further the process of relapse, rather than making 'relapse' something that we all do with our resolutions.

Apart from questioning whether 'relapse' really is a two-staged process, this aside was also included as an introduction to a related issue. Some commentators have argued that 'addicts' and 'alcoholics' are different from ordinary folk, and are made so by virtue of their addiction, drug dependence or addiction being a 'super-added' process that changes the relationship the individual has with drugs, and thus the processes that mediate that relationship.

What's dependence got to do with it?

This raises the issue of the importance of dependence in the 'relapse' process and whether 'relapse proneness' is determined by the extent of the individual's dependence on her/his preferred substance. Central to this discussion is the Alcohol Dependence Syndrome and its derivation the Drug Dependence Syndrome. Proposed in provisional form by Edwards and Gross (1976), the Alcohol and Drug Dependence Syndromes have been internationally accepted (WHO 1981).

The concept of the Alcohol Dependence Syndrome has been described by Edwards (1982) as 'an idea roughly coterminus with what many people would call the disease of alcoholism or with the AA notion of what counts as alcoholism'. From this view the Alcohol Dependence Syndrome may have little to offer in understanding the 'relapse' process, because if it is an idea 'coterminus' with 'alcoholism' then the principles that underpin relapse are presumably deemed as being those factors central to the 'disease concept', namely 'craving' and 'loss of control', both of which have been severely criticized (see, e.g., Heather and Robertson 1981).

Additionally, from a psychological perspective the use of the term dependence as a marker of an abnormal state is unfortunate. Kozlowski and Wilkinson (1987) have noted that scientists occasionally take a word that has served the community well and haul it off to the laboratory, where it is given a new and technical meaning. Unfortunately, neither the word, nor at times the scientists, behave themselves, and old uses and new meanings become mixed together. While Kozlowski and Wilkinson (1987) were referring to the term 'craving', the word dependence is no less open to this criticism. It seems more helpful, as some psychologists have argued, to view dependence as a normal part of the human condition. For example Peele has noted that:

> Psychological dependence may be said to exist with respect to anything which is part of one's preferred way of life. In our society this kind of dependency occurs regularly with respect to such things as television, music, books, religion, sex, money, favourite foods, psychoactive drugs, hobbies, sports and often other persons.
>
> (Peele 1985)

Thus, being dependent on alcohol or heroin is no more a concern than relying on one's friends, spouse, salary, car, or enjoying sunshine, physical exercise, Stoke City football club, and specific television programmes. The issue is, of course, that such reliances can become overstated. Undue regard, time, endeavour, and money may be expended in the pursuit and enjoyment of a specific behaviour. As the importance of the behaviour increases so other activities may be dropped from one's behavioural repertoire and more reliance placed upon the preferred behaviour for making one feel good or, later on, just normal. This gradual escalation of behaviour, from a modest, take-it-or-leave-it level to total involvement has been well described by Stewart.

> Normal life becomes a thing of the past for junkies. The losing of friends and acquaintances is an everday reality. Hobbies and sport are abandoned, and outside interests go by the board as energy and time are poured into the hunt for drugs. Talents and abilities waste away. The drug user finds that she cannot make arrangements to stray far from home and her supplies. Those who do attempt to carry on as normal and try taking holidays wish they had not bothered. They find that suffering cold turkey on a hot beach is considerably worse than staying at home. Junkies learn that lesson fast. They free themselves from all interference and make sure that new acquaintances find room in their lives only if they know a new place to score.
>
> (Stewart 1987: 137)

Obviously this level of involvement is much more than an ordinary dependence or reliance. The issue for this chapter is how does this overinvolvement influence outcome or 'relapse' if the user decides to stop. In terms of the Alcohol and Drug Dependence Syndromes the issue is clear – the greater the severity of dependence the quicker the reinstatement of symptoms. For example, Edwards has written:

> Typically the patient who has only a moderate degree of dependence will take weeks or months to reinstate it, perhaps pulling back once or twice on the way. A severely dependent patient typically reports that he is again 'hooked' within a few days of starting to drink.
>
> (Edwards 1982: 29)

One difficulty, however, is that the Dependence Syndrome is a descriptive rather than explanatory model. Based on clinical formulation, there is no clear message as to what mechanisms are supposed to underpin dependence, and hence 'relapse'. Barbor *et al.*, who have suggested that the Drug Dependence Syndrome is valuable as an organizing principle for understanding relapse, have addressed this issue: 'What ties together the elements of the syndrome and helps to account for their interrelationships is an often unstated set of assumptions about the learning processes behind the acquisition and maintenance of drug dependence' (Barbor *et al.* 1986: 21).

There is indeed 'an unstated set of assumptions' about the basis of the dependence syndrome and it is not clear from the work of the progenitors of the Dependence Syndrome (e.g., Edwards *et al.* 1977; Edwards 1986) whether learning processes or other mechanisms underpin the syndrome. Given this lack of specific proposals of the mechanisms for the acquisition and maintenance of the syndrome, dependence is, from the perspective of relapse, of very restricted utility because, even if an association between relapse and severity of dependence is found, the why of the relationship is not. Barbor *et al.* (1987) in a series of careful studies have attempted to assess this specific question. In one study of 266 patients, abstainers and relapsers were compared on a variety of social, psychological, and dependence measures. 'Relapsers', or those who had consumed any alcohol in the year of follow-up, were found to be different from abstainers in that they had a greater prior history of treatment for alcohol problems, a higher number of lifetime psychiatric diagnoses, greater social problems, increased rate of familial alcohol problems, and higher life time (but not current) levels of dependency. These differences were found only for the males in the study. Dependence levels had no influence on the 'relapses' of women.

In further analysis of reinstatement of problematic alcohol use, it was found that for males the severity of dependence (lifetime and current) was a predictor, along with other factors such as previous treatments, lifetime social problems, number of psychiatric diagnoses, and beliefs about loss of control. Again, the findings for women were dissimilar, with social problems being the major discriminator and recent dependence only a modest predictor of reinstatement. Barbor *et al.* are cautious in their conclusions, rightly pointing out that their analysis was one of association rather than cause and effect, and that for their female sample, dependence was not a significant predictor. They concluded that 'alcohol dependence is not a robust predictor of initial alcohol use following treatment . . . different mechanisms may be involved in initial relapse and subsequent reinstatement and variables other than dependence may contribute substantially to the prediction of both' (Barbor *et al.* 1987: 403).

Elsewhere, Barbor *et al.* (1986) have lamented the difficulties inherent in attempting to define operationally the elements of the Drug Dependence Syndrome and we cannot but have some sympathy for them. In the above research, their fifteen-point dependence index was concerned with tolerance, withdrawal, and loosely structured assessments of salience and compulsion. Narrowing of the drinking repertoire was omitted and it is possible to argue that neither the salience nor the compulsion questions reflect those elements as described by Edwards *et al.* (1977). More seriously however, in the study it was assumed that all patients were identical in terms of motivation, commitment, and ability to change their drug-taking behaviour. The tendency to study 'relapse' in isolation from other aspects in the cycle of change needs to be avoided. Studying relapse in this way is akin to understanding Shakespearian tragedy by watching the last ten minutes of *Hamlet* or *Macbeth*. One does get a view but a distorted and incomplete one without a sense of the development of motives for the behaviour.

Dependence, or degree of one's involvement with drugs, is only part of why people resume use. Of course at one level the involvement one has with any activity, be it the stock market, property speculation, a long-term relationship, or drinking, influences the degree of difficulty one has in getting out, or the rapidity with which after a break one re-adopts old habits, but care is needed not to elevate dependence beyond this mundane level. In our view then, there are more crucial determinants of relapse and its sister state, resolution maintenance.

A model of relapse

Having expressed our ideas and given some vent to our prejudices, we are now in a position to speculate further and unveil an alternative model of 'relapse'. A model, as even cursory examination will show, from which 'relapse' is omitted. This is deliberate. As argued above, much can be learned about 'relapse' from the study of people who don't. We contend that models of 'relapse' encourage a focusing down, a reductionism and neglect of the proper context, that of the individual drug user as an actor in a social setting, beset by economic, familial, occupational, psychological, drug-use career, and physiological forces. Hence 'relapse' or more pertinently its opposite – behaviour change – is orchestrated and sustained by a complex intervention of factors.

We have divided the process of successful behaviour change into four stages. The predisposing factors for initiating behaviour change are essentially the individual's drug-use career to date, the values placed on continuing to be a user, and the converse values placed on stopping; the quality of the individual's lifestyle and the influence of family and friends upon the user. All may encourage or restrain drug use and the sum of these influences – which might be labelled 'motivation' – will determine whether a resolution to change is precipitated. As noted above, resolutions will vary in quality, in type, and in robustness, and it may well be that for the giving up of drug use the decision to stop will be a much conflicted and emotional one – hence the flash of lightning in the model.

However, once embraced, the action of carrying out the resolution – in our terms the commitment – is itself influenced by cognitive, social, and lifestyle considerations. The literature is replete with references to self-efficacy, the value one places on the resolution, cognitive, vigilance, coping skills, and high-risk situations. They have their place but these psychological constructs need to be tempered by an appreciation that they are fluid variables open to influence by the individual's day to day existence. Rather than being the engine-room of action they are correlates of the social milieu of the behaviour change. If the individual's environment is well endowed with, or has the potential for, good-quality interpersonal relationships, agreeable employment, and supportive familial contacts then successful outcome is more likely than if the individual is locked into bad housing, unemployment, and fractured relationships. The degree of plasticity, or potential for change within the existing lifestyle is important, and will influence the psychological state of the person concerned.

In emphasis of this we have labelled our final stage as lifestyle

PROS
CONS
OF USING
CAREER
PROS
CONS
OF STOPPING
RESOLUTION
PSYCHOLOGICAL
SELF-EFFICACY SUBJECTIVE EXPECTED UTILITY
COGNITIVE VIGILANCE OUTCOME EXPECTANCY
COMMITMENT
AVOIDANCE
COPING SKILLS
SOCIAL MILIEU
SOCIAL SUPPORT
FAMILY MARITAL
PLASTICITY
LIFE SATISFACTION
OCCUPATIONAL
LIFESTYLE CHANGE
QUALITY OF LIFE

Model

change, since our clinical and research experience dictates to us that maintaining a drug-free or markedly reduced pattern of drug use is only achieved if such a shift occurs. As for relapse, the giving up on a resolution can occur at any stage, and can be induced by a shortfall or adverse change in any of the factors contained within the model. From this perspective the issue of why people 'relapse' is a very difficult one. The components in any 'relapse' formula are many, are difficult to measure, and probably impossible to weight or prioritize. Any 'relapse-proneness' assessment questionnaire derived from this framework will be comprehensive but arduous to complete.

In a study we are currently undertaking into the 'relapses' of women with alcohol problems (a much neglected area), we included the usual components – self-efficacy, relapse precipitants inventory, coping skills, cognitive impairment, intention, drug-use history, demographics, 'relapse' history, and some gauge of motivation, and were then forced to add scales measuring life satisfaction, psychological well being, quality of partner support, and family interaction. Yet this list is not exhaustive and eventually we will have obtained only a partial explanation of why some women 'relapse'.

A further comment is also necessary. We have recently completed a controlled trial of 'relapse' management and prevention techniques. Based on motivational interviewing and problem solving (see chapter 2), those subjects receiving the active cognitive-behavioural strategies were, on six-month follow-up, more abstinent and less 'relapsed' than either a treatment control group or a discussion-based 'relapse' prevention group. At one year, however, these significant differences were no longer present.

One commentator on the research marvelled that, given the social conditions to which our subjects returned – a locale dominated by chronic unemployment, slum-like housing, atrocious weather, poverty, and much interpersonal abuse, our psychological interventions had had any impact at all. The surprise, he argued, was not that our efforts had faded, but that against such odds we had achieved any impact at all. He then asked us why we had not invested some effort and ingenuity in attempting to rectify the social circumstances of our patients. Relapse prevention might, he argued, be better achieved by social rather than clinical intervention. It was a good question. It still is.

Relapse prevention and management – individual restraint or structural change?

It has become increasingly well recognized that exhortation and instruction to individuals on the need for restraint in undertaking health-compromising behaviours can be augmented by structural change. In Britain the possibility of a fine for non-compliance with seat-belt legislation effectively enhanced media cajoling to clunk-click every trip, and the advent of random breath testing has convinced Finns and residents of New South Wales in Australia that 'Don't drink and drive' needs to be taken seriously. Pictures of healthy hearts on menus in Minnesotan restaurants may have prompted change, but lowered cholesterol levels were made more likely by arguments with meat suppliers to provide less fatty meat and with supermarkets to restrict the availability of high-cholesterol foods.

If such amalagams of instruction and structural restraints can reduce the incidence of heat disease, of serious head injuries in road traffic accidents, and prevent drunken driving, then perhaps those of us concerned with preventing 'relapse' might consider what social initiatives can be undertaken to assist people who are attempting to quit. Reducing the availability of alcohol, ensuring the adequate supply of attractive alternatives to alcohol at social events, and reducing the perceived pressure to drink alcohol may maintain a faltering resolution. The removal of untruthful and misleading alcohol advertising, the abolition of 'happy hours', or two-for-the-price-of-one promotions, and stricter controls on the capricious serving of alcohol to already intoxicated patrons may do much to help the clients help themselves. The wider social cnvironment may also need to be addressed. Employment, housing, and opportunities for personal development do matter.

Similarly, the introduction of workplace practices to restrict the areas in which smoking is permitted and removal of alcohol from the working day may well shore up and sustain those individuals attempting to quit. If every waking minute is a challenge to one's sobriety, it is not surprising that the task is perceived as enormous and the effort needed to recover as being great and debilitating. Currently in Western Australia there is a well-promoted, annual, mass-media-based Quit programme for smokers, which this year was launched by the state's Premier (an ex-smoker), and supplemented with self-help quit manuals, General Practitioners' kits, and community action guides. The impact of four years of such Quit programmes is that the overall smoking rate has declined significantly and ex-smokers abound. Quit Week has almost become part of the social calendar, and social events during and immediately after Quit Week are made compelling because of the small, conspicuous knots of people discussing how they are doing with their resolves. Support and encouragement are given; strategies and temptations eagerly debated. In Western Australia stopping smoking is a community activity. This theme has been noted by Grabowski in his writing about smoking and relapse:

> the major problem confronting therapists and scientist-clinicians is the . . . anomalous environment in which tobacco use is not only legal but substantially encouraged on the one hand and deemed hazardous and unacceptable on the other. This issue is not resolvable by better theory. The greatest increments in enhancement of the diverse interventions will come less from future refinements in the techniques . . . but more through changes in the social environment via legislation and social policy.
>
> (Grabowski 1986: 44)

We agree and not just in terms of tobacco. 'Relapse' prevention work has been concerned with increasing individuals' ability to resist temptations, yet has not addressed the issue that the temptations themselves have become bigger and more prevalent. Increasing 'moral fibre' is of limited value if the environment is allowed to become increasingly amoral. Attempts to induce better coping skills are irrelevant if we simultaneously permit the challenges to become more taxing, and the drug-related stresses of everyday life more burdensome. The campus on which we write this has recently become a no-smoking one – this policy has assisted secretary and research fellows to quit smoking and stay stopped. The university's regulations about alcohol use are now under review, and if certain of the recommendations are implemented, drinking and working will become separate activities, to the benefit of social and problem drinkers alike. Resisting temptation is made easier if there are few, or very few temptations. Perhaps the work of the next decade is not the further refinement of clinical interventions but implementation of social preventions.

Significantly, some health promotion practitioners have recognized that programmes that are individually focused are not enough. Wallack has written:

> Health educators should not only seek to empower individuals to change themselves, but provide skills for changing conditions that are central to the problem. If the large environment is not changed, then individual change, when it does occur, simply will not be sufficient.
>
> (Wallack 1984)

In similar vein but with an added important message Perry and Jessor have noted:

> Although we have argued that health promotion must ultimately come to rest on behaviour change, we do not wish to be understood as urging only a proximal focus for intervention, one that only deals with individuals and only with the immediate context of their lives . . . . On the contrary the immediate context of lives and the patterning of personality are both shaped by larger and more distal social, economic and political forces and the general promotion of health probably faces insuperable obstacles and countervailing pressures unless the distal environment is also changed. Changes in cultural values, social norms, and the socioeconomic structure of opportunity – for education, employment, recreation, and self-development – must be considered as an essential part of any broad approach to the promotion of health. Failure to recognize the necessity for such distal and macro-environmental changes, while at the same time emphasizing personal responsibility for health, seems tantamount to blaming the victim.
>
> (Perry and Jessor 1985: 183)

We contend that Perry and Jessor's perspective and accusation are very relevant to the prevention of 'relapse'. But will the next decade see 'relapse' prevention taking on a broader, social focus, and one in which activity in the clinic is augmented by activist behaviour to change our drug saturated environment? We hope so, but we doubt it.

Acknowledgements: The preparation of this chapter was much assisted by the helpful critical advice of Sue Helfgott and John O'Connor; Arie Valkoff's artistry and Jan Matthew-Stubbs' care and patience in typing the manuscript was much appreciated. The clinical trial conducted by the authors and reported in this paper was supported by the Alcohol Education and Research Council (London) and the study of relapse and women is supported by the Commonwealth Department of Health, Canberra.

References

Allsop, S., Saunders, B., and Carr, A. (1989) 'Relapse prevention and management: a controlled trial with problem drinkers', in preparation.

Barbor, T., Cooney, N., and Lauerman, R. (1987) 'The Dependence Syndrome concept as an organizing principle in the explanation and prediction of relapse', in F.M. Tims and C.G. Leukefeld (eds) *Relapse and Recovery in Drug Abuse*, National Institute on Drug Abuse

Research Monograph 72, Rockville, Maryland: Department of Health and Human Services.

Barbor, T., Cooney, N., and Lauerman, R. (1987) 'The Dependence Syndrome concept as a psychological theory of relapse behaviour: an empirical evaluation of alcoholic and opiate addicts', *British Journal of Addiction* 82 (4): 393–405.

Billings, A. and Moos, R. (1983) 'Psychological processes of recovery among alcoholics and their families: implications for clinicians and programme evaluators', *Addictive Behaviors*, 8: 205–18.

Brandon, T., Tiffany, S., and Baker, T. (1986) 'The process of smoking relapse', in F.M. Tims and C.G. Leukefeld (eds) *Relapse and Recovery in Drug Abuse*, National Institute on Drug Abuse Research Monograph 72, Rockville, Maryland: Department of Health and Human Services.

DiClemente, C. (1981) 'Self-efficacy and smoking cessation maintenance: a preliminary report', *Cognitive Theory and Research* 5: 175–87.

Edwards, G. (1982) *The Treatment of Drinking Problems*, London: Grant McIntyre.

Edwards, G. (1986) 'The Alcohol Dependence Syndrome: a concept as stimulus to enquiry', *British Journal of Addiction*, 81 (2): 171–83.

Edwards, G. (1987) book review of *Relapse Prevention*, edited by G.A. Marlatt and J.R. Gordon, *British Journal of Addiction* 82: 319–23.

Edwards, G. and Gross, M. (1976) 'Alcohol dependence: provisional description of a clinical syndrome', *British Medical Journal* 1: 1058–61.

Edwards, G., Gross, M., Keller, M., Moser, J., and Room, R. (1977) *Alcohol-Related Disabilities*, WHO Offset Publication No. 32, Geneva: WHO.

Grabowski, J. (1986) 'Acquisition, maintenance, cessation and reacquisition: an overview and behavioural perspective of relapse to tobacco use', in F.M.Tims and C.G. Leukefeld (eds) *Relapse and Recovery in Drug Abuse*, National Institute on Drug Abuse Research Monograph 72, Rockville, Maryland: Department of Health and Human Services.

Heather, N. and Robertson, I. (1981) *Controlled Drinking*, London: Methuen.

Kozlowski, L. and Wilkinson, D.A. (1987) 'Use and misuse of the concept of craving by alcohol, tobacco and drug researchers', *British Journal of Addiction*, 82 (1): 31–6.

Lichtenstein, E. and Weiss, S. (1986) 'Task Force 3: patterns of smoking relapse', *Health Psychology* 5 (supplement): 29–40.

Litman, G. (1980) 'Relapse in alcoholism: traditional and current approaches', in G. Edwards and M. Grant (eds) *Alcoholism: Treatment in Transition*, London: Croom Helm.

Litman, G. (1986) 'Alcoholism survival: the prevention of relapse', in W. Miller and N. Heather (eds) *Treating Addictive Behaviors* New York: Plenum.

Litman, G., Eiser, J., Rawson, N., and Oppenheim, A. (1977) 'Towards a typology of relapse: a preliminary report', *Drug and Alcohol Dependency* 2: 157–62.

Litman, G., Eiser, J., Rawson, N., and Oppenheim, A. (1979) 'Towards a typology of relapse: differences in relapse and coping behaviours between alcohol relapsers and survivors', *Behavior Research and Therapy* 17: 89–94.

Marlatt, G.A. and Gordon, J.R. (1985) *Relapse Prevention: Maintenance Strategies in the Treatment of Addictive Behavior*, New York: Guilford Press.

Murdoch, I. (1981) *Nuns and Soldiers*, Harmondsworth: Penguin.

Orford, J. (1985)*Excessive Appetites: A Psychological View of Addiction*, Chichester: Wiley.

Orford, J. and Edwards, G. (1977) *Alcoholism*, Oxford: Oxford University Press.

Peele, S. (1985) *The Meaning of Addiction*, Massachusetts: Lexington Books.

Perry, C. and Jessor, R. (1985) 'The concept of health promotion and the prevention of adolescent drug abuse', *Health Education Quarterly*, 12 (2): 169–84.

Polich, J., Armor, D., and Braiker, H.B. (1980) *The Course of Alcoholism: Four Years After Treatment*, Santa Monica, California: The Rand Corporation.

Prochaska, J. and DiClemente, C. (1983) 'Stages and processes of self-change of smoking: toward an integrative model of change', *Journal of Consulting and Clinical Psychology* 51: 390–5.

Prochaska, J. and DiClemente, C. (1986) 'Toward a comprehensive model of change', in W. Miller and N. Heather (eds) *Treating Addictive Behaviors*, New York: Plenum.

Saunders, B. and Allsop, S. (1987) 'Relapse: a psychological perspective', *British Journal of Addiction* 82: 417–29.

Shiffman, S. (1986) 'Task Force 2: models of smoking relapse', *Health Psychology* 5 (supplement): 13–27.

Stall, R. and Biernacki, P. (1986) 'Spontaneous remission from the problematic use of substances: an inductive model derived from a comparative analysis of the alcohol, opiate, tobacco and food/obesity literature', *International Journal of the Addictions* 21: 1–23.

Stewart, T. (1987) *The Heroin Users*, London: Pandora.

Stimson, C. and Oppenheimer, E. (1982) *Heroin Addiction: Treatment and Control in Britain*, London: Tavistock.

Sutton, S. (1986) 'Trying to stop smoking: a decision making perspective', in W. Miller and N. Heather (eds) *Treating Addictive Behaviors*, New York: Plenum.

Sutton, S.R. (1987) 'Social-psychological approaches to understanding addictive behaviours: attitude-behaviour and decision making models', *British Journal of Addiction* 82 (4): 355–70.

Taylor, C., Brown, D., Duckitt, A., Edwards, G., Oppenheimer, E., and Sheehan, M. (1986) 'Multivariate description of alcoholism careers: a 10 year follow up', in F.M. Tims and C.G. Leukefeld (eds) *Relapse and Recovery in Drug Abuse*, National Institute on Drug Abuse Research Monograph 72, Rockville, Maryland: Department of Health and Human Services.

Tuchfeld, B. (1981) 'Spontaneous remission in alcoholics – empirical observations and theoretical implications', *Journal of Studies on Alcohol* 42: 626–41.

Wallack, L. (1981) 'Alcohol and the mass media', in D. Gerstein (ed.) *Prevention of Alcohol Problems*, Washington, DC: National Academy Press.

WHO (1981) 'Nomenclature and classification of drug-and alcohol-related problems', *Bulletin of the World Health Organization* 59 (2): 225–42.

Chapter Fourteen

Relapse prevention: future directions

G. Alan Marlatt and Judith R. Gordon

Relapse prevention (RP) provides the framework for a general model of habit change. Although the foundations of RP were established in the addictions field (in which relapse is a frequent and visible process), the model has been expanded to include other behaviours in which habit change is often subject to periodic setbacks. These behaviours (some of which have been described in earlier chapters) include eating disorders and weight change, anger control and abusive behaviours, compulsive sexual habits (paedophilia and exhibitionism), and other problems of 'impulse control'. In the second half of this chapter, Judith Gordon will describe one such application of the RP model: to change the sexual habit patterns of individuals at risk of acquiring or transmitting AIDS. The purpose of the first part of the chapter is to discuss two general issues related to future directions of the RP model: (a) the focus and timing of RP interventions and their relation to other therapeutic approaches, and (b) treatment matching for stages in the habit change process.

The focus and timing of RP intervention

Although 'relapse' has traditionally been defined as a treatment *outcome* variable (e.g., relapse as an index of treatment failure), the RP model views relapse as part of the *process* of behaviour change. The habit change process involves a series of interlocking stages, including motivation and preparation for change, the active change stage (treatment-aided or self-initiated without formal treatment), and the maintenance or stabilization stage. Matching prevention and intervention methods to the appropriate stage in the change process is described in a subsequent section of this chapter. The point we wish to make here is that the 'bottom line' of RP remains the same at each stage of change – to apply clinical procedures towards the prevention of relapse and/or intervention when relapse occurs. The emphasis on relapse provides both the therapist and the client with a framework to select an appropriate intervention strategy. Relapse dictates the choice of treatment methods at each stage of change; it provides a focus by telling us 'when to do what' to maximize progress and minimize setbacks.

The RP procedures described in our book (Marlatt and Gordon 1985) are designed with the following goals in mind: (a) to *enhance awareness* of the vicissitudes of change (thereby facilitating the navigational ability of the individual embarking upon the journey of habit change); (b) to assist in the development of cognitive and behavioural *coping skills* to deal effectively with hindrances and blocks in the attempt to change; (c) to facilitate the acquisition of a *balanced lifestyle* to maintain and integrate productive habit change. The ultimate goal of RP extends beyond the immediate need to intervene regarding the occurrence of a specific lapse or relapse at a given point in the change process. Ultimately we would like to help individuals to develop their own self-management strategies to improve the overall quality of their life experience. Quality of life experience as it relates to habit change transcends the dichotomous outcome criterion that characterizes traditional treatment efficacy studies – that the person is either 'abstinent' (or some other absolute measure of outcome) or 'relapsed'. Strict adherence to abstinence is not a guarantee for enhanced life experience.

Many therapeutic modalities are relevant to the development of quality of life experiences, including cognitive–behavioural therapy, lifestyle modification, psychodynamic approaches to personality change, methods to enhance spiritual values (including twelve-step, self-help fellowship groups), marital and family therapy, and community-based approaches (including modifying the sociocultural environment). Where does RP fit into this wide-ranging therapeutic armamentarium? Any of the above-mentioned approaches may be enlisted as a means of helping prevent relapse. Although each therapeutic approach may play an important role in this regard, the question arises of when to do what? The diagram in figure 14.1 represents one approach to this question.

The purpose of figure 14.1 is to draw a metaphorical parallel between a lapse and a diamond stylus that 'jumps off the record' that is being played on a phonograph. The stylus moves along the spiral groove from the 'past' to the 'future' – but the 'lapse' of the needle displaced from the groove occurs in the immediate present moment. In a similar vein, a lapse is a discrete event that disrupts the overall programme of habit change at least temporarily. As with the stylus supported by the cartridge and the phonograph arm, there are many forces that come to bear on the interplay of needle and groove. Many determinants of a particular lapse (the stylus jump) may be

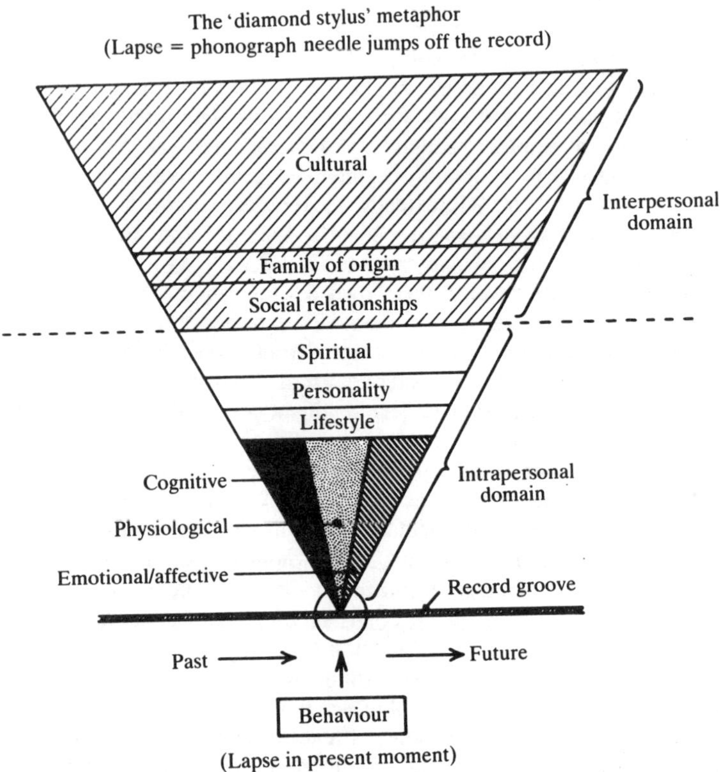

Figure 14.1 The 'diamond stylus' metaphor

involved, as figure 14.1 indicates. Yet the most important focus at the time of the lapse itself is the *behaviour* of the stylus as it skips the groove: the jump needs immediate attention to get the needle back in the groove (or get the behaviour back on the right track).

The behavioural lapse itself, although determined in part by distal causes, has its immediate (proximal) determinants in one or more of the following systems: cognitive, physiological, and emotional reactions. In other words, the 'triggering' mechanism associated with the lapse may be the final common causative pathway, even though the precipitating factors are often influenced by distal events removed in time and place from the trigger situation. As an example, consider a smoker who attempts to quit smoking, only to experience an initial lapse after five days of abstinence. He experiences his first lapse after a hectic work day at the office. After drinks and a pleasant restaurant meal, our ex-smoker experiences a strong urge to smoke when his companion lights up after dinner. After a moment or two of hesitation, he 'gives in' and smokes a cigarette (the needle skips). What 'caused' the slip? Many factors probably influence this type of event, some distal, some proximal in their determination. Distal factors might include, among others, the individual's stressful work lifestyle, the strength of his past dependence on nicotine (physical dependence and associated withdrawal), personality factors (e.g., impulsivity, dependence, sensation-seeking, etc.), lack of social support for remaining an ex-smoker, and possibly even the impact of cultural factors associated with smoking (e.g. advertisements that link smoking with dining out and good times). These determinants may manifest themselves as proximal factors active at the time of the lapse (e.g., the stress of the day may have undermined the resistance to smoking). In addition, there are a number of determinants that may or may not be linked to the more distal factors. Having consumed alcohol and being in the company of a friend who smokes, to take but two examples, will increase the intensity of the urge, regardless of the relative impact of distal causes.

This combination of distal and proximal factors associated with the lapse is experienced in one or more of the following response system domains: (a) *cognitive*, including positive outcome experiences associated with smoking, level of self-efficacy associated with remaining an ex-smoker, etc.; (b) *physiological*, including stress-induced fatigue, the disinhibiting influence of alcohol, conditioned 'craving' responses elicited by the friend's lighting up, etc.; (c) *emotional/affective*, including mood level, emotional residue of the day's experiences coupled with the pleasant evening meal, and so on. In addition, *reactions* to the lapse also occur in the same systems, including the effects of nicotine (physiological), a possible abstinence violation effect or 'AVE' (cognitive–affective), and a sense of low-efficacy or helplessness (cognitive).

When a lapse appears imminent or has already happened, the first line of defence in the RP model lies in these three systems. The choice of a particular system or access (intervention method) for the therapist and/or the individual experiencing the lapse depends to a large extent on what is modifiable in the particular situation. Interventions may be possible on the physiological/biological level (e.g., the use of nicotine chewing-gum to control physiological withdrawal). Avenues of intervention are often more readily accessible in the cognitive and affective systems, however. Helping the person cope with the guilt and self-blame associated with the AVE is one example, involving the use of cognitive restructuring (lapse = mistake vs. personal failure), plans to cope effectively so as to keep the lapse from escalating into a relapse, and strategies to strengthen self-efficacy. These procedures take precedence whenever a lapse is imminent or has already happened.

Once the lapse has been coped with in this way and the individual's habit pattern has restabilized, the course of therapy can focus on other factors further 'up the line' (or into the upper part of the diamond stylus depicted in figure 14.1). There are both intrapersonal and interpersonal domains (below and above the dotted line in figure 14.1) that may provide the arena for further clinical intervention. In the *intrapersonal* domain, the next area to work on (following stabilization of the needle back in the groove) is *lifestyle*, including such stress-reduction procedures as exercise, relaxation, and the development of a balanced daily lifestyle. Moving up, the next intrapersonal level of intervention is *personality*; here the therapist may focus on personality issues (from a variety of theoretical approaches, including insight-oriented psychodynamic therapy) that influence relapse risk. Another intrapersonal level that is often important to consider is the individual's *spiritual* values and interests. Spiritual issues are often involved in many addiction treatment programmes (e.g., many twelve-step programmes such as Alcoholics Anonymous rely on a 'higher power').

Many factors are also open to change on the *interpersonal* level – interventions here may occur concomitantly with those at the intrapersonal level, depending on the particular case. Personal and *social relationships*, including the influence of peers, family members, and appropriate social-support figures, play a predominant role in influencing relapse. Interventions at this level range from marital and/or family therapy to placing the client in touch with mutual self-help groups. In some cases, it may be useful to work with the *family of origin*, either in terms of making contacts with parents and other family members or by therapy that is geared towards insight into familial determinants of relapse risk. Finally, interventions may be possible at the broader *community* and sociocultural level, including legal restrictions, the alteration of community norms (e.g., the anti-smoking movement), or changing the larger cultural setting (e.g., moving away).

Treatment matching and stages of habit change

In the previous section, we discussed the focus and timing of RP methods for individuals who have already developed an addiction problem. As such, the use of RP to prevent an established addictive behaviour from worsening (by reducing relapse risk) can be considered a *tertiary prevention* approach. A related issue concerns the application of RP principles to the various *stages of change* that characterize recovery from addiction. Another important future direction is that of exploring whether the cognitive-behavioural strategies espoused by the RP model can be successfully applied to primary and secondary prevention efforts (i.e., to prevent addictive behaviours or to intervene in the early stages of addiction). Both of these questions are addressed in the following discussion.

A recent conceptual advance in the field of addictions treatment is the notion of *stages of change*. Originally developed with reference to the stages that people appear to go through in smoking cessation (Prochaska and DiClemente 1983; Shiffman and Wills 1985), this approach has merit for understanding the stages of recovery associated with a variety of addiction problems, including both self-initiated and treatment-aided change (Brownell *et al.* 1986).

The basic idea is that individuals proceed through a series of relatively discrete stages in the change process. First is the *precontemplation* stage, which characterizes the ongoing addiction pattern *prior to* any active consideration of change (this period may last for several months or years before the addict recognizes a need for change or is forced to consider change based on external pressure or events). Next comes the *contemplation* stage (also called the motivation and commitment stage), in which the individual considers doing something about the problem. Some people remain in the contemplation stage indefinitely (the 'I'll quit tomorrow' syndrome), presumably reflecting the motivational conflict and ambivalence about change that characterize this stage. The next stage is called the *action* stage, in which the individual makes an active attempt to change, either on his or her own or by seeking outside help. Most addiction treatment programmes are geared toward the action stage, and represent attempts to inculcate abstinence (e.g., to stop all drug use) or moderation (e.g., as in some eating disorders). The final stage, often neglected because of our usual focus on the action stage, is the *maintenance* stage. Whether or not the results of the action stage will be maintained over time (stable recovery vs. relapse) depends largely on what happens during the critical maintenance stage. As has been noted in recent research by Moos and his colleague (Finney *et al.* 1980), most of the 'variance' in treatment outcome in the addictions field can be accounted for by events that transpire *after* the completion of a formal treatment programme. The RP model is particularly relevant to the selection of strategies in the maintenance stage.

The 'stages of change model' is applicable to addiction treatment *regardless* of the type of interventions employed during the action phase (e.g., whether treatment is medical, psychosocial, spiritual, or community based). Matching strategies can be employed with each stage in the change process. Adherence or compliance with a particular treatment regimen may reflect problems associated with the contemplation or motivation stage, rather than with the type of treatment employed. Clients may be more willing to stick with treatment, regardless of format, if they are given assistance or guidance to help them overcome their motivational conflicts and uncertainties. In this regard, a number of motivation-enhancing strategies can be matched to the individual's particular deficit, once a detailed assessment has been made (Miller 1983). For some, education and information about the positive health consequences of quitting may be essential, whereas for others, resolving an underlying conflict may be the key. Still others may benefit from rallying social support.

The addiction treatment field continues to be permeated with 'uniformity myth' problems, stemming from the traditional idea that each addiction is a unique and uniform disorder (e.g., alcoholism vs. heroin addiction vs. smoking, etc.). Corollaries of this myth include the notion that addictions such as alcoholism represent unidimensional diseases that follow a specific course (usually downward, as in the progressive disease model). From this perspective, treatment itself is considered a uniform 'entity' and is recommended for everyone who exhibits signs of the particular addiction problem. The ubiquitous thirty-day in-patient treatment programme favoured by many experts in the United States for a variety of addiction problems (e.g., alcoholism, cocaine dependence, bulimia, etc.) is a manifestation of this uniformity assumption – as is the recommendation that in-patient treatment be followed by lifelong participation in one of the many 'anonymous' self-help groups. All too often, however, the data on recovery and relapse do not support the effectiveness of the uniformity approach to treatment.

One alternative to the uniformity concept is the notion that treatment for addiction problems should be *graded in intensity* relevant to the magnitude of the presenting problem. A good example of this *stepped-care approach* comes from the field of hypertension treatment research. Hypertension, like addiction, is a multidetermined problem (it has both biopsychosocial and genetic determinants), with serious associated health risks (e.g., cardiovascular disease). Treatment for this problem, unlike present treatment for the addictions, is geared toward the severity of the problem. For borderline hypertension cases, for example, the treating physician may begin by asking the patient to make specified changes in his or her lifestyle (e.g., to cut down on salt, exercise regularly, avoid excessive use of alcohol, learn a relaxation technique, etc.). If the problem does not improve after a monitored period, the physician may recommend that the patient take a relatively mild medication (usually a diuretic) for several weeks or months, again under continued monitoring to see how the blood pressure responds. Finally, if these secondary prevention efforts fail to make an impact, more intensive medication may be required (e.g., beta-blocker). And so on: each intervention is tested for efficacy before the next more intensive procedure is introduced and evaluated (Marlatt 1988).

A similar graded series of interventions would seem appropriate for many addiction problems. Since many people give up addictive habits on their own, without costly and lengthy professional assistance, why not begin by asking the client first to attempt to change on his or her own with the help of a *minimal intervention* procedure, such as reading a self-help manual and/or attending a self-help group? If a positive change is made on this basis, it may not be necessary to proceed to the next, more intensive step. If progress is not made, however, a more intensive form of treatment (e.g., out-patient professional treatment coupled with a self-help group) can be tried. Finally, if all else fails, the use of long-term in-patient treatment programmes can be implemented as a last resort. Careful assessment of the nature and severity of the addictive behaviour pattern will be necessary at each stage of the graded intervention process in order to monitor progress and select a matched treatment strategy. Choice of treatment goal (abstinence vs. moderation) can also be made on this basis. For less dependent clients (e.g., problem drinkers), moderation may be the most appropriate goal to begin with. If a client does not respond well to this approach, it may be necessary to recommend total abstinence (a goal that may be accepted more readily by some clients *after* they have been unsuccessful with a moderation approach).

The application of cognitive-behavioural programmes similar to the

RP model has already been tested in the secondary prevention arena with excessive drinking among young adults (Baer *et al.* 1988; Kivlahan *et al.* 1988), with encouraging results. A related area of application of the RP model is in the modification of behaviours that increase the risk of physical disease. In the concluding section of this chapter, Judith Gordon describes one such programme in which RP strategies were employed as a means of modifying sexual behaviours associated with the risk of acquiring the AIDS virus.

AIDS prevention and the RP model

Our newest project is a secondary prevention programme for gay and bisexual men who are compulsively engaging in sexual behaviours that facilitate transmission of the AIDS virus (Roffman *et al.* 1988). Based on the relapse prevention model, individuals wanting to develop greater control over their sexual behaviour receive training in a variety of self-management skills, including cognitive-behavioural strategies, modification of lifestyle balance, and the utilization of social support. In this section we briefly describe the population who came in for a demonstration treatment project and give an overview of the programme, focusing on treatment modalities, components, strategies, and clinical issues.

From March 1987 through August 1988, gay and bisexual men wanting help changing compulsive unsafe sexual behaviours were recruited through public service announcements, paid advertisements, and community networking, for free anonymous treatment. Pre-treatment data were collected on sixty-four individuals who met the eligibility requirements (adult, gay or bisexual, currently engaging in high-risk sexual activities, not untreated for a current dependence on alcohol or other drugs). The modal subject was 36 years of age (range 18–61), white (90.5 per cent), a college graduate (40.6 per cent), employed (78.1 per cent), and never married (79 per cent). A majority defined themselves as exclusively homosexual (57.8 per cent).

Of these, forty-four began treatment: twenty-four received group counselling in three cohorts, fourteen received individual counselling, and six received a self-help manual with limited therapist contact. With the exception of the initial pilot group, all subjects worked with the self-help materials (Gordon, Craver, and Roffman 1988). Group and individual counselling subjects met for seventeen weekly sessions and three monthly follow-ups; self-help subjects received five sessions over a five-month period. Subjects completed extensive pre- and post-treatment and follow-up questionnaires and submitted weekly records of all sexual activities, but, as of this writing, no data analyses have been completed, so the comments and preliminary conclusions below are based on clinical experience and impressions.

Most subjects showed a high level of knowledge about AIDS and risk factors involved in infection and had extensive personal experience with friends who had died of AIDS. None the less, they typically reported high levels of unsafe sexual activities (e.g., unprotected anal and oral sex with multiple unknown partners). Unlike the changes reported by the majority of gay men, who have succeeded in changing their risk behaviours (Becker and Joseph 1988), primary prevention via community education and public health efforts have not been effective with this group. Although we do not have summaries of pre-treatment levels of high-risk sexual activity, an earlier survey we conducted with a similar population indicated that 47 per cent of respondents never used condoms and 30 per cent used them less than half the time (Roffman *et al.* 1988).

They were highly motivated to change, as evidenced by self-report measures, willingness to participate in a research protocol that required daily records on sexual behaviours for four months, and completion of detailed questionnaires asking for intimate information over a period of seven months. Only one subject had ARC, though many were HIV-positive and some were symptomatic. They described their risky sexual behaviour as having a compulsive or addictive quality, rather than simply being a matter of preference and personal inclination. Many reported previous struggles with eating disorders, alcohol, and other drug abuse and experienced their problems with sexual control as being very similar to difficulties controlling these other behaviour patterns.

Our clinical impression is that what drives the compulsive high-risk sexual behaviours is a combination of old habitual sexual patterns developed prior to AIDS, low self-esteem, and a strong desire for intimacy coupled with inadequate relationship skills. These individual factors operate in the context of a society that does not support long-term homosexual relationships. The uncontrolled sexual behaviours were consistently described by our subjects as attempts to cope with negative emotions, feelings of loneliness and unworthiness, and an inability to create positive nonsexual experiences. Sex, particularly anonymous sex, is a 'quick fix' that temporarily gives pleasure, reassures insecurity, creates the illusion of connectedness, intimacy, caring, and acceptance. It is similar to the 'PIG effect' or 'problem of immediate gratification' that we have described elsewhere as a facet of the addictive experience (Marlatt and Gordon 1985). (For a discussion of the conceptualization of problems of sexual control in homosexual and bisexual men and the relationship to addictive behaviour disorders, see Quandlund and Shattls 1987.) Thus for this population, the relapse prevention approach includes the following goals: to help develop specific skills for coping with high-risk situations that otherwise lead to unsafe sex, and to develop healthier, more satisfying lives and relationships in order to reduce vulnerability to relapsing back into unsafe sexual behaviour patterns.

Treatment components were arranged in a sequence suggested by these stages of change model (Prochaska and DiClemente 1983). In the therapist-led conditions, we spent about a month each on the contemplation and action stages and about two months on the maintenance stage. Below we discuss selected issues associated with each stage.

Contemplation stage

One of the first issues to arise regards goals. The primary goal, of course, is to stop engaging in unsafe sexual activities: namely, any act that facilitates exposure to bodily fluids that may contain the HIV. But what does this mean? Individuals must choose whether to use the strict 'risk elimination' standard or the more moderate 'risk reduction' standard (Goedert 1987). The former requires either celibacy or abstinence from all sexual practices involving any possible risk of exposure to HIV. The latter requires avoiding highly risky behaviours, such as unprotected anal intercourse, but allows for activities carrying some degree of risk, such as anal intercourse with a condom. This choice parallels the abstinence vs. moderation debate in treatment for substance abuse and chemical dependency (see e.g., Marlatt 1983). Another choice regards anonymous sexual partners: strictly speaking, anonymous partners do not increase risk levels as long as safe sex guidelines are adhered to, although it may be easier to maintain limits with known partners with whom one can negotiate more comfortably. These and other discriminations in safety levels demand personal judgements regarding risks individuals are willing to take. Our general position is that since sex is a biological drive that can be expressed in a variety of ways but which individuals seldom choose to suppress voluntarily, we prefer to view people with problems of compulsive unsafe sex much as we do people with eating disorders: the aim is not to eliminate sexual activity for most people but to make it safe and healthy.

A second significant theme that emerges during this initial phase of treatment involves motivational factors and conflicts. We use a modified version of the decision matrix (Marlatt and Gordon 1985; Gordon, Craver, and Roffman 1988) to help people identify the personal benefits and costs of giving up favoured or familiar sexual activities in order to be sexually safer. Although preservation of life and health is a powerful motivator, people tend to perceive the costs or losses, described below, as enormous. The sexual behaviours that have been identified as unsafe did not necessarily pose a health threat prior to AIDS, so that gay men are having to change patterns that were once considered normal and safe by their own community norms. These perceived losses are factors that are frequently associated with high-risk situations that threaten the commitment to safe sex. Two broad categories of losses commonly associated with changing are (1) fears of loss of pleasure, comfort, and identity (negative outcome expectations for safe sex), and (2) fears of failure (negative efficacy expectations). During contemplation, we encourage people to identify them, explore their emotional impact and personal meaning, and mourn and grieve; in the action stage, we work more actively to reduce their power to precipitate lapses.

Action stage

Once having clarified their motivation for and commitment to specific sexual behaviour changes, individuals assess their personal high-risk situations or triggers associated with unsafe sexual activities and receive instruction and practice in specific behavioural, cognitive, and assertiveness skills to help them avoid designated undesirable sexual behaviours and expand their repertoire of safe positive sexual practices. Subjects report making major changes at the beginning of treatment, eliminating most episodes of unprotected anal and oral sex, but lapses are common. They are usually associated with loneliness, lack of assertiveness, or desire for particular sexual experiences.

High-risk situations or triggers to high-risk sex cluster in categories similar to those we have observed with other addictive problem behaviours. *Affective states* include negative effect in particular: loneliness, boredom, depression, anxiety. *Interpersonal factors* include old lovers with whom the individual has a history of unsafe sex; any partner who exerts pressure to do unsafe activities; difficulty asserting one's desire to have safe sex; fear of rejection or abandonment; concern that safe sex interferes with intimacy and spontaneity. *Physical factors* include urges, fantasy, sexual arousal, and drug use. *Cognitive factors* include low self-esteem, low self-efficacy, motivational conflict, internalized homophobia, and an identity that has been largely based hitherto on sexual orientation and lifestyle. *Lifestyle balance factors* include poor stress management skills and a limited repertoire of nonsexual ways of achieving stimulation, satisfaction, and pleasure. Finally, *environmental 'hot spots'* include parks, baths, tea-rooms, adult book-stores, bars.

Behavioural and cognitive self-control strategies are relevant and useful to people during this stage, including stimulus control, avoidance, delay, substitution, and self-talk. Most of the strategies we teach are grasped easily, with the exception of assertiveness training, since gay men (indeed most people in our culture) are typically unaccustomed to assertive verbal communication about sexual behaviour. In addition, we emphasize experimenting with lower-risk sexual activities; for example, mutual masturbation, massage, use of condoms, and nongenital sensual acts.

Maintenance stage

This stage of treatment emphasizes establishing nonsexual behaviours and habits to gain more satisfaction and better balance (e.g., through stress management, working on self-esteem, and personal development that could include hobbies, job changes, making new friends, improving intimate relationships, developing 'positive addictions') so that subjects are less likely to act out sexually. The development of personal connections and support systems that are not based on sexual relationships is a major focus.

Although we have not yet analysed our data on the relative efficacy of the different treatment modalities, some treatment-matching issues did emerge in this study. The self-help condition attracted very few subjects, because they were seeking to break out of their sense of isolation. Some subjects felt that a group was too threatening and preferred to work individually. The group condition created a powerful sense of support and connectedness, and facilitated working on issues that gay men typically struggle with, such as negative self-image, lack of positive role models, emotionally unavailable fathers and partners, as well as creative problem solving (e.g., where do you meet gay men if not at gay bars?). Also nonspecific therapeutic factors – warmth, acceptance, and positive regard experienced not only with the therapist but with peers – increased self-acceptance, inner healing, and the courage and strength to give up old familiar ways and try new ones. Whereas the individual therapist can meet some of these needs, our experience is that a group modality is the most powerful once the individual is able to function in that setting.

The clinical reports of the therapists in this project, based on client contact, are that most subjects showed a gradual steady decline in unsafe sex. Increases in self-esteem, improved interpersonal relations, particularly a greater capacity for developing friendships, a growing sense of self-efficacy regarding assertiveness in sexual situations, and increased capacity to achieve greater overall life satisfaction were commonly reported and observed. Subjects were enthusiastic about the programme, participated actively in treatment, and frequently referred friends or requested extra copies of the materials for them.

An overriding goal of all our subjects, in addition to achieving sexual safety, was to experience more intimacy, preferably by getting into a monogamous relationship. Similarly many subjects expressed a desire to 'de-sexualize' their lives, to expand their focus of attention and energy beyond their sexual compulsion to a broader range of meaningful experiences. But it seems clear that to sustain such individual changes, the emotional and structural support of the immediate community is needed: the gay community needs to develop new social norms and institutions that facilitate them – for example, ways of meeting that don't rely on sex and drugs as bath houses and bars do. Furthermore, since individual changes in high-risk sexual behaviours seem to be influenced by self-worth, the support of the society at large for homosexuality and alternative lifestyles is critical. As long as gay men feel inferior because of their sexual orientation they may be more susceptible to developing unhealthy behavioural patterns associated with low self-esteem.

The relapse prevention model seems well suited to help individuals initiate and implement necessary behavioural changes to reduce health risk. As we discussed in the first section of this chapter, it is by no means intended as an exhaustive, self-sustaining treatment approach, but is compatible with many therapeutic modalities and orientations that focus on enhancing quality of life, and its greatest strength is in its objective to empower individuals in stabilizing new learning. It provides a scaffolding or framework and a language that individuals can use to understand the nature of behaviour change, develop their own resources and utilize their experiences constructively, and connect with appropriate external supports. What relapse prevention cannot do is redress those social, community, and societal factors that hamper individual progress. In reality, no clinical interventions can provide the ongoing support or substitute for the broader psychosocial changes necessary to maintain deep individual change. Future research needs to focus on developing the most effective ways to give individuals the understanding, the motivation, the encouragement, and the efficacy-enhancing experiences to change from the role of victim to that of initiator of personal and social changes that will help them lead healthy lives.

References

Baer, J.S., Kivlahan, D.R., Fromme, K., and Marlatt, G.A. (1988) 'Secondary prevention of alcohol abuse with college student populations: a skills-training approach', in press.

Becker, M.H. and Joseph, J.G. (1988) 'AIDS and behavioral change to reduce risk: a review', *American Journal of Public Health* 78: 394–410.

Brownell, K.D., Marlatt, G.A., Lichtenstein, E., and Wilson, G.T. (1986) 'Understanding and preventing relapse', *American Psychologist* 41: 765–82.

Finney, J.W., Moos, R.H., and Newborn, C.R. (1980) 'Posttreatment experiences and treatment outcome of alcoholic patients six months and two years after hospitalization', *Journal of Consulting and Clinical Psychology* 48: 17–29.

Goedert, J. (1987) 'Sounding board: what is safe sex? *The New England Journal of Medicine* May 21: 1340.

Gordon, J.R., Craver, J.A., and Roffman, R.A. (1988) *Safer Sex: A Self-Help Manual*, unpublished manuscript, University of Washington, in preparation.

Kivlahan, D.R., Coppel, D.B., Fromme, K., Williams, E., and Marlatt, G.A. (1988) 'Secondary prevention of alcohol-related problems in young adults at risk', in K.D. Craig and S.M. Weiss (eds) *Prevention and Early Intervention: Biobehavioral Perspectives*, New York: Springer, in press.

Marlatt, G.A. (1983) 'The controlled drinking controversy: a commentary', *American Psychologist* 38: 1097–110.

Marlatt, G.A. (1988) 'Matching clients to treatment: treatment models and stages of change', in D.M. Donovan and G.A. Marlatt (eds) *Assessment of Addictive Behaviors*, New York: Guilford Press.

Marlatt, G.A. and Gordon, J.R. (eds) (1985) *Relapse Prevention: Maintenance Strategies in the Treatment of Addictive Behavior*, New York: Guilford Press.

Miller, W.R. (1983) 'Motivational interviewing with problem drinkers', *Behavioural Psychotherapy* 11: 147–72.

Prochaska, J.O. and DiClemente, C.C. (1983) 'Stages and processes of self-change of smoking: towards a more integrative model of change', *Journal of Consulting and Clinical Psychology* 51: 390–5.

Quandlund, M.C. and Shattls, W.D. (1987) 'AIDS, sexuality, and sexual control', *Journal of Homosexuality* 14: 277–98.

Roffman, R.A., Gilchrist, L.D., Gilmore, M.R., Stephens, R., and Mathias, S. (1988) *Relapse Prevention Training as a Means of AIDS Risk Reduction*, manuscript in preparation, University of Washington.

Roffman, R.A., Gordon, J.R., and Craver, J.A. (1988) *AIDS Risk Reduction: Preventing Relapse to Unsafe Sex*, manuscript in preparation, University of Washington.

Shiffman, S. and Wills, T.A. (eds) (1985) *Coping and Substance Use*, New York: Academic Press.

Name index

Subject index